AutoCAD 14

NO EXPERIENCE REQUIRED

AutoCAD® 14

NO EXPERIENCE REQUIRED™

David Frey

SYBEX®

San Francisco • Paris • Düsseldorf • Soest

Associate Publisher: Amy Romanoff
Contracts and Licensing Manager: Kristine Plachy
Acquisitions & Developmental Editor: Melanie Spiller
Editor: Davina Baum
Technical Editor: Sam Sol Matzkin
Book Designers: Patrick Dintino and Catalin Dulfu
Graphic Illustrator: Andrew Benzie
Electronic Publishing Specialists: Cyndy Johnsen and Robin Kibby
Production Coordinator: Charles Mathews
Production Assistant: Beth Moynihan
Indexer: Lynnzee Elze
Cover Designer: Ingalls + Associates

Screen reproductions produced with Collage Complete.

Collage Complete is a trademark of Inner Media Inc.

SYBEX is a registered trademark of SYBEX Inc.

No experience required. is a trademark of SYBEX Inc.

TRADEMARKS: SYBEX has attempted throughout this book to distinguish proprietary trademarks from descriptive terms by following the capitalization style used by the manufacturer.

Library of Congress Card Number: 97-81246
ISBN: 0-7821-2199-3

Manufactured in the United States of America

10 9 8 7

*To Esther, for her patience,
wisdom, and encouragement.*

Acknowledgments

There are many people who deserve acknowledgment and gratitude for their contribution to the development and publication of this book.

First, many thanks to the folks at Sybex who were involved in this project. Kristine Plachy, acquisitions manager, was my first contact at Sybex and patiently negotiated with me to finalize the contract. Melanie Spiller, acquisitions and developmental editor, conceptualized a 100-page booklet into this title and sold the concept to the marketing people. Then she taught me enough about writing for me to believe such a book could really be written. Davina Baum has served as editor and has been a true pleasure to work with. Besides doing an excellent job of editing, she has gently guided me through the developmental process of reviews and submissions, while somehow finding a way to keep track of all the figures and details.

Thanks also to Amy Romanoff, associate publisher, as well as to the production team at Sybex: Charles Mathews, production coordinator, Cyndy Johnsen and Robin Kibby, electronic publishing specialists, and Beth Moynihan, production assistant. They've been successful in maintaining the standards of high quality that Sybex is known for, and I appreciate their ability and effort in putting together such a good-looking book.

A special thanks to my technical editor, Sam Sol Matzkin, who took on the daunting and tedious task of checking the book for accuracy. He's done a superb job and provided many insights and suggestions that I feel have increased the quality of the information presented here.

I also would like to acknowledge the following three people—Jerry Warren, Dan Losee, and Bill Costello. They are all talented educators who gave me not only the opportunity, but also the support and encouragement I needed to get involved in teaching.

Thank you to Larry Davis for his ideas and vision of education in the community of the future.

Finally, I want to thank Judy Morgan of the Autodesk Foundation for her unflinching support and encouragement over the years to pursue my goals in education.

Contents at a Glance

Table of Contents

Foreword

In the early 1980s I was drafting architectural plans using technical pens on mylar. It was painstaking work, but clarity and precision was, and still is, one of the basic requirements of architectural drafting. Today, AutoCAD has made its way into nearly every major architectural firm, offering that needed precision and clarity, and removing the endless hours bent over a drafting table. We still use the old tried-and-true methods of quick sketches on tracing paper to convey and develop design ideas, but, more and more, architects are turning to AutoCAD as a tool to help nurse their design ideas along and to get buildings built.

Over the past few releases, AutoCAD has become much easier to use. You used to have to memorize volumes of command names to make the simplest of drawings. But Autodesk has been quite successful in turning a DOS-based, command-driven program into an intuitive, easy-to-understand Windows application. As I use AutoCAD today, I still rely on memorized keyboard shortcuts, but it's much easier to remember those less frequently used commands and settings, largely due to AutoCAD's generous use of dialog boxes, help messages, and tool tips.

Today, AutoCAD learning tools need to offer new ways to teach AutoCAD. David Frey's new book takes a look at AutoCAD from a fresh perspective. In *AutoCAD 14: No experience required*, David explores the potential of this powerful and sometimes intimidating tool, and, at the same time, provides a wonderful introduction to the complicated craft of architectural drafting. He offers a clear and uncomplicated look at AutoCAD, and the sample cabin project provides an overview of architectural drafting methods. It is really very satisfying to spend a few evenings with this book and create the cabin, even if you have as much experience with AutoCAD as I do.

David also provides a useful survey of the tools and features in this latest release of AutoCAD. Long after you've worked your way through it, you will probably find yourself referring to this book for quick reminders. And while the examples are specific to a small project, you'll be able to adapt the skills you learn to your own work. I would have loved to have had David's book when I was first learning AutoCAD. It offers clear instruction and plenty of illustrations at each step.

I hope you find this book as satisfying to read and use as I did. And welcome to the world of AutoCAD.

George Omura

Author of Sybex's
Mastering AutoCAD Release 14
Mastering AutoCAD Release 14, for Mechanical Engineers (with Steven Keith)
AutoCAD 14 Instant Reference (with B. Robert Callori)
Mastering AutoCAD Release 13 for Windows
Mastering AutoCAD Release 13 for DOS
AutoCAD 13 Instant Reference (with Paul Richardson)
Mastering AutoCAD Release 12 for Windows
Mastering AutoCAD Release 12 for DOS
AutoCAD 12 Instant Reference
Mastering AutoCAD 3D
Mastering AutoCAD LT

Introduction

This book was born out of the need for a simple yet engaging tutorial that would help beginners step into the world of AutoCAD without feeling intimidated. That tutorial has evolved over the years into a full introduction to the way in which architects and civil and structural engineers use AutoCAD to increase their efficiency and capacity to produce state-of-the-art computerized production drawings and designs.

This book is directed towards AutoCAD novices—users who know how to use a computer and do basic file-managing tasks like create new folders and save and move files, but who know nothing or very little about AutoCAD. If you are new to the construction and design professions, this book will be an excellent companion as you're learning AutoCAD. If you're already practicing in those fields, you'll be immediately able to apply the skills you'll pick up from this book to real-world projects. The exercises included herein have been successfully used to train architects, engineers, and contractors, as well as college and high school students in the basics of AutoCAD.

What Will You Learn from This Book?

Learning AutoCAD, as in learning any complex computer program, requires a significant commitment of time and attention, and, to some extent, repetition. Although there are new concepts you must understand to operate the program and appreciate its potential as a drafting and design tool, becoming proficient at AutoCAD requires that you use the commands enough times to gain an intuitive sense of how they work and how parts of a drawing are constructed.

In this tutorial, each chapter is designated as a *skill*. At the end of each skill you will find a checklist of the tools you have learned (or should have learned!). The steps in the tutorial have a degree of repetition built into them that allows you to work through new commands several times and build up confidence before you move on to the next skill.

Progressing through the book, the skills break into four general areas of study:

- Skills 1 through 3 will familiarize you with the organization of the screen, go over a few of the most basic commands, and equip you with the tools necessary to set up a new drawing.

- Skills 4 and 5 develop drawing strategies that will help you use commands efficiently.

- Skills 6 through 11 work with the major features of AutoCAD.

- Skills 12 through 14 and Appendix A look into more intermediate and advanced features of AutoCAD.

In the process of exploring these elements, you will follow through the steps involved in laying out the floor plan of a small, three-room cabin. Then you will learn how to generate elevations from the floor plan and, eventually, set up a title block and print out your drawing. Along the way, you will learn how to:

- use the basic drawing and modifying commands in a strategic manner

- set up layers and put color into your drawing

- define and insert blocks

- generate elevation views

- place hatch patterns and fills on building components

- use text in your drawing

- dimension the floor plan

In the latter part of the book, the skills touch on some of the more intermediate and advanced features of AutoCAD, including:

- drawing a site plan

- using external references

- setting up a drawing for printing with Paper Space

- making a print of your drawing

- working in three dimensions

All of these features are taught with the cabin as a continuing project. As a result, you will build up a set of drawings that document your progress through the project and that can be used as reference material later, if you find that you need to refresh yourself with material in a specific skill. If you are already somewhat familiar with AutoCAD and are reading only some of the skills included, you can pull accompanying files for this book off Sybex's Web page, at http://www.sybex.com.

At the end of the book is a glossary of terms used in the book that are related to AutoCAD and building design, and, finally, an index.

Hints for Success

Because this book is essentially a step-by-step tutorial, it has a feature in common with any tutorial of this type: You may finish a skill and see that you have progressed further through the cabin project, but you have no idea how you got there and are sure you couldn't do it again without the help of the step-by-step instructions. This feeling is a natural result of this kind of learning tool, and there are a couple of things you can do to get past this feeling. You can do the chapter over again. This may seem tedious but it has a great advantage: You gain speed in drawing. You'll accomplish the same task in half the time it took you the first time, and, if you repeat a skill for the third time, you'll halve your time again. Each time you repeat a skill, you can skip more and more of the explicit instructions and eventually you'll be able to execute the commands and finish the skill by just looking at the figures and reading a minimum of the text. In many ways, this is just like learning a musical instrument: You must go slowly at first, but over time and through practice, your pace picks up.

Another suggestion for honing your skills is to follow the course of the book, but apply the steps to a different project—possibly draw your own living space, or design a new one. If you have a real design project that is not too complex, that's even better. The probability of learning AutoCAD or any computer program is greatly increased when you are highly motivated, and a real project of an appropriate size can be the perfect motivator.

Ready, Set...

When I started learning AutoCAD 12 years ago, I was surprised how long I could sit at a workstation and be unaware of time passing. And, at first, I experienced a level of frustration that I never thought I was capable of feeling. When I finally "got over the hump" and began feeling that I could successfully draw with this program after all, I told myself that I would someday figure out a way to help others get over the hump. That was the primary motivating force for writing this book. I hope it works for you and that you too get some enjoyment while learning AutoCAD. As the title says... no experience is required... only an interest in the subject, and a willingness to learn!

Getting to Know AutoCAD

- ➔ **Opening a new drawing**
- ➔ **Getting familiar with the AutoCAD Graphics window**
- ➔ **Modifying the display**
- ➔ **Calling up and arranging toolbars**

Your introduction to AutoCAD begins with a tour of the features of the AutoCAD screen. In this skill, you will also learn some tools to help you control its appearance, and how to find and start commands. Starting up AutoCAD is the first task at hand.

Starting Up AutoCAD

If you have loaded AutoCAD using the default settings for location, start AutoCAD by selecting Programs ➤ AutoCAD R14 ➤ AutoCAD R14 from the Start menu. If you have customized your installation, find and select the AutoCAD R14 icon to start the program.

When AutoCAD first opens, the Start Up dialog box appears (Figure 1.1). Dialog boxes are used extensively in AutoCAD, for many different functions. They have various combinations of buttons and text boxes which you will learn about as you progress through the book.

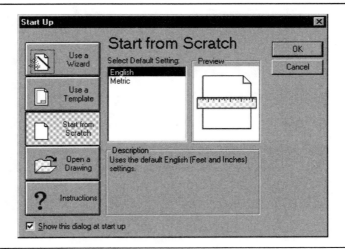

FIGURE 1.1:   The Start Up dialog box

The five buttons on the left side of the Start Up dialog box give you options for setting up a new drawing or choosing an existing drawing to revise or update.

The middle portion of the dialog box changes depending on which of the five buttons you choose.

Click the Start from Scratch button. Be sure that English is highlighted in the box titled Select Default Setting and click OK. The dialog box disappears and your monitor displays the AutoCAD Graphics window, sometimes called the Graphical User Interface or GUI (see Figure 1.2).

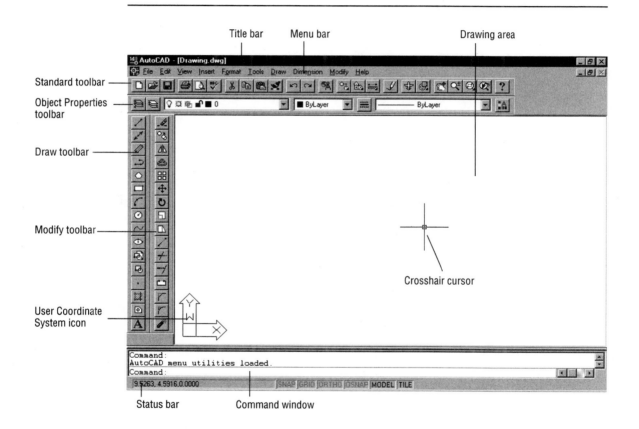

FIGURE 1.2:   The AutoCAD Graphics window

Introduction to the AutoCAD Graphics Window

At the top of the Graphics window sits the *title bar*, the *menu bar*, and two *toolbars*.

Title bar

Menu bar

Standard toolbar

Object Properties toolbar

The title bar is analogous to the title bar on any Windows program. It contains the program name (AutoCAD) and the title of the current drawing. Below the title bar is the menu bar, where you will see the drop-down menus, the first two and the last of which are Microsoft menus (meaning that they appear on most Windows applications). They also contain a few commands specific to AutoCAD. The rest of the menus are AutoCAD menus. Below these menus is the *Standard toolbar*, which contains 24 command buttons. Several of these buttons will be familiar to Windows users; the rest are AutoCAD commands. Just below this toolbar is the *Object Properties toolbar* containing four command buttons and three drop-down lists.

The blank middle section of the screen is called the *drawing area*. Notice the movable *crosshair cursor*.

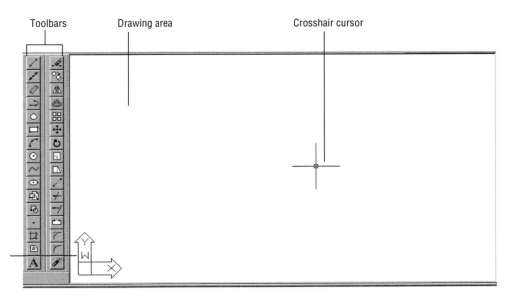

Toolbars   Drawing area   Crosshair cursor

User Coordinate System icon

Notice the little box at the intersection of the two crosshair lines. This is one of several forms of the AutoCAD cursor which is moved and controlled by the mouse. When you move the cursor off the drawing area, it changes to the standard Windows pointing arrow. As you begin using commands, it will take on other forms, depending on which step of a command you are in. There is also an icon with a double arrow in the lower-left corner of the drawing area. This is called the *User Coordinate System icon* and is used to indicate the positive direction for *x* and *y* coordinates. You won't need it for most of the skills in this book, so you'll learn how to make it invisible when you start Skill 5. Our example shows no toolbars in the drawing area, but there are two docked toolbars on the left of the drawing area. Your screen may or may not have them, or they may be in a different position. If the toolbars are on top of the drawing area, they will have a colored title bar. For more specifics, see the section titled "Toolbars" later in this skill.

Below the drawing area is the *Command window*.

The Command window is where you tell the program what to do, and where the program tells you what's going on. It's an important area and you will need to learn about how it works in detail. There should be three lines of text visible. If your screen has fewer than three lines showing, you will need to make another line or two visible. You'll learn how to do this later in this skill (see "The Command Window").

Below the Command window is the status bar.

On the left end of the status bar, you'll see a coordinate readout window. In the middle there are six readout buttons that indicate various drawing modes. It is important to learn about the coordinate system and most of these drawing aids (Snap, Grid, Ortho, and Osnap) early on as you learn to draw in AutoCAD as they will help you create neat and accurate drawings. The other buttons (Model and Tile) are advanced aids which will be covered later in Skill 13, *Getting Familiar with Paper Space*.

This has been a quick introduction to the various parts of the Graphics window and there are a couple of items I didn't mention which may be visible on your screen. You may have slide bars below and to the right of the drawing area. And you may have a menu on the right side of the drawing area. Both of these features can be useful, but they may also be a hindrance and can take up precious space in the drawing area.

To temporarily remove these features:

1. From the menu bar, click Tools ➤ Preferences. The Preferences dialog box appears (shown in Figure 1.3). It has eight tabs across the top that act like tabs on file folders.

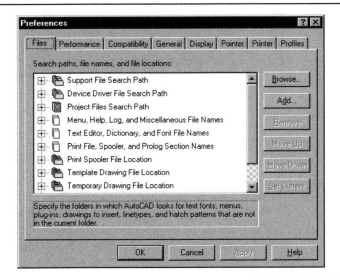

FIGURE 1.3:   The Preferences dialog box

2. Click the Display tab. The display settings come up (Figure 1.4). If you have a screen menu (a column on the right side of your drawing area headed by four stars) visible on your screen, the first checkbox ("Display AutoCAD Screen menu in drawing window") should be checked.

3. Click the checkbox to remove the checkmark, as you will not be using the screen menu. This turns off the screen menu. Do the same for the second checkbox to turn off the scroll bars. Don't click the OK button yet.

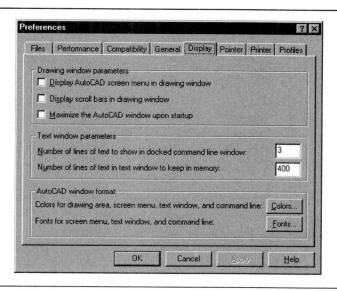

FIGURE 1.4:   The Display tab of the Preferences dialog box

Another display setting which you may want to change at this point controls the color of the cursor and the drawing area background. The illustrations in this book show a white background and black crosshair cursor, but you may prefer to have the colors reversed. To do this:

1. Click the Colors button in the bottom section of the Display tab in the Preferences dialog box. The AutoCAD Window Colors dialog box comes up (Figure 1.5). In the upper-right corner, there is a drop-down list titled Window Element, where Graphics window background should be visible and highlighted.

2. From the group of Basic Colors below this box, click the color you want to have as the background color of the drawing area. The drawing area will now have that color.

3. Next, to change the color of the cursor, click the arrow at the right end of the drop-down list. A list of Window element options will appear.

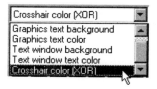

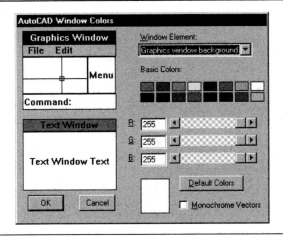

FIGURE 1.5:   The AutoCAD Window Colors dialog box

4.   Scroll down the list and select Crosshair color (XOR). Then pick another
     color from the same group of Colors for the crosshair cursor. Click OK to
     close the AutoCAD Window Colors dialog box and click OK again to close
     the Preferences dialog box.

Your screen and crosshair cursor will take on their newly assigned colors.

The Command Window

Just below the drawing area is the Command window. This window is actually
separate from the drawing area and behaves like a Microsoft Windows window;
that is, you can drag it to a different place on the screen and resize it, although
I don't recommend you do this at first. If you currently have fewer than three
lines of text in the window, you will need to increase its vertical size. To do this,
move the cursor to the horizontal boundary between the drawing area and the
Command window until it changes to an up-and-down arrow broken by two
parallel horizontal lines.

Hold down the left mouse button and drag the cursor up about the amount that one or two lines of text would take up, then release the mouse. You should get more lines of text showing, but you may have to try it a couple of times to get exactly three lines visible. When you close the program the new settings will be saved and it will be right the next time you start up AutoCAD.

The Command window is very important. It is here where you will give information to AutoCAD, and where AutoCAD will prompt you as to the next step in executing a command. It is a good practice to get into the habit of keeping one eye on it as you work on your drawing. Most errors are made from not watching it often enough.

Before you begin to draw, you should take a close look at the menus, toolbars, and keyboard controls.

NOTE   In many cases, AutoCAD offers you a number of ways to start up commands. There are ways to get to most of the commands either from drop-down menus, from the toolbars, or from the keyboard. When you get used to drawing with AutoCAD, you will learn some of the shortcuts available to start commands quickly, and you will find the way that is most comfortable for you.

Drop-Down Menus

The menu bar, just below the title bar (see Figure 1.2), consists of ten words and an icon. Click any of these and you will find a drop-down menu. The icon, as well as the File, Edit, and Help options are Microsoft menus that come with all Windows-compatible applications, although they are somewhat customized to work with AutoCAD. The menu associated with the icon contains commands which allow you to control the appearance and position of the drawing area. Commands in the File menu are for opening and saving new and existing drawing files, printing, exporting files to another application, basic utility options, and exiting the application. The Edit menu contains the Undo and Redo commands, the Cut and Paste tools, and options for creating links between AutoCAD files and other files. The Help menu, which is the button with the arrow and question mark, works like all Windows help menus.

The other seven menus contain the most often-used AutoCAD commands. You will find that if you can master the logic of how the commands are organized by menu, it will be immensely helpful in finding the command you want. Here is a short description of each of the AutoCAD drop-down menus:

View contains tools for controlling the display of your drawing file.

Insert has commands for placing drawings or parts of drawings inside other drawings.

Format is where you'll find commands for setting up the general parameters for a new drawing.

Tools contains special tools for use while you are working on the current drawing, such as those for finding how long a line is or for running a special macro.

Draw holds the commands for putting new objects (like lines or circles) on the screen.

Dimension is where you'll find commands for dimensioning a drawing.

Modify has the commands for making changes to objects already existing in the drawing.

Toolbars

Just below the drop-down menus is the most extensive of the toolbars—the Standard toolbar.

Almost half of the buttons on the Standard toolbar are for commands used in all Windows-compatible applications, so you may be familiar with them. The other buttons are AutoCAD commands that you will use with your regular drawing activities for a variety of tasks. These commands can do a number of things, including:

- change the view or orientation of the drawing on the screen

- change the properties of an object, such as color or linetype

- force a line you are drawing to meet another line or geometric feature at specified points

Toolbar Flyouts

Notice that some command buttons on the Standard toolbar have a little triangular arrow in the lower-right corner. These arrows indicate that more than one command can be found through these buttons. Follow the next few steps to see how these buttons work.

1. Move the cursor up to the Standard toolbar and place the arrow on the icon that has a yellow ruler with a dimension line above it.

2. Rest the arrow on the button for a moment without clicking. A small window opens just below it, revealing what command the button represents. In this case, the window should say "Distance." This is a tool tip—all buttons have them. Notice the small arrow in the lower-right corner of the icon. This is the multiple command arrow mentioned above.

3. Place the arrow cursor on the button and hold down the left mouse button. As you hold the mouse button down, a row of five buttons drops down vertically below the original button. The top button in the row is a duplicate of the button you clicked. This row of buttons is called a *toolbar flyout*.

4. While still holding the mouse button down, drag the arrow down over each button until you get to the one that has a white paper scroll on it. Hold the arrow there until you see the tool tip. It should say "List." Now release the mouse button. The flyout disappears and the List command has started. Look in the Command window at the bottom of the screen.

 NOTE   The List command queries AutoCAD about the objects you select after the command has started. AutoCAD then displays information about the selected objects.

The middle line of text says Command: _list. This tells you that you have started the List command. The bottom line says Select objects:. This prompt tells you what you need to do next: select the objects about which you want information. This flyout is called the Inquiry flyout because it contains tools for asking questions about parts of the drawing.

5. Look at the Standard toolbar where the Distance button was previously located. Notice that it's been replaced by the List button.

On a toolbar flyout, the button you select replaces the button that was on the toolbar. This is handy if you are going to be using the same command several times, because now the button for the command is readily available and you don't have to open the flyout to select it again. The order of the flyout buttons remains the same, so when you open the Inquiry flyout again, the Distance button will be at the top of the list. You will need to become familiar with any flyout buttons you use, because they become the representative button on the home toolbar after being used.

6. Press Esc to cancel the List command.

By taking a look at the Inquiry flyout on the Standard toolbar, you have been introduced to the mechanisms which govern the behavior of flyouts in general.

NOTE Whenever you start up AutoCAD for a new drawing session, the toolbars will be reset and contain the flyout buttons which were originally there.

The toolbar flyouts are actually regular toolbars which have been attached to another toolbar. There are 17 toolbars in all and only five have been made into flyouts. Four of them have been attached to the Standard toolbar and one to the Draw toolbar. Any of these flyouts can be called up as a regular toolbar, independent from the Standard or Draw toolbars.

Calling Up and Arranging Toolbars

We'll use the Inquiry toolbar as an example of some ways in which toolbars can be controlled and manipulated.

1. From the View menu, select Toolbars. The Toolbars dialog box comes up (Figure 1.6). On the left side is a scrolling list box with all 17 toolbars listed.

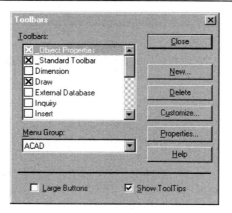

FIGURE 1.6: The Toolbars dialog box

2. In the Toolbars list box, find Inquiry and click the checkbox to select it. The Inquiry toolbar will appear in the form of a floating box in front of the Toolbars dialog box (Figure 1.7).

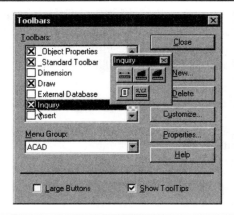

FIGURE 1.7:   The Inquiry toolbar

3. Click the Close button in the Toolbars dialog box. Notice that the Inquiry toolbar now has a title bar. Toolbars which are positioned on the drawing area have title bars. By putting the cursor on the title bar and holding down the left mouse button, you can drag the toolbar around on the screen. Try this with the Inquiry toolbar.

4. Click and drag the Inquiry toolbar to the top of the screen. You will notice that as you drag it, the toolbar stays put and you are dragging a rectangle of the same size as the toolbar (see Figure 1.8). As you drag the rectangle to the top of the drawing area and begin to move it off the drawing area onto the upper-right corner of the screen, the rectangle changes size to become shorter and wider.

5. Release the left mouse button once the toolbar is out of the drawing area. The rectangle changes to the Inquiry toolbar, now positioned off the drawing area and without its title bar.

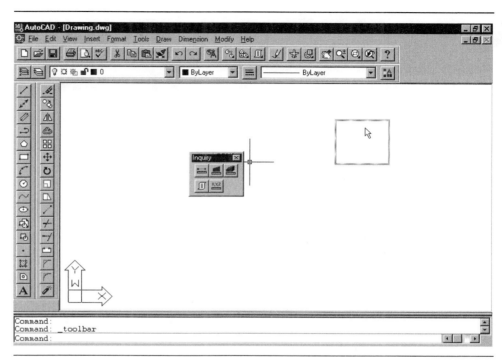

FIGURE 1.8:   Dragging the Inquiry toolbar

This procedure is called *docking* a toolbar. Notice how the Standard and Object Properties toolbars have no title bars—they are docked.

6. Move the cursor arrow to the edge of the Standard toolbar so the point of the arrow is still within the toolbar border but not on any buttons.

7. Hold down the left mouse button and drag the Standard toolbar onto the drawing area. Release the mouse button. The Standard toolbar now has a title bar, and the space it was occupying at the top of the screen has been filled in, making the drawing area a little larger, as you will see in Figure 1.9. The Standard toolbar is now a *floating* toolbar and can be moved around the drawing area.

Floating toolbars don't affect the size of the drawing area but they cover your drawing. Each docked toolbar takes up a little space that would otherwise be drawing area. You have to decide how many docked and floating toolbars you need on the screen at a time. A good way to start out is to leave the Standard and Object Properties toolbars docked at the top of the screen, and the Draw and Modify ones docked on the left side of the screen, as in Figure 1.2.

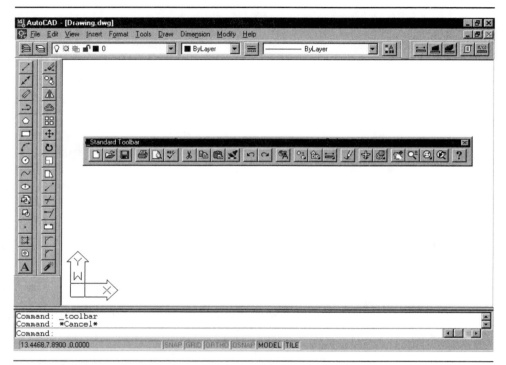

FIGURE 1.9: The Standard toolbar on the drawing area

Now, to put the Standard toolbar back where it was, and delete the Inquiry toolbar, follow these steps:

1. Drag the Standard toolbar up to its former position above the Object Properties toolbar.

2. Drag the Inquiry toolbar back onto the drawing area. You can change the shape of a floating toolbar by moving the cursor to the far-right edge of the Inquiry toolbar until the crosshair cursor changes into a two-way arrow.

3. Hold down the left mouse button with the cursor on the right edge of the toolbar and drag the arrow to the right until the rectangle changes shape. Then release the mouse button.

Each floating toolbar can be reshaped and repositioned to fit on the drawing area just how you like it. You won't need the Inquiry toolbar just now, so remove it.

4. Move the cursor up to the title bar and click the box with an × in it. The Inquiry toolbar disappears.

If your Draw and Modify toolbars are positioned on the left side of the drawing area as in Figure 1.2, go on to the next section. If these toolbars are in another location on the drawing area, try out the steps you have used in this section to dock them on the left side. If the toolbars are not visible, select View ➤ Toolbars and use the Toolbars dialog box to bring them onto the screen. Then drag the Draw toolbar to the left side of the drawing area and dock it. Do the same with the Modify toolbar, positioning it next to the Draw toolbar.

This arrangement of the toolbars will be convenient because commands on these four toolbars are used often. When you need other toolbars temporarily, you can use the Toolbars dialog box to bring them onto the drawing area.

Custom Toolbars

Each toolbar can be customized and you can build your own custom toolbars with only the command buttons you need for your drawing. You can even design your own buttons for commands that aren't already represented by toolbars. These activities are for more advanced users, however, and are not covered in this book. To find out more about how to work with toolbars, see *Mastering AutoCAD 14*, by George Omura (Sybex, 1997).

The Keyboard

Getting used to using the keyboard with AutoCAD is a good skill to master. The keyboard is an important tool for entering data and commands. If you are a good typist, you will gain a lot of speed in working with AutoCAD by learning how to use keyboard commands. AutoCAD provides what are called *alias keys*—single keys or key combinations that will start any of several often-used commands, and you can add more or change the existing aliases as you get more familiar with the program.

In addition to the alias keys, several of the F keys (function keys) on the top of the keyboard can be used as two-way or three-way toggles (switches) to turn AutoCAD functions on and off. Although there are buttons on the screen which duplicate these functions (Snap, Grid, etc.), it is often faster to use the F keys.

Finally, as mentioned in the "Drop-Down Menus" section, you can activate commands on these menus from the keyboard, rather than using the mouse. Notice that each menu has an underlined letter, called a *hotkey*. By holding down the Alt key while pressing the underlined letter, the menu is activated. Each command on the menu also has a hotkey. Once you have activated the menu with the hotkey combination, you can type in the underlined letter of these commands without using the Alt key to execute them. For some commands, this method can be the fastest way to start them up and select options.

While working in AutoCAD, you will need to enter ample amounts of data through the keyboard, such as dimensions and construction notes, answer questions with "yes" or "no," and use the keyboard arrow keys. The keyboard will be used constantly. It may help to get into the habit of keeping the left hand on the keyboard and the right hand on the mouse—if you are right-handed—and the other way around, if you are left-handed.

The Mouse

Your mouse will most likely have two or three buttons. So far in this skill, you have used only the left mouse button, for choosing menus, commands or command options, or for holding down the button and dragging a menu, toolbar, or window. That button is the one you will be using most frequently.

While drawing, the right mouse button will be used for the following three operations:

- as a substitute for the Enter key

- to use in combination with the Shift key to bring up a special menu called the Cursor menu (see Skill 10, *Controlling Text in a Drawing*)

- to access customization dialog boxes. (This is an advanced use and won't be covered in this book.)

If you have a three-button mouse, the third button is usually programmed to bring up the Cursor menu mentioned above, instead of using the second button with the Shift key.

The next skill will familiarize you with a few basic commands which will enable you to draw a small diagram. If you are going to take a break and want to close down AutoCAD, click File ➢ Exit and choose not to save the drawing.

Are You Experienced?

Now you can. . .

☑ **open a new drawing using the Start Up dialog box**

☑ **recognize the elements of the AutoCAD Graphics window**

☑ **understand how the Command window works and why it's important**

☑ **use drop-down menus**

☑ **call up and control the positioning of toolbars**

☑ **use the keyboard and mouse with AutoCAD**

Basic Commands to Get Started

- ➔ Understanding coordinate systems
- ➔ Drawing your first figure
- ➔ Erasing, offsetting, filleting, extending, and trimming lines in a drawing

Now that you have taken a quick tour of the AutoCAD screen, you are ready to begin drawing. In this skill you will be introduced to the most basic commands used in drawing with AutoCAD. To get you started, I will guide you through the process of drawing a box (Figure 2.1).

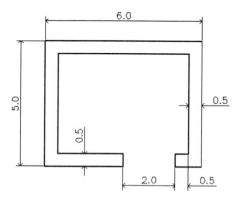

FIGURE 2.1: The box to be drawn

You only need to use five or six commands to draw the box. First, you'll become familiar with the Line command and how to make lines a specific length. Then I'll go over the strategy for completing the box.

The Line Command

In traditional architectural drafting, lines were often drawn to extend slightly past their endpoints (Figure 2.2). This is no longer done in CAD except for special effects.

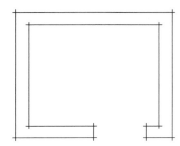

FIGURE 2.2: Box drawn with overlapping lines

The *Line command* draws a line between locations on existing lines, between geometric figures, or between two points which you can choose anywhere within the drawing area. These points can be designated by either clicking them on the screen, by entering the *x* and *y* coordinates for each point in the Command window, or by entering distances and angles at the command line. After the first segment of a line is drawn, you have the option of ending the command or drawing another line segment from the end of the first one. You can continue to draw adjoining line segments for as long as you like. Let's see how it works.

1. Click File ➤ New and then click the Start from Scratch button in the Create New Drawing dialog box to start a new drawing.

2. Be sure that the Draw and Modify toolbars have been docked on the left side of the drawing area, as in Figure 2.3. Refer to Skill 1, *Getting to Know AutoCAD*, if you need a reminder on how to bring up or move toolbars.

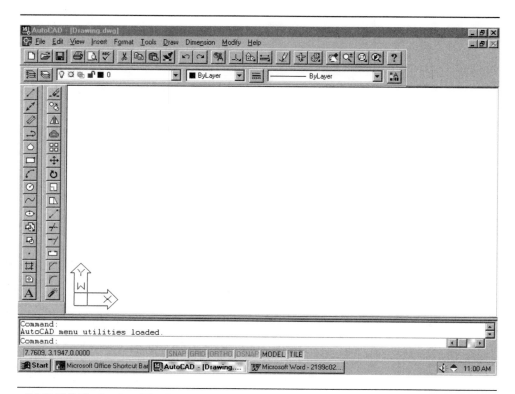

FIGURE 2.3: The Draw and Modify toolbars docked on the left side of the drawing area

3.   Click the Line button at the top of the Draw toolbar.

NOTE   The Line command can also be started by picking Draw ➢ Line on the Menu bar, or by typing l ↵.

Look at the bottom of the Command window and see how the Command: prompt has changed.

The prompt now tells you that the Line command has been started (Command: _line) and that AutoCAD is waiting for you to designate the first point of the line (From point:).

 **WARNING**   As important as it is to keep an eye on the Command window, some of the prompts may not make sense to you until you get used to them.

4. Move the cursor onto the drawing area and, using the mouse, click a random point to start a line.

5. Move the cursor away from the point you clicked and notice how a line segment appears which rubberbands from the point you just picked to the cursor. The line changes length and direction as you move the cursor.

6. Look at the Command window again and notice that the prompt has changed.

It now is telling you that AutoCAD is waiting for you to designate the next point (To point:).

7. Continue picking points and adding lines as you move the cursor around the screen (see Figure 2.4). Note that the Command window now repeats the To point: prompt each time you pick another point.

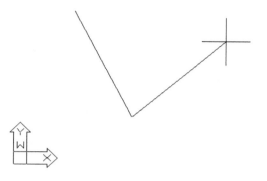

FIGURE 2.4: Drawing the second line segment

8. When you've drawn six or seven line segments, click the right mouse button to end the Line command. The cursor separates from the last drawn line segment. Look at the Command window once again.

The Command: prompt has returned to the bottom line. This tells you there is no command running.

 TIP You could have also pressed Enter to end the command. The right mouse button serves as the Enter key when commands are running, and when the cursor is in the drawing area.

In this exercise, you used the left mouse button to select the Line button from the Draw toolbar and also to pick several points in the drawing area to make the line segments. Then you clicked the right mouse button (or Enter on the keyboard) to end the Line command.

> **NOTE** In the exercises that follow, the Enter symbol (⏎) will be used when you are asked to press the Enter key or click the right mouse button while a command is running.

Coordinates

Try using the Line command again, but instead of picking them in the drawing area with the mouse as you did before, this time enter x and y coordinates for each point from the keyboard. To see how, follow these steps:

First, you'll clear the screen using the Erase command.

1. Type **erase** ⏎.

2. Type **all** ⏎.

3. Press ⏎.

Now start drawing lines again.

1. Start the Line command again by clicking the Line button on the Draw toolbar.

2. Type **2,2** ⏎.

3. Type **6,3** ⏎.

4. Type **4,6** ⏎.

5. Type **1,3** ⏎.

6. Type **10,6** ⏎.

7. Type **10,1** ⏎.

8. Type **2,7** ⏎.

9. Press ⏎ again to end the command.

The lines will be similar to those you drew previously, but this time you know where each point is located relative to the 0,0 point. In the drawing area, every point has an x and y coordinate. In steps 4–9 above you entered the x and y coordinates for each point. For a new drawing, like this one, the 0,0 point is in the lower-left corner of the drawing area and all points in the drawing area are positive (Figure 2.5).

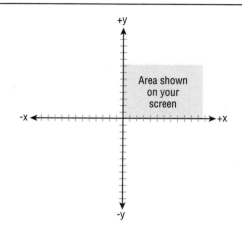

FIGURE 2.5: The x and y coordinates on the drawing areas

1. Move the cursor around and notice the coordinate readout on the left end of the status bar at the bottom of the screen, which displays the coordinates of the cursor's position.

2. Move the cursor as close to the lower-left corner of the drawing area as you can without it changing into an arrow. The coordinate readout should be close to 0.0000,0.0000,0.0000.

NOTE   You will see a readout for the z coordinate as well, but we can ignore it for now as you will be working only in two dimensions for the majority of this book. The z coordinate will always read as 0 until we work in three dimensions (see Appendix A, *A Look at Drawing in 3D*).

3. Move the cursor to the top-left corner of the drawing area. The readout will change to something close to 0.0000,9.0000,0.0000, indicating that the top of the screen is nine units away from the bottom.

4. Move the cursor one more time to the upper-right corner of the drawing area. The readout will still have a *y* coordinate of approximately 9.0000 and the *x* coordinate will now have a value of somewhere between 12.0000 and 16.0000, depending on the size of your monitor and how the various parts of the AutoCAD Graphics window (see Skill 1 for a recap) are laid out on your screen.

The drawing area of a new drawing is preset to be 9 units high and 12–16 units wide, with the lower-left corner of the drawing at the coordinates 0,0.

 NOTE For the moment, it doesn't matter what measure of distance these units represent. Those decisions will be addressed in Skill 3, *Setting Up a Drawing*. And don't worry about the four decimal places in the coordinate readout, which is controlled by a setting you will learn about in the next skill, as well.

Relative Coordinates

With knowledge of the coordinate system used by AutoCAD, you can draw lines of any length and in any direction you desire. Look at the box in Figure 2.1. Because you know the dimensions, you could calculate, by adding and subtracting, the absolute coordinates for each vertex and then use the Line command to draw the shape by entering these coordinates from the keyboard. But AutoCAD offers you two much easier tools for drawing this box: the relative Cartesian and relative polar coordinate systems.

When drawing lines, these systems use a set of new points based on the last point designated, rather than the 0,0 point of the drawing area. They are called "relative" coordinate systems because the coordinates used are *relative* to the last point specified. If you have the first point of a line located at the coordinate 4,6 and you want the line to extend 8 units to the right, the coordinate that is relative to the first point is 8,0 (8 units in the positive *x* direction and 0 units in the *y* direction), while the actual—or *absolute*—coordinate of the second point would be 12,6.

The *relative Cartesian coordinate system* uses relative *x* and *y* coordinates in just the manner shown above, while the *relative polar coordinate system* relies on a distance and an angle relative to the last point specified. You will probably favor one system over the other, but you need to know both systems because there will be times when, due to limitations created by known or unknown information, you will have no choice. A limitation of this nature will be illustrated in Skill 4, *Gaining Drawing Strategies: Part 1*.

When entering the relative coordinates, you need to enter an "at" symbol (@) before the coordinates. In the above example, the relative Cartesian coordinates would be entered as **@8,0**. The @ symbol lets AutoCAD know that the numbers following that symbol represent coordinates which are relative to the last point designated.

Relative Cartesian Coordinates

The Cartesian system of coordinates, named after the philosopher René Descartes, who invented the x,y coordinate system in the 1600s, uses a vertical (x) and horizontal (y) component to locate a point relative to the 0,0 point. The relative Cartesian system uses the same components to locate the point relative to the last point picked, so it's a way of telling AutoCAD how far left or right and up or down to extend a line or move an object from the last point picked (Figure 2.6). If the direction is to the left, the x coordinate will be negative. Similarly, if the direction is down, the y coordinate will be negative. Use this system when you know the horizontal and vertical distances from point 1 to point 2. To enter data using this system, use this form: **@x,y**.

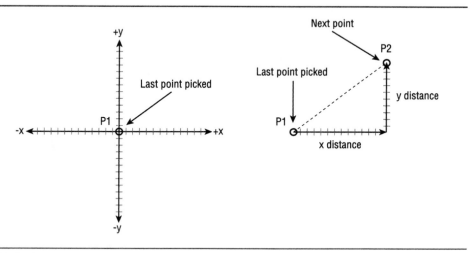

FIGURE 2.6: The relative Cartesian coordinate system

Relative Polar Coordinates

This system requires a known distance and direction from point 1 to point 2. Calculating the distance is pretty straightforward: it's always positive and is simply the distance away from point 1 that point 2 will be placed. The direction requires a convention for determining an angle. AutoCAD defines right (three o'clock) as the direction of the 0°angle, and all other directions are determined from a counter-clockwise rotation (Figure 2.7). Up is 90°, left is 180°, down is 270°, and a full circle is 360°. To let AutoCAD know that you are entering an angle and not a relative *y* coordinate, use the "less than" symbol (<) before the angle and after the distance. So in the example above, designating a point 8 units to the right of the first point, you would enter **@8<0**.

NOTE   Remember, use this method to draw a line from the first point when you know the distance and direction to its next point. For entering data using relative polar coordinates, use this form: ***@distance<angle***.

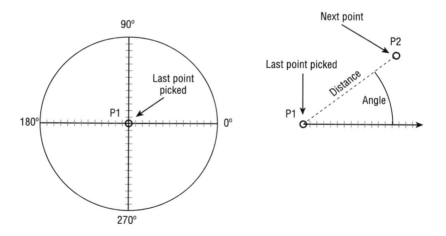

FIGURE 2.7: The relative polar coordinate system

Drawing the Box

Now that you have the basics down, the following exercises will take you through the steps to draw the four lines comprising the outline of the box using both relative coordinate systems.

Using Relative Cartesian Coordinates

1. Click File ➤ New. You will be prompted to save your last drawing: Click no.

2. In the Create New Drawing dialog box, click Start from Scratch, then click OK.

3. Select the Line button from the top of the Draw toolbar.

4. At the From point: prompt in the Command window, type in **3,3** ↵. This is an absolute Cartesian coordinate and will be the first point.

5. Type **@6,0** ↵.

6. Type **@0,5** ↵.

7. Type **@-6,0** ↵.

8. Type **c** ↵. The letter *c* stands for *close*. Entering this letter after drawing several lines closes the shape by making the next line segment extend from the last point specified to the first point (Figure 2.8). It also ends the Line command. Notice the Command: prompt signifying that AutoCAD is ready for a new command.

Erasing Lines

To prepare to draw the box again, use the Erase command to erase the four lines you have just drawn.

1. Click Modify ➤ Erase. Notice how the cursor changes from the crosshair to a little square. This is called the *pickbox*. When you see it on the screen, it's a sign that AutoCAD is ready for you to select objects on the screen. Also, notice the Command window. It is prompting you to select objects.

2. Place the pickbox on one of the lines and click. The line changes into a dashed line. This is called *ghosting* or *highlighting*.

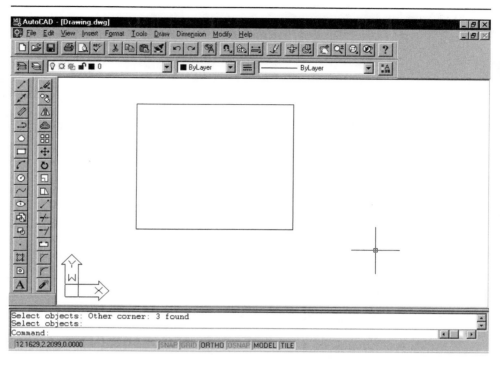

FIGURE 2.8: The first four lines of the box

3. Do the same thing for the rest of the lines.

4. Press ⏎. The objects are erased and the Erase command ends.

Using Relative Polar Coordinates

Now draw the box again using the polar method.

1. Start the Line command (choose the Line button from the Draw toolbar).

2. Type in **3,3** ⏎ to start the box at the same point.

3. Type **@6<0** ⏎.

4. Type **@5<90** ⏎.

5.   Type **@6<180** ↵.

6.   Type **c** ↵ to close the box and end the Line command. Your box will once again resemble the box in Figure 2.8.

You can see from this simple exercise that either method can be used to draw a simple shape. When the shapes you are drawing get more complex and the amount of available information about the shapes varies from segment to segment, there will be situations where one of the two relative coordinate systems will turn out to be more appropriate. As you start drawing the floor plan of the cabin in Skills 3 and 4, you will get more practice using these systems.

The Offset Command

The next task is to create the lines which represent the inside walls of the box. Because they are all equidistant from the lines you have already drawn, the *Offset command* is the appropriate command to use. You will offset the existing lines 0.5 units to the inside.

The Offset command has three steps:

- setting the offset distance

- picking the object to offset

- indicating the offset direction

Here's how it works:

1.   At the Command: prompt, click Modify ➢ Offset, or click the Offset button on the Modify toolbar. The prompt changes to Offset distance or Through <1.0000>:. This is a confusing prompt—you really have three choices for setting the offset distance:

- enter a distance on the keyboard

- pick two points on the screen to establish the offset distance as the distance between those two picked points (the Through option)

- accept the default offset distance of 1.0000 in the brackets (< >)

2.   Enter **0.5** ↵ to move to the second stage of the command.

NOTE When I say to "Enter" something, it means to type the data that follows the word Enter and then press the Enter key (↵) or the right mouse button.

Note that the cursor has changed to a pickbox, and the prompt changes to say Select object to offset:.

3. Place the pickbox on one of the lines and click. The selected line ghosts (Figure 2.9), the cursor changes back to the crosshair and the prompt changes to Side to offset?. AutoCAD is telling you that to determine the direction of the offset, you have two choices: toward one side of the line or the other. You make the choice by picking, anywhere in the drawing area, on the side of the line you want.

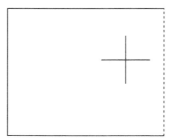

FIGURE 2.9: The first line to be offset is selected.

4. Pick a point somewhere inside the box. The offset takes place and the new line is exactly 0.5 units to the inside of the chosen line (Figure 2.10). Notice that the pickbox comes back on. The Offset command is still running and you can offset more lines the same distance.

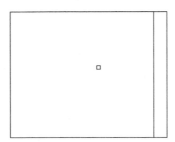

FIGURE 2.10: The first line is offset

 NOTE   You can cancel a command at any time by pressing Esc.

You have three more lines to offset.

5.   Click another line, then click inside the box again. The second line is offset.

6.   Click a third line, click inside the box, then click the fourth line and then again inside the box (Figure 2.11).

 NOTE   The offset distance stays set at the last distance you specify for it—0.5, in this case—until you change it.

7.   Press ↵ to end the Offset command. This command is similar to the Line command in that it keeps running until it is stopped. With Offset, after the first offset, the prompts switch between Select object to offset: and Side to offset? until you press ↵ to end the command.

The inside lines are now drawn, but to complete the box, you need to clean up the intersecting corners. To handle this task efficiently, we will use a new tool called the Fillet command.

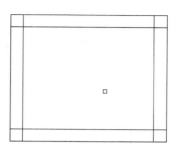

FIGURE 2.11: Four lines have been offset.

The Fillet Command

The *Fillet command* allows you to round off a corner formed by two lines. You control the radius of the curve, so if you set the curve's radius to 0 the lines will form a sharp corner. In this way you can clean up corners like the ones formed by the lines inside the box.

1.   At the Command: prompt, click the Fillet button on the Modify toolbar.

TIP   You can also start the Fillet command by selecting Modify ➤ Fillet from the menu bar, or by typing **f** ↵.

Notice the Command window:

```
Command: _fillet
(TRIM mode) Current fillet radius = 0.5000
Polyline/Radius/Trim/<Select first object>:
```

The default fillet radius is 0.5 units, but you want to use a radius of 0 units.

2. Type **r** ↵ **0** ↵ to change the radius to 0. This has the effect of ending the Fillet command while setting the new radius to 0 units. Press ↵ to restart it.

3. Move the cursor—now a pickbox—to the box and click two intersecting lines as shown in Figure 2.12. The intersecting lines will both be trimmed to make a sharp corner (Figure 2.13). The Fillet command automatically ends.

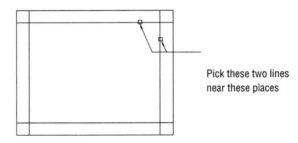

Pick these two lines
near these places

FIGURE 2.12: Pick two lines to execute the Fillet command.

4. Press ↵ to restart the command and fillet two more lines in a similar fashion.

5. Continue restarting the command and filleting the lines for each corner until all corners are cleaned up (Figure 2.14).

 WARNING   If you make a mistake and pick the wrong part of a line or the wrong line, press Esc to end the command and then type **u** ↵. This will undo the effect of the last command.

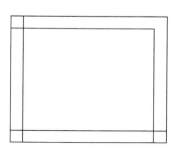

FIGURE 2.13: The first cleaned-up corner

FIGURE 2.14: The box with all corners cleaned up

Used together like this, the Offset and Fillet commands are a powerful combination of tools to lay out walls on a floor plan drawing. Since these commands are so important, let's take a closer look at them to see how they work. Both commands are found on the Modify toolbar or drop-down menu, both initially require you to enter a numerical value—for offset distance and fillet radius—and both hold that value as the default until it is changed. However, the Offset command keeps running until you stop it, and the Fillet command stops after each use and must be restarted for multiple fillets. These two commands are probably the most frequently used tools in AutoCAD. You will learn about more of their uses in later skills.

Completing the Box

The final step in completing the box (Figure 2.1) is to make an opening in the bottom wall. From the diagram, you can see that the opening is 2 units wide and set off from the right inside corner by 0.5 units. To make this opening, you will use the Offset command twice, changing the offset for each distance.

Offsetting Lines to Mark an Opening

Follow these steps to establish the precise position of the opening:

1. At the Command: prompt, start the Offset command, either from the Modify toolbar or the Modify menu. Notice the Command window. The default distance is now 0.5, the offset distance you previously set to offset the outside lines of the box to make the inside lines. You want to use this distance again. Press ↵ to accept this default distance.

2. Pick the inside vertical line on the right, and then pick a point to the left of this line. The line is offset to make a new line 0.5 units to its left (Figure 2.15).

3. Press ↵ to end the Offset command, then press it again to restart the command. This will allow you to reset the offset distance.

4. Enter **2.5** as the new offset distance and press ↵.

5. Click the new line then pick a point to the left (Figure 2.16).

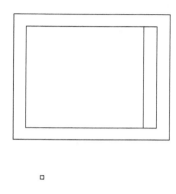

FIGURE 2.15: Offsetting the first line of the opening

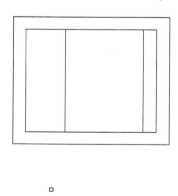

FIGURE 2.16: Offsetting the second line of the opening

You now have two new lines indicating where the opening will be. You can use these lines to form the opening using the Extend and Trim commands.

Extending Lines

The *Extend command* is used to lengthen (extend) lines to meet other lines or geometric figures (called *boundary edges*). The execution of the Extend command may be a little tricky at first until you see how it works. Once you understand it, however, it will become automatic. The command has two steps: First, you will pick the boundary edge or edges, and second, you will pick the lines you wish to extend to meet those boundary edges. After selecting the boundary edges, you must press ↵ before you begin selecting lines to extend.

1. At the Command: prompt, go to the Modify menu and select Extend. Notice the Command window.

```
Command: _extend
Select boundary edges: (Projmode = UCS, Edgemode = No extend)
Select objects:
```

2. The bottom line says to select objects, but, in this case, you need to observe the bottom two lines of text in order to know that AutoCAD is prompting you to select boundary edges.

3. Pick the very bottom horizontal line (Figure 2.17) and press ↵.

TIP The Select Objects: prompt would be more useful if it said "Select objects, and press Enter when finished selecting objects." But it doesn't. You have to train yourself to press Enter when you are finished selecting objects for a particular step—in this case, selecting objects to serve as boundary edges—in the execution of a command, in order to get out of the selection mode and move on to the next step in the command.

4. Pick the two new vertical lines created by the Offset command. Be sure to place the pickbox somewhere on the lower halves of these lines, or AutoCAD will ignore your picks. The lines are extended to the boundary edge line. Press ↵ to end the Extend command (Figure 2.18).

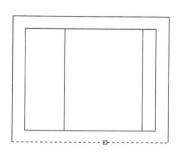

FIGURE 2.17: Selecting a line to be a boundary edge

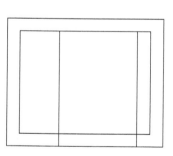

FIGURE 2.18: The lines are extended to the boundary edge.

Trimming Lines

The final step is to trim away the horizontal lines to complete the opening. To do this, you will use the *Trim command*. As with the Extend command, there are two steps to trimming. The first one is to select reference lines—in this case, they're called *cutting edges* because they determine the edge or edges to which a line is trimmed.

1. At the Command: prompt, select Modify ➤ Trim from the menu bar, click the Trim button from the Modify toolbar, or type **tr** ↵. Any of these will start the Trim command.

   Notice the Command window. Similar to the Extend command, the bottom line prompts you to select objects, but the second line up tells you to select cutting edges.

2. Pick the two vertical offset lines which were just extended as your cutting edges. Then press ↵ (Figure 2.19).

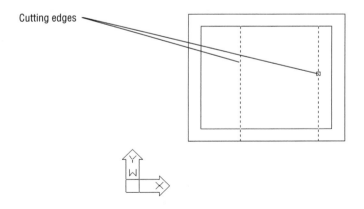

Cutting edges

FIGURE 2.19: Lines selected to be cutting edges

3. Pick the two horizontal lines across the opening somewhere between the cutting edge lines (Figure 2.20).

   The opening is trimmed away (Figure 2.21).

Lines to be trimmed

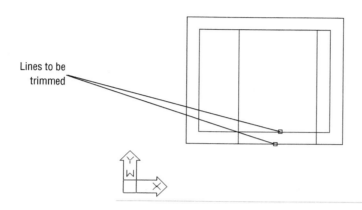

FIGURE 2.20: Lines selected to be trimmed

 NOTE   If you trim the wrong line or wrong part of a line, you can click the Undo button on the Standard toolbar. This will undo the last trim without canceling the Trim command and you can try again.

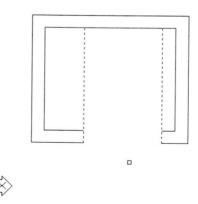

FIGURE 2.21: Wall lines are trimmed to make the opening.

Now let's remove the extra part of our trimming guide lines.

1. Press ↵ twice—once to end the Trim command and again to restart it. This will allow you to pick new cutting edges for another trim operation.

2. Pick the two upper horizontal lines in the lower wall as your cutting edges, shown in Figure 2.22, and press ↵.

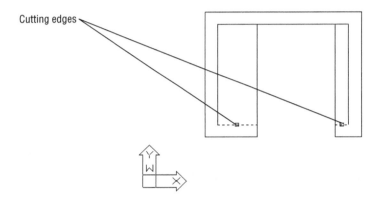

Cutting edges

FIGURE 2.22: Lines picked to be cutting edges

3. Pick the two vertical lines that extend above the new opening. Be sure to pick them above the opening (Figure 2.23). The lines are trimmed away and the opening is complete. Press ↵ to end the Trim command (Figure 2.24).

Congratulations! You have just completed the first drawing project in this book and have covered all the tools in Skill 2. As you will see in later sections of the book, these skills will be invaluable to you as you learn how to work on drawings for actual projects.

A valuable exercise at this time would be to draw this box two or three more times, until you can do it without the instructions. This will be a confidence builder and will get you ready to take on new information in the next skill, in which you will set up a drawing for a building.

Lines to be trimmed

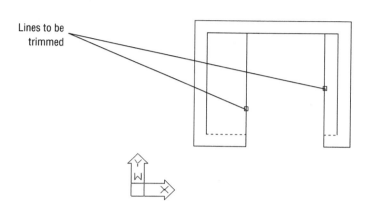

FIGURE 2.23: Lines picked to be trimmed

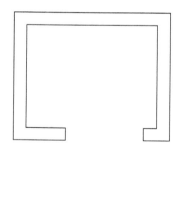

FIGURE 2.24: The completed trim

The box you drew was 6 units by 5 units, but how big was it? You really don't know at this time, because the units could represent any actual distance: inches, feet, meters, miles, etc. Also, the box was positioned conveniently on the screen so you didn't have any problem viewing it. Consider the situation if you were drawing a building that was 200 feet long and 60 feet wide. The next skill to be tackled is how to set up a drawing for a project of a specific size.

You can exit AutoCAD now without saving this drawing. To do this, click File ➤ Exit. When the dialog box comes up asking if you want to save changes, click No. Or you can leave AutoCAD open and go on to the following practice section or the next skill.

If You Would Like More Practice...

Draw the following object (Figure 2.25).

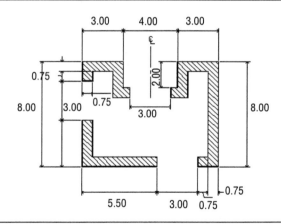

FIGURE 2.25: Practice drawing

You can use the same tools and strategy used to draw the box. Use File ➤ New to start a new drawing and click the Start from Scratch button in the Create New Drawing dialog box.

Are You Experienced?

Now you can...

- ☑ understand the basics of coordinates
- ☑ discern between the two relative coordinate systems used by AutoCAD
- ☑ use the Line, Erase, Offset, Fillet, Extend, and Trim commands to manipulate lines in a drawing

Setting Up a Drawing

- ⊙ Setting up drawing units
- ⊙ Using a grid
- ⊙ Zooming in and out of a drawing
- ⊙ Naming and saving a file

In Skill 2 you explored the drawing area as it is set up by default when a new drawing is opened. It is probably 9 units high by 12 to 16 units wide, depending upon the size of your monitor. You drew the box within this area. If you drew the additional diagram offered as a supplemental exercise, the drawing area was set up the same way.

For most of the rest of this book you will be developing drawings for a cabin with outside wall dimensions of 25' × 16'. In this skill, you will learn how to set up the drawing area to lay out the floor plan for a building of a specific size. The decimal units with which you have been drawing until now will be changed to feet and inches and the drawing area will be transformed so that it can represent an area large enough to display the floor plan of the cabin you will be drawing. You will be introduced to some new tools that allow you to visualize the area your screen represents and to draw within a specified incremental distance. Finally, you will save this drawing to a floppy disk or to a special directory on the hard disk.

Drawing Units

When you draw lines of a precise length in AutoCAD, you will use one of five kinds of linear units. Angular units can also be one of five different types. You can select the type of units to use, or accept the default decimal units that you used in the last chapter.

When you start a new drawing, AutoCAD brings up a blank drawing called `drawing.dwg` with the linear and angular units set to decimal numbers. The units and other basic setup parameters applied to this new drawing are based on a prototype drawing, or drawing template, with default settings—including those for the units—which are stored with the drawing template file `Acad.dwt`. You can choose another template file as a prototype drawing, or you can create your own set of prototype drawings.

Skill 3 will cover some of the tools for changing the basic parameters of a new drawing so you can tailor it to the cabin project. You will start by setting up new units.

1. Start up AutoCAD and, in the Start Up dialog box, click the Start from Scratch button. Be sure English is selected and click OK.

2. From the Format menu, select Units. The Units Control dialog box appears (Figure 3.1). In the Units area, there are five choices for linear units, and

Decimal is currently selected. Similarly, in the Angles area, of the five choices, Decimal Degrees is the default.

NOTE The white circles next to the choices are called *radio buttons*. Only one in each list may be selected at a time.

FIGURE 3.1:   The Units Control dialog box

3. In the Units area, click the radio button next to Architectural. These units are feet and inches, which you will be using for the cabin project. Notice the two Precision drop-down lists at the bottom of the Units and Angles areas. When the linear units specification was changed from Decimal to Architectural, the number in the Precision drop-down list on the left changed from 0.0000 to 0'-0 ¹⁄₁₆". At this level of precision, linear distances will be displayed to the nearest ¹⁄₁₆".

4. Click some of the other radio buttons in the Units area and note the way the units appear in the Precision drop-down list. Then click the Architectural radio button again.

NOTE Drop-down lists are lists of choices with only the selected choice displayed. When you click the arrow the list opens and you can select another choice. The list closes and the one chosen is now displayed. Like radio buttons, only one choice from the list can be made at a time.

5. Click the arrow in the Precision drop-down list for Units. The drop-down list appears, showing the choices of precision for Architectural units (Figure 3.2). This setting controls the degree of precision to which AutoCAD will *display* a linear distance. If set to ⅟₁₆", this means any line which is drawn more precisely—such as a line 6'-3 ½" long—will be displayed to the nearest ⅟₁₆" or, in the example, as 6'-3 ⅟₁₆". But the line will still be 6'-3 ½" long. If you change the precision setting to ½" and then use the Distance command (explained in Skill 7, *Using Blocks and Wblocking*) to measure the line, you will see that its length is 6'-3 ½".

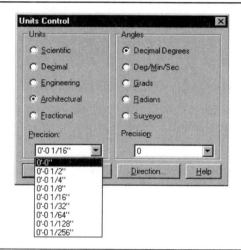

FIGURE 3.2:   The Precision drop-down menu for Architectural units

6. Click 0'-0 ⅟₁₆ to maintain the precision for display of linear units at ⅟₁₆".

In the Angles area, you can see that there is a choice between Decimal Degrees and Deg/Min/Sec, among others. Most drafters find the decimal angular units the most practical, but the default precision setting is to the nearest degree. This might be too restrictive, so you should change that to the nearest hundredth of a degree.

1. Click the arrow in the Angles Precision drop-down list.

2. Click 0.00.

The Units Control dialog box will now indicate that in your drawing you plan to use Architectural units with a precision of 1/16", and Decimal angular units with a precision of 0.00 (Figure 3.3).

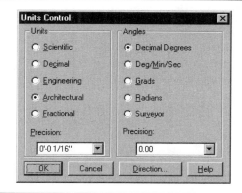

FIGURE 3.3:   The Units Control dialog box after changes

NOTE   You will have a chance to work with the Surveyor angular units later in the book, in Skill 12, *Managing External References,* when you develop a site plan for the cabin.

The Direction button at the bottom of the dialog box takes you to another dialog box which has settings to control the direction of 0 degrees and the direction of angular rotation. There is no need to change these from the defaults, so, if you want to take a look, open the Direction Control dialog box, note the choices and then click OK to close it. You won't have occasion in the course of this book to change any of those settings.

3. Click OK in the Units Control dialog box to close it. Notice the coordinate readout in the lower-left corner of the screen. It now reads out in feet and inches.

This tour of the Units Control dialog box has introduced you to the choices you have for the type of units and degree of precision for linear and angular measurement. The next step in setting up a drawing is learning how to determine the size of a drawing.

Drawing Size

As you discovered earlier, the default drawing area on the screen for a new drawing is 12–16 units wide and 9 units high. After changing the units to Architectural, the same drawing area is now 12–16 *inches* wide and 9 *inches* high. You can check this by moving the crosshair cursor around on the drawing area and looking at the coordinate readout, as you did in the previous skill.

TIP When Decimal units are changed to Architectural units, one Decimal unit translates to one inch. Some industries use Decimal units to represent feet instead of inches. If their drawing's units are switched to Architectural, the drawing must be scaled up by a factor of 12 to be the accurate size.

The drawing area is defined as the part of the screen in which you draw. The distance across the drawing area can be made larger or smaller through a process known as zooming in or out. To see how this works, you'll learn about a tool called the grid that helps you to draw and visualize the size of your drawing.

The Grid

The grid is a pattern of regularly spaced dots used as an aid to drawing. You can set the grid to be visible or invisible. The area covered by the grid depends on a setting called *drawing limits*. To learn how to manipulate the grid size, you'll make the grid visible, use the Zoom In and Zoom Out commands to vary the view of the grid and then change the area over which the grid extends by resetting the drawing limits.

1. At the Command: prompt, move the crosshair cursor to the status bar at the bottom of the screen, and double-click the Grid button. The word GRID will darken and dots will appear on most of the drawing area (Figure 3.4). These dots are the grid. They are preset by default to be 0.5" apart and they extend from the 0,0 point out to the right and up to the coordinate point 1'-0",0'-9". Notice that rows of grid dots run right along the left edge, top and bottom of the drawing area, but the dots don't extend all the way to the right side. The grid dot at the 0,0 point is positioned exactly at the lower-left corner of the screen, and the one at 1'-0",0'-9" is on the top edge not too far from the upper-right corner.

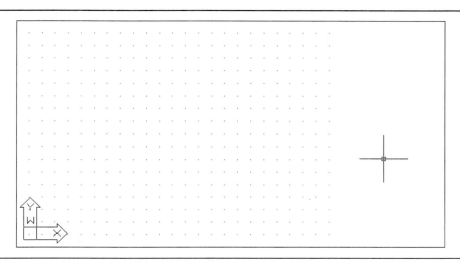

FIGURE 3.4:   The AutoCAD default grid

2. For a better view of the entire grid, use the *Zoom Out* command. From the drop-down menus, select View ➤ Zoom ➤ Out. The view changes and the grid appears smaller (Figure 3.5). Move the crosshair cursor to the lower-left corner of the grid, then to the upper-right corner and note the coordinate readout in the lower-left of your screen. These two points should read as approximately 0'-0",0'-0" and 1'-0",0'-9" respectively.

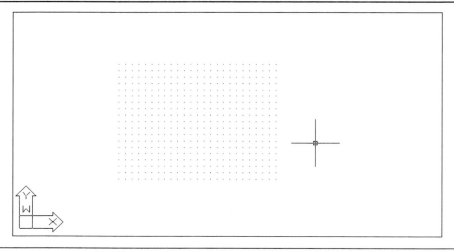

FIGURE 3.5:   The grid after zooming out

3. On the status bar, next to the Grid button, double-click the Snap button, then move the cursor back onto the grid and look at the coordinate readout again. The cursor stops at each grid point and the readout is to the nearest half inch. Now when you place the crosshair cursor on the lower-left corner of the grid, the readout is exactly 0'-0",0'-0", and 1'-0",0'-9" for the lower-left and upper-right corners. The Snap tool locks the cursor onto the grid dots, and even when the cursor is not on the grid but somewhere outside it on the drawing area, the cursor maintains the grid spacing.

4. Use the Zoom Out command two more times. The first time the grid gets even smaller and then, after the second use of the command, the grid disappears and you get a message on the second line of the Command window: "Grid too dense to display." Once the dots get too close together, the monitor cannot display them and AutoCAD lets you know.

5. On the same menu, use the Zoom In tool twice to bring the view of the grid back to the way it was in Figure 3.5. You are not changing the size of the grid, just the view of it. It's like switching from a wide-angled to a telephoto lens on a camera.

The grid is more of a guide than an actual boundary of your drawing. You can change a setting to force lines to be drawn only in the area covered by the grid, but this is not ordinarily done. For most purposes, you can draw anywhere on the screen. The grid merely serves as a tool for visualizing how your drawing is going to be laid out.

Because it will serve as a layout tool for this project, you need to increase the area covered by the grid from its present size of 1' × 9" to 60' × 40'. Because the drawing limits control the size of the grid, you need to change this setting.

Drawing Limits

The Drawing Limits setting records the coordinates of the lower-left and upper-right corners of the grid. The coordinates for the lower-left corner are 0,0 by default, and are usually left at that setting. You only need to change the coordinates for the upper-right corner.

1. At the Command: prompt, pick Format ➤ Drawing Limits from the drop-down menus. Notice the Command window:

```
Command: '_limits
Reset Model space limits:
ON/OFF/<Lower left corner> <0'-0",0'-0">:
```

The bottom command line tells you that the first step is to decide whether to change the default coordinates for the lower-left limits, which are presently set at 0,0. There is no need to change these.

2. Press ↵ to accept 0,0 for this corner. The bottom command line changes and is now allowing you to change the coordinates for the upper-right corner of the limits. This is where you want to change the settings.

3. Type **60',40'** ↵. Be sure to include the foot sign (').

NOTE   AutoCAD requires that you always indicate when a distance is feet by using the foot sign ('). You do not have to use the inch sign (").

The grid now appears to extend to the top-right edge of the drawing area (Figure 3.6), but it actually extends way past the edges. It was one foot wide and now it's 60 times that, but the drawing area is only showing us the first foot or so. To bring the whole grid onto the screen, use the Zoom command again, but this time you will use the All option.

4. Select View ➤ Zoom ➤ All. The grid disappears and you get the "Grid too dense to display" message in the Command window.

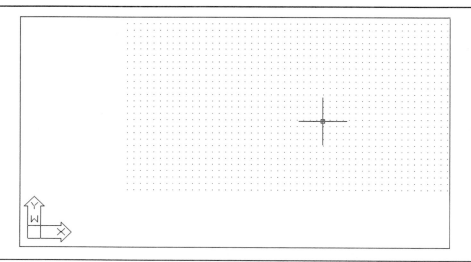

FIGURE 3.6:   The same view with the grid extended to 60'×40'

Remember that you found the grid spacing to be 0.5", by default. If the drawing area is giving us a view of a 60' × 40' grid with dots at 0.5", the grid is 1440 dots wide and 960 dots high. If the whole grid were to be shown on the screen, the dots would be so close together that they would only be about one pixel in size and would solidly fill the drawing area. So AutoCAD won't display them at these settings.

You need to change the spacing for the dots for two reasons: first, the spacing needs to be larger so that AutoCAD will display them; and second, for the drawing task ahead, it will be more useful to have the spacing set differently. Remember how we turned Snap on, and the cursor stopped at each dot? If you set the dot spacing to 12", you can use Grid and Snap modes to help you draw the outline of the cabin, because the dimensions of the outside wall line are in even feet: 25' × 16'. Here's how:

1. At the Command: prompt, select Tools ➤ Drawing Aids. The Drawing Aids dialog box appears (Figure 3.7). The settings for the Grid and Snap aids are in the middle and on the right. Notice that they are both set for an *x* and *y* spacing of 0.5".

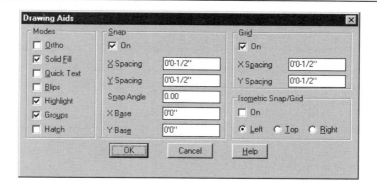

FIGURE 3.7: The Drawing Aids dialog box

2. In the Grid section, click in the X Spacing box and change it to 0. If you set the grid spacing to 0, it will then take on whatever spacing you set for the 'Snap. This is how you lock the two together. When the X spacing reads 0, press ↵. The Grid Y Spacing changes to match the X Spacing.

3. In the Snap section, click in the X Spacing box and change the setting to 12. The inch sign is not required. Then press ↵. The Y Spacing for the Snap changes to automatically match the X Spacing.

4. Click OK. The grid is now visible (Figure 3.8). Move the cursor around on the grid—be sure Snap is on—and notice the coordinate readout. It is displaying coordinates to the nearest foot, to conform to the new grid and snap spacing.

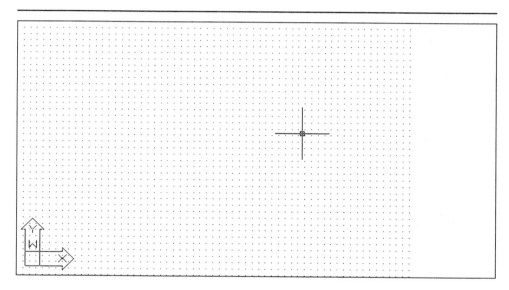

FIGURE 3.8:   The new 60'×40' grid with 12" dot spacing

Drawing with Grid and Snap

Your drawing area now has the proper settings and is zoomed to a convenient magnification. You should be ready to draw the first lines of the cabin.

1. At the Command: prompt, start the Line command (choose the Line button on the Draw toolbar) and pick a point on the grid in the lower-left quadrant of the drawing area (Figure 3.9).

2. Hold the crosshair cursor to the right of the point just picked and look at the coordinate readout.

3. Double-click the coordinate readout and note the change. The coordinates are frozen and ghosted out.

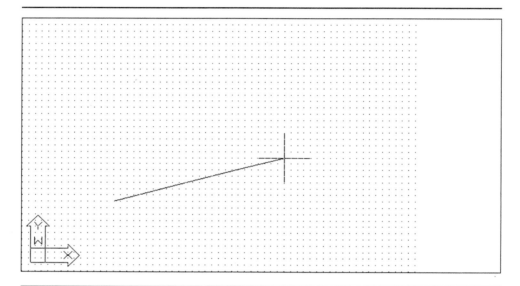

FIGURE 3.9: One point picked on the grid

4. Double-click the coordinate readout again, move the cursor back onto the grid and note how the readout has changed this time. Now it's displaying relative polar coordinates from the first point picked.

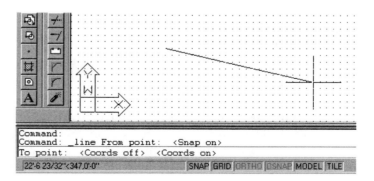

5. Hold the crosshair cursor directly out to the right of the first point picked and look at the coordinate readout. It will be displaying a distance in even feet and should have an angle of 0.00. (Ignore the extra *z* coordinate.)

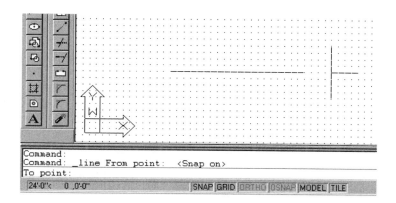

6. Continue moving the crosshair cursor left or right until the readout displays 25'-0"<0.00. At this point, click the left mouse button. The first line of the cabin wall is drawn (Figure 3.10).

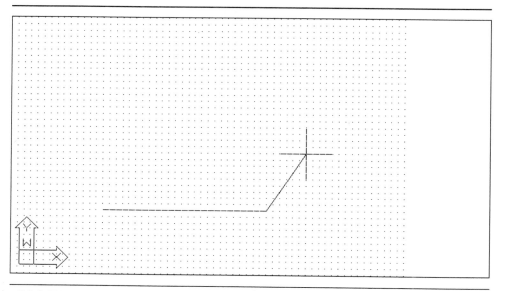

FIGURE 3.10:   The first line of the cabin wall is drawn.

7. Move the crosshair cursor directly above the last point picked to a position such that the coordinate readout displays 16'-0"<90.00, and pick that point.

8. Move the crosshair cursor directly left of the last point picked until the coordinate readout displays 25'-0"<180.00, and pick that point (Figure 3.11).

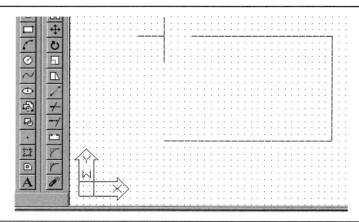

FIGURE 3.11: Drawing the second and third wall lines

9. Finally, type **c** ↵ for close. This tells AutoCAD to draw a line from the last point picked to the first point picked and, in effect, closes the box. Then AutoCAD automatically ends the Line command (Figure 3.12).

This method of laying out building lines by using Snap and Grid, and the coordinate readout is quite useful if the dimensions all conform to a convenient rounded-off number like the nearest 6 inches or, as in this case, the nearest foot. It is not necessary to keep Snap and Grid set to the same spacing, as they were in this example, as long as the grid spacing is an even multiple of the snap spacing. In this project, you could have kept the snap spacing at 1 foot and set the grid spacing to 4 feet. Then you wouldn't have so many dots on the screen and snap would have forced the crosshair cursor to stop at quarter intervals (12") between the 4-foot-spaced grid dots. This would have been a slightly more elegant way to accomplish the same thing.

The key advantage to this method over just typing in the relative coordinates—as was done with the box in Skill 2—is that you avoid having to type in the numbers. You should, however, assess whether the layout you need to draw has characteristics which lend themselves to using grid, snaps and the coordinate readout, or whether just typing in the relative coordinates would be more efficient. As you get more comfortable with AutoCAD, you will see that this is the sort of question that comes up often: which way is the most efficient? This happy dilemma is inevitable in an application with enough tools to give you many strategic choices.

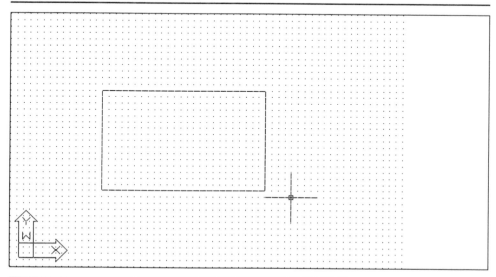

FIGURE 3.12: The completed outside wall lines

Saving Your Work

Like all Windows-compatible applications, when you save a file for the first time by clicking Save, you are given the opportunity to designate a name for the file and a directory or folder to store it in. Later in this book, you will learn how to designate file and directory information before you start a new drawing, but for the cabin project, you will do that now, after the drawing has been started.

If you intend to save the file onto your hard disk or a network server, you should first set up a directory in which to place the file. You can usually do this while AutoCAD is running by minimizing AutoCAD and using Windows Explorer or My Computer to set up a new directory or folder. I recommend that you create a special folder called something like "TrainingData" for storing the files you will generate as you work your way through this book. This will keep them separate from project work already on your computer, and you will always know where to save or find a training drawing. When you return to AutoCAD:

1. Click the Save button on the Standard toolbar or select File ➤ Save.

   The Save Drawing As dialog box comes up.

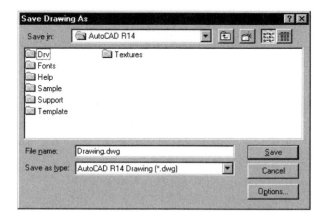

 NOTE The actual directories and files may be different on your computer.

2. In the Save In drop-down list, designate the drive where you wish to save the drawing. If you are saving it on the hard drive or server, navigate to the directory you have designated to hold your training files.

3. In the File name box, change the name from the default name (drawing.dwg) to Cabin3. You're not required to enter the .dwg extension in this case.

 NOTE From now on, when you are directed to save the drawing, you should save it as Cabinx, with x indicating the number of the skill. This way, you will know where in the book to look to for review, if necessary. Multiple saves within a skill should be called Cabinxa, Cabinxb, etc.

4. Click Save. It is now safe to exit AutoCad.

5. If you want to shut AutoCAD down at this time, click File ≻ Exit. Otherwise, keep your drawing up and read on.

The tools covered in this skill will be your key to starting up a new drawing from scratch and getting it ready for a specific project.

The next skill will focus on adding to the drawing and modifying commands you learned as part of Skill 2 and develop strategies for solving problems that occur in the development of a floor plan.

Are You Experienced?

Now you can...

☑ set up linear and angular units for a new drawing

☑ make the grid visible and modify its coverage

☑ use the Zoom In and Zoom Out features

☑ activate the Snap mode and change the snap and grid spacing

☑ use the Zoom All function to fit the grid on the drawing area

☑ draw lines using grid, snap, and the coordinate readout

☑ name and save your file

SKILL 4

Gaining Drawing Strategies: Part 1

- → **Making interior walls**
- → **Zooming in on an area using various zoom tools**
- → **Making doors and swings**
- → **Using Object Snaps**
- → **Using the Copy and Mirror commands**

Assuming that you have worked your way through the first three skills, you have now successfully drawn a box (Skill 2) as well as the outer wall lines of the cabin (Skill 3). From here on, you will develop a floor plan for the cabin and, ultimately, elevations (views of the front, back, and sides of the building which show how the building will look if you're standing facing it). Elevations will be drawn in Skill 8, *Generating Elevations*. The focus in Skill 4 is on gaining a feel for the strategy of drawing in AutoCAD, and on how to solve drawing problems that may come up in the course of laying out the floor plan. Working your way through this skill, your activities will include making the walls, cutting doorway openings, and drawing the doors (Figure 4.1). In Skill 5, *Gaining Drawing Strategies: Part 2*, you will add steps and a balcony, and place fixtures and appliances in the bathroom and kitchen.

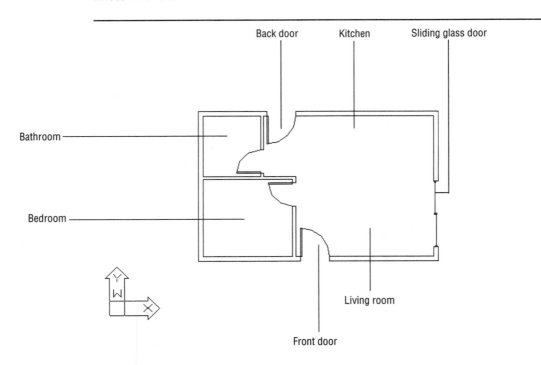

FIGURE 4.1: The basic floor plan of the cabin

Each of the exercises in this skill will present opportunities to practice using commands you already know from previous skills and to learn a few new ones. The most important goal is to begin to use strategic thinking as you develop methods for creating new objects in the floor plan.

Laying Out the Walls

For any floor plan, the walls come first. The first lesson of this skill is that you will not be putting very many new lines in the drawing, at least not as many as you might be expecting. Most new objects in this skill will be created from items already in your drawing. In fact, no new lines will be drawn to make walls. All new walls will be generated from the four exterior wall lines you drew in the last skill.

You will need to create an inside wall line for the exterior walls (because the wall has thickness), and then make the three new interior walls (Figure 4.2). The wall thickness will be 4 inches for interior walls and 6 inches for exterior walls, as exterior walls have an additional layer or two of weather protection, such as shingles or stucco. Finally, you will need to cut five openings in these walls (interior and exterior) for the doorways.

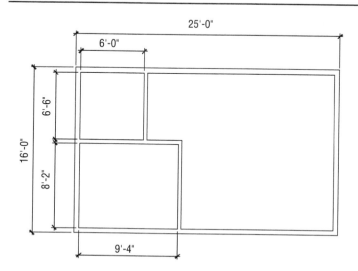

FIGURE 4.2: The wall dimensions

The Exterior Wall Lines

The first step is to offset the existing four wall lines to the inside to make the inside wall lines for the exterior walls. Then you will need to fillet them to clean up their corners, just like you did for the box in Skill 2.

TIP   Buildings are usually—but not always—dimensioned to the outside edge of exterior walls and to the centerline of interior walls. Wood frame buildings are dimensioned to the outside edges of their frames, stud faces, and the centerlines of interior walls.

1. If AutoCAD is already running, select File ➢ Open, open the folder you have designated as your training folder, and select your cabin drawing (you named it Cabin3.dwg at the end of Skill 3). If you are starting up AutoCAD, the Start Up dialog box will appear. Be sure the Open a Drawing button is selected, then look for the Cabin3 drawing in the Select a File box. This box keeps a list of the most recently opened .dwg files and a "More files" option. If you don't find your file in the list, double-click More files. The Select Files dialog box will open. Find and open your training folder, select your drawing file and click Open. The drawing should consist of four lines making a rectangle (Figure 4.3).

2. On the status bar, double-click the Grid and Snap buttons to turn them off. Then start the Offset command by clicking the Offset button on the Modify toolbar.

NOTE   You can also start the Offset command by typing **o** ↵, or selecting Modify ➢ Offset from the drop-down menus.

3. At the Offset distance: prompt, type **6** ↵.

NOTE   Remember: You do not have to enter the inch sign (") but you are required to enter the foot sign (').

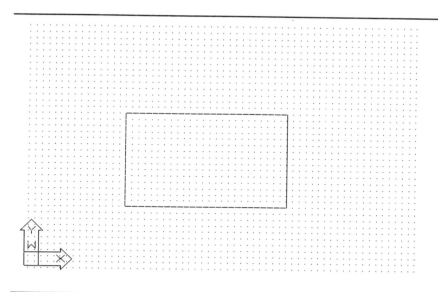

FIGURE 4.3: The cabin as you left it in Skill 3

4. At the Select object to offset: prompt, click one of the four lines.

5. Click in a blank area inside the rectangle. The first line is offset 6 inches to the inside (Figure 4.4). The Offset command is still running and the Select object to offset: prompt is still in effect.

FIGURE 4.4: The first line is offset.

6. Select another outside wall line and click in a blank area on the inside again. Continue doing this until you have offset all four outside wall lines to the inside at the set distance of 6 inches. Then press ↵ to end the Offset command (Figure 4.5). Now you will clean up the corners with the Fillet command.

FIGURE 4.5: All four lines are now offset 6 inches to the inside.

7. Start the Fillet command by clicking the Fillet button on the Modify toolbar.

NOTE Look at the Command window to see whether or not the radius is set to 0. If it is, go on to step 8. Otherwise, type **r** ↵ then type **0** ↵ to set the Fillet radius to 0. The Fillet command will end after a new radius is set. Press ↵ one more time to restart the Fillet command.

8. Click any two lines that form an inside corner. Be sure to click the part of the lines you want to remain after the fillet is completed. (Refer to Skill 2 to review how the Fillet command is used in a similar situation.) Both of the two lines will be trimmed to make an inside corner (Figure 4.6). The Fillet command automatically ends after each fillet.

9. Press ↵ to restart the Fillet command.

filleted corner

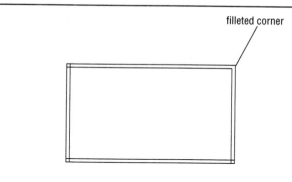

FIGURE 4.6: The first corner is filleted.

 TIP   You can restart the most recently used command by pressing ↵ at the Command: prompt.

10. Pick two more lines to fillet, then press ↵ to restart the Fillet command. Continue doing this until all four corners have been cleaned up (Figure 4.7). After the last fillet, the Fillet command will end automatically.

FIGURE 4.7: The four inside corners have been cleaned up.

NOTE   This procedure was identical to the one you performed in Skill 2 on the box.

CHARACTERISTICS THAT OFFSET AND FILLET HAVE IN COMMON

- Both are found on the Modify toolbar and on the Modify drop-down menu.
- Both have a default distance setting—offset distance and fillet radius—that can be accepted or reset.
- Both require you to select object(s).

CHARACTERISTICS THAT ARE DIFFERENT IN OFFSET AND FILLET

- You select one object with Offset and two with Fillet.
- Offset keeps running until you stop it. Fillet ends after the radius is changed and after each fillet operation, and Fillet needs to be restarted to be used again.

You will find several uses for Offset and Fillet in the subsequent sections of this skill and throughout the book.

The Interior Walls

The interior wall lines will be created by offsetting the exterior wall lines.

1. At the Command: prompt, start the Offset command by typing **o** ↵ (the letter *o*, not the number *0*) or by selecting Offset from the Modify toolbar.

2. At the Offset distance: prompt, type **9'4** ↵. Leave no space between the foot sign (') and the 4.

NOTE   AutoCAD requires that you enter a distance containing feet and inches in a particular format: no space between the foot sign (') and the inches, and a hyphen (-) between the inches and the fraction. So if you were entering 6'-4 3/4", you would type **6'4-3/4**. The measurement will be displayed in the normal way, like 6'-4 3/4", but it must be entered in this format.

3. Click the inside line of the left exterior wall (Figure 4.8).

Pick this line to offset ——————

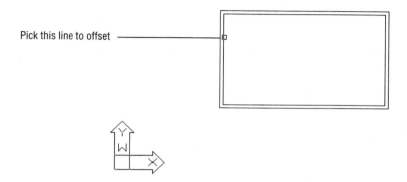

FIGURE 4.8: Selecting the wall line to offset

4. Click in a blank area to the right of the selected line. The line is offset 9'-4" to the right.

5. Press ⏎ twice. The Offset command is now restarted and you can reset the offset distance.

 TIP   In the Offset command, your opportunity to change the offset distance comes right after you start the command. So if the Offset command is already running and you need to change the offset distance, you need to stop and then re-start the command. This is easily done by pressing ⏎ twice.

6. Type **4** ⏎ to reset the offset distance.

7. Click the new line that was just offset, and then click in a blank area to the right of that line. You have created a vertical interior wall (Figure 4.9). Press ⏎ twice to stop and restart the Offset command.

8. Type **6.5'**⏎. This sets the distance for offsetting the next wall.

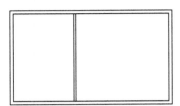

FIGURE 4.9: The first interior wall

 NOTE With Architectural units set, you can still enter distances in decimal form for feet and inches, and AutoCAD will translate them into their appropriate form. So 6'6" can be entered as 6.5' and 4 ½" can be entered as 4.5 without the inch sign. Remember that when entering figures, the inch sign (") can be left off, but the foot sign (') must be included.

9. Pick a point on the inside, upper exterior wall line (Figure 4.10).

Pick this line to offset

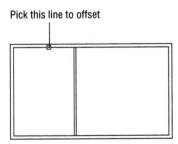

FIGURE 4.10: Selecting another wall line to offset

10. Pick in a blank area below the line selected. The inside exterior wall line is offset to make a new interior wall line. Press ↵ twice to stop and restart the Offset command.

11. Type 4 ↵. Click the new line and click again below it. A second wall line is made and you now have two interior walls. Press ↵ to end the Offset command.

These interior wall lines form the bedroom and one side of the bathroom. Their intersections with each other and with the exterior walls need to be cleaned up. If you take the time to do this now, it will be easier to make the last interior wall and complete the bathroom.

Cleaning Up Wall Lines

Earlier, you used the Fillet command to clean up the inside corners of the exterior walls. You can use that command again to clean up some of the interior walls, but you will have to use the Trim command to do the rest of them. You'll see why as you progress through the next set of steps.

1. It will be easier to pick the wall lines if the drawing is made larger on the screen. Type **z** ↵, then type **e** ↵. Press ↵, then type **.6x** ↵. The drawing is bigger. You've just used two options of the Zoom command: First you zoomed to *extents* to fill the screen with your drawing. Then you zoomed to a scale (.6x) to make the drawing 0.6 the size it had been after zooming to extents. This is a change in magnification on the view only, as the drawing is still 25 feet long by 16' wide.

2. Pick the Fillet button from the Modify toolbar to start the Fillet command and, after checking the Command window to be sure that the radius is still set to 0, click two of the wall lines as shown in Figure 4.11a. The lines will be filleted, and the results will look like Figure 4.11b.

3. Press ↵ to restart the Fillet command. Select the two lines as shown in Figure 4.12a. The results are shown in Figure 4.12b.

The two new interior walls are now the right length, but you will have to clean up the area where they form T intersections with the exterior walls. The Fillet command won't work in T intersections because too much of one of the wall lines gets trimmed away. You'll have to use the Trim command in T intersection cases. The Fillet command does a specific kind of trim and is easy and quick to execute, but its uses are limited (for the most part) to single intersections between two lines.

TIP   The best rule for choosing between Fillet and Trim is the following: If you need to clean up a single intersection between two lines, use the Fillet command. For other cases, use the Trim command.

Select these lines to fillet.

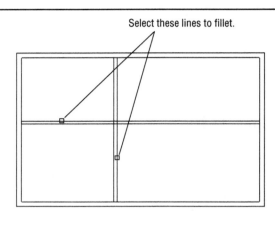

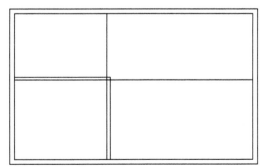

FIGURE 4.11: Selecting the first two lines to fillet (a) and the result of the fillet (b)

Select these lines to fillet

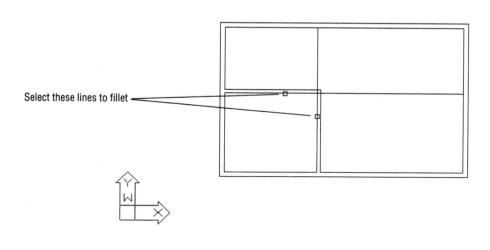

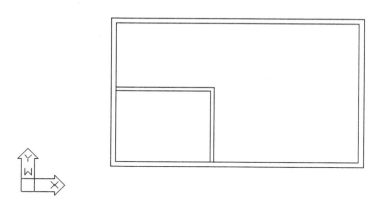

FIGURE 4.12: Selecting the second two lines to fillet (a) and the result of the second fillet (b)

Using the Zoom Command

To do this trim, you need to have a closer view of the T intersections. Use the Zoom command to get a better look.

1. Type **z** ↵. Then move the crosshair cursor to a point slightly above and to the left of the upper T intersection (Figure 4.13) and click in a blank area outside the floor plan.

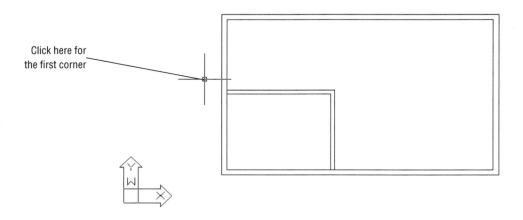

Click here for
the first corner

FIGURE 4.13: Positioning the cursor for the first click of the Zoom command

2. Move the cursor down and to the right, and notice a rectangle with solid lines being drawn. Keep moving the cursor down and to the right until the rectangle encloses the upper T intersection (Figure 4.14a).When the rectangle fully encloses the T intersection, click again. The view changes to a closer view of the intersection of the interior and exterior wall (Figure 4.14b). The rectangle you've just created is called a *zoom window*. The part of the drawing enclosed by the zoom window becomes the view on the screen. This is one of several zoom options for changing the magnification of the view. Other zoom options are introduced later in this skill and throughout the book.

NOTE When you start the Zoom command by typing **z** ↵ and then pick a point on the screen, a zoom window begins.

3. On the Modify toolbar, click the Trim button. In the Command window, notice the second and third lines of text. You are being prompted to select cutting edges, or objects to use as limits for the lines you want to trim.

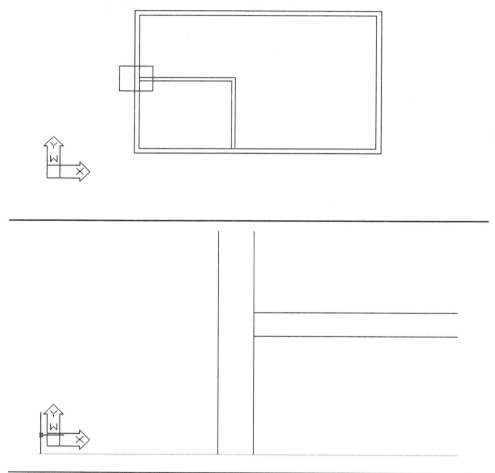

FIGURE 4.14: Using the Zoom Window option: positioning the rectangle (a), and the new view after the Zoom command (b)

4. Select the two interior wall lines and press ↵. The prompt changes, now asking you to select the lines to be trimmed.

5. Select the inside exterior wall line at the T intersection, between the two intersections with the interior wall lines that you have just picked as cutting edges (Figure 4.15a). The exterior wall line is trimmed at the T intersection (Figure 4.15b). Press ↵ to end the Trim command.

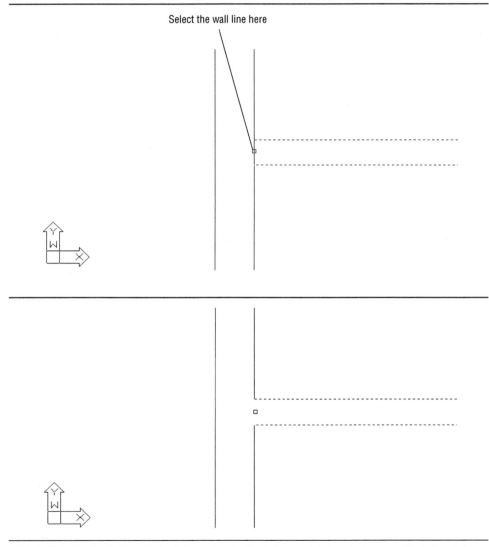

FIGURE 4.15: Selecting a line to be trimmed (a) and the result of the Trim command (b)

> **TIP** In the Trim command, when picking lines to be trimmed, select the part of the line which needs to be trimmed. In the Fillet command, select the part of the line you want to keep.

6. Return to a view of the whole drawing by typing **z** ↵, then **p** ↵. This is the Zoom command's Previous option, which restores the view that was active before the last use of the Zoom command (Figure 4.16).

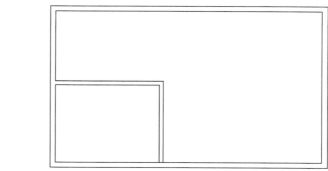

FIGURE 4.16: The result of the Zoom Previous command

7. Repeat this procedure to trim the lower T intersection. Follow these steps:

    *   Type **z** ↵ and click two points to make a rectangular zoom window around the intersection.

    *   Start the Trim command by choosing Modify ➢ Trim, select the interior walls as cutting edges, and press ↵.

    *   Select the inside exterior wall line between the cutting edges.

    *   Press ↵ to end the Trim command.

    *   Zoom Previous by typing **z** ↵ **p** ↵.

    Figure 4.17 shows the results.

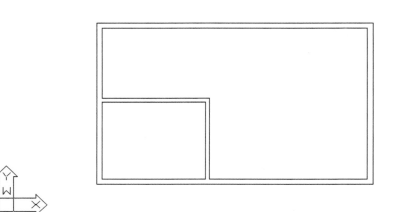

FIGURE 4.17: The second trim is completed.

You need to create one more interior wall to complete the bathroom.

Finishing the Interior Walls

You will use the same method to create the last bathroom wall that you used to make the first two interior walls. Briefly, this is how it's done:

1. Offset the inside line of the left exterior wall 6 feet to the right, then offset this new line 4 inches to the right.

2. Use the zoom window to zoom into the bathroom area.

3. Use the Trim command to trim away the short portion of the intersected wall lines between the two new wall lines.

4. Use Zoom Previous to restore the full view.

The results should look like Figure 4.18. You used Offset, Fillet, Trim, and a couple of Zooms to create the interior walls. The next task is to create five doorway openings in these walls.

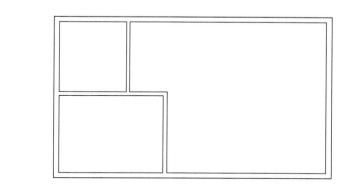

FIGURE 4.18: The completed interior walls

Cutting Wall Openings

Of the five doorway openings needed, there are two on the interior and three on the exterior walls (Figure 4.19). Four of them will be for swinging doors and one will be for a sliding glass door.

The procedure used to make each doorway opening is the same one that you used to create the wall opening for the box in Skill 2. First, you establish the location of the *jambs*, or edges, of an opening. One jamb for each swinging door opening will be 6 inches away from an inside corner. This allows the door to be positioned next to a wall and out of the way when swung open. When the jambs are established, you will trim away the wall lines between the edges. The commands used in this exercise are Offset, Extend, and Trim. You'll make openings for the 3'-0" exterior doorways first.

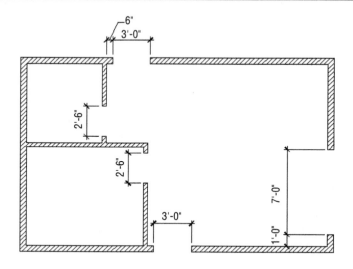

FIGURE 4.19: The drawing with doorway openings

The Exterior Openings

These openings are on the front and back walls of the cabin and have one edge set 6 inches in from an inside corner.

1. At the Command: prompt, click the Offset button on the Modify toolbar to start the Offset command, then type **6** ↵ to set the distance.

2. Click one of the two lines indicated in Figure 4.20, then click in a blank area to the right of it. Now do the same thing to the second of the two lines. You have to offset one line at a time, because of the way the Offset command works.

3. End and restart the Offset command by typing ↵ twice, then type **3'**↵ to set a new offset distance and offset the new lines to the right (Figure 4.21). Next, you will need to extend these four new lines through the external walls to make the jamb lines.

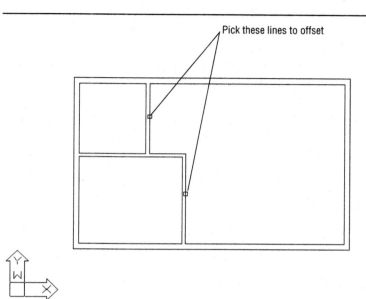

Pick these lines to offset

FIGURE 4.20: Lines to offset for 3'-0" openings

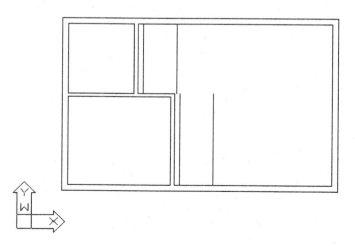

FIGURE 4.21: Offset lines for 3'-0" openings

4. Be sure to end the Offset command by pressing ↵, then type **ex** ↵ to start the Extend command. Extend is used here exactly as it was used in Skill 2. Select the upper and lower horizontal outside external wall lines as boundary edges for the Extend command, and press ↵.

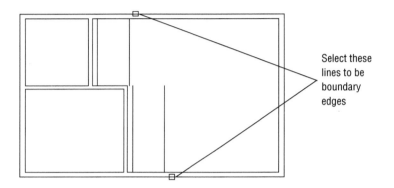

Select these lines to be boundary edges

5. Click the four lines to extend. The lines are extended through the external walls to make the jambs (Figure 4.22). End the Extend command by pressing ↵.

  TIP   The lines to be extended must be picked on the half of them nearest the boundary's edge, or they will be extended to the opposite boundary edge.

To complete the openings, trim away (a) the excess part of the jamb lines and (b) the wall lines between the jamb lines. Use the Trim command the same way you used it in Skill 2, but this time do a compound trim to clean up the wall and jamb lines in one cycle of the command.

6. Type **tr** ↵ to start the Trim command and select the three lines at each opening as shown in Figure 4.23. Then press ↵ to tell AutoCAD you are finished selecting objects to serve as cutting edges.

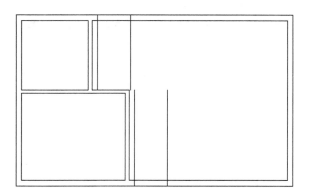

FIGURE 4.22: The lines after being extended through the external walls

Select these lines to be cutting edges

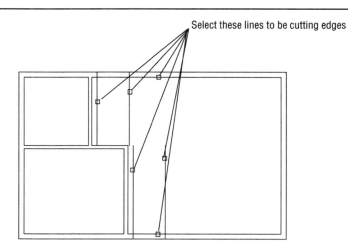

FIGURE 4.23: Selecting the cutting edges

7. Pick the jamb lines—the lines you just extended to the outside exterior walls—and the wall lines between the jamb lines. Each time you pick a line, it is trimmed. Press ↵ to end the command. Your drawing should look like Figure 4.24.

The two interior openings can be constructed using the same procedure.

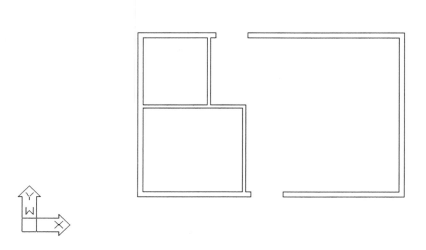

FIGURE 4.24: The finished 3'-0" openings

The Interior Openings

These doorways are 2'-6" wide and also have one jamb set in 6" from the nearest inside corner. Figure 4.25 shows the three stages of fabricating these openings. Refer to the previous section on making openings for step-by-step instructions.

Construct the 7'-0" exterior opening using the same commands and technique.

The 7'-0" Opening

Notice the opening on the right side of the building has one jamb set 12 inches in from the inside corner. This will be the sliding glass door.

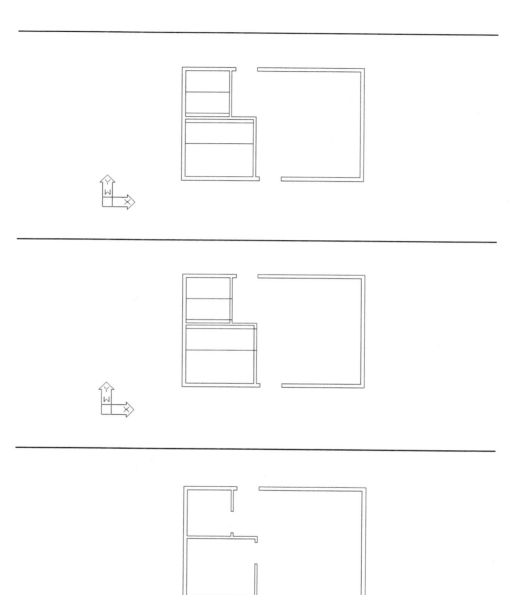

FIGURE 4.25: Creating the interior openings: the offset lines which locate the jamb lines (a), the extended lines which form the jamb lines (b), and the completed openings after trimming (c)

You've done this before, so here's a summary of the steps:

- Offset a wall line 12 inches.
- Offset the new line 7'-0".
- Extend both new lines through the wall.
- Trim the new lines and the wall lines to complete the opening.

Save this drawing now as Cabin4a. This completes the openings. The results should look like Figure 4.26.

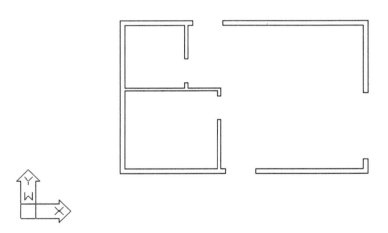

FIGURE 4.26: The completed doorway openings

As you gain more control over the commands you used here, you will be able to anticipate how much of a task can be done for each use of a command. Each opening required offsetting, extending, and trimming. You constructed these openings by drawing two at a time except for the last one, thereby using each of the three commands three times. It is possible to do all the openings using each command only once. In this way, you would do all the offsetting, then all the extending, and finally, all the trimming. In cutting these openings, however, the arrangement of the offset lines determined how many cycles of the Trim command were most efficient to use. If lines being trimmed and used as cutting edges cross each other, the trimming gets complicated. For these five openings, the most efficient procedure was to use each command twice. In Skill 8, when you draw the elevations, you'll get a chance to work with more complex multiple trims.

Now that the openings are complete, doors and door swings can be placed in their appropriate doorways. In doing this, you'll be introduced to two new objects and a few new commands, and there will be an opportunity to use the Offset and Trim commands in new, strategic ways.

Creating Doors

In a floor plan, doors are usually indicated by a rectangle for the door and an arc showing the path of the door swing. The door's position varies, but it's most often shown at 90° from the closed position (Figure 4.27). The best rule I have come across is to display them in such a way that others working with your floor plan will be able to see how far the door will swing open.

FIGURE 4.27: Possible ways to illustrate doors

The cabin has five openings, four of which need swinging doors that open 90°. The fifth is a sliding glass door. Drawing the sliding glass door will require a different approach.

Drawing Swinging Doors

The swinging doors are of two widths: 3' for exterior and 2'-6" for interior (refer to Figure 4.1). In general, doorway openings leading to the outside are wider than the interior doors, with bathroom and closet doors usually being the most narrow. For the cabin, we'll use two sizes of swinging doors. You will draw one door of each size, and then just copy these to the other openings as required. Start with the front door at the bottom of the floor plan. To get a closer view of the front door opening, use the Zoom Window command.

1. At the Command: prompt, move the cursor to the Standard toolbar and click the Zoom Window button. This has the same effect as typing **z** ↵, used earlier in this skill.

2. Pick two points to form a window around the front doorway opening, as shown in Figure 4.28a. The view changes, and you now have a close-up view of the opening (Figure 4.28b). You'll draw the door in a closed position and then rotate it open.

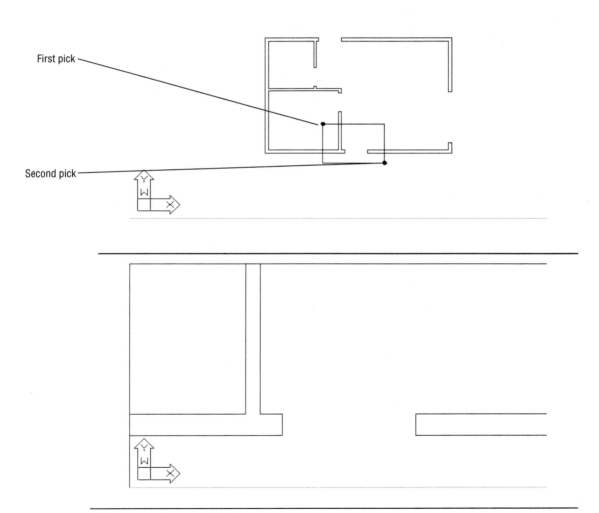

FIGURE 4.28: Forming a zoom window at the front door opening (a) and the results (b)

3. To draw the door, use the Rectangle command. It is found on the Draw toolbar and the Draw drop-down menu. The command can also be started by typing **rec** ↵ in the Command window. Start the command by any of these means.

   Notice the Command window prompt. There are several options, but <First corner> as the default is the one you want. The rectangle is formed like the zoom window—by picking two points to represent opposite corners of the rectangle. You need the door to fit exactly between the jambs and on the inside corners. To be exact, you will use an Object Snap to assist you. *Object Snaps* (or *Osnaps*) allow you to pick specific points on objects like endpoints, midpoints, the center of a circle, etc.

4. Move the cursor onto the Tracking button on the Standard toolbar and hold down the left mouse button. The Object Snap flyout opens and you see all the Object Snap options (Figure 4.29).

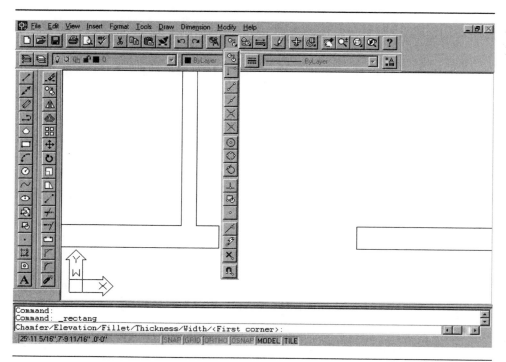

FIGURE 4.29: The Object Snap flyout

5. Holding the left mouse button down, drag the cursor down the column to the Endpoint button, and release the mouse button. A large box is now on the crosshair cursor and the prompt line now says _endp of. Both these changes are signals to you that an Object Snap has been activated.

6. Move the cursor near the upper end of the left jamb line. When the box on the cursor touches a line, a colored rectangle appears at the nearest endpoint. This shows you which endpoint in the drawing is closest to the position of the crosshair cursor at that moment.

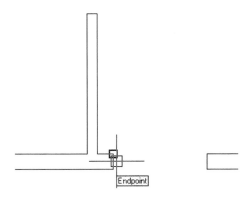

7. Move the cursor until the square is positioned on the upper end of the left jamb line, as shown above, and then click that point. The first corner of the rectangle now is located at that point. Drag the cursor to the right and slightly down to see the rectangle being formed (Figure 4.30). To locate the opposite corner, let's use the relative Cartesian coordinates discussed in Skill 2.

8. When the Command window shows the Other corner: prompt, type @3',-1.5 ↵ in the command line. The rectangle is drawn across the opening, creating a door in a closed position (Figure 4.31). The door now needs to be rotated around its hinge point to an open position.

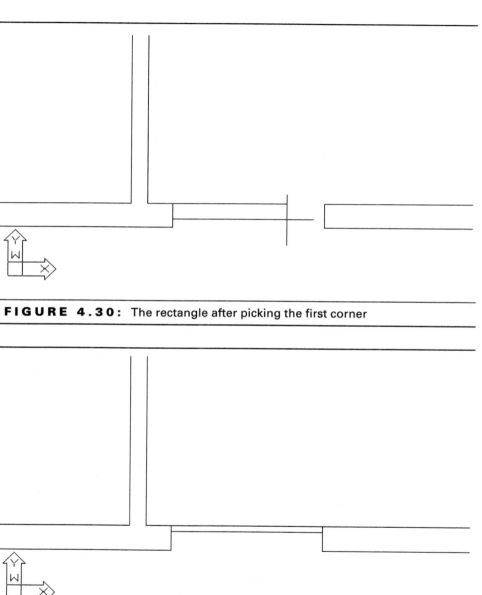

FIGURE 4.30: The rectangle after picking the first corner

FIGURE 4.31: The completed door in a closed position

Rotating the Door

This will be a 90° rotation in the counter-clockwise direction, making it a rotation of +90. You'll use the *Rotate command* to rotate the door. This command can be found on the Modify drop-down menu or the Modify toolbar, and it can also be started by typing **ro** ↵.

 TIP   Counter-clockwise rotations are positive and clockwise rotations are negative.

1. Pick the Rotate button from the Modify toolbar. You'll see a prompt to select objects. Click the door and press ↵.

 NOTE   Note that when you select the door, one pick selects all four lines. Rectangles are made of a special line called a *Polyline* that connects all segments into one object. You will learn more about them in Skill 10, *Controlling Text in a Drawing*.

You will be prompted for a base point. You need to indicate a point around which the door will be rotated. To keep the door placed correctly, pick the hinge point for the base point.

2. Return to the Standard toolbar and select the Endpoint Osnap button. Endpoint Osnap has replaced the Tracking button, because it was the last Osnap button selected.

3. Move the cursor near the upper-left corner of the door. When the colored square is displayed at that corner, left-click to locate the base point.

4. Check the status bar to be sure the Ortho button is ghosted out. If it's not, double-click it to turn it off. When the Ortho button is on, the cursor is forced to move in a vertical or horizontal direction. This is very useful at times, but in this instance, such a restriction would keep you from being able to see the door rotate. You'll learn more about Ortho in Skill 5, *Gaining Drawing Strategies: Part 2*.

5. Move the cursor away from the hinge point and see how the door rotates as the cursor moves (Figure 4.32). If the door swings properly, you are reassured that you correctly selected the base point. The prompt reads `<Rotation angle>/reference`, asking you to enter an angle.

6. Type **90** ↵. The door is rotated 90° to an open position (Figure 4.33).

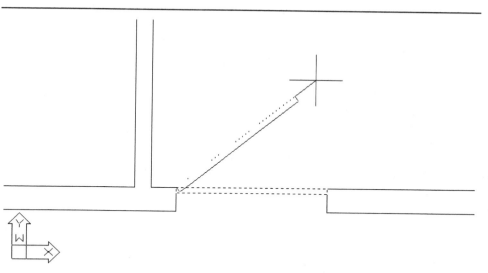

FIGURE 4.32: The door rotating with movement of the cursor

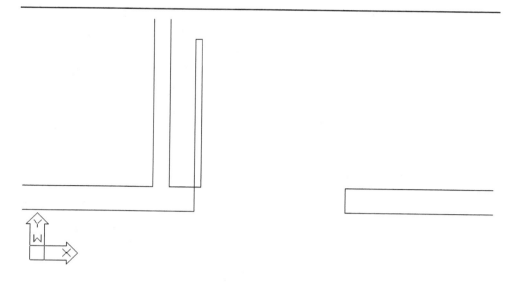

FIGURE 4.33: The door after the 90° rotation

To finish this door, you need to add the door's swing. You'll use the Arc command for this.

Drawing the Door Swing

The *swing* shows the path that the outer edge of a door takes when it swings from closed to fully open. Including a swing in a floor plan with the door helps to resolve clearance issues. The swings are drawn with the *Arc command*, in this case using the Endpoint Osnap. When you are learning AutoCAD, it is best to start the Arc command from the Draw menu, because this gives you all the Arc options. An abbreviated version of the command can be started from the Draw toolbar, or by typing **a** ↵.

1. From the Draw menu, select Arc. The Arc menu is displayed. An arc needs to be drawn from the upper end of the right jamb line through a rotation of 90°, and the center point of the arc is the hinge point of the door.

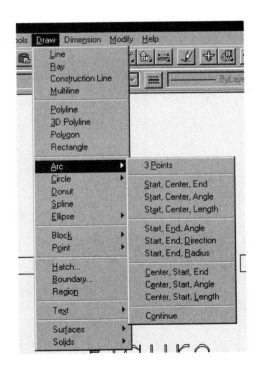

TIP   An arc can be defined by a combination of its components, some of which are starting point, ending point, angle, center point, and radius. The Arc command gives you eleven options, each of which uses three components. With a little study of the geometric information available to you on the drawing, you can choose the option that best fits the situation. In this case, the arc needs to be drawn from the upper end of the right jamb line through a rotation of 90°, and the center point of the arc is the hinge point of the door. Thus you know the start point, center point, and angle.

2. From the Arc menu, select Start, Center, Angle. The prompt now reads: `Center/ <Start point>:.` The angle brackets enclose the default option: selecting the starting point of the arc. There is also the option to start with the center point, but you would have to type **c** ↵ before picking a point to be the center point.

3. Activate the Endpoint Osnap and pick the upper endpoint of the right jamb line. The prompt changes to read: `Center/End/<Second Point>: _c Center:.`

   This may be confusing at first. The prompt shows you three options to choose: Center, End, and Second Point in brackets. Because you have previously chosen the Start, Center, Angle option, AutoCAD chooses Center for you.

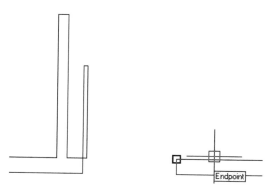

4. Activate the Endpoint Osnap again and select the hinge point. The arc is now visible, and its endpoint follows the cursor's movement (Figure 4.34a). The prompt displays a different set of options, then selects the Included angle option.

5.   Type **90** ↵. The arc is completed and the Arc command ends (Figure 4.34b).

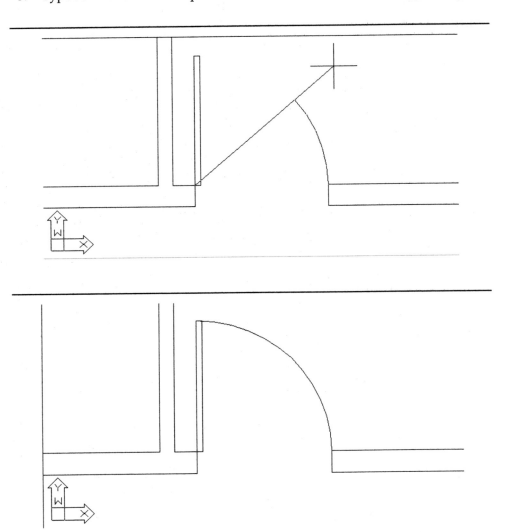

FIGURE 4.34: Drawing the arc: the ending point of the arc follows the cursor's movements (a) and the completed arc (b)

The first door is completed. Since there is another doorway of the same size, you can save time by copying this door to the other opening.

Copying Objects

The *Copy command* makes a copy of the objects you select. This copy can be located either by a point you pick or by relative coordinates which you enter from the keyboard. For AutoCAD to position these copied objects, you must designate a base point, which serves as a point of reference for where the move starts, and then a second point. The copy is moved the same distance and direction from the original that the second point is from the first point. When you know the actual distance and direction to move the copy, the base point isn't critical because you will specify the second point with relative polar or Cartesian coordinates. But in this situation, you don't know the exact distance or angle to move a copy of the front door to the back door opening, so you need to choose a base point for the copy carefully.

In copying this new door and its swing to the back door opening of the cabin, you need to find a point somewhere on the existing door or swing which can be located precisely on a point at the back door opening. There are two points like this to choose from: the hinge point or the start point of the door swing. Let's use the hinge point. You usually know where the hinge point of the new door belongs, so this is easier to locate than the start point of the arc.

The Copy command can be started three ways: from the drop-down menus, by picking Modify ➤ Copy; from the Modify toolbar, by clicking the Copy button; or from the keyboard, by typing **cp.⏎**.

1. Select the Copy button on the Modify toolbar. The prompt asks you to select objects to copy. Pick the door and swing, then press ⏎. The prompt reads `<Base point or displacement>/Multiple:`. Activate the Endpoint Osnap and pick the hinge point. A copy of the door and swing is attached to the crosshair cursor at the hinge point (Figure 4.35). The prompt changes to `Second point of displacement:`. You need to pick where the hinge point of the copied door will be located at the back door opening. To do this, you need to change the view back to what it was before you zoomed into the doorway opening.

2. From the Standard toolbar, click the Zoom Previous button. The full view of the cabin is restored. Move the crosshair cursor with the door in tow up to the vicinity of the back door opening. The back door should swing to the inside and be against the wall when open, so the hinge point for this opening will be at the lower end of the left jamb line.

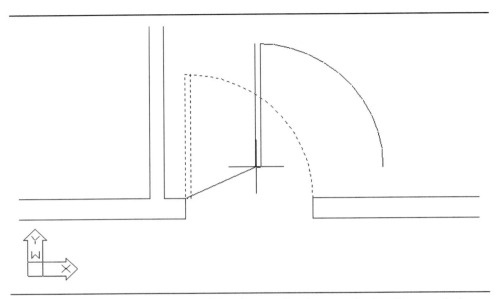

FIGURE 4.35: The copy of the door and swing attached to the crosshair cursor

3. Activate the Endpoint Osnap and pick the lower end of the left jamb line on the back door opening. The copy of the door and swing is placed in the opening (Figure 4.36) and, by looking at the Command window, you can see that the Copy command has ended.

TIP The Copy command ends when you pick or specify the second point of the move, unless you're copying the same object to multiple places. You'll do that in Skill 5, when you draw the stovetop.

The door is oriented the wrong way, but you'll fix that next.

When you copy doors from one opening to another, often the orientation may not match. The best strategy is to use the hinge point as a point of reference and place it where it needs to go, as you have just done, then flip and/or rotate the door and swing so it sits the right way. The flipping of an object is known as mirroring.

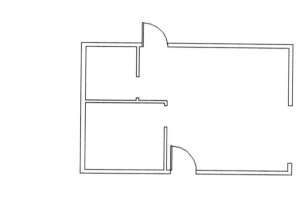

FIGURE 4.36: The door is copied to the back door opening

Mirroring Objects

You have located the door in the opening, but it needs to be flipped so it swings to the inside of the cabin. To do this, we'll use the *Mirror command*.

The Mirror command allows you to flip objects around an axis called the *mirror line*. You define this imaginary line by designating two points to be the endpoints of the line. Strategic selection of the mirror line ensures the accuracy of the mirroring action, so it's critical to visualize where the proper line lies. Sometimes you will have to draw a guideline in order to designate one or both of the endpoints.

1. Choose the Zoom Window icon from the Standard toolbar, and create a window around the back door.

2. Pick the Mirror button on the Modify toolbar. (This command can also be found on the Modify drop-down menu or can be started by typing **mi** ↵.) Select the back door and swing, and press ↵. The prompt changes to read `First point of mirror line:`.

3. Activate the Endpoint Osnap, then pick the hinge point of the door. The prompt changes to read `Second point:`, and you will see the mirrored

image of the door and the swing moving as you move the cursor around the drawing area. You are rotating the mirror line about the hinge point as you move the cursor, and, as the mirror line moves, the location of the mirrored image moves (Figure 4.37).

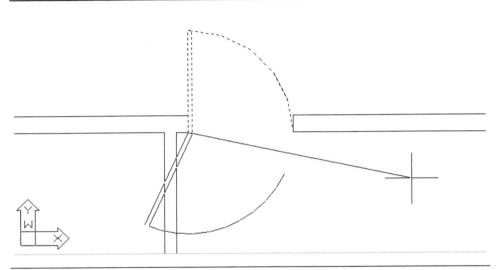

FIGURE 4.37: The mirror image moves as the mirror line moves.

4. Hold the crosshair cursor directly to the right of the first point picked, along the inside wall line. The mirror image appears to be where you want the door to be.

5. Activate the Endpoint Osnap again and pick the lower end of the right jamb line. The mirror image disappears and the prompt changes to read Delete old objects? <No>. You have the choice of keeping both doors by pressing ↵ and accepting the default No, or discarding the original one by typing **y** (for yes) in the command line and pressing ↵.

6. Type **y** ↵. The flipped door is displayed and the original one is deleted (Figure 4.38). The Mirror command ends. Like the Copy command, the Mirror command ends automatically after one mirroring operation.

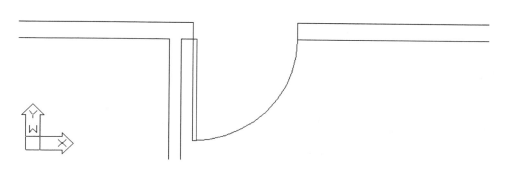

FIGURE 4.38: The mirrored door and swing

It may take some practice to become proficient at visualizing and designating the mirror line, but once you are used to it, you will have learned a very powerful tool. Because many building layouts have some symmetry to them, wise use of the Mirror command can save you a significant amount of drawing time.

You have two more swinging doors to place in the floor plan.

Finishing the Swinging Doors

You cannot copy the existing doors and swings to the interior openings because the sizes don't conform, but you can use the same procedure to draw one door and swing, and then copy it to the other opening. There will be a discussion on door sizes in Skill 7, *Using Blocks and Wblocking.*

NOTE   We could have used the Stretch command to lengthen the door, but it's an advanced Modify command, and won't be introduced until Skill 9, *Working with Hatches and Fills.* Besides, the arc would have to be modified to a larger radius. It turns out to be easier to draw another door and swing to a different size.

1. Click the Zoom Previous button on the Standard toolbar. Then click the Zoom Window button right next to the Zoom Previous button, and make a zoom window to zoom into the area of the interior door openings. Be sure to make the zoom window large enough to leave some room for the new doors to be drawn (Figure 4.39).

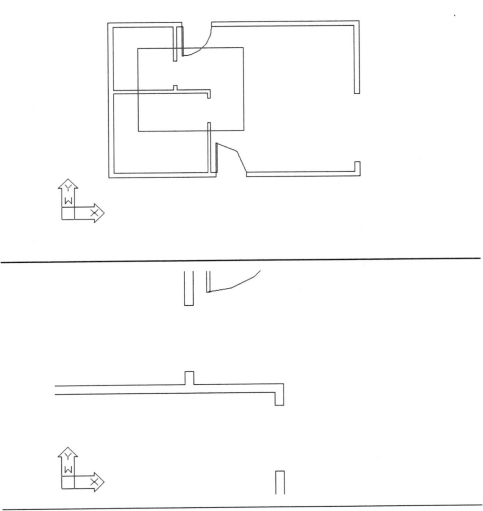

FIGURE 4.39: Zooming into the interior door opening area (a) and the results of the zoom (b)

2. Follow the same procedure to draw the door and swing in the lower opening. Here is a summary of the steps:

    - Use the Rectangle command and Endpoint Osnap to draw the door from the hinge point to a point @1.5,-2'6.

    - Rotate the door around the hinge point to an open position. You will have to use a rotation angle of -90.

    - Use the Start, Center, Angle option of the Arc command to draw the door swing, starting at the upper-left corner of the door, and using Endpoint Osnap for the two picks.

 NOTE   The Start, Center, Angle option—as well as a few others—of the Arc command requires that you choose the start point for the arc in such a way that the arc is drawn in a counter-clockwise direction. If you progress in a clockwise direction, use a negative number for the angle.

3. Use the Copy command to copy this door and swing to the other interior opening. The base point will be the hinge point, and the second point will be the left end of the lower jamb line in the upper opening. Use the Endpoint Osnap for both picks.

4. Use the Mirror command to flip this copy of the door and swing up. The mirror line will be different from the one used for the back door, because for this one, the door and its swing must flip in a direction parallel to the opening, while the geometrical arrangement at the back opening required that the door and its swing be flipped across the opening. For this opening, the mirror line is the lower jamb line itself, so pick each end of this line (using Endpoint Osnap) to establish the mirror line.

5. Zoom Previous to see the four swinging doors in place (Figure 4.40).

The last door to draw is the sliding glass door. This kind of door requires an entirely different strategy, but you'll use commands familiar to you by now.

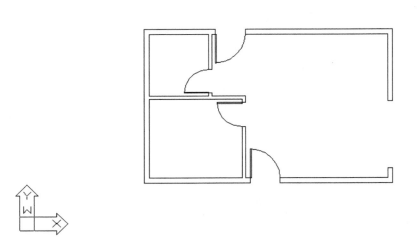

FIGURE 4.40: The four swinging doors in place

Drawing a Sliding Glass Door

Sliding glass doors are usually drawn to show their glass panels within the door frames.

To draw the sliding door, you will apply the Line, Offset, and Trim commands to the 7' opening you made earlier.

1. Pick the Zoom Window button on the Standard toolbar and make a zoom window closely around the 7' opening. In making the zoom window, pick one point just above and to the left of the upper door jamb and below and to

the right of the lower jamb. This will make the opening as large as possible while including everything you will need in the view (Figure 4.41).

FIGURE 4.41: The view when zoomed in as close as possible to the 7' opening

2. You will be using several Osnaps for this procedure, so it will be convenient to have the Osnap Flyout toolbar more immediately available. Here's how:

   - From the View menu, pick Toolbars. The Toolbars dialog box appears.

   - Scroll down the list and click in the box next to Object Snap. The Object Snap toolbar will appear.

   - Click the Close button of the Toolbars dialog box.

   - Put the cursor on the colored title bar of the Object Snap toolbar, and, holding down the left mouse button, drag the toolbar to the right side of the drawing area and dock it there by releasing the mouse button (Figure 4.42). Now all Object Snaps can easily be selected as needed.

Object Snap
toolbar docked

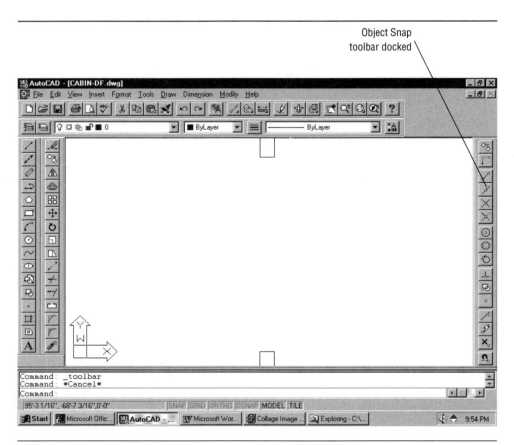

FIGURE 4.42: The Object Snap toolbar docked to the right of the drawing area

3. Offset each jamb line 2" into the doorway opening (Figure 4.43).

4. Type **l** ↵ to start the Line command. Pick the Midpoint Osnap button from the Object Snap toolbar, then place the cursor near the midpoint of the upper door jamb line. Notice how a colored triangle appears when your cursor gets in the vicinity of midpoint. Each Osnap has a distinctive shape and color. When the triangle appears at the midpoint of the jamb line, left-click. Click the Midpoint Osnap button again, move the cursor to the bottom jamb line, and, when the triangle appears at that midpoint, click again. Press ↵ to end the Line command.

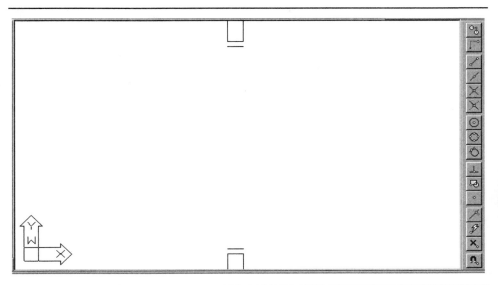

FIGURE 4.43: Jamb lines offset 2" into the doorway opening

5. Start the Offset command and type **1.5** ↵ to set the offset distance. Pick the newly drawn line, then pick a point anywhere to the right side. Then, while the Offset command is still running, pick the line again and pick another point in a blank area somewhere to the left side of the original line (Figure 4.44). Press ↵ to end the Offset command.

 TIP   A line *offset* from itself, that is, a copy of the selected line, is automatically made at a perpendicular specified distance from the selected line.

6. Make sure Ortho is activated and type **l** ↵ to start the Line command. Click the Midpoint Osnap button and then move the cursor near the midpoint of the left vertical line. When the colored triangle appears at the midpoint of this left-most line, click. Hold the cursor out directly to the right of the point you just selected to draw a horizontal line through the three vertical lines. When the cursor is about two feet to the right of the three vertical lines, pick a point to set the endpoint of this guideline. Press ↵ to end the Line command (Figure 4.45).

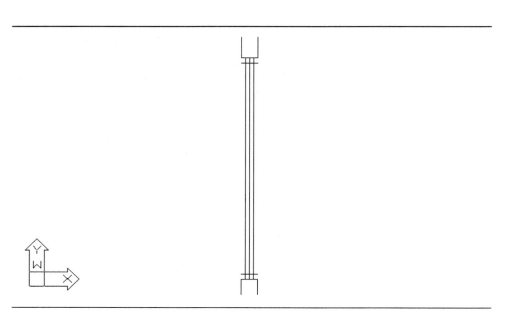

FIGURE 4.44: Offset vertical line between jambs

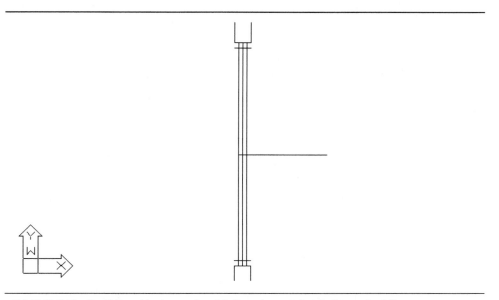

FIGURE 4.45: Horizontal guideline drawn through vertical lines

7. Type **o** ↵ to start the Offset command. Type **1** ↵ to set the offset distance. Pick this new line, and then pick a point in a blank area anywhere above the line. Pick the original line again and then pick anywhere below it. The new line has been offset 1" above and below itself (Figure 4.46). Now you have placed all the lines necessary to create the sliding glass door frames in the opening. You still need to trim some of these lines back and erase others. Press ↵ to end the Offset command.

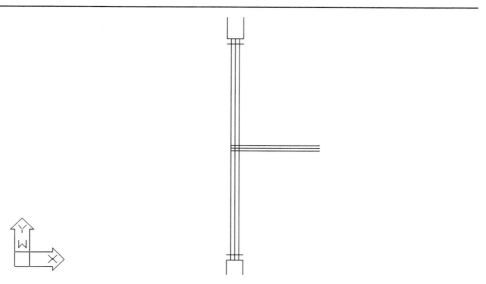

FIGURE 4.46: Offset horizontal guideline

8. Start the Trim command by typing **tr** ↵ and, when you are prompted to select cutting edges, pick the two horizontal lines which were just created with the Offset command. Then press ↵.

9. Now trim the two outside vertical lines by picking them as shown in Figure 4.47a. The result is shown in Figure 4.47b.

10. Press ↵ twice to stop and restart the Trim command, and, when you are prompted to select cutting edges, use a special window called a *crossing window* to select all the lines visible in the drawing. A crossing window will select everything within the window or crossing it. Here's how to do it:

    • Pick a point above and to the right of the opening.

- Move the cursor to a point below and to the left of the opening, forming a window with dashed lines.

- Pick that point. Everything inside the rectangle or crossing an edge of it is selected.

- Press ↵.

11. To trim the lines, pick them at the points noted in Figure 4.48a. When you finish trimming, the opening should look like Figure 4.48b. Be sure to press ↵ to end the Trim command.

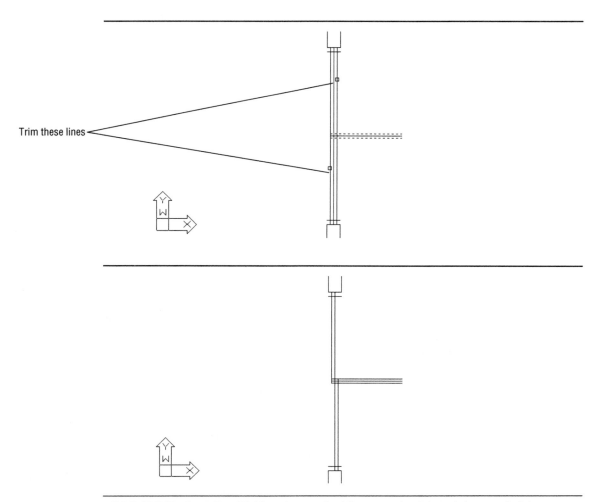

FIGURE 4.47: Picking the vertical lines to trim (a) and the result (b)

NOTE   If all lines don't trim the way you expect them to, you may have to change the setting for the Edgemode variable. This is easy to do. Cancel the trim operation and undo any trims you've made to the sliding glass door. Type **edgemode** ↵, then type **0** ↵. Now start the trim command and continue trimming

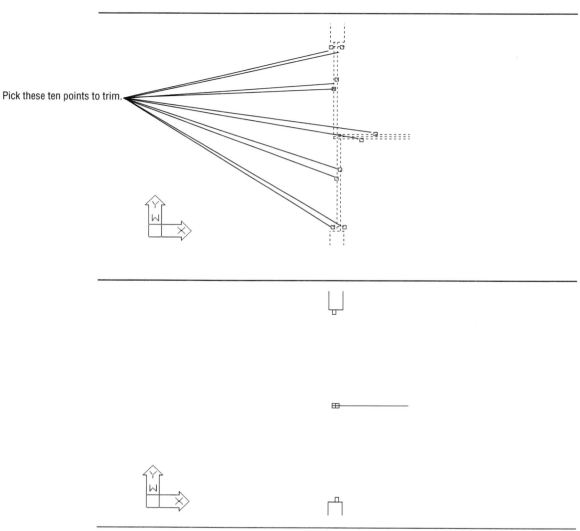

Pick these ten points to trim.

FIGURE 4.48:   Lines to trim (a) and the result (b)

12. Start the Erase command and erase the remaining horizontal guide line.

To finish the sliding glass doors, you need to draw in two lines to represent the glass panes for each door panel. Each pane of glass is centered inside its frame, so the line representing the pane will run between the midpoints of the inside edge of each frame section.

13. Type l ↵ to start the Line command and pick the Midpoint button on the Object Snap toolbar.

14. For each of the two sliding door frames, put the cursor near the midpoint of the inside line of the frame section nearest the jamb. When the colored triangle appears there, click. Then select the Perpendicular Osnap button from the Object Snap toolbar and move the cursor to the other frame section of that door panel. When you get near the horizontal line that represents both the inside edge of one frame section and the back edge of the frame section next to it, the colored perpendicular symbol will appear on that line. When it does, select that point.

15. Press ↵ to end the Line command.

16. Press ↵ to restart the Line command and repeat the procedure described in step 14 for the other door panel, being sure to start the line at the frame section nearest the other jamb. The finished opening should look like Figure 4.49.

17. Zoom Previous to see the full floor plan with all doors (Figure 4.50).

18. Save this drawing as Cabin4b.

This completes the doors for the floor plan. The focus here has been on walls and doors, and the strategies for drawing them. As a result, you now have a basic floor plan for the cabin, and you will continue to develop this plan in the next skill.

By working with the tools and strategies in this skill, you now should have an idea of an approach to drawing many objects. In the next skill, you will continue in this same vein, learning a few new commands and strategies as you add steps, a balcony, a kitchen, and a bathroom to the floor plan.

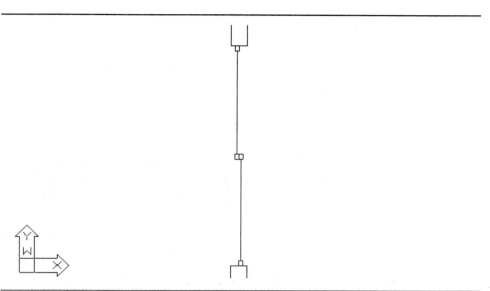

FIGURE 4.49: The finished sliding glass doors

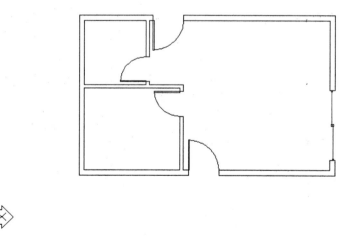

FIGURE 4.50: The floor plan with all doors finished

Are You Experienced?

Now you can...

- ☑ offset exterior walls to make interior walls
- ☑ zoom in on an area with a zoom window and zoom back out with the Zoom Previous command
- ☑ use the Rectangle and Arc commands to make a door
- ☑ use the Endpoint, Midpoint, and Perpendicular Object Snap modes
- ☑ use the crossing window selection tool
- ☑ use the Copy and Mirror commands to place an already-existing door and swing in another opening
- ☑ use the Offset and Trim commands to make a sliding glass door

Gaining Drawing Strategies: Part 2

- ➔ **Using Object Snaps**
- ➔ **Zooming with Realtime and Pan**
- ➔ **Copying and moving objects**
- ➔ **Creating circles and ellipses**

Developing a drawing strategy begins with determining the best way to start, or when to start, a command. AutoCAD provides several ways to start most of the commands you will be using. You have seen how the Offset, Fillet, Trim, and Extend commands can be found on either the Modify toolbar or Modify drop-down menu. They can also be started by typing in the first letter or two of the command then pressing Enter.

TIP For a quick recap, to start the Offset and Fillet commands, enter **o** or **f**, respectively. To execute the Trim command, enter **tr**, and for Extend, **ex**. Remember also that the drop-down menus may be activated by holding down the Alt Key while pressing the hotkey—the letter that is underlined in the menu name. For example, to open the Modify drop-down menu enter **Alt+m**.

The choice of which method to use will be determined to an extent by what you were doing at the time, as well as your command of the keyboard. Keyboard entry when using the abbreviations is generally the fastest method, but if your hand is already on the mouse and the Modify toolbar is docked on the screen, selecting commands from there may at times be faster.

There are also usually several drawing strategies which can be used in any particular situation to accomplish the same goal. For example, in the last skill you could have used the Line command to draw the doors, instead of the Rectangle command. Or the openings could have been made by copying the jamb lines from one completed opening to another. One of the key elements for efficient drafting on the computer is being able to observe what objects currently in your drawing can serve as aids in accomplishing your next task. In the previous skill, we used the outer wall lines to create the rest of the wall lines, including the door jambs, thereby avoiding having to draw any new lines. As you get more familiar with the commands and techniques for computer drafting, you will start looking more carefully at the geometry of your drawing to see what help it can offer you.

In this chapter, you will be introduced to several new commands and, through the step-by-step instructions, be shown some alternate methods for accomplishing tasks similar to those you have previously completed. In this skill, you will add front and back steps, a balcony and threshold, and kitchen and bath fixtures to the floor plan of the cabin (Figure 5.1). In each of these tasks, the focus will be on noticing what is already in the drawing that can make your job easier.

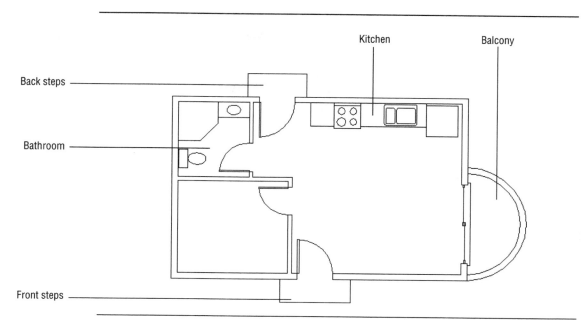

FIGURE 5.1: The cabin with front and back steps, balcony, kitchen, and bathroom

Drawing the Steps

The steps and threshold are drawn with simple lines. The trick is to see what part of the drawing can be effectively used to generate those lines. Use a width of 2 feet for the front and back step, and lengths of 6 and 5 feet, respectively. The threshold at the sliding glass door extends 3 inches beyond the outside wall line and runs 2 inches past either jamb line (Figure 5.2).

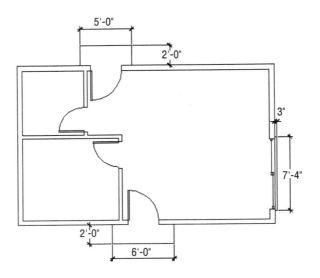

FIGURE 5.2: The steps and threshold with their dimensions

These are simple shapes to draw, but you will learn a few new techniques as you create them.

The Front Step

As you can see in Figure 5.2, the front step is 2 feet wide and 6 feet long. Because you know the width of the doorway opening, you can determine how far past the opening the step extends, assuming it to be symmetrical. A line can then be drawn from the endpoint of one of the jamb lines, down 2 feet, then offset the proper distance left and right to create the sides of the step. Here's how it's done:

1. With AutoCAD running, bring up your cabin drawing (last saved as Cabin4b) and use the Zoom command options to achieve a view similar to Figure 5.3. The Object Snap toolbar may be docked on the right side of the drawing area. If not, you can either bring it up and dock it or just use the Object Snap flyout, which is activated by holding down the left mouse

button when the cursor is on the Tracking button on the Standard toolbar. The cursor menu also has the Object Snaps on it. You can open this menu by holding down the Shift key and clicking the right mouse button.

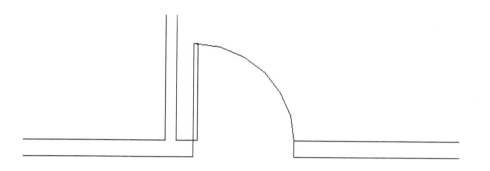

FIGURE 5.3: Zoomed into the front opening

2. The User Coordinate System (UCS) icon in the lower-left corner of the drawing area may start getting in your way as more precise zooms become necessary. It is really of no use to you until later in the book, so now is a good time to suppress it. You can always display it again later. Type **ucsicon** ↵, then type **off** ↵.

3. Start the Line command, activate the Endpoint Osnap and pick a point at the lower end of the left jamb line.

4. Double-click the Ortho button on the status bar at the bottom of the screen to turn on Ortho mode (if it's not already on) and hold the crosshair cursor so it is directly below the first point picked. Do not pick a point yet (Figure 5.4).

NOTE   When Ortho mode is on, lines you draw are forced to be horizontal or vertical.

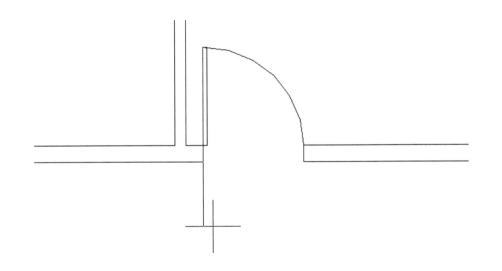

FIGURE 5.4: Line command running with Ortho on

5. Type **2'** ⏎. A vertical line is drawn two feet long. When the line command is running and the cursor is held away from the last point picked in a particular direction, you can enter a distance and the line will be drawn to the desired length in the direction of the cursor. Because you want the line to be vertical, Ortho assisted you by forcing the line to be drawn in the vertical direction.

6. Press ⏎ to end the Line command, and type **o** ⏎ to start the Offset command. Type **1'6** ⏎ for an offset distance, and offset this line to the left.

7. Press ⏎ twice to stop and restart Offset, type **6'**⏎, and offset this new line to the right (Figure 5.5). Press ⏎ to end the Offset command.

8. Erase the original line and draw a line from the lower endpoints of these two new lines to represent the front edge of the step. Use Endpoint Osnap for each point picked. Press ⏎ to end the Line command. Your drawing should look like Figure 5.6.

9. Zoom Previous to view the entire floor plan.

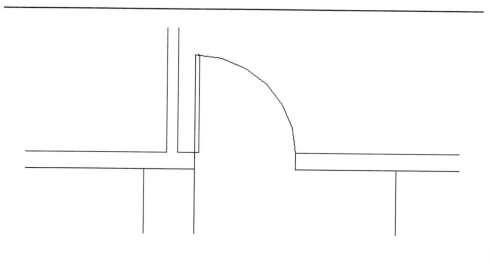

FIGURE 5.5: The sides of the front step after offsetting

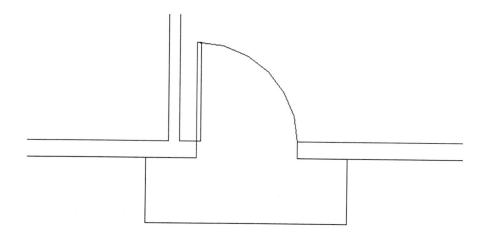

FIGURE 5.6: The completed front step

Skill 5

The strategy here was to recognize that a line drawn from the jamb line could be used to determine the location of the sides of the step. The new technique of using the Ortho mode to draw showed you a quick method for entering distances when the lines are horizontal or vertical. For the back step, you'll build on this by adding the From Osnap drawing aid to your bag of tools.

The Back Step

The method used on the front step can be applied here as well. The situation is identical: you will be working with the same geometry in the drawing and will accomplish the same thing. This time, however, you'll use From Osnap to locate the side of the step. Remember that the step in the back is 5 feet wide.

1. Zoom into the back step. Start the Line command and pick the Snap From button on the Object Snap toolbar.

    The prompt line in the Command window will read: `_line From point: _from Base point:`. This is actually four prompts grouped together:

    - `_line` signifies the starting of the Line command
    - `From point:` is the first prompt for the Line command
    - `_from` signifies that the From Osnap has been selected
    - `Base point:` is the first prompt for the From Osnap option

    The From Osnap enables you to pick a point a specified distance from a known point. In this case, because the step is 5 feet long, we want to begin the side of the step one foot to the left of the doorway opening. So the "Base point" AutoCAD is prompting you for is the upper end of the left jamb line.

2. Pick the Endpoint Osnap and pick the upper end of the left jamb line. The prompt line now has `_endp of <Offset>:` added to it. This is two more prompts:

    - `_endp` signifies that the Endpoint Osnap has been selected
    - `<Offset>:` is the second prompt for the From Osnap option. It means that you now need to enter the relative coordinates from this last point picked to the point at which you want to start the line.

3. Type **@-12,0** ↵ . A line begins one foot to the left of the opening, on the outside wall line (Figure 5.7). Making sure that Ortho is still on, hold the cursor directly above the point picked, and type **2'** ↵. The side of the step is drawn.

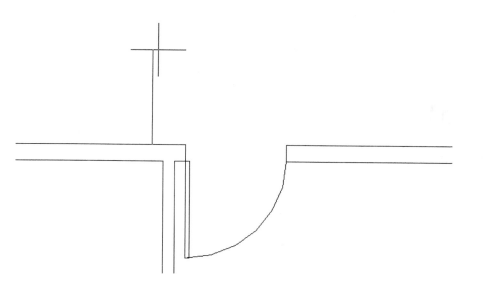

FIGURE 5.7 The line for the side of the step

4. Hold the cursor directly to the right from the last point, then type **5'** ↵. The front edge of the step is drawn.

5. Pick Perpendicular Osnap from the Object Snap toolbar and move the cursor to the outside wall line (Figure 5.8). When the perpendicular icon appears on the wall line, click the mouse. The right edge of the step is drawn and the back step is complete. Press ↵ to end the Line command.

6. Zoom Previous.

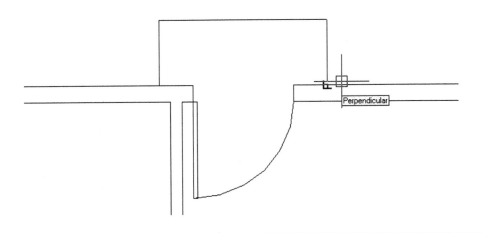

FIGURE 5.8: Completing the back step with the Perpendicular Osnap

The From Osnap is a welcome new tool to AutoCAD users. It will be used often in the rest of the book. When you combine it with the technique of using Ortho to help enter distances, as you have for the back step, you will be surprised how quickly you can lay out orthogonal walls in a floor plan. The Ortho technique used by itself powerfully facilitates drawing the footprint of a building.

You now have the threshold for the 7 foot opening, outside the sliding glass door, to do.

The Balcony Threshold

Though quite different in shape, the threshold has the same geometry as the steps and is drawn using the same techniques. Remember that it is offset three inches from the outside wall, and is 7'-4" long. Try it on your own:

- Use the From Osnap to start the first line.

- Either offset the side line *OR* draw all three lines using the Ortho technique.

- When finished, Zoom Previous and your drawing should look like Figure 5.2 (without the dimensions).

The Balcony: Drawing Circles

A glance at Figure 5.1 will tell you the balcony is made up of two semi-circles. Of the several ways these could be drawn, you will form them from a circle. Often the easiest way to draw an arc is to draw a circle which contains the arc segment; then trim the circle back.

1. Select Draw ➤ Circle and look at the Circle menu for a moment.

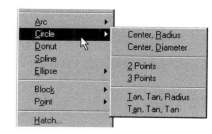

There are six options for constructing a circle. Two require you to specify a point to be the center of the circle and enter a radius or diameter. The next two are used when you know two or three points the circle must intersect, and finally the last two use tangents and a radius, or just tangents to form a circle.

2. The balcony has a radius of 5 feet, so select the Center, Radius option. The Command window will prompt you to specify a point to be the center of the circle. The actual center for the balcony will be 5 feet above the lower-right corner of the outside wall line but, since there is no way we can snap to that point, the circle can be drawn anywhere for now. You will move it into position later.

3. Pick a point in the middle of the largest room of the cabin. The center is established and, as you move the cursor, the circle changes size and becomes attached to the crosshair cursor (Figure 5.9). You could pick a point to establish the radius, but you know exactly what you want the radius to be.

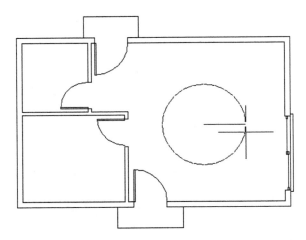

FIGURE 5.9: The circle attached to the crosshair cursor

4. Type **5'** ↵. The circle is drawn and the command ends.

5. Select the Move button on the Modify toolbar. The cursor changes to a pick-box. Select the circle and press ↵.

6. On the Object Snap toolbar or flyout, pick the Quadrant button.Select the circle somewhere near its bottom extremity (Figure 5.10). An image of the circle is attached to the cursor. Turn Ortho off by double-clicking the Ortho button on the status bar.

7. Move the cursor around to see that the lowest point on the circle is attached (Figure 5.11). This point on the circle needs to be placed at the lower-right corner of the outside wall line.

8. Select Endpoint Osnap, then pick the lower-right corner of the cabin. The circle is positioned correctly for the balcony (Figure 5.12). Now you can use the existing wall lines to trim the circle into a semi-circle.

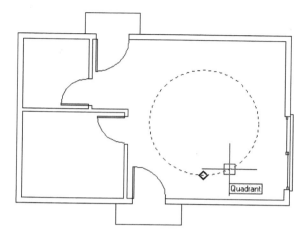

FIGURE 5.10: Selecting the circle with Quadrant Osnap

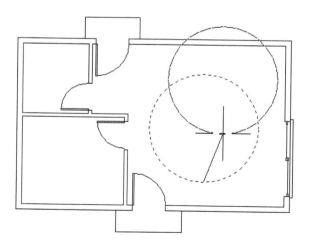

FIGURE 5.11: The circle attached to the crosshair cursor at lowest point

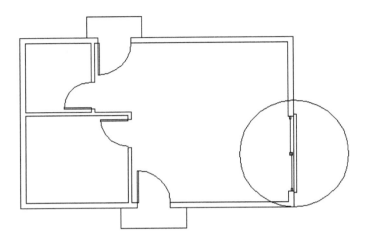

FIGURE 5.12: The circle positioned for the balcony

9. Zoom into the area of the balcony and start the Trim command.

10. Select the two outside wall lines on the far right, as shown in Figure 5.13.
    Then press ↵.

11. Select the portion of the circle that is inside the cabin. The circle is trimmed
    into a semi-circle. Press ↵ to end the Trim command.

12. Start the Offset command, set the distance for 6" and offset the semi-circle to
    the inside. Press ↵ to end the Offset command. The balcony is complete.
    Zoom Previous and save the drawing as Cabin5a (Figure 5.14).

As mentioned at the beginning of this section, there are several techniques for
drawing the balcony. The one you used gave you the opportunity to use the
Move command and the Quadrant Osnap, and allowed you to see how using the
lowest quadrant snap point on the circle is an easy way to locate the balcony on
the building. No entry of relative coordinates was required.

In the next section, you will continue to develop drawing strategies as you
focus on creating a counter and fixtures to comprise a kitchen.

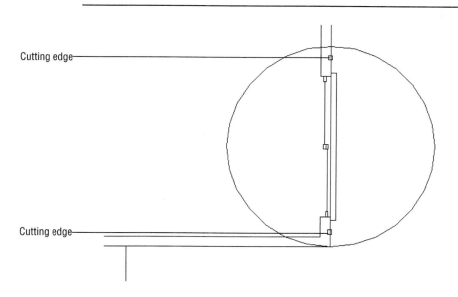

Cutting edge

Cutting edge

Skill 5

F I G U R E   5 . 1 3 : Selecting wall lines to be cutting edges

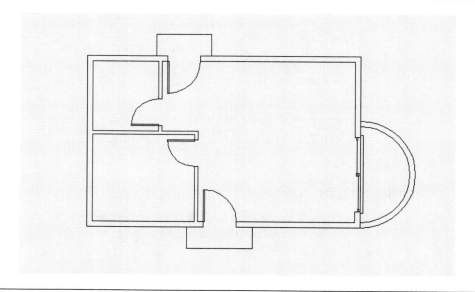

F I G U R E   5 . 1 4 : The floor plan with the balcony completed

Laying Out the Kitchen

The kitchen for the cabin will have a stove, refrigerator, and counter with sink (Figure 5.15). The refrigerator is set 2 inches away from the back wall. Approaching this drawing task, your goal is to think about the easiest and fastest way to complete it. The first step in deciding on an efficient approach is to ascertain what information you have about the various parts, and what geometry in the drawing will be able to assist you. The basic dimensions are given and you will get more detailed information about the sink and stove below.

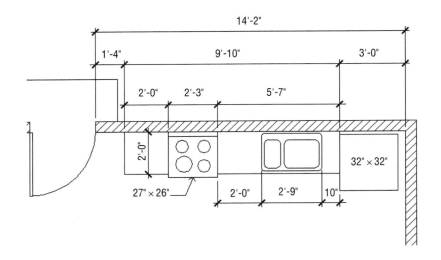

FIGURE 5.15: The general layout of the kitchen

The Counter

Although the counter is in two pieces, you will draw it as one piece and then cut out a section for the stove. Try two ways to draw the counter to see which method is more efficient.

Using Ortho

1. Use a zoom window to zoom your view so it is about the same magnification as Figure 5.15.

2. Start the Line command, activate the From Osnap and click Endpoint Osnap. Then pick the lower end of the right back-door jamb line. Then type **@1'4<0** ↵. The line for the left side of the counter is begun.

3. Be sure Ortho is turned on, then hold the cursor directly below the first point of the line and type **2'** ↵. Hold the cursor to the right and type **9'10** ↵ (Figure 5.16). Select Perpendicular Osnap and pick the inside wall line again. Press ↵ to end the Line command. The counter is drawn.

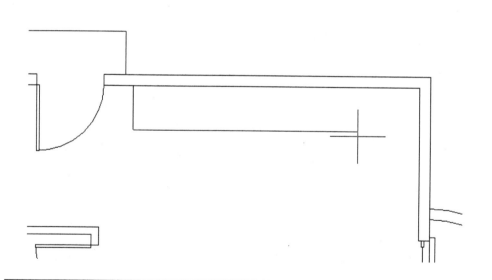

FIGURE 5.16: Drawing the counter using the Ortho technique

Using Offset

To do the same thing using the Offset command, you'll need to undo the effects of the previous command. Since all lines were drawn in one cycle of the Line command, one use of the U command will undo the entire counter.

1. Click the Undo button on the Standard toolbar. The counter you just drew should disappear. If you ended the Line command while drawing the counter, and had to restart it before you finished, you may have to click the Undo button more than once. If you undo too much, click the Redo button just to the right of the Undo button. The Redo command will undo the effect of only one Undo, so if you used undo one step too many you can still get the last one back. Undoing more than one step has the effect of deleting work permanently. Your work will then have to be redrawn.

> **WARNING** AutoCAD has two undo commands and they operate quite differently. When you click the Undo button on the Standard toolbar, you are using the U command. It can also be started by typing **u** ↵. The U command works like the undo command for Windows-compatible applications, by undoing the results of commands one step at a time. The Undo command in AutoCAD has many options and is started by typing **undo** ↵. This is used when you want to undo everything you've done since you last saved your drawing, or back to a point in your drawing session that you marked earlier. Be careful when you use the Undo command, as you could easily lose a lot of your work.

Now draw the counter again, this time using the Offset and Fillet commands.

2. Offset the right inside wall line 3 feet to the left, then offset this line 9'-10" to the left. Finally, offset the upper inside wall line 2 feet down (Figure 5.17).

3. Use the Fillet command with a radius of 0 to clean up the two corners.

You can decide which of the two methods—Ortho or Offset—is more practical for you. Both are powerful techniques for laying out orthogonal patterns of lines for walls, counters, and other objects.

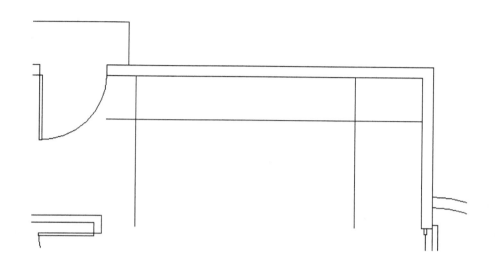

FIGURE 5.17: Offsetting wall lines to create the counter

The Stove and Refrigerator

The stove and refrigerator are simple rectangles. Use the From Osnap to locate the first corner of each shape.

1. For the refrigerator, select the Rectangle button on the Draw toolbar, then select the From Osnap option and use Endpoint Osnap to select a base point at the upper end of the right side of the counter. Then, for the offset, type **@2<270** ↵. This starts the rectangle 2 inches away from the back wall along the side of the counter. To specify the opposite corner of the rectangle, type **@32,-32** ↵.

2. For the stove, start the Rectangle command again and use the same technique, but pick the upper end of the left side of the counter as the base point, and, for the offset, type **@ 1'6<0** ↵. Then type **@27,-26** to complete the rectangle.

3. Use the Trim command to trim away the front edge of the counter at the stove (Figure 5.18).

NOTE Because the stove rectangle is drawn as a *polyline*, that is, one unique entity, you only need to select it once for all sides of the rectangle to be cutting edges.

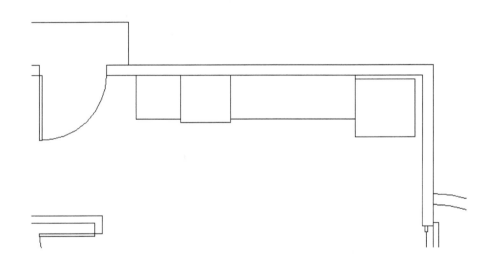

FIGURE 5.18: Using rectangles and the From Osnap to make the stove and refrigerator

Completing the Stove

The stove needs a little more detail. You will need to add circles to represent the burners and a line off the back to indicate the control panel (Figure 5.19). The burners are located by their centers.

1. Zoom into a closer view of the stove using the zoom window. You need to draw a line along the back of the stove 2.5 inches in from the wall line. Offsetting seems like the right command to use.

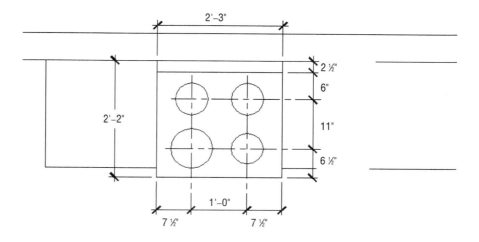

FIGURE 5.19: The details of the stove

2. Offset the wall line 2.5 inches down, then trim it back to the sides of the stove (Figure 5.20).

 **WARNING**   When you pick the wall line to offset it, choose a location on either side of the stove, but not where the back of the stove coincides with the wall. You don't want to offset a line of the stove, because it was made with the Rectangle command and is therefore a polyline. When any side of a polyline is offset, all sides are offset and all corners are filleted automatically. This would be an inconvenience in this situation because you need only one line offset.

3. The next step is to lay out guidelines to locate the centers of the burners. Offset the line for the control panel down 6 inches. Then offset this line down 11 inches. Next you need vertical guide lines.

4. Draw a line from the upper-left corner of the stove, using Endpoint Osnap and with Ortho on, down to a point about 1 foot below the front stove line (Figure 5.21).

Skill 5

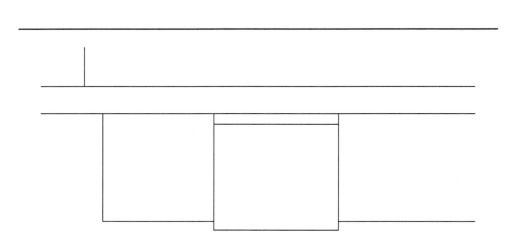

FIGURE 5.20: The stove with the control panel drawn

5. Offset this line 7.5 inches to the right, then offset that line a further 12 inches to the right (Figure 5.22). The guidelines have been set in place.

6. Using Intersection Osnap, draw a circle with its center at the lower-left intersection of the guidelines and a radius of 4.5 inches. Then draw another circle with its center at the upper-left guideline intersection and a radius of 3.5 inches (Figure 5.23). Copy the 7-inch circle to the other two intersections indicated by the guidelines on the right half of the stovetop.

7. Start the Copy command, select the 7-inch (3-1/2" radius) circle and then press ↵.

8. Type **m** ↵, which starts the Multiple option, then pick Intersection Osnap and select the intersection of the guidelines at the center of the 7-inch circle as a base point. Press ↵.

9. Select Intersection Osnap again and pick the top intersection of guidelines on the right half of the stovetop. Pick Intersection Osnap one more time and select the intersection below the one you just picked. The burners are in place.

10. Erase the guidelines and the stove is completed (Figure 5.24). Zoom Previous.

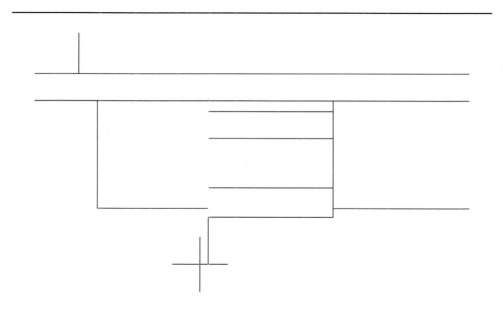

FIGURE 5.21: Drawing a vertical guide line

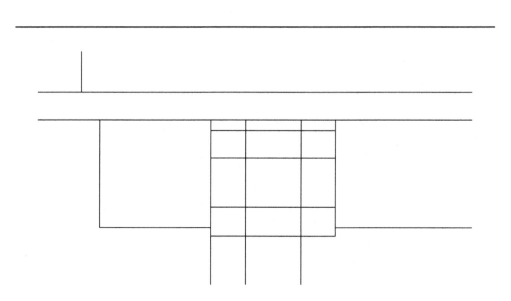

FIGURE 5.22: The guidelines for the centers of the burner circles

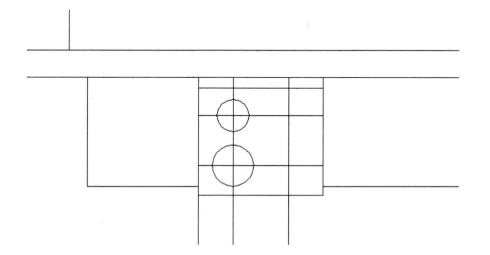

FIGURE 5.23: The 9-inch and 7-inch burners

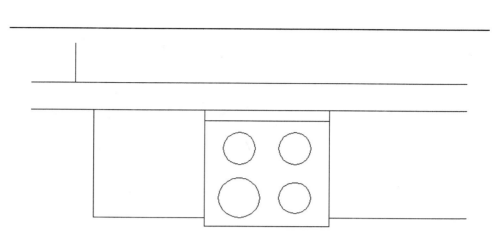

FIGURE 5.24: The completed stove

With the stove finished, the final task in the kitchen is to draw the sink.

The Kitchen Sink

The sink you will draw is a double sink, with one larger than the other (Figure 5.25). You will use Offset, Fillet, and Trim to create it from the counter and wall lines.

1. Zoom into the sink area, keeping the edges of the refrigerator and stove in view. Offset the wall line 1 inch down and the front edge of the counter 1.5 inches up.

2. Offset the right side of the counter 10 inches to the left. When you pick this line to offset, be sure to click it on the 2-inch segment between the refrigerator and the wall line, because the rest of this line coincides with the left line of the refrigerator. You can't always control which line you'll pick when two lines coincide.

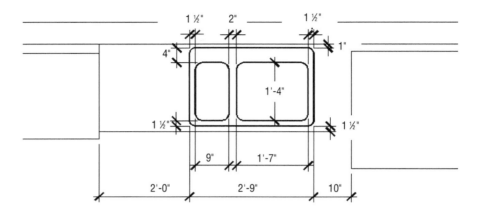

FIGURE 5.25: The sink with dimensions

3. Offset this new line 2'-9" to the left. This forms the outside edge of the sink (Figure 5.26a).

4. Fillet the corners of this rectangle to clean them up, using a radius of 0.

5. Offset the left side, bottom and right side of the sink 1.5 inches to the inside, and offset the top side 4 inches to the inside. Then offset the new line on the left 9 inches to the right, and then again, 2 inches further to the right. This forms the basis of the inside sink lines (Figure 5.26b).

6. Trim away the horizontal top and bottom inside sink lines between the two middle vertical sink lines, then fillet the four corners of each sink with a 2-inch radius to clean them up.

7. Fillet all outside sink corners with a 1.5-inch radius. This will finish the sink (Figure 5.26c). Zoom Previous.

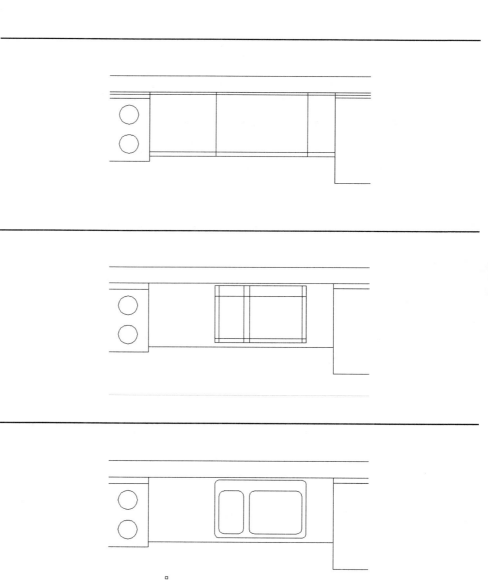

Skill 5

FIGURE 5.26: The offset lines to form the outside edge of the sink (a), the offset lines to form the inside edges of the sink (b), and the finished sink (c)

This completes the kitchen area. Very few new lines were drawn to accomplish this task because most of them were created by offsetting existing lines, then trimming or filleting them. Keep this in mind as you move on to the bathroom.

Constructing the Bathroom

The bathroom has three fixtures: sink, shower, and toilet (Figure 5.27). In drawing these fixtures, you will be using Object Snaps over and over again. You can set one or more of the Osnap choices to be continually running until you turn them off. Then you won't have to pick them each time.

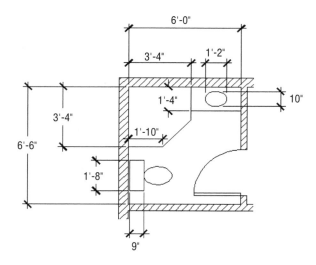

FIGURE 5.27: The bathroom fixtures with dimensions

Setting Running Object Snaps

You will set only two Osnaps running for now, until you get used to how they work.

1. Select Tools ➤ Object Snap Settings. The Osnap Settings dialog box comes up.

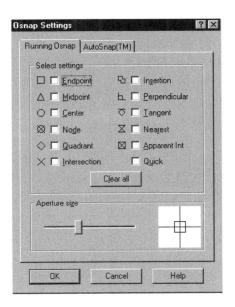

The 12 Osnap options are listed with a checkbox and their symbol to the checkbox's left. Each Osnap option has a different symbol, which appears in the drawing when a particular Osnap has been selected and the cursor is near a point where that Osnap can be used. You can check any number of Osnaps to be running at a time.

TIP   The symbols or icons that appear on an object when an Osnap is active and you move the cursor near the object are called *Autosnaps*. They're quite helpful and you can choose a different color for them if you wish. Click Tools ➢ Object Snap Settings. In the Object Settings dialog box, click the AutoSnap(TM) tab at the top. Then open the Marker Color drop-down list and select a color. Click OK.

2. To start out, click in the checkboxes next to Endpoint and Midpoint, then click OK. These Osnaps will be active any time you are prompted to select a point on the drawing.

NOTE   Osnap is a nickname for Object Snap. The two terms are used interchangeably.

Now you are ready to begin drawing the three fixtures for the bathroom. The shower determines the placement of the other two, so you will start there.

Skill 5

Drawing a Shower Unit

You will start the shower unit with a rectangle, then trim away one corner.

1. Zoom to extents, then use the zoom window and zoom into a view of the bathroom. Start the Rectangle command. For the first point, move the cursor to the upper-left inside corner of the room. Notice the square appears at the corner. This is the symbol for the Endpoint Osnap. As soon as it appears on the endpoint you want to snap to, click the left mouse button and the first corner of the rectangle is placed. For the second point, type **@40,-40** ↵.

2. Start the Line command and move the cursor to the bottom line of the rectangle. Notice how a triangle, the Midpoint Osnap symbol, appears when you get near the midpoint of the line. When you see the triangle on the midpoint you want, click it.

3. Be sure that Ortho is off, then move the cursor near the midpoint of the right side of the rectangle until you see the triangle appear at the midpoint location (Figure 5.28). Click again. Press ↵ to end the Line command.

4. Use this line as a cutting edge and trim the lower-right corner. Press ↵ to stop the Trim command. This completes the shower.

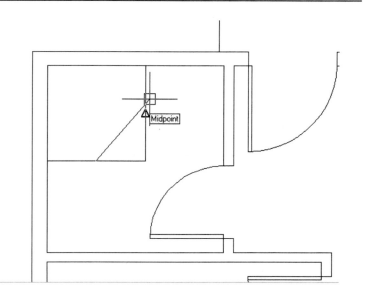

FIGURE 5.28: Using Midpoint Osnap to complete a line across the corner of the shower

Next, draw the sink to the right of the shower.

The Bathroom Sink

You will offset a line and draw an ellipse for this fixture, practicing the From Osnap option in the process. The Endpoint and Midpoint Osnaps are still running.

1. Zoom into the sink area with a zoom window. Offset the top-inside wall line 16 inches down, then use the shower wall as a cutting edge and trim the line back.

2. Click the Ellipse button on the Draw toolbar. Type **c** ⏎ to select the Center option.

3. Click the From Osnap button and then click the newly offset line near its midpoint.

When you have Osnaps running, you can still use an Osnap that is not running. Just click the Osnap button you want to use and the Osnaps running will be suspended for the next pick. In this case, the From Osnap first requires you to pick a base point. After selecting From, the Osnaps running are restored and you can use Midpoint Osnap to locate the base point.

4. Type **@8<90** ⏎ to locate the center of the counter. The Command window will prompt you for the location of the ends of two perpendicular axes. You will start with the left/right axis and enter the distance using the Ortho technique used for the steps earlier in the skill.

5. Be sure Ortho is on, then hold the cursor directly to the right of the center point, being careful to not touch any lines with the cursor's target box. Type **7** ⏎. Hold the cursor directly above the center and, being careful again, type **5** ⏎. The ellipse is constructed and the sink fixture is complete (Figure 5.29).

WARNING   When you have running Osnaps and you are entering distances and/or angles on the keyboard, you have to be careful to keep the cursor with its target box away from any objects, or AutoCAD may ignore what you type in and snap to the objects touching the target box.

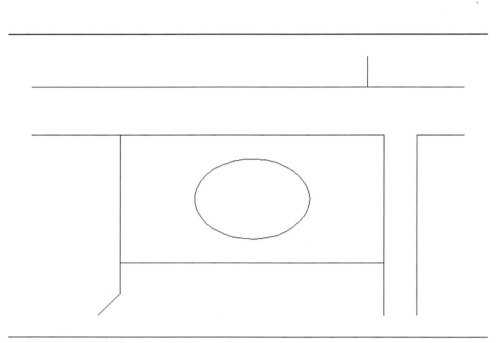

FIGURE 5.29: The completed sink fixture

Drawing the toilet will be the final task in this chapter. You will use the Ellipse command again, along with Rectangle. And you will be introduced to a couple of new display options.

Positioning a Toilet

The toilet consists of a rectangle and an ellipse centered between the shower and the wall, and offset 1 inch from the back wall. The tank is 9 inches by 20 inches, while the seat measures 18 inches in one direction and 1 foot in the other.

1. On the Standard toolbar, click the Pan Realtime button. The cursor changes to a small hand when you return it to the drawing area. Position it in the lower-left corner of the drawing area with the view still zoomed in on the sink.

2. Hold down the left mouse button and drag the hand up and to the right. At the upper-right edge of the drawing area, release the mouse button. The drawing slides along with the movement of the cursor. If necessary, do this again until you have the toilet area centered in the drawing area.

3. Go back to the Standard toolbar and click the Zoom Realtime button. The cursor back on the drawing has been changed to a magnifying glass with a plus and minus sign.

4. Position the Zoom Realtime cursor near the top of the drawing and hold down the left mouse button. Drag the cursor down and watch the view being zoomed out in real time. Move the cursor up, still holding the mouse button down. Position the cursor in such a way that you have a good view of the toilet area, then release the mouse button. Press Esc to exit the Zoom Realtime command.

TIP   With Zoom Realtime, moving the cursor to the left or right has no effect on the view. The magnification is controlled purely by the up-and-down motion.

These zooming options are convenient tools for adjusting the view of your drawing. Move on to the toilet. You need to find a way to position the toilet accurately, centered between the wall and shower. The midpoint of the left wall line won't be useful because the wall line runs behind the shower. You will have to construct a guideline.

1. With the Rectangle command, draw the toilet tank a few inches to the right of the wall, not touching any lines. (See Figure 5.27 for the dimensions.) Then offset the left wall line 1 inch to the right to make a guideline. Use the shower as a cutting edge and trim this guideline down to the shower (Figure 5.30).

2. Start the Move command and select the tank, then press ↵.

3. For the base point, move the cursor to the middle of the left side of the tank and click. When you see the triangle at the midpoint, click the left mouse button.

4. For the second point, move the cursor onto the guideline. When it gets closer to the midpoint than the endpoint, the triangle will appear at the midpoint. At this point, click the left mouse button. The rectangle is positioned accurately 1 inch from the left wall and centered between the shower and lower wall (Figure 5.31).

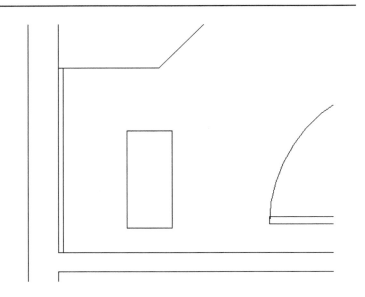

FIGURE 5.30: The toilet tank with an offset guideline

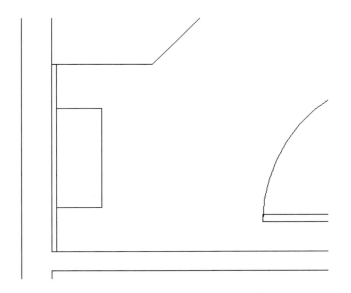

FIGURE 5.31: The tank correctly positioned

5. Erase the guideline.

6. Start the Ellipse command. The Command window displays a default prompt of Axis endpoint 1. Using this option rather than Center, you can define the first axis from one end of the ellipse to the other. This will help you here.

7. Move the cursor near the midpoint of the right side of the tank and, when the triangle shows up there, click. This starts the ellipse.

8. With Ortho on, hold the cursor out to the right of the rectangle and type **1'6** ↵. The first axis is positioned. Now as you move the cursor, you will see that a line starts at the center of the ellipse and the cursor's movement controls the size of the other axis (Figure 5.32). To designate the second axis, you need to enter the distance from the center to the end of the axis, or half the overall length of the axis.

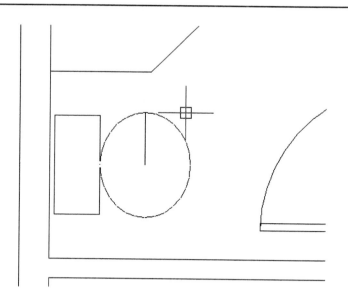

FIGURE 5.32: The cursor controlling the size of the second axis

9. Hold the cursor directly above the center point and type **6** ↵. The ellipse is complete and the toilet is finished.

10.   Select Tools ➤ Object Snap Settings from the drop-down menu. In the dialog box, click the Clear All button, then click OK. This turns off all running Osnaps.

11.   Before you save this drawing, use the Pan Realtime and Zoom Realtime commands to zoom out and pan your drawing until the whole floor plan fills the drawing area except for a thin border around the outside of the plan (Figure 5.33). Save this drawing as Cabin5b.

The bath is complete and you now have a fairly complete floor plan for the cabin. In accomplishing the drawing tasks for Skill 5, you have been exposed to several new commands and techniques that will add to those introduced in Skill 4. Combined, you now have a set of tools for drawing that will take you a long way towards being able to layout a floor plan of any size.

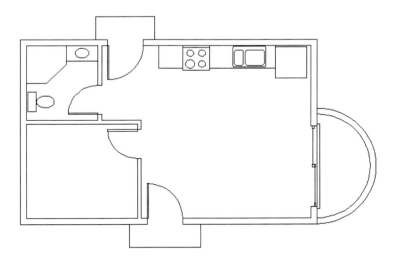

FIGURE 5.33: The completed floor plan zoomed and panned to fill the screen

As is true for almost any computer skill, the key to mastery is practice. Redrawing the entire cabin may seem like a daunting task at this point because you may be thinking about how long it took you to get to this point. But if you try it all again, you will find it will take you about half the time it did the first time, and if you do it a third time, half the time again. Once you understand the techniques used and how the commands work, feel free to experiment with alternative techniques to accomplish tasks and other options on the commands. If you have a specific project in mind you would like to draw in AutoCAD, so much the better—try it out.

Skills 1 through 5 fill out the basic level of skills in AutoCAD that allow you to draw on the computer approximately like you would with pencil and vellum, though you may already be seeing some of the advantages CAD offers over traditional board drafting. Beginning with the next skill, you will be introduced to concepts of AutoCAD that do not have a counterpart in board drafting. These features will take you to a new level of knowledge and skill, and you will start to get an idea of what sets computer drafting apart.

Are You Experienced?

Now you can...

- ☑ pick a point from a specified distance with the From Osnap option
- ☑ use Quadrant and Intersection Osnaps
- ☑ use running Object Snaps
- ☑ move around the drawing area with Realtime Zoom and Pan
- ☑ use the Circle and Ellipse commands
- ☑ move and duplicate objects with the Move and Copy Multiple commands
- ☑ calculate the difference between a doorway opening width and step width to find where to start the side of the step
- ☑ use a circle to make a semi-circle arc
- ☑ use guidelines to locate the center of circles for a stove top

Using Layers to Organize Your Drawing

- ➔ Creating new layers
- ➔ Assigning a color and linetype to layers
- ➔ Moving existing objects onto a new layer
- ➔ Freezing and thawing layers
- ➔ Working with linetypes

In pre-computer days, drafters used a set of transparent overlays on the drafting table. They were sheets that stacked on top of one another and the drafters could see through several at a time. Specific kinds of information were drawn on each overlay, all related spatially so that several overlays might all be drawn to the same floor plan. Each overlay had small holes punched into it near the corners so the drafter could position it onto buttons, called registration points, which were taped to the drawing board. Because all overlays had holes punched at the same locations with respect to the drawing, information on the set of overlays was kept in alignment.

To help you organize your drawing, AutoCAD provides you with an amazing tool, called *layers*, which is a computerized metaphor for the transparent overlays, only much more powerful and flexible. In manual drafting, you could use only four or five overlays at a time before the information on the bottom overlay became unreadable. In AutoCAD, you are not limited in number of layers. You can have hundreds of layers, and complex CAD drawings often do.

Layers as an Organization Tool

To understand what layers are and why they are so useful, think again about the transparent overlay sheets in hand drafting. Each overlay was designed to be printed. The bottom sheet may have been a basic floor plan. To create an overlay sheet for a structural drawing, the drafter would trace over the lines of the floor plan that they needed in the overlay, then add new information pertinent to that sheet. For the next overlay, the same thing was done again. Each sheet, then, contained some information in common plus data unique to that sheet.

In AutoCAD, using layers will allow you to generate all the sheets for a set of overlays from one file (Figure 6.1). Nothing needs to be drawn twice or traced. The wall layout will be on one layer and the roof lines on another. Doors will be on a third. The visibility of layers can be controlled so that all objects residing on a layer can be made temporarily invisible. This feature provides you with the means to put all information keyed to a particular floor plan in one DWG file and, from that drawing, produce a series of derived drawings such as the foundation plan, the second floor plan, the reflected ceiling plan, and the roof plan by making different combinations of layers visible for each drawing. When you make a print, you decide which of the layers will be visible in the print. Consequently, in a set of drawings, each sheet based on the floor plan will display a unique combination of layers, all of which are in one file.

Layers, as an organization tool, allow you to classify the various objects in a computerized drawing—lines, arcs, circles, etc.—according to the component of

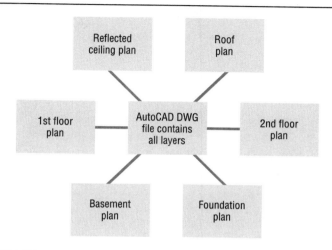

FIGURE 6.1: Diagram of several drawings coming from one file

the building they represent, such as doors, walls, and windows. Each layer is assigned a color and all objects placed on the layer take on that assigned color. This allows you to easily distinguish between objects that represent separate components of the building (Figure 6.2), and you can quickly tell what layer a given object, or group of objects, is on.

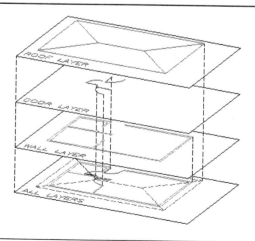

FIGURE 6.2: Separate layers combined to make a drawing

The procedure for achieving this level of organization is to set up the new layers, and then move existing objects onto them. Following that, you will learn how to create new objects on a specific layer.

Setting Up Layers

All AutoCAD drawings have one layer in common—the 0 layer. The 0 layer is the default layer in all new drawings, so if you don't add any new layers on a drawing, everything you create in that drawing will be on the 0 layer. Everything you have drawn so far in the cabin drawing has been drawn on the 0 layer.

TIP A good way to think about objects and layers is the analogy of people and countries: Just as all persons must reside in some country, so must all objects be on some layer.

All objects in AutoCAD are assigned a layer, and in this book, I will refer to objects assigned to a particular layer as "being on" that layer. Objects get placed on a layer in two ways: either they are moved to the layer or they are created on the layer in the first place. You will learn to do both in this chapter. But first you need to learn how to set up layers. To see how this is done, you will create seven new layers for your cabin drawing—Walls, Doors, Steps, Balcony, Fixtures, Headers, and Roof—then move the existing objects in your drawing onto the first five of these layers. Finally, you will create new objects on the Header and Roof layers.

1. If you have taken a break and shut down your system, bring up AutoCAD and open Cabin5b.dwg. The Object Properties toolbar, just above the drawing area on your screen, contains all the buttons and drop-down lists for controlling layers, linetypes, colors, and object properties. On the left half of the toolbar are the layer controls.

Layer controls

2. Click the Layers button on the Object Properties toolbar. It's the second button from the left. The Layer & Linetype Properties dialog box is

displayed (Figure 6.3). Notice the large open area in the middle of the dialog box with the 0 layer listed at the top. This is called the Layer List box. All of the layers in a drawing are listed here along with their status and characteristics. For Cabin5b, there is only one layer so far.

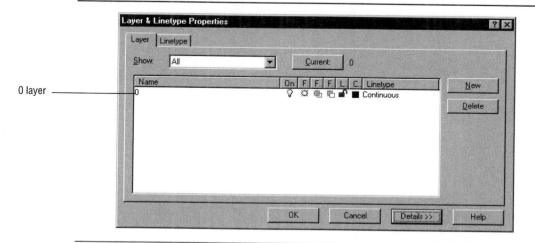

FIGURE 6.3: The Layer & Linetype Properties dialog box

The Layer & Linetype Properties Dialog Box

Besides the Layer List box, there are the Layer and Linetype tabs, a drop-down list titled Show, and several command buttons in the dialog box. Before setting up new layers, look for a moment at the Layer List box.

The Layer List Box

The Layer List box lists all the layers in the drawing along with each layer's properties and modes.

Each layer has two properties: a color and a linetype. Look at the 0 layer row in the list and notice the square and the word "Continuous" at the far right. The square is black (or white if you have a black background for your drawing area) and is in a column headed up by a C (for color). Continuous is in the Linetype column. This tells us that the 0 layer is assigned to be black and the linetype Continuous, by default.

The rest of the columns to the left of the Color column are headed with On, three Fs, and L, and have picture icons in the 0 layer row. These columns represent the status modes of the layer, and control whether objects on a layer are visible or can be changed. The visibility status of a layer will be covered below and the changeability of objects will be discussed later in this skill.

Creating New Layers and Assigning Colors

Let's create a few new layers, name them, and assign them colors.

1. In the upper-right corner of the dialog box, click New. A new layer called Layer1 appears in the list. The layer's name is highlighted, which means that it can be renamed by entering another name now (Figure 6.4a).

2. Type **walls** ↵. Layer1 changes to Walls. Walls should still be highlighted (Figure 6.4b).

3. Click the square in the C column in the Walls row. The Select Colors dialog box comes up (Figure 6.5). There are four areas of color choices. In the Standard Colors area, click the blue square. In the Color text box, under the Full Color Palette, white has changed to blue and the square just to the right has taken on the color blue.

4. Click OK. The Select Colors dialog box disappears and now, in the layer list in the Layers & Linetype Properties dialog box, you can see that the color square for the Walls layer has changed to blue.

As you saw in the Select Colors dialog box there are—besides the nine standard colors—six gray shades, two logical colors and a full color palette containing as many colors as your video card and driver can support, up to 256. Most computers running AutoCAD 14 will support 256 colors. With one color as the background, that leaves 255 colors for you to choose from. Colors 1–7, all in the Standard Colors palette, have names. Those numbered 8–255 have numbers only. Color number 7 is named white, but will be black if you are using a white background color.

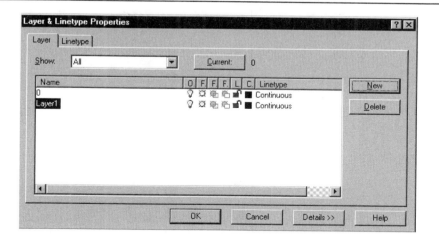

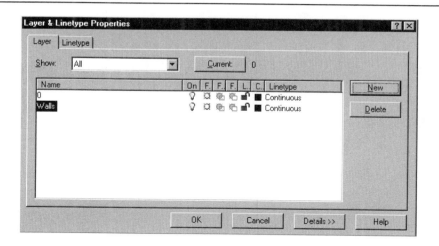

FIGURE 6.4: The Layer & Linetype Properties dialog box with a new layer called Layer1 (a) and with Layer 1 renamed to Walls (b)

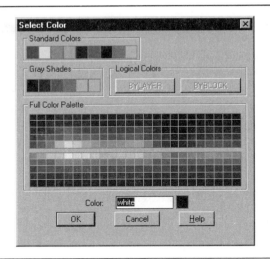

FIGURE 6.5: The Select Color dialog box

When we assign the color blue to the Walls layer and place all objects representing walls on that layer, all wall objects will be blue. In this way you will be able to easily distinguish which objects in your drawing represent walls. In addition to helping you distinguish between building components, colors are also involved in controlling line weight, so the choice you make of a color for a layer can be an important one. Most offices have a standard they follow for organizing layers by name, color and linetype. The American Institute of Architects publishes their Layering Standards, which is often adapted by architecture firms to fit their specific needs. With the cabin drawing you will start out developing a basic set of layers. Once you learn how to manage this set, tackling more complex layering systems will come naturally.

As you create your new list of layers and assign them colors, notice how each color looks in your drawing. Some are easier to see on a screen with a light background and others do better on a black screen.

1. In the Layers & Linetype Properties dialog box, click New.

2. Type **doors** ↵ to change the name of the layer.

3. Pick the color square in the Doors row and, when the Select Colors dialog box comes up, click the red square in the Standard Colors area, then click OK.

4. Repeat the steps above for each of the following layers and their assigned colors. Pick the colors from the Standard Colors area of the Select Colors dialog box.

Layer Name	Color
Steps	Light Gray
Balcony	Green
Fixtures	Magenta
Headers	Yellow
Roof	Cyan

When finished, the layer list should have eight layers listed with their assigned colors in the color squares of each row (Figure 6.6). All layers are assigned the Continuous linetype by default. This is convenient since most building components are represented in the floor plan by continuous lines, but the roof—because of its position above the walls—needs to be represented by a dashed line. So you need to assign a Dashed linetype to the Roof layer.

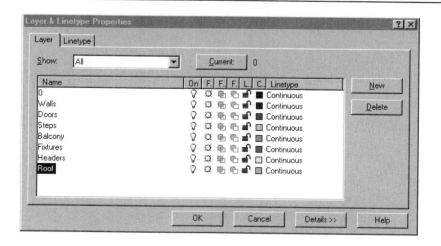

FIGURE 6.6: The Layer List box in the Layer & Linetype Properties dialog box, with the seven new layers and the 0 layer

NOTE In more complex drawings, you may need to have several layers for variations of the same building components, such as Existing Walls to Remain, Walls to Be Demolished and New Walls. Once you acquire the skills presented here, you will have no difficulty progressing to a more complex layering system.

Assigning Linetypes to Layers

When you assigned a color to a layer, all colors supported by your system were available to choose from. Not so with linetypes. Each new drawing has only one linetype loaded into it by default (the Continuous linetype). You must load in any other linetypes you need from an outside file.

1. In the Layer & Linetype Properties dialog box, click Continuous in the row for the Roof layer. The Select Linetype dialog box comes up (Figure 6.7). In the Loaded linetypes list, only Continuous is displayed. No other linetypes have been loaded into this drawing.

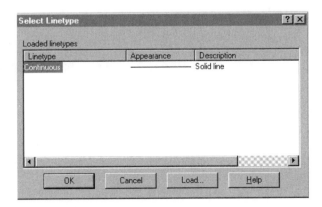

FIGURE 6.7: The Select Linetype dialog box

2. Click Load. The Load or Reload Linetypes dialog box comes up (Figure 6.8a). In the Available Linetypes list, there are 45 linetypes listed, and they fall into three groups. The first 14 linetypes are in the Acad_iso family

(International Standards Organization). Below these are eight families of three linetypes each and seven special linetypes with symbols in them. Scroll down the list to where the Dashed, Dashed2 and Dashedx2 linetypes are located (Figure 6.8b). Notice how in this family the dashed lines are different sizes.

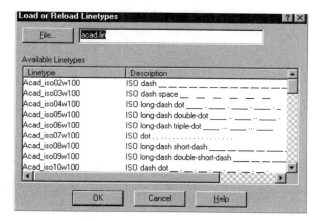

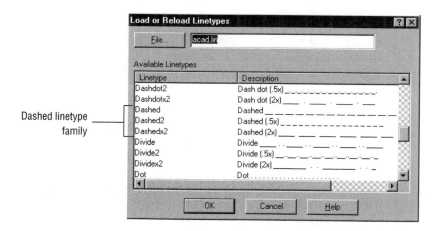

FIGURE 6.8: The Load or Reload Linetypes dialog box (a) with the list scrolled to the three Dashed linetypes (b)

3. Select Dashed, then click OK. You are returned to the Select Linetype dialog box. In the Select Linetype dialog box, the Dashed linetype has been added to the Linetypes list, under Continuous (Figure 6.9). Click Dashed to highlight it and click OK. In the Layer & Linetype Properties dialog box, the Roof layer has been assigned the Dashed linetype (Figure 6.10).

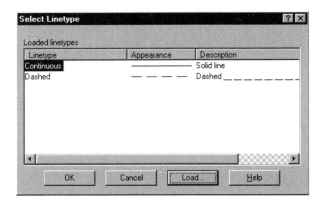

FIGURE 6.9: The Select Linetype dialog box with the Dashed linetype loaded

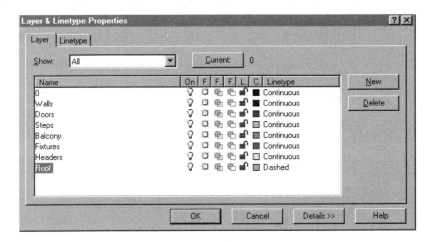

FIGURE 6.10: The Layer & Linetype Properties dialog box with the Roof layer assigned the Dashed linetype

The eight families of three linetypes each are the standard AutoCAD linetypes. The Dashed line family, like the others, has one basic linetype and two which are multiples of it: one twice the size (2×) and one half the size (.5×). (See Figure 6.8b.) You have an assortment of different sizes of one style of linetype. This will be helpful for distinguishing between building components, such as foundation walls and beams, which, in addition to roof lines, may also need dashed lines.

Now is a good time to look at what it means for a layer to be current.

The Current Layer as a Drawing Tool

Notice the Current button in the top center of the Layers & Linetypes dialog box, just above the layer list. Next to it is the name of the current layer, in this case, 0.

At any one time there is always one—and only one— layer that is set to be the current layer. When a layer is current, all objects you draw will be assigned to that layer and take on the Object Properties assigned to it. Because the 0 layer is current, all objects in your drawing are on the 0 layer and thereby have the linetype and color that were specified by default for the 0 layer: Continuous and White, respectively. If you make the Walls layer current, any new lines you draw while the Walls layer is current will be Blue and Continuous. If the Roof layer is current, any new lines will be Cyan and Dashed.

1. Click the Walls layer in the layer list to highlight it, then click Current. The Walls layer becomes the current layer and replaces the 0 layer next to the Current button.

2. Click OK at the bottom of the Layer & Linetype Properties dialog box. The dialog box closes and you are returned to your drawing.

3. Look at the drop-down layers list on the Object Properties toolbar. Most of the symbols you saw in the layers list in the Layers & Linetypes dialog box are here on this drop-down list, and the Walls layer is the visible entry on the list with a blue square (the color you assigned to the Walls layer earlier). This list always shows you the current layer.

4. Look at the drawing. Nothing has changed because the objects in the drawing are still on the 0 layer.

You need to move the objects in the drawing onto their proper layers. To do this, you'll use the Properties button to assign a different layer to each object.

Assigning Objects to Layers

The Properties button works in two modes, depending on whether you select only one, or more than one object.

1. Click the Properties button at the right end of the Object Properties toolbar. The cursor turns into a pickbox and the Command window prompts you to Select objects:.

2. Pick the outer arc of the balcony, then press ↵. The Modify Arc dialog box comes up (Figure 6.11). In the top half of the dialog box there are buttons and text boxes for the basic properties common to all objects. The bottom half contains information specific to arcs and about this arc in particular.

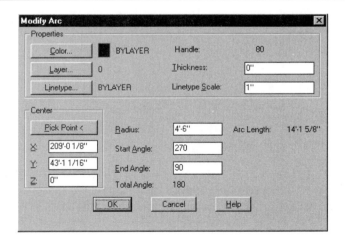

FIGURE 6.11: The Modify Arc dialog box

3. Click Cancel, then press ↵ again to restart the Properties command. This time click both arcs of the balcony, then press ↵. The Change Properties dialog box comes up (Figure 6.12). The buttons and text boxes are the same ones as are in the top half of the Modify Arc dialog box.

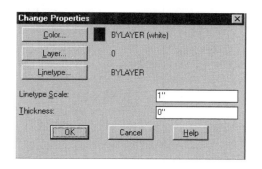

FIGURE 6.12: The Change Properties dialog box

 TIP When using the Properties command, if only one object is selected, a dialog box comes up which is named after the object chosen and which contains information pertinent to that particular object, including properties shared by all objects. If more than one object is selected, the Change Properties dialog box comes up instead, which contains only the properties shared by all objects.

4. Click Layer. The Select Layer dialog box comes up (Figure 6.13). It looks like the layer list in the Layer & Linetype Properties dialog box, and it contains a list of the layers in your drawing.

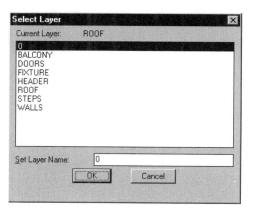

FIGURE 6.13: The Select Layer dialog box

5. Click Balcony in the list of layers. Balcony appears in the Set Layer Name box. Click OK. Back in the Change Properties dialog box, the Balcony now appears next to the Layer button, and the color (green) and linetype (continuous) assigned to the Balcony layer appear next to the Color and Linetype buttons, respectively, along with the word "Bylayer."

 NOTE When a color and linetype are assigned to a layer, objects on that layer take on the Bylayer color and linetype. This means their color and linetype are controlled "by the layer" the objects are on.

6. Click OK to accept the way things are currently set up in this dialog box. You are returned to your drawing, and the two arcs representing the balcony are now green.

This is the process you need to go through for each layer, so that each of the remaining four new layers can receive objects currently on the 0 layer (Steps, Doors, Fixtures, and Walls). This time, move the threshold and steps to the Steps layer. You will select them using a selection window.

Selecting Objects with Windows

AutoCAD provides many tools for selecting objects in your drawing. Two of the most powerful among these tools are the crossing and regular selection windows. The size and location of these selection windows are determined by picking points on your drawing to be opposite corners of a rectangle that serves as the window. The regular window selects any objects completely enclosed by the window. The crossing window selects objects that are completely enclosed by, or cross through an edge of, the window. The crossing window is represented by dashed lines and the regular window by solid lines.

By default, the application is set up in such a way that, whenever the prompt in the Command window is Select objects:, you can pick objects one at a time or start a regular or crossing window. The pickbox becomes the cursor. If you pick an object, it is selected and the same prompt returns. If you select a blank area of the drawing, a selection window is started. If you then move the cursor to the right of the point just picked, a regular window is started. If you move the cursor to the left, a crossing window is started.

1. Press ↵ to restart the Properties command. Use crossing windows to select the threshold and the front and back steps.

2. At the Select objects: prompt, hold the pickbox cursor above and to the right of the upper-right corner of the balcony threshold—still inside the balcony wall—as shown in Figure 6.14a. Click that point, then move the cursor down and to the left until you have made a tall, thin crossing window which completely encloses the right edge of the threshold and is crossed on its left edge by the short horizontal connecting lines, as shown in Figure 6.14b. Then click again.

3. Make similar crossing windows to select the front and back steps. Be sure your first pick starts a window at the right and finishes to the left of each step, so the window completely encloses the horizontal line and is crossed by the vertical lines on its upper or lower edge. Press ↵ when both steps and the threshold have been selected. The Change Properties dialog box comes up.

4. Click the Layer button, then, in the Select Layer dialog box, click Steps, then click OK.

5. Click OK again to close the Change Properties dialog box. You are returned to your drawing. The steps and threshold are now light gray.

You can also specify a regular or crossing window by typing **c** ↵ (for crossing) or **w** ↵ (for regular) before you pick the first point of the window. Then you can drag the window out in either direction, and it remains the type of window you specified. You'll see how this works when we select doors and swings to move onto the Doors layer.

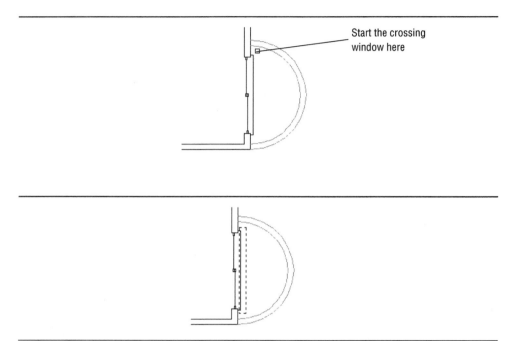

Start the crossing window here

FIGURE 6.14: Starting the crossing selection window (a) and completing it (b).

Selecting the Doors and Swings

To accomplish this task you can use the same kind of crossing window to select the objects. Let's examine it closely to learn more valuable skills in selecting objects.

1. Press ⏎ to restart the Properties command.

2. At the Select Objects: prompt, place the pickbox in a clear space below and to the right of the back door, then pick that point. This starts the selection window. Move the cursor up and to the left until the crossing window crosses the back door and swing, but does not cross the wall line, as in Figure 6.15a.

3. When you have the crossing window positioned correctly, click in a clear space again. This selects the back door and its swing.

4. Move to the bathroom and position the pickbox cursor in the clear space directly above the swing. When the pickbox is positioned, click in a clear

space. Then move the cursor down and to the left until the window you are creating crosses the bathroom door and swing, without crossing any wall lines (Figure 6.15b), then click in a clear space again. The bathroom door and swing are selected.

5. Continue this procedure to select the other two doors and their swings. For the bedroom door, start the crossing window directly below the door swing. For the front door, start a crossing window above and to the right of the door. Figure 6.15c shows the two crossing windows that will select the bedroom and front doors.

For the sliding glass door, it will be not be easy to create a crossing window from left to right, because it may be difficult to position the pickbox between the threshold lines and the sliding door. In situations like this one, you can manually start a crossing window and move the cursor to the left or right after the first point is picked and still make a crossing window.

1. At the Select objects: prompt, type c ⏎ to manually start a crossing window. Pick a point to the left of the balcony opening, just below the upper jamb line. The pickbox changes to the crosshair. Move the crosshair down and to the right, forming a crossing window. When the crossing window looks like Figure 6.16, click. The entire sliding glass door assembly will be selected, but not the jambs, walls, threshold, or balcony.

2. Press ⏎ to end the selection process. The Change Properties dialog box comes up. Click the Layer button. In the Select Layer dialog box, click Doors, then click OK. Click OK again to close the Change Properties dialog box. Back in your drawing, the doors have become red.

The next task is to move the kitchen and bathroom counters and fixtures onto the Fixtures layer. To do this, you need to know how to undo selections.

Removing Objects from the Selection Set

Previously, when you moved the doors and swings onto the Doors layer, you first selected the five doors and then you pressed ⏎ to end the selection process. That procedure is known as building up a *selection set*. The selection set, in this case, contains the five doors and four swings. It will often happen that, as you build up a selection set, you will find it easier to select more objects than you want to be in the selection set, and then remove the unwanted ones before continuing on with the command that is currently running. You'll see how this is done when you select the bathroom fixtures.

Selection window

Selection window

Selection windows

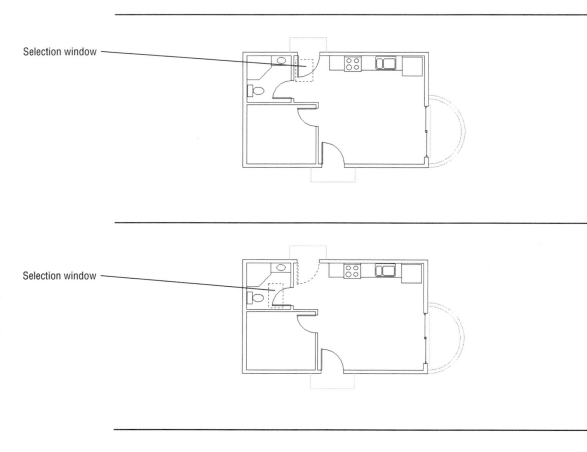

FIGURE 6.15: Using a crossing window to select the doors and swings: the back door (a), the bathroom door (b), and the bedroom and front doors (c)

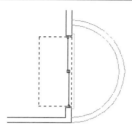

FIGURE 6.16: Using a Crossing Window to select the sliding glass door

1. Click the Properties button. At the Select objects: prompt, pick a point in the kitchen area just below the refrigerator to start a crossing window.

2. Move the cursor to the left and up until the upper-left corner of the crossing window is to the left of the left edge of the counter, and inside the back wall as in Figure 6.17a. When you have it right, click that point. The entire kitchen counter area and the back wall line are selected.

3. Now move over to the bathroom and pick a point in the middle of the bathroom sink, being careful to not touch any lines with the pickbox.

4. Move the cursor down and to the left until the lower-left corner of the crossing window is in the middle of the toilet tank (Figure 6.17b). When you have it positioned this way, click that point. All the bathroom fixtures and the door swing are selected.

5. Type **r** ↵, then pick the selected door swing in the bathroom and the back wall line in the kitchen. As you pick them, their lines become solid again, letting you know they have been de-selected or removed from the selection set (Figure 6.17c).

6. Press ↵ to end the selection process. In the Change Properties dialog box, click Layer, then select Fixtures from the list of layers in the Select Layers dialog box. Click OK twice to get back to your drawing. The fixtures are now magenta.

The last objects to move onto a new layer are the wall lines. As the drawing is now, it will not be easy to select the wall lines because there are so many other objects in the drawing that are in the way. However, these other objects are now on their own layers while the wall lines are still on the 0 layer. If you make all of your layers temporarily invisible except for the 0 and Walls layers, selection of the wall lines will be easy.

Skill 6

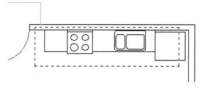

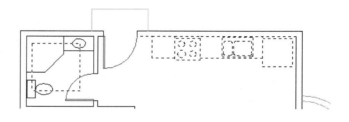

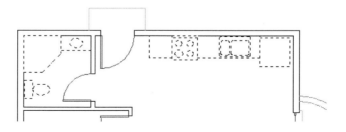

FIGURE 6.17: A crossing window to select the kitchen objects (a), another crossing window to select the bathroom objects (b), and the completed selection set after removing the door swing and back wall line (c)

Freezing and Turning Off Layers

Layers can be made invisible either by freezing them or turning them off. These two procedures operate the same way and do about the same thing. The difference between freezing and turning a layer off is technical and beyond the scope of this book, but, in general, freezing layers has the effect of minimizing the amount of time needed by AutoCAD to make the geometrical calculations for a drawing, so for our purposes, freezing is preferable to turning layers off. We will freeze all the layers except the 0 layer and the Walls layer, then move the wall lines onto the Walls layer.

1. Click the Layers button on the Object Properties toolbar. The Layer & Linetype Properties dialog box comes up. Notice that the 0 layer is still first in the list and the others have been reorganized alphabetically (Figure 6.18). Layers beginning with numbers are listed first in numerical order. Following them, the rest of the layers are listed alphabetically.

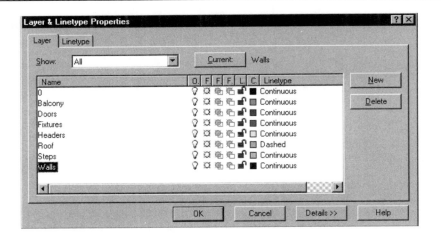

FIGURE 6.18: The layers, now listed alphabetically

2. Click the Balcony layer to highlight it. Then hold down the Shift key and click the Walls layer. All layers have been selected except the 0 layer (Figure 6.19).

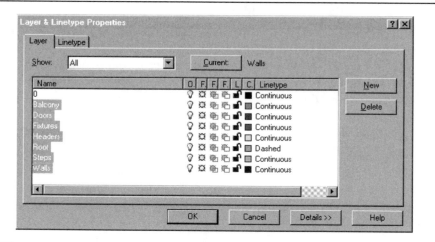

FIGURE 6.19: Selecting all layers except the 0 layer

3. Move the arrow cursor over to the second column from the left—the first one to begin with "F"—which has yellow suns as symbols for each layer row.

4. Click one of the suns. A warning box comes on and tells you that you cannot freeze the current layer, which at the moment is Walls in your drawing. Click OK to close this box. The sun symbols have all changed to snowflakes except the ones for the 0 layer and the Walls layer (Figure 6.20).

5. Click OK. All objects in your drawing are invisible except the wall lines (Figure 6.21). They are still on the 0 layer, and nothing is on the Walls layer yet.

6. Click the Properties button on the Object Properties toolbar. Make a regular selection window around the cabin wall lines. Click in the upper-left corner of the drawing area, above and to the left of any lines, then click in the lower-right corner in the same way. All the wall lines are selected. Press ↵. The Change Properties dialog box comes up.

7. Click the Layer button. Then click the Walls layer. Click OK twice. The walls are now blue.

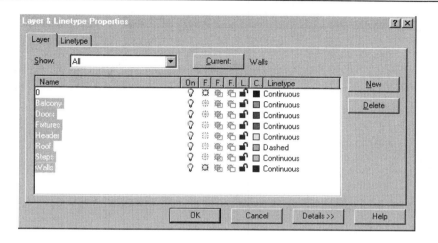

FIGURE 6.20: The frozen layers are signified by snowflakes.

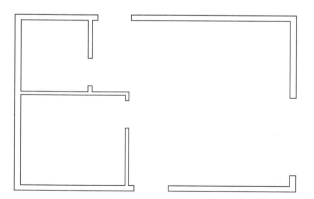

FIGURE 6.21: The floor plan with all layers frozen except the Walls and 0 layer

8. Click the Layers button on the Object Properties toolbar. In the Layers & Linetype Properties dialog box, click the Balcony layer, then hold down the Shift key and click the Steps layer. All layers are highlighted except the 0 layer and the Walls layer.

9. Click one of the snowflakes in the first F column. All snowflakes become suns. Click OK. Back in your drawing, all objects are now visible (*thawed*) and on their correct layers (Figure 6.22).

10. Save this drawing in your training folder as Cabin6a.

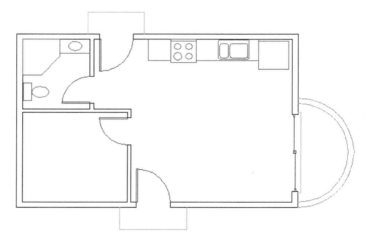

FIGURE 6.22: The floor plan with all layers visible and all objects on their correct layer

Two of your layers, Roof and Header, still have no objects on them because these components haven't been drawn yet. We'll draw the headers now.

Drawing the Headers

Most door and window openings do not extend to the ceiling. The portion of the wall above the opening and below the ceiling is the *header*. The term comes from the name of the beam inside the wall that spans across the opening. In a floor plan, wall lines usually stop at the door and window openings, but you need lines across the gap between jamb lines to show that an opening does not extend to the ceiling; hence, the header.

To draw the headers you need to make the Header layer current. As you've seen above, this can be done in the Layer & Linetype Properties dialog box, but there is a shortcut—the Layer drop-down list on the Object Properties toolbar.

Look at the Layer drop-down list for a moment. The name of the current layer is displayed in the box along with a color square showing the current color, and four status icons.

1. Click anywhere in the box or on the down arrow button on the right end. The drop-down list opens, displaying a list of the layers in your drawing (Figure 6.23). If you have more than 10 layers, a scroll bar becomes operational, giving you access to all layers.

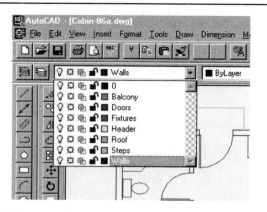

FIGURE 6.23: The Layer drop-down list

2. Click the Header layer. The list closes and Header is now in the box, telling you that the Header layer has replaced Walls as the current layer.

3. Type **Alt+t**, then type **n**. The Osnap Settings dialog box comes up. Click in the checkbox next to Endpoint to place a checkmark in the box, then click OK.

4. Type l ↵ to start the Line command. The doors and steps may be in your way. Click the Layer drop-down list. When the list of layers appears, click the sun icons for the Doors and Steps layers, to freeze them. Then click Header at the top of the list. The drop-down list closes, the Header layer is still current, and the doors, steps, and threshold have disappeared.

    You need to draw two parallel lines across each of the five openings, from the endpoint of one jamb line to the corresponding endpoint of the jamb on the opposite side of the opening.

5. Move the cursor with its target box near the upper end of the left jamb for the back door until the blue square appears at the upper endpoint of the jamb line, then click.

6. Move the cursor to the upper end of the right jamb and do the same thing as you did in the previous step.

7. Right-click twice—once to end the Line command, and once to restart it. This will allow you to start a new line segment that won't be connected to the last segment you drew.

8. Move to the lower endpoint of the right jamb line for the back door and—with the same technique used in Steps 5, 6, and 7—draw the lower header line across the opening. The results are shown in Figure 6.24a.

    Keep using the same procedure to draw the rest of the header lines for the remaining four doorway openings. Use a *click, click, right-click, right-click* pattern on your mouse until the last segment is drawn. Then right-click once to end the Line command. The floor plan will look like Figure 6.24b.

9. Thaw the Doors and Headers layers.

The Layer drop-down list box is a shortcut which allows you to quickly pick a different layer to be the current layer and to freeze or thaw individual layers. To create new layers, or to freeze many layers at a time, use the Layer & Linetype dialog box, accessed by clicking the Layer button on the Object Properties toolbar. You'll learn another tool for changing the current layer as you draw the roof lines.

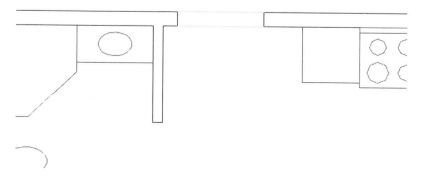

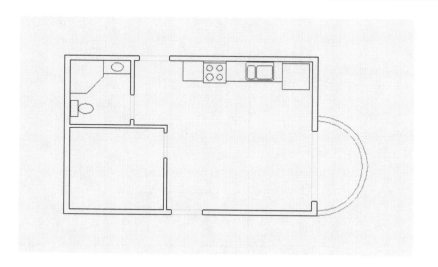

FIGURE 6.24: The header lines drawn, for the back door opening (a) and for the rest of the doorway openings (b)

Drawing the Roof

Before starting to draw the roof lines, refer to Figure 6.25 and note the lines representing different parts of the roof:

- four *eaves lines* around the perimeter of the building, representing the lowest edge of the roof

- one *ridge line*, representing the peak of the roof

- four *hip lines* which connect the endpoints of the eaves lines to an endpoint of the ridge line

The roof for the cabin is called a *hip roof* because the end panels slope down to the eaves just as the middle panels do. The intersections of the sloping roof planes form the hip lines. We'll start with the eaves.

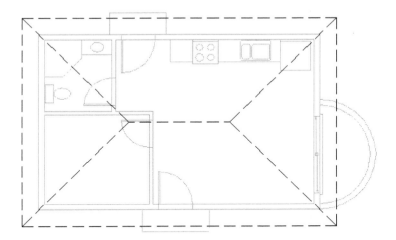

FIGURE 6.25: The floor plan with the roof lines

Creating the Eaves

Because the roof cantilevers beyond the exterior walls the same distance on all sides of the building, we can generate the eaves lines by offsetting the outside wall lines.

1. Type **o** ↵ to start the Offset command, then type **1'-6"**↵ to set the offset distance. Pick the left outside wall lines and then pick a point to the left of that line to offset it to the outside.

2. Move to another side of the building and pick one of the outside wall lines on that side and offset it to the outside as well.

3. Repeat this for the other two sides of the building until you have offset one outside wall line to the outside of the building on each side of the cabin (Figure 6.26). Press ↵ to end the Offset command. Be sure you have only one line offset on each side of the building. If you offset too many lines on one side, erase one.

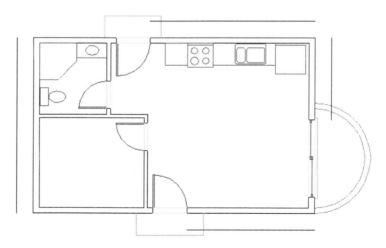

FIGURE 6.26: One outside wall line is offset to each side of the building.

4. Type **f** ↵ to start the Fillet command. Make sure that the radius is set to 0. If it is, go on to step 5. If not, type **r** ↵, then type **0** ↵ ↵ to set the radius and restart the Fillet command.

5. Click any two of these newly offset lines that are on adjacent sides of the building. Click the half of the line nearest the corner that the two selected lines will meet (Figure 6.27a). The lines extend to meet each other and form a corner (Figure 6.27b). The Fillet command ends.

6. Press ↵ to restart the Fillet command. Pick two more adjacent lines that will meet at another corner.

7. Start the Fillet command again, and keep picking pairs of lines until all corners are filleted and the result is a rectangle, which represents the eaves of the roof surrounding the building, offset 1'-6" from its outside exterior walls (Figure 6.28).

Because the eaves lines were offset from wall lines, they are on the Walls layer. You need to move them onto the Roof layer. Then you'll make the Roof layer current so when you draw the hip lines and the ridge line, they will be on the Roof layer.

1. Click the Properties button on the Object Properties toolbar.

2. Select the four eaves lines, then press ↵. In the Change Properties dialog box, click the Layer Button.

3. In the Select Layer dialog box, click Roof. Click OK, then click OK again. The eaves lines are now on the Roof layer.

The eaves lines are still solid lines, even though the Roof layer has been assigned a dashed linetype. Actually, the lines are dashed, but the dashes are so small the monitor can't display them.

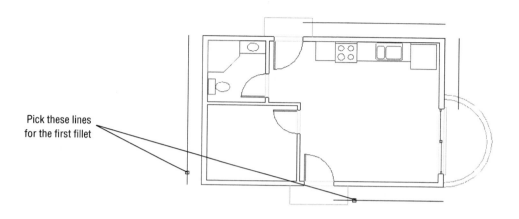

Pick these lines
for the first fillet

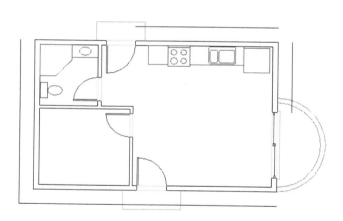

FIGURE 6.27: Picking lines to fillet one of the eaves corners (a) and the result (b)

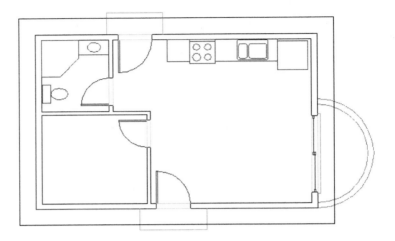

FIGURE 6.28: The eaves lines after filleting

Setting a Linetype Scale Factor

By default, the dashes are set up to be ½ inch long with ¼ inch spaces. This is the right size for a drawing that is close to actual size on your screen, like the box you drew in Skill 2, but for something the size of your cabin, you must increase the linetype scale to make the dashes large enough to see. If the dashes were a foot long with six-inch spaces, they would at least be visible, though possibly not exactly the right size. To make such a change in the dash size, ask what you must multiply ½ inch by to get 12 inches. The answer is 24: that's your scale factor. AutoCAD stores a Linetype Scale Factor setting that controls the size of the dashes and spaces of non-continuous linetypes. The default is 1.00 which gives you the ½ inch dash, so we need to change it to 24.00.

1. Type **ltscale** ↵. The prompt in the Command window reads New scale factor <1.0000>:.

2. Type **24** ↵ to set the linetype scale factor to 24. Your drawing changes and you can see the dashes (Figure 6.29). If you are not satisfied with the dash size, restart the Ltscale command and increase the scale factor for a longer dash or decrease it for a shorter one. This linetype scale factor is a global one, meaning it affects every non-continuous line in the drawing. There is also an individual scale factor for linetypes. You'll see that after you finish the roof.

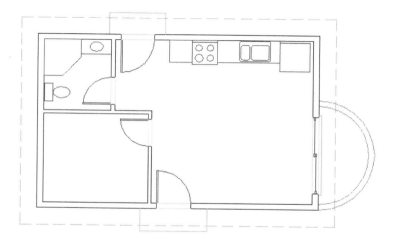

FIGURE 6.29: The eaves lines on the roof layer with visible dashes

Drawing the Hip and Ridge Lines

Next, you'll draw one of the diagonal hip roof lines, then use the Mirror command to create the other three. To do this you need to assign the Roof layer to be the current layer. Because you have moved the lines you just offset to the Roof layer, you can use the Make Object's Layer Current button to make the Roof layer current.

1. Click the Make Object's Layer Current button on the left end of the Object Properties toolbar. You will get the `Select object whose layer will become current:` prompt.

2. Pick one of the dashed eaves lines. The Roof layer replaces Header in the Layer drop-down list, telling you the Roof layer is now the current layer. Look at the Linetypes drop-down list on the Object Properties toolbar. A dashed line with the name "ByLayer" appears there. ByLayer tells you that the current linetype is going to be what ever linetype has been assigned to the current layer, and, in the case of the Roof layer, the assigned linetype is dashed. You will read more about ByLayer at the end of this chapter.

3. The Endpoint Osnap should still be running. How can you tell? Type **os** ↵. The Osnap Settings dialog box comes up and you can easily see which osnaps are checked. If Endpoint is checked, click OK. Otherwise, click in the checkbox next to Endpoint and then click OK.

4. Start the Line command by typing l ↵. Move the cursor to the lower-left corner of the rectangle representing the roof, until the square appears on the corner, then click. A line is started.

5. Be sure Ortho is off by checking to see if the Ortho button on the status bar is ghosted out. If it is, go on to step 6. Otherwise, double-click the Ortho button to turn it off.

6. Move the crosshair to the middle of the bedroom but don't click. Type **@10'<45**↵. Then press ↵ again to end the Line command. A diagonal line is drawn part way across the floor plan (Figure 6.30).

This line can be flipped to the upper-left corner with the Mirror command. To do this successfully, you need to imagine a mirror line that this hip line can flip around, and then decide if there is some point in the drawing which can be snapped to, to create the mirror line. The mirror line you need runs horizontally across the floor plan from the midpoint of the left eaves line of the roof.

1. Type **mi** ↵ to start the Mirror command. When asked to select objects, pick the diagonal hip line and press ↵. For the first point of the mirror line, pick the Midpoint Snap button on the Object Snap toolbar or the Object Snap flyout on the Standard toolbar.

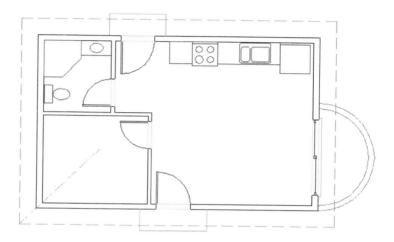

FIGURE 6.30: A diagonal hip line is drawn from the lower-left corner of the eaves.

2. Move the cursor to the left eaves line of the roof. When the triangle appears at the midpoint of this eaves line, click. The mirror line is begun. As you move the cursor to the right, a mirror image of the selected diagonal line appears on the opposite side of the mirror line from the original diagonal line (Figure 6.31a).

3. Double-click the Ortho button on the status bar, then hold the cursor to the right of the first point of the mirror line (Figure 6.31b). The endpoint of the mirrored line is forced to coincide with the upper-left corner of the roof rectangle.

4. Move the cursor to the middle of the living room and pick a point there. The ghosted image disappears and the prompt changes to `Delete old objects? <N>`.

5. Press ↵ to accept the default. The mirrored diagonal line is drawn from the upper-left corner (Figure 6.31c).

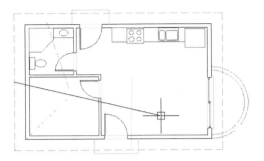

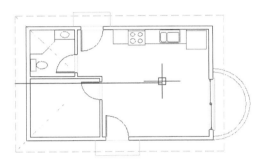

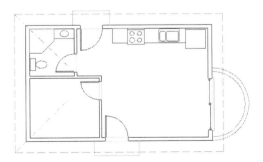

FIGURE 6.31: The mirror line is begun (a), the mirror line with Ortho on (b), and the mirroring completed (c)

6.   Type **f** ↵ to start the Fillet command. The radius should still be set to 0. Click the two diagonal lines somewhere on the half of them that is closer to the other line. The lines are filleted together (Figure 6.32). Now you need to mirror these two diagonal lines to the right side of the roof.

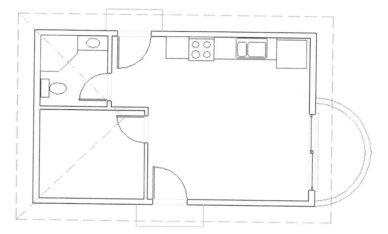

FIGURE 6.32: The two diagonal hip lines after filleting

7.   Type **mi** ↵ to start the Mirror command again. At the prompt to select objects, select the two diagonal lines, then press ↵. Pick the Midpoint Osnap button again and select the upper roof eaves line near its midpoint.

8.   Hold the cursor down into the living room at a place where the target box is not touching any objects, and click in a clear space. Press ↵ when asked whether to delete old objects. The diagonal lines from the left are mirrored to the right (Figure 6.33). The Mirror command automatically ends. To finish the roof, draw in the ridge line.

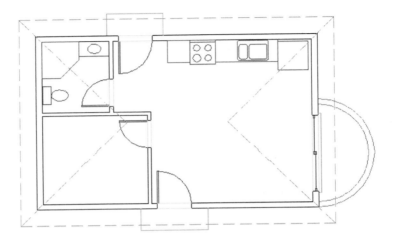

FIGURE 6.33: The two diagonal hip lines are mirrored to the right.

9. Type **l** ↵ to start the Line command. Endpoint Osnap is still running. Pick
    the intersection of the diagonal lines on the right. Move the cursor to the left
    and position it on the lower diagonal line just below the door swing, but
    not touching the door or door swing. When you see the square appear at the
    intersection of the two diagonal lines (Figure 6.34a), click. Press ↵ to end the
    Line command. The roof is complete (Figure 6.34b).

    Save this drawing as Cabin6b.

By drawing the roof lines, you have completed the exercises for this chapter.
The cabin floor plan is almost complete. In the next skill, you will complete the
floor plan by placing windows in the external walls using a new tool called the
block. The rest of this chapter contains a short discussion on color and linetypes,
and how they work with layers and objects.

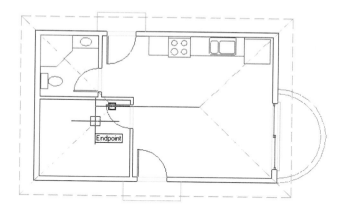

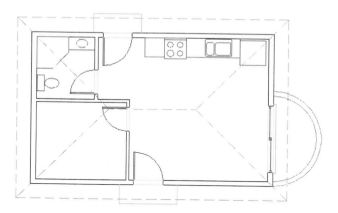

FIGURE 6.34: Positioning the cursor to pick the second point of the ridge line (a) and the completed roof (b)

Color, Linetypes, and Layers

First, look at the colors in your drawing. If the background of your drawing area is white, notice which colors are the easiest to read. For most monitors, the yellow, light gray, and cyan are partially faded out, while the blue, green, red, and magenta read very well. If the drawing area background is black, the blue is sometimes too dark to read easily, but the rest of the colors usually read very well. This is one reason most people prefer the black, or at least dark, background color. The other consideration is the lighting in your work area. Bright work areas usually make it difficult to read monitors easily, and, with a dark background, you will often get sharp contrast between the screen and your surroundings, and distracting reflections on the screen. Eyestrain can result. Darkening your work area will usually mollify these effects.

Assigning a Color or Linetype to an Object

While you have been taught to assign colors and linetypes to layers, in order to control the way objects on those layers appear, colors and linetypes can be individually assigned to objects and made to be current in the drawing.

If an object is assigned a color which is different from the color assigned to the object's layer, that object will be a different color from the rest of the objects on the layer. The same thing is true for linetypes. There may be an occasion where it makes sense to do this, especially for linetypes, but that would be the rare exception, rather than the rule. Changing the color of an object could result in confusion. If you do need to make such a change, you would use the Properties button, select the object and then pick the Color or Linetype button (rather than the Layers button as you have been doing in this chapter), and make the reassignment. The danger in doing this is that, if the color of an object is changed from the color assigned to the whole layer, you won't be able to tell which layer the object belongs to as easily. If the new color matches that of another layer, you may mistake the object for being on that layer.

Making a Color or Linetype Current

If you look at the Object Properties toolbar for a moment, you will see the Color Control drop-down list, the Linetype button, and the Linetype Control drop-down list. These tools allow you to set a color or linetype to be current. When this is done, each object subsequently created will be assigned the current linetype and/or color, regardless of which linetype and color has been assigned to the current layer. If, for example, the Doors layer were set to be the current layer, and the dashed linetype and green color were also assigned to be current, any lines drawn would be dashed and green but still on the Doors layer. This is not a good way to set up the system of layers, linetypes, and colors because of the obvious confusion it would create in your drawing, but beginners often accidentally do this without knowing what they've done.

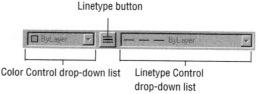

Linetype button

Color Control drop-down list   Linetype Control drop-down list

The best way to keep all this straight is to keep the current linetype and color set to ByLayer, as it is by default. When you do this, colors and linetypes are controlled by the layers and objects take on the color and linetype of the layers they are on. If this configuration is accidentally disturbed and objects are created with the wrong color or linetype, you can correct the situation without too much trouble. First, reset the current color and linetype to ByLayer by using the Color Control and Linetype Control drop-down lists on the Object Properties toolbar. Then use the Properties button to change the linetype or color of the problem objects to ByLayer. They will then take on the color and linetype of the layer to which they have been assigned.

Assigning an Individual Linetype Scale Factor

Although the Ltscale command sets a linetype scale factor for all non-continuous lines in the drawing, you can adjust the dash and space sizes for individual lines by using the Properties button to change the linetype scale of a particular object or group of objects. If you want to change the dash and space size for the ridge line of the roof to make them larger, this could be done in the following way:

1. Click the Properties button on the Object Properties toolbar.

2. Select the ridge line and press ↵.

3. In the top portion of the Modify Line dialog box, click in the textbox next to Linetype Scale.

4. Delete what's there and type **3** ↵, then click OK. Back in your drawing, notice how the dashes and spaces of the ridge line are three times larger than those for the rest of the roof lines.

5. Click the Properties button and use the same procedure to change the individual linetype scale factor for the ridge line back to 1.

This tool allows you to get subtle variations in the size of dashes and spaces for individual, non-continuous lines. But remember that a line which has an individual linetype scale factor is also controlled by the global linetype scale factor. The actual size of the dashes and spaces for a particular line is a result of the two linetype scale factors working together. So the additional flexibility requires you to keep careful track of the variations you are making.

Are You Experienced?

Now you can...

☑ **create new layers and assign them a color and linetype**

☑ **load a new linetype into your current drawing file**

☑ **move existing objects onto a new layer**

☑ **freeze and thaw layers**

☑ **make a layer current and create objects on the current layer**

☑ **reset the linetype scale factor to make non-continuous lines visible**

☑ **use the individual linetype scale factor to adjust the size of one dashed line**

Using Blocks and Wblocking

- ➔ Creating and inserting blocks
- ➔ Using the Wblock command
- ➔ Detecting blocks in a drawing
- ➔ Using point filters and blips

Computer drafting gains a significant portion of its efficiency from features that allow you to group a collection of objects into one object, and to repeatedly use this new object in your current drawing as well as importing it to other drawings. AutoCAD calls the grouped objects a *block*, and calls the process of moving blocks outside your current drawing *wblocking*.

These features allow you to:

- create a block in your current drawing
- repeatedly place copies of the block in precise locations in your drawing
- save a copy of the block on the hard disk as a drawing file
- insert a copy of this new drawing file into a different drawing

In general, objects best suited to becoming part of a block are the components of your building which are repeatedly used in drawing, such as doors, windows and fixtures, or those serving as drawing symbols, like a North arrow or labels for a section cut line (Figure 7.1). In your cabin drawing, you will convert the doors with swings and the kitchen and bath fixtures into blocks. Then you will create a new block to serve as the windows in the drawing.

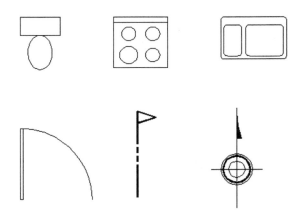

FIGURE 7.1: Examples of blocks often used in drawings

Making a Block for a Door

When making a block, you will create a *block definition* which will consist of:

- the block name
- an insertion point to help place the block in the drawing
- the objects to be grouped into the block

You will specify each of these in the course of using the Block command. When the command is completed, the block definition is stored with the drawing file. The objects included in the block may now be erased, and you can insert the object (as a block) back into the drawing using the Insert command.

Before you create a block, you must consider the layers on which the objects to be blocked reside. When objects on the 0 layer are grouped into a block, they will take on the color and linetype of the layer which is current when the block is inserted. Objects on other layers retain the properties of their original layers, regardless of which color or linetype has been assigned to the current layer. This characteristic distinguishes the 0 layer from all other layers.

As you define a block, you must decide which—if any—of the objects to be included in the block will need to be on the 0 layer before they are blocked. If a block is always going to be on the same layer, the objects making up the block can remain on that layer. On the other hand, if a block may be inserted on several layers, objects to be in the block will need to be moved to the 0 layer before the block definition is created, so as to avoid confusion of colors and linetypes.

As you learn to make blocks for the doors, you will get to see how the layers work in the process of creating block definitions. We'll create a block for the exterior doors first, using the front door, and call it Door3_0 to distinguish it from the smaller, interior door. For the insertion point, you will need to assign a point on or near the door that will facilitate its placement as a block in your drawing. The hinge point will make the best insertion point.

For this skill, the Endpoint Osnap should be running at all times. To be sure it is running, click Tools ➤ Object Snap Settings and be sure there is a check in the checkbox next to Endpoint.

1. If you are continuing on from the last skill, go on to step 2. If you are starting up a new session, start AutoCAD. In the Start Up dialog box, click Open a Drawing. In the Select a File list, highlight Cabin6b and click OK.

2. The Roof layer should be visible on the Layers drop-down list on the Object Properties toolbar. Click the list to open it, then click Doors to make the Doors layer current. The list will close. Click the drop-down list again and this time click the sun icons for the Roof and Header layers to freeze them, then click the Doors layer to close the list. The Doors layer is now current, and the Headers and Roof are no longer visible in the drawing (Figure 7.2).

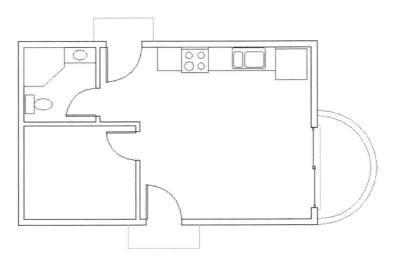

FIGURE 7.2: The floor plan with the Headers and Roof layers frozen

3. Click the Block button on the Draw toolbar. (The Block command can also be started by picking Draw ➢ Block ➢ Make, or by typing **b** ↵.) The Block Definition dialog box comes up (Figure 7.3). Notice the flashing cursor in the text box next to Block name. Type **door3_0**.

4. Click Select Point. The dialog box momentarily disappears and you are returned to your drawing.

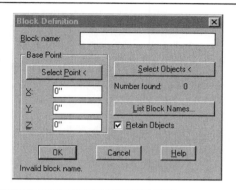

FIGURE 7.3: The block definition dialog box

5. You need to zoom into the front door area. In your drawing, click the Zoom Window button on the Standard toolbar and make a window around the front door area. The area in the window will fill the screen.

6. Move the cursor to the front door area and position the target box on the cursor near the hinge point of the door. When the square appears on the hinge point (Figure 7.4a), click it. This selects the insertion point for the door, and the Block Definition dialog box returns.

7. Click Select Objects. You are returned to the drawing again. The cursor changes to a pickbox, and the Command window displays the Select objects: prompt.

8. Select the door and swing, then press ↵. You are returned to the Block Definition dialog box. Under the Select Objects button, the count of selected objects is displayed next to "Number found:" Click OK, and the dialog box disappears.

9. Erase the door and swing by typing **e** ↵, picking the door and swing, then pressing ↵. The door and swing are erased (Figure 7.4b).

You have now created a block definition, called Door3_0. Block definitions are stored electronically with the drawing file. You need to insert the Door3_0 block (known formally as a *block reference*) into the front door opening to replace the door and swing that were just erased.

Skill 7

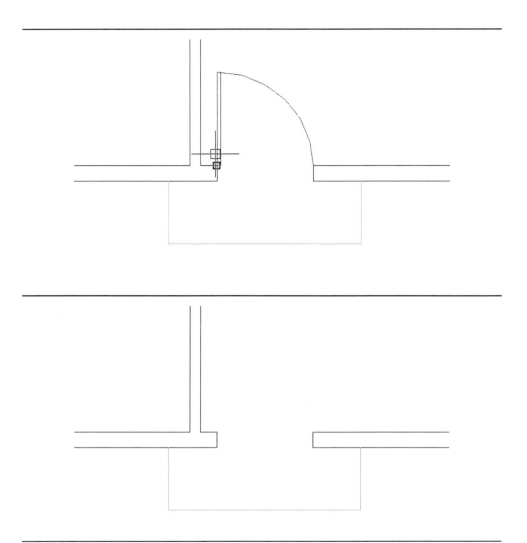

FIGURE 7.4: The front door opening when picking the hinge point to be the insertion point (a) and after creating the Door3_0 block and erasing the door and swing (b)

Inserting the Door Block

You will use the Insert command to place the Door3_0 block back into the drawing.

1. On the Draw toolbar click Insert. (The Insert command can also be started by selecting Insert ➢ Block, or by typing **i** ↵.) The Insert dialog box comes up (Figure 7.5). Notice at the top are two buttons: Block and File. We will use the File button later in the skill. For now we want the Block button.

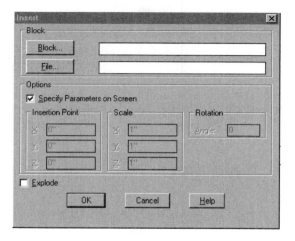

FIGURE 7.5: The Insert dialog box

2. Click the Block button. The Defined Blocks dialog box comes up (Figure 7.6). In the large list area you will see the Door3_0 block definition listed. Select it. Door3_0 will appear in the Selection text box. Click OK.

3. You are returned to the Insert dialog box and Door3_0 is now displayed in the text box next to the Block button. Click OK again. You are returned to your drawing and the Door3_0 block is now attached to the cursor, with the hinge point coinciding with the intersection of the crosshairs (Figure 7.7). The Command window reads Insertion point:.

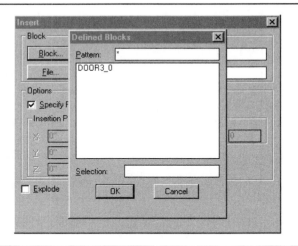

FIGURE 7.6: The Defined Block dialog box

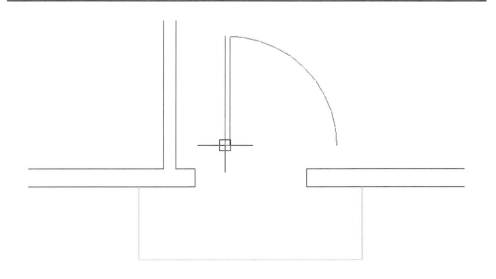

FIGURE 7.7: The Door3_0 block attached to the cursor

4. With Endpoint Osnap running, move the cursor towards the upper end of the left jamb line in the front door opening. When it gets close enough that a colored square appears at the jamb-line upper endpoint, click the mouse. The insertion point has been positioned and the Command window now displays an additional prompt: X Scale factor <1>/Corner / XYZ:.

5. Press ↵ to accept the default of 1 for the X Scale factor. The prompt changes to: Y Scale factor (default = X):.

6. Press ↵ again to accept the default for this option. Be sure Ortho is off. The Door3_0 block comes into view, and you can see that its insertion point has been placed at the upper end of the left jamb line, and that the block rotates as you move the cursor (Figure 7.8a). Another prompt comes up: Rotation angle <0>:. Press ↵ again to accept the default of 0. The Door3_0 block is placed in the drawing (Figure 7.8b).

Each time a block is inserted, you must go through the following procedure:

-   Select the block from a list of defined blocks.
-   Specify the location of the insertion point of the block.
-   Enter an X scale factor or accept the default of 1.
-   Enter a Y scale factor or accept the default of having the Y scale factor conform to the X scale factor.
-   Enter a rotation angle or accept the default rotation of 0.

When blocks are inserted, they can be stretched horizontally (the X scale factor) or vertically (the Y scale factor), or they can be rotated from their original orientation. Because the Door3_0 block was created from the door and swing that occupied the front door opening, inserting this block back into the front door opening required no rotation, and the size was the same, so we followed the defaults. When you insert the same block into the back door opening, you will have to change the Y scale factor, because the door will be flipped.

Skill 7

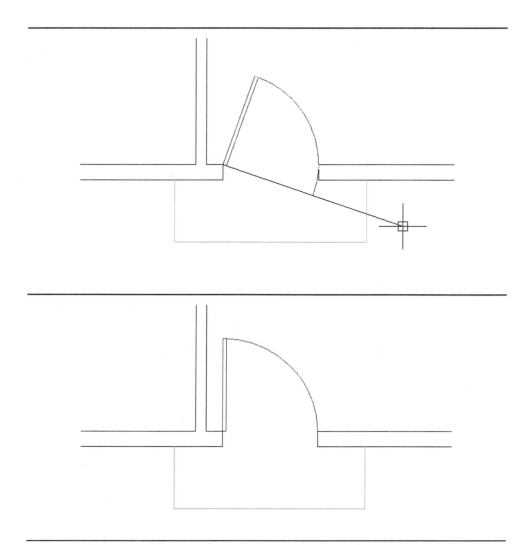

FIGURE 7.8: The rotation option (a) and the final placement (b)

Inserting a Block while Flipping It

The X scale factor controls the horizontal size and orientation. The Y scale factor mimics the X scale factor unless you change it. For the next insertion, you will make such a change.

1. Click the Zoom Previous button of the Standard toolbar to zoom back out to a full view of the floor plan.

2. Click the Zoom Window button and make a window around the back door area (Figure 7.9a), leaving plenty of room inside and outside the opening to see the Door3_0 block as it is being inserted. You will be zoomed into a close view of the back door (Figure 7.9b).

3. Use the Erase command to erase the door and swing from the back door opening.

4. Click Insert ➤ Block. In the block area of the Insert dialog box, Door3_0 should still be in the text box next to the block button.

5. Click OK. You are returned to your drawing and the Door3_0 block is attached to the cursor.

6. Move the cursor to the lower end of the left jamb line, and, when the colored square appears at that endpoint (Figure 7.10a), click. The insertion point has been placed and the prompt reads X scale factor <1> / Corner / XYZ:.

7. Press ↵ to accept the default X scale factor of 1. The prompt changes to read Y scale factor (default=X):. In order to flip the door down to the inside of the cabin, you need to give the Y scale factor a value of -1.

8. Type **-1** ↵. Then press ↵ again to accept the default rotation angle of 0. The Insert command ends and the Door3_0 block is placed in the back door opening (7.10b).

 NOTE   Figure 7.10b will look exactly like Figure 7.9b.

9. Click the Zoom Previous button on the Object Properties toolbar to zoom back out to a full view of the floor plan.

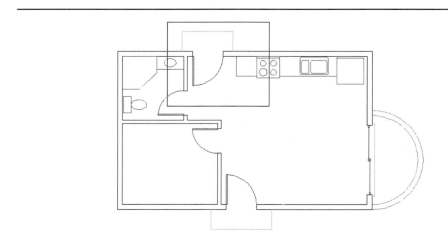

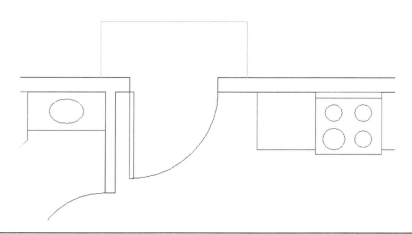

F I G U R E   7 . 9 : Using a zoom window to make a window around the back door area (a) and the result of the zoom (b)

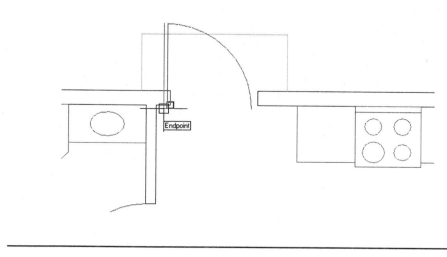

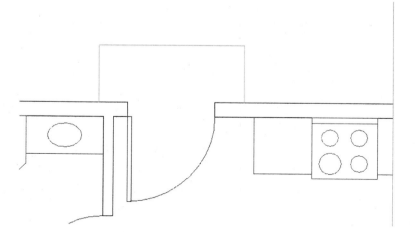

F I G U R E 7 . 1 0 : Placing the DOOR 3_0 insertion point (a) and the block after insertion (b)

NOTE Giving a value of -1 to the X or Y scale factor when inserting a block has the effect of flipping the block, much like the Mirror command did in Skill 4 when you first drew the doors. Because you can flip or rotate the Door3_0 block as it is inserted, it can be used to place a door and swing in any 3'-0" opening, regardless of its orientation.

Doors are traditionally sorted into four categories, which are determined by which side the hinges and doorknob are on and by which way the door swings open. To be able to use one door block for all openings of the same size, you need to know:

- how the door and swing in the block is oriented

- where the hinge point is to be in the next opening

- how the block has to be flipped and/or rotated during the insertion process to properly fit in the next doorway opening

Blocking and Inserting the Interior Doors

Because the interior doors are smaller, you will need to make a new block for them.

1. Click the Zoom Window button on the Standard toolbar, and pick two points to define a window which encloses both the bathroom and bedroom doors (Figure 7.11a). The view will change to a close up view of the area enclosed in your window (Figure 7.11b).

2. Follow the steps above to make a block out of the bathroom door and swing. Here is a summary of the steps:

   - Start the Block command (type **b** ↵).

   - In the dialog box, type **door2_6** ↵ to name the block.

   - Click Select Point and pick the hinge point of the door.

   - Click the Select Objects button and pick the door and swing, then press ↵.

   - Click OK.

   - Erase the bathroom and bedroom doors and swings (type **e** ↵, pick the doors and swings, then press ↵).

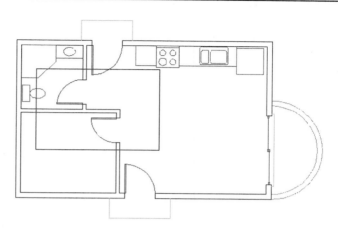

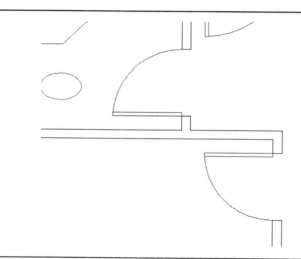

FIGURE 7.11: Creating a zoom window (a) and the result (b)

3. Now insert the new block back into the bath doorway opening. Here are the steps:

   - Type **i** ↵ to start the Insert command.
   - Click the Block button.
   - Click Door2_6.
   - Click OK.
   - Click OK again.
   - Pick the left end of the lower jamb line as the insertion point.
   - Press ↵ three times to accept all defaults for scale factor and rotation.

   The Door2_6 block is inserted in the doorway opening.

4. Restart the Insert command and insert the Door2_6 block into the bedroom doorway opening. Here's a summary of the steps:

   - Press ↵ to restart the Insert command.
   - Click OK.
   - Pick the left end of the upper jamb line.
   - Press ↵ to accept the default of 1 for the X scale factor.
   - Type **-1** ↵ to give the Y scale factor a value of -1.
   - Press ↵ to accept the default rotation of 0.
   - Zoom Previous to view the full floor plan (Figure 7.12).

This view looks the same as the view you started with at the beginning of this skill. Blocks look the same as other objects and can't be detected by viewing only. The next section will go into how you can detect a block.

Finding Blocks in a Drawing

There are three ways of detecting blocks in a drawing: with grips, with the List command, or with the Properties button. Each method is detailed below.

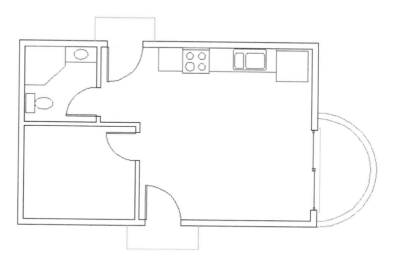

FIGURE 7.12: The floor plan with all swinging doors converted into blocks

Using Grips to Detect a Block

1. At the Command: prompt, click one of the door swings. The door and swing ghost and a colored square appears at the hinge point. The square is a *grip*. Grips appear on objects that are selected when no command has been started. We'll look at grips in more detail in Skill 11, *Dimensioning the Floor Plan*.

2. Click one of the arcs that represent the balcony wall. Three grips appear on the arc: one at each end and one at the midpoint.

3. Press Esc twice to clear the grips.

> **TIP** When an object that is not a block is selected in the above manner, grips appear in several places. But if you select a block, only one grip appears and it's always located at the block's insertion point. Selecting an object with no command started is a quick way to see if it is a block.

You may need to know more about a block than just whether or not it is one. If that is the case, you will need to use the List command.

Using the List Command to Detect a Block

1. Move the cursor to the Distance button on the Standard toolbar and hold down the mouse button. The Inquiry flyout appears.

2. Move the cursor down the flyout to the List button, then release the mouse button. The List command is started and you are prompted to select objects.

3. Click the bedroom door block, then press ↵. The AutoCAD Text Window temporarily replaces the drawing (Figure 7.13). In the text window you can see the words BLOCK REFERENCE Layer: DOORS, followed by eight lines of text. These nine lines describe the block you selected.

> **NOTE** Each time you use the List command and select an object, the text screen will display information which is tailored to the kind of object selected.

Some of the information stored here about the selected object is:

- what the object is (*Block Reference*)
- the layer the object is on (*Doors layer*)
- the name of the block (*DOOR2_6*)
- the coordinates of the insertion point in the drawing
- the X and Y scale factors
- the rotation angle

```
AutoCAD Text Window                                              _|□|×|
Edit
Command: '_zoom
All/Center/Dynamic/Extents/Previous/Scale(X/XP)/Window/<Realtime>: _w
First corner: Other corner:
Command: '_zoom

All/Center/Dynamic/Extents/Previous/Scale(X/XP)/Window/<Realtime>: _p
Command:
Command:
Command: _list
Select objects: 1 found

Select objects:
                    BLOCK REFERENCE  Layer: DOORS
                          Space: Model space
                  Handle = 17E
                  DOOR2_6
           at point, X=12'-5 1/16"  Y=11'-2 1/8"  Z=    0'-0"
              X scale factor    1.0000
              Y scale factor   -1.0000
          rotation angle        0
              Z scale factor    1.0000


Command:
```

FIGURE 7.13: The AutoCAD text window

4. Press F2. The drawing area returns.

TIP   The F2 key toggles the screen back and forth between the drawing area and the
text screen.

5. Move the cursor back up to the Standard toolbar. The List button has
    replaced the Distance button on the flyout. Click the List button.

6. At the Select objects: prompt, click one of the arcs that represent the
    balcony, then click one of the wall lines, then press ↵.

7. The text screen comes up again, and you see information about the arc you
    selected, followed by information about the selected wall line.

8. Press F2, then slowly press it a few more times. As you switch back and forth between the text screen and the drawing, notice that the last three lines on the text screen are the three lines of text in the Command window of the drawing (Figure 7.14). The Command window is displaying a strip of text from the text screen, usually the last three lines.

9. Press F2 to display the drawing.

Using the Properties Button to Detect a Block

The Properties button on the Object Properties toolbar was used extensively in the last skill to move objects onto layers. It can also be a tool for investigating objects in your drawing. When the Properties command is started and only one object is selected, AutoCAD will display a dialog box, the bottom half of which is tailored to the kind of object selected.

1. Click the Properties button on the Object Properties toolbar.

2. Click one of the door blocks, then press ↵. The dialog box that comes up is titled after the type of object selected, in this case, a block, so it's called "Modify Block Insertion" (Figure 7.15).

 TIP   *Block insertion* means the same thing as block reference, and they are both casually called blocks.

3. In the dialog box, just below the Properties section, is information specific to the block selected, including the coordinates of the insertion point, the X and Y scale factors, and the rotation angle, all of which may be modified.

4. Click Cancel without making any changes.

If you are ever working on a drawing that you did not draw, these tools for finding out about objects will be invaluable. The next exercise on working with blocks will involve the placement of windows in the walls of the cabin.

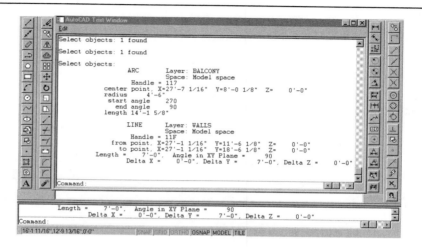

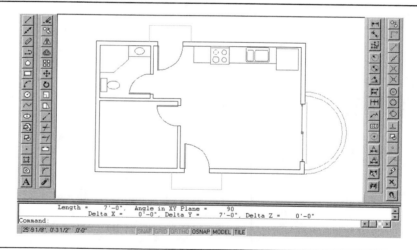

FIGURE 7.14: Toggling between the text window (a) and the drawing with its Command window (b)

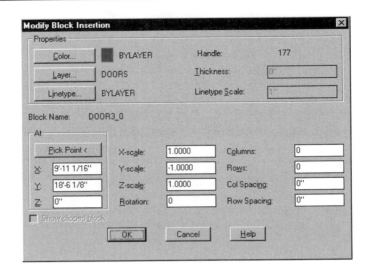

FIGURE 7.15: The Modify Block Insertion dialog box

Creating a Window Block

The windows in the cabin floor plan can all be created from one block, even though there are four different sizes (Figure 7.16). You'll create a window block, then we'll go from room to room to insert the block into the walls.

1. Click the Layers list on the Object Properties toolbar to open the drop-down list and click the 0 layer in the list to make it current.

2. Zoom into a section of wall where there are no jamb lines or intersections with other walls, by clicking the Zoom Window button on the Standard toolbar and picking two points to be opposite corners of the zoom window (Figure 7.17). Because the widths of the windows in the cabin are multiples of 12", a block made from a 12" wide window can be inserted for each window, and an X scale factor can be applied to the block to make it the right width. The first step is to draw a 12" wide window inside the wall lines.

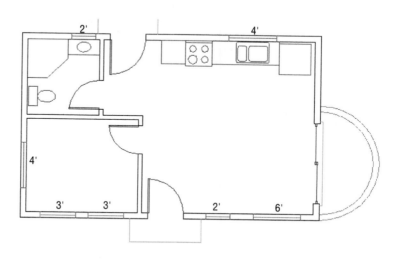

FIGURE 7.16: The cabin windows in the floor plan

3. Start the Line command by typing l ↵, then pick the Nearest Osnap button from the Object Snap toolbar or the Osnap flyout on the Standard toolbar. The Nearest Osnap will allow you to start a line on one of the wall lines. It finds the point on the wall line nearest to the point you pick.

4. Move the cursor to the upper wall line. When the target box on the cross-hairs is on the wall line, a colored hourglass-type symbol appears. Move a little to the left of the center of the screen and, with the hourglass symbol still displayed, click. A line is begun.

5. Click the Perpendicular Osnap on the Object Snap toolbar, then move the cursor so the target box is on the lower wall line. A colored perpendicular icon will appear directly below the point you previously picked. When it is displayed, click. The line is drawn between the wall lines. Press ↵ to end the Line command.

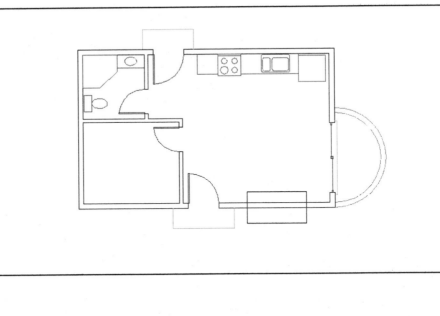

6. Start the Offset command by typing **o** ↵. Type **12** ↵ to set the offset distance to 12". Pick the line you just drew, then pick a point to the right of that line. The line is offset 12" to the right. Press ↵ to end the Offset command.

7. Start the Line command again by typing **l** ↵, then pick the Midpoint Osnap button from the Object Snap toolbar. Click the line you first drew, and a line will begin at its midpoint. Select the Midpoint Osnap button again and click the line that was just offset. Press ↵ to end the Line command. Your drawing should look like Figure 7.18.

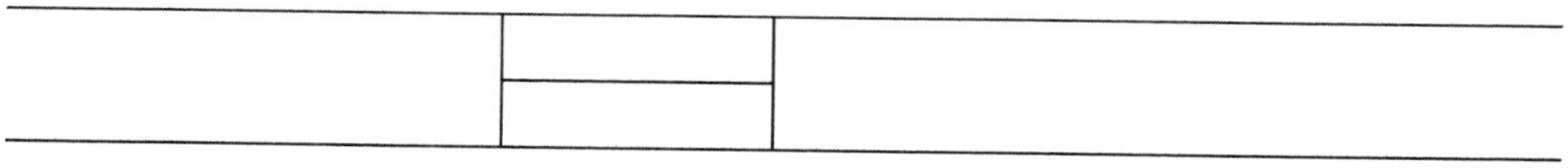

FIGURE 7.18: Completed lines for the window block

The three lines you've drawn will make up a window block. They represent the two jamb lines and the glass (usually called *glazing*). When inserted, by varying the X scale factor from 2 to 6, you will be able to create windows 2', 3', 4', and 6' wide.

Before you create the block, you need to decide the best place for the insertion point. For the doors, you chose the hinge point because you always know where it will be in the drawing. Locating a similar strategic point for the window is a little more difficult, but certainly possible. We know the insertion point can't be on the horizontal line representing the glazing, because it will always rest in the middle of the wall, and there is no guideline in the drawing for the middle of the wall. Windows are usually dimensioned to the midpoint of the glazing line rather than to either jamb line, so we don't want the insertion point to be at the endpoint of a jamb line. The insertion point will need to be positioned on a wall line but also lined up with the midpoint of the glazing line.

To locate this point, draw a guideline from the midpoint of the glazing line straight to one of the wall lines.

1. Press ↵ to restart the Line command. Pick the Midpoint Osnap button and click the glazing line.

2. Pick the Perpendicular Osnap button and click the bottom wall line. A guideline is drawn from the midpoint of the glazing line perpendicular to the lower wall line (Figure 7.19). The lower endpoint of this line is the location of the window block insertion point. Press ↵ to end the Line command. Now you are ready to define the window block.

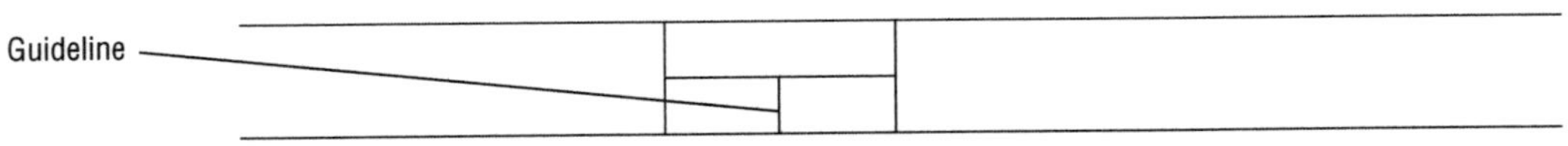

Guideline

FIGURE 7.19: The guideline is completed.

3. Type **b** ↵ to start the Block command. In the dialog box, type **win-1** for the block name, then click the Select Point button.

4. Back in the drawing, with Endpoint Osnap running, move the cursor to the lower end of the guideline you just drew and, when the colored square appears at that location, click.

5. In the dialog box, click the Select Objects button.

6. Back in the drawing again, select the two jamb lines and the glazing line, but do not select the guideline whose endpoint locates the insertion point.

7. Press ↵. In the dialog box, click OK. The Win-1 block has been defined.

8. Erase the window and guideline with the Erase command.

9. Zoom Previous to zoom out to a view of the whole floor plan.

This completes the definition of the block, which will represent the windows. The next task is to insert the Win-1 block where the windows will be located.

Inserting the Window Block

Several factors come into play when deciding where to locate windows in a floor plan:

- the structure of the building

- appearance of windows from outside the building

- appearance of windows from inside the room

- location of fixtures that may block or interfere with placement

- sun angle and climate considerations

For this exercise, we will work on the windows for each room, starting with the bedroom.

Rotating a Block during Insertion

The bedroom has windows on two walls: two 3-foot windows centered in the front wall 12 inches apart, and one 4-foot window centered in the left wall (Figure 7.20). You'll make the 4-foot window first.

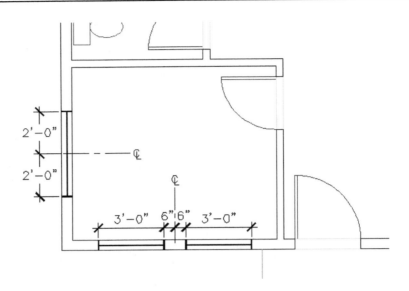

FIGURE 7.20: The bedroom windows

1. Use a zoom window to zoom into a view of the bedroom similar to that of Figure 7.20.

2. Create a new layer by clicking the Layer button and then clicking the New button in the Layer & Linetype Properties dialog box. Layer1 will appear and be highlighted. Type **windows** ↵ to rename Layer1.

3. Click the color square in the Windows row. When the Select Color dialog box comes up, White will be highlighted in the Color text box near the bottom. Type **30** ↵ to change the color to a bright orange. (If you don't have 256 colors available, choose any color that's not too light.) The Select Color dialog box will close.

4. With Windows still highlighted in the Layers & Linetype Properties dialog box, click the Current button to make the Windows layer current, then click OK. You return to your drawing, and Windows is the current layer.

5. Type **i** ↵ to start the Insert command. Click the Block button in the Insert dialog box. In the list of blocks, click Win-1 and, when it shows up in the Selection text box, click OK. Back in the Insert dialog box, Win-1 now is displayed in the text box next to the Block button. Click OK.

6. In your drawing, the 12-inch window block is attached to the cursor at the insertion point (Figure 7.21). Note that it is still in the same horizontal orientation it was when you defined the block. You will need to rotate it to fit into the left wall.

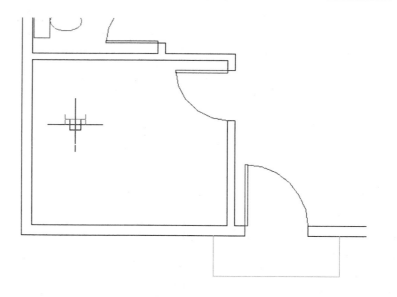

FIGURE 7.21: The Win-1 block attached to the cursor

7. Pick Midpoint Osnap from the Object Snap toolbar. Move the cursor to the left wall and put the target box on the inside wall line. When a colored triangle appears at the midpoint of the wall line, click.

8. You will be prompted for an X scale factor. This is a 4-foot window, so type **4** ↵. For the Y scale factor, type **1** ↵.

 NOTE The Y scale factor will be 1 for all the Win-1 blocks because all walls that have windows are 6 inches wide—the same width as we made the Win-1 block.

9. Then you are prompted for the rotation angle. Turn Ortho off if it's on. The window block is now 4 feet wide and rotates with movement of the

cursor. Move the cursor so it's directly to the right of the insertion point (Figure 7.22a). This will show you how the window will be positioned if the rotation stays at the 0° default. Obviously, you don't want this.

10. Move the cursor so it is directly above the insertion point. This shows what position a 90° rotation will result in (Figure 7.22b). The window fits nicely into the wall here.

11. Type **90** ↵. The Win-1 block is placed in the left wall and the Insert command ends (Figure 7.22c).

Using Guidelines when Inserting a Block

The pair of windows in the front wall of the bedroom are 3 feet wide and 12 inches apart, centered horizontally in the bedroom wall. You can use a guideline to locate the insertion points for these two windows.

1. Type **l** ↵ to start the Line command, and pick Midpoint Osnap from the Object Snap toolbar. Locate the cursor with its target box on the inside horizontal exterior wall line. When the colored triangle appears at the midpoint of this line, click. A line is started.

2. Double-click the Ortho button on the status bar to turn Ortho on, then pick a point a few feet below the first point of the line. Press ↵ to end the Line command. This establishes a guideline at the center of the wall. The insertion points for the windows will be at their centers. The distance between the center of the wall and the insertion point will be half the width of the window plus half the distance between the windows, or 2 feet.

3. Offset the line that you just drew 2 feet to the right and left (Figure 7.23). Now you have established the locations for the insertion points of the Win-1 blocks, and you are ready to insert them.

4. Select the Insert button on the Draw toolbar to start the Insert command. In the Insert dialog box, the Win-1 block will still be displayed in the text box next to the Block button, because it was the last block inserted. Click OK.

Back in the drawing, the Win-1 block is again attached to the cursor. To locate the insertion point, you can choose the upper endpoint of one of the outer guidelines, or the intersection of this guideline with the exterior outside wall line. Which one would be better? The second choice requires no rotation of the block, so it's easier and faster to use that intersection.

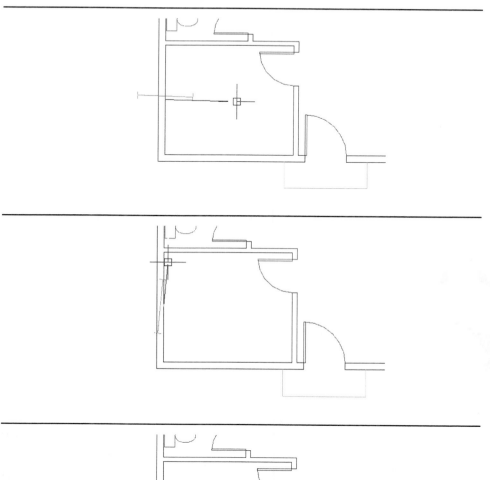

FIGURE 7.22: Rotating the Win-1 block 0 degrees (a), 90 degrees (b), and the final position (c)

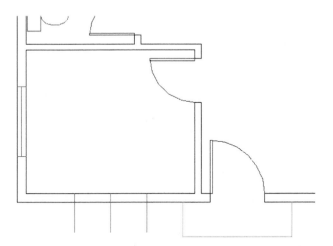

FIGURE 7.23: Guidelines for the pair of window blocks

5. Pick the Intersection Osnap button from the Object Snap toolbar and position the target box of the cursor on the outside wall line without touching any other lines (Figure 7.24a). A colored x appears with three dots to its right. Click. Now hold the target box on the lower portion of the left-most offset guideline, again without touching any other lines. The x will appear, this time at the intersection of this guideline with the outside wall line, and without the three dots (Figure 7.24b). Click again. The insertion point has been set at the intersection of the guideline and the outside wall line.

6. Type **3** ↵ for the X scale factor, then type **1** ↵ for the Y scale factor. At the rotation angle prompt, press ↵ to accept the default of 0 degrees. The 3-foot window on the left is inserted in the front wall.

7. Repeat this procedure for the other 3-foot window.

8. Erase the three guidelines.

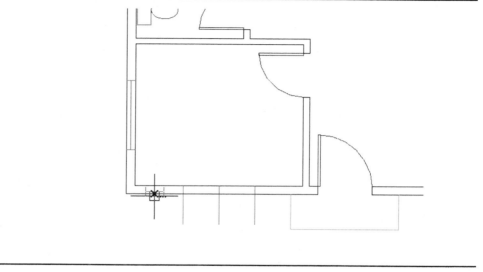

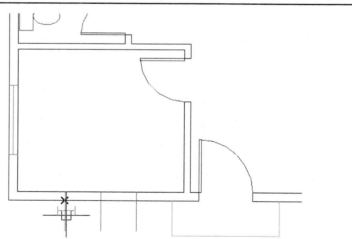

FIGURE 7.24: Selecting the first line (a) and the second (b)

Because you chose the lower of the two wall lines on which to locate the insertion point, the block needed no rotation. When finished, the bedroom will look like Figure 7.25.

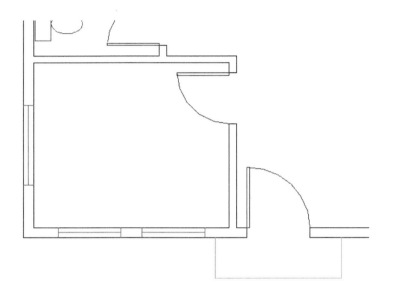

FIGURE 7.25: The bedroom with all windows inserted

Using Point Filters to Insert a Block

The next room to work on is the bathroom.

1. Click the Pan button on the Standard toolbar. The cursor changes to a hand.

2. Position the hand on the wall between the bedroom and bathroom, then hold down the left mouse button and drag the drawing down. When the

bathroom is in the middle of the drawing area, release the mouse button. Press Esc to cancel the Pan command. You want one 2-foot window in the bathroom, centered over the sink. This time you'll insert the block without the use of guidelines.

3. Start the Insert command (type **i** ↵) and then type **.x** ↵ to start point filters. *Point filters* allow you to locate a point by picking two points, one the *x* coordinate you want, and the other the *y* coordinate you want. If this sounds confusing, it will become clearer once you use the feature.

4. Select the Midpoint Osnap and position the target box on the line representing the front edge of the sink counter. A colored triangle will appear at the midpoint of that line (Figure 7.26a). When it does, click—you have selected the x coordinate. Now the prompt in the Command window reads (need YZ):. This means that AutoCAD wants you to specify the *y* coordinate (we'll ignore the Z coordinate). You can do this in two ways: type in a relative coordinate based on the previously specified *x* coordinate, or pick a point in the drawing that has the value for the *y* coordinate you need. We'll use the second option.

5. The target box is still attached to the crosshair cursor because the Endpoint Osnap is running. Move the cursor to the upper-left corner of the counter top. This corner has the *y* coordinate you want, because it is on the inside wall line. When the colored square appears on the corner (Figure 7.26b), click. The insertion point has been placed on the inside wall line, centered over the sink.

NOTE   No mark is left at this point. You have to wait until the insertion process is over to see if everything has been done correctly. When I walk you through the next insertion, you'll learn how to change a setting so AutoCAD will leave a mark.

Skill 7

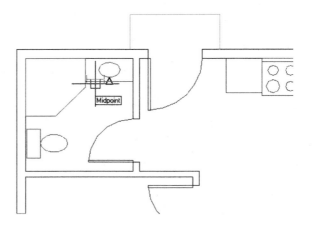

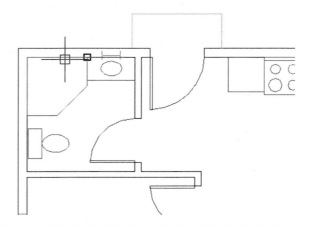

FIGURE 7.26: Using point filters to select a point to get the *x* coordinate (a) and the *y* coordinate (b)

6. At the X scale factor prompt, Type **2** ↵, then, at the Y scale factor prompt, type **1** ↵. Press ↵ again to accept the default rotation angle of 0. The 2-foot window is inserted into the wall behind the sink (Figure 7.27). Press Esc to cancel Pan Realtime.

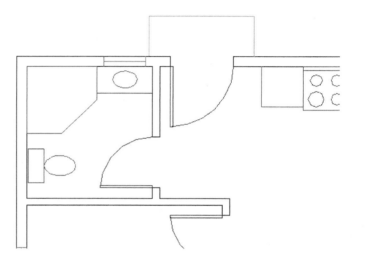

FIGURE 7.27: The 2-foot window after insertion

Using Blips to Help in Inserting Blocks

You're over half way done with the windows—just three remain to be inserted: one in the kitchen and two in the living room.

1. Click the Pan button on the Standard toolbar, then position the hand cursor on the back door swing. Hold down the left mouse button and drag the drawing over to the left until the kitchen is in the middle of the drawing area. Release the mouse button.

2. Click Tools ➤ Drawing Aids. The Drawing Aids dialog box comes up. On the left, in the Modes area, click in the checkbox next to Blips, then click OK. The Blips mode has been activated.

3. You need to insert a 4-foot window in the back wall, centered behind the sink (See Figure 7.16). Start the Insert command and click OK when the Insert dialog box comes up. The Win-1 block appears on the cursor.

4. At the Insertion point: prompt, type .x ↵ to activate the point filters. You need to pick the midpoint of the back or front edge of the sink. Since the front edge is more accessible, select that one.

5. Select the Midpoint Osnap and put the target box on the front edge of the sink. When the colored triangle appears on the front edge, click. A small + is placed at the midpoint of the front edge of the sink (Figure 7.28a). This is called a *blip*.

6. Position the target box on the inside wall line of the back wall where it's not touching any other lines. Because Endpoint Osnap is running, a colored square should show up at one of the endpoints of this wall line. When it does, click. The + is placed at the endpoint of the wall line and at a position on the wall line directly behind the midpoint of the sink's back edge (Figure 7.28b). This assures you that the point filters worked successfully to set the insertion point exactly where you need it.

7. Type 4 ↵ for the X scale factor, then type 1 ↵ for the Y scale factor. For the rotation angle, press ↵ again to accept the default angle of 0. The window is placed in the back wall, centered behind the sink (Figure 7.29).

When the Blips mode is on, a + is placed wherever you pick in the drawing area, whether you are drawing or selecting objects. They are temporary markers and are not saved with the drawing file, nor do they show up in prints. As they accumulate, you can delete them by typing **r** ↵ at the Command: prompt, or by picking View ➤ Redraw. Using blips is up to you—some people find them irritating and would rather not see them. Others find them useful because they are a record of what you've done, as you've seen when placing an insertion point. Leave them visible for the rest of the skill and see how you feel about them.

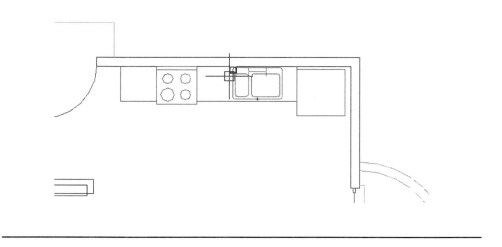

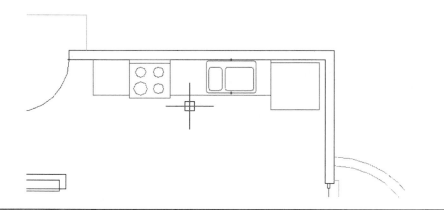

FIGURE 7.28: A blip marks the midpoint of the front edge of the sink (a) and the endpoint and resulting insertion point location (b)

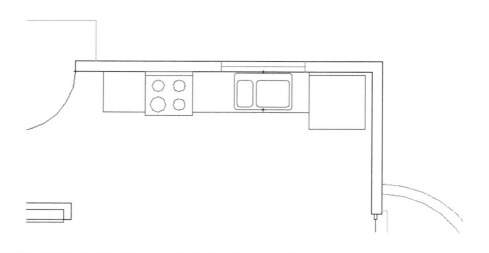

FIGURE 7.29: The inserted window behind the sink

Finishing the Windows

The last two windows to insert are both in the front wall of the living room. You will use skills you've already worked with to place them.

1. Use the Pan command to move the drawing down to the front wall of the living room. One window is 6 feet wide. Its right jamb is 12 inches to the left of the inside corner of the wall. The other one is a circular window, 2 feet in diameter, positioned halfway between the 6-foot window jamb and the front door jamb (Figure 7.30).

2. Start the Insert command and click OK in the Insert dialog box to select the Win-1 block.

3. Select the From Osnap button, then, with Endpoint Osnap running, pick the lower-right inside corner of the cabin. The insertion point will be positioned to the left of this corner a distance of 12 inches plus half the width of the 6-foot window, or 4 feet from the corner.

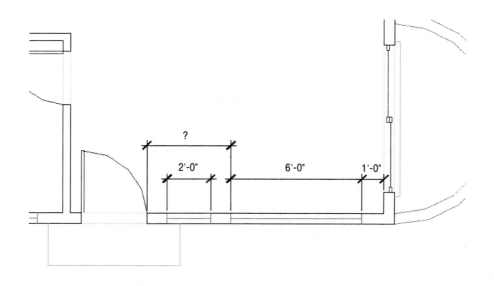

FIGURE 7.30: The windows in the front wall of the living room

4. Type **@4'<180** ↵. This sets the insertion point 4 feet to the left of the corner, on the inside wall line.

5. For the scale factors, type **6** ↵, then type **1** ↵.

6. For the rotation angle, turn Ortho off if it's not already off. Hold the cursor directly to the right of the insertion point to see the position of the window at 0 rotation, then hold the cursor directly above the insertion point to see how a 90° rotation would look. Finally, hold the cursor directly to the left for a view of the effect of a 180° rotation. The 180° view is the one you want.

7. Type **180** ↵. The 6-foot window is placed in the front wall.

Finally, you need to locate the 2-foot circular window halfway between the left jamb of the 6-foot window and the right jamb of the front door opening. Use the Distance command to find out the distance between the two jambs. Then offset one of the jambs half that distance to establish the location of the insertion point on the wall lines. Of the two jamb lines, you must offset the door jamb because the window jamb is part of the window block and can't be offset.

1. Type **di** ↵ to start the Distance command. With Endpoint Osnap running, pick the upper end of the front door jamb, then the upper end of the left window jamb. In the Command window, the distance is displayed as 3'-10". You need to offset the door jamb half that distance to locate the insertion point for the 2-foot window.

2. Start the Offset command, then type **1'-11** ↵ to set the offset distance.

3. Pick the door jamb, type **non** ↵, and then pick a point to the right of the door jamb. Press ↵ to end the Offset command.

NOTE Typing **non** ↵ cancels any running osnaps for one pick.

4. Start the Insert command. Click OK to accept the Win-1 block. Pick the bottom endpoint of the offset jamb line to establish the insertion point.

5. Type **2** ↵ for the X scale factor, then type **1** ↵ for the Y scale factor.

6. For the rotation angle, press ↵ to accept the default of 0. The last window is inserted in the front wall and the Insert command ends (Figure 7.31). Erase the offset jamb line.

NOTE Notice how the blips have been appearing on and near the wall as you've been working.

7. Type **r** ↵ to use the Redraw command to refresh the screen. The blips disappear.

8. Type **z** ↵ **e** ↵ to zoom out to the Extents view of the drawing. This changes the view to include all visible lines and fills the drawing area (Figure 7.32a).

NOTE Zooming to *Extents* is one of the zoom options, and is the bottom button on the Zoom flyout on the Standard toolbar.

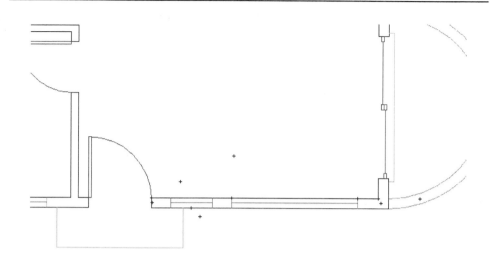

FIGURE 7.31: The two windows inserted in the front wall of the living room

9. Type **z** ↵ **.85x** ↵ to zoom out a little from the Extents view, so all objects are set in slightly from the edge of the drawing area (Figure 7.32b).

10. Save this drawing as Cabin7a.

You have inserted seven windows into the floor plan, each of them generated from the Win-1 block. You created the Win-1 block on the 0 layer, and then made the Windows layer current, so each window block reference took on the characteristics of the Windows layer when it was inserted.

Blocks can be ungrouped by using the *Explode command*. Exploding a block has the effect of reducing the block to the objects that made up the block. For the Win-1 block, exploding it would reduce it to three lines, all on the 0 layer. If you exploded one of the door blocks, it would be reduced to a rectangle and an arc, with both objects on the Doors layer, because these components of the door block were on the Doors layer when the block was defined.

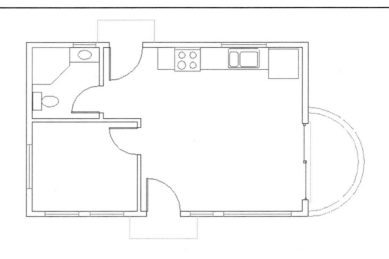

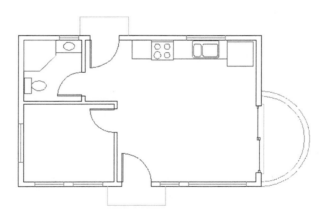

FIGURE 7.32: Zooming to extents (a) and then to .85x (b)

Revising a Block

If you need to revise a block that has already been inserted several times, you will need to use the Explode command to unblock one of the block references. Then you can make changes to the objects that formerly made up the block reference. When finished with the changes, use the Block command to re-block the objects, using the same name as before. This redefines the block.

Let's say that the client who's building the cabin finds out that double glazing is required in all windows. You want the windows to show two lines for the glass. You cannot make such a change in each window block because blocks can't be modified in this way, and you don't want to have to change seven windows separately. If you revise the Win-1 block, the changes you make in one block will be made in all seven windows.

 NOTE   Blocks can be moved, rotated, copied, erased, scaled, and exploded, but they can't be trimmed, extended, offset, or filleted, and you can't erase or move part of a block. All objects in a block are grouped together and behave as if they were one object.

1. Start the Insert command and click OK to accept the Win-1 block to be inserted.

2. Pick a point in the middle of the living room. This establishes the insertion point location.

3. Press ↵ three times to accept the defaults for X and Y scale factors and rotation. The Win-1 block is inserted in the living room (Figure 7.33). You need to place a mark on the insertion point so you'll know where it is after the block is exploded.

4. Zoom into a closer view of the window. Start the Line command. On the Object Snap toolbar, pick Insert Osnap. Put the target box anywhere on the window in the living room and click. A line is started from the insertion point of the block.

5. Pick a second point about a foot or two below the insertion point. Press ↵ to end the Line command. The upper endpoint of this line marks the location of the insertion point (Figure 7.34).

Skill 7

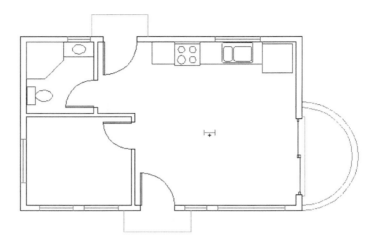

FIGURE 7.33: The Win-1 block inserted into the living room

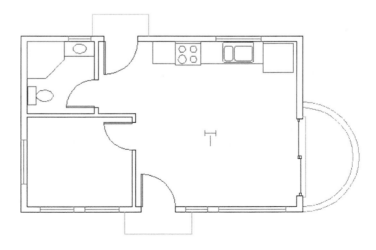

FIGURE 7.34: The guideline drawn to mark the Win-1 block insertion point

6. Click the Explode button on the Modify toolbar. Click anywhere on the window block in the living room, then press ↵. The Win-1 block is exploded. The lines that made up the Win-1 block change to black (or white), because they were originally drawn on the 0 layer.

NOTE   When a block is exploded, the objects that made up the block revert to the layer they were on before the block was defined. If objects were on the 0 layer, they may change color after the block is exploded.

7. Use the zoom window to zoom into the middle of the living room (Figure 7.35a).

NOTE   Anytime you zoom or pan, the Redraw command is executed automatically and all blips are deleted.

8. Use the Offset command to offset the horizontal line 0.5" up and down, then erase the original horizontal line (Figure 7.35b). The window block now has double glazing.

9. Click the Make Object's Layer Current button on the left end of the Object Properties Toolbar, then click any line in the revised window. This makes the 0 layer current.

10. Click the Block button on the Draw toolbar to start the Block command.

11. In the Block Definition dialog box, type **win-1**, then click the Select Point button. In the drawing, pick the upper endpoint of the guideline you drew before you exploded the block.

12. Click the Select Objects button. Pick the four lines that make up the revised block (do not pick the guideline). Press ↵ when finished. Then click OK. A message appears to warn you that a block called Win-1 already exists in this drawing and to ask you if you want to redefine the original block. Click Redefine to approve the redefinition.

13. Back in the drawing, erase the guideline and the window you have been altering. Then Zoom Previous to see the whole floor plan. All of the window blocks have been updated and now have two lines for the glazing.

Skill 7

TIP In the Block Definition dialog box, if you click in the Retain Object checkbox to remove the checkmark, objects selected to be part of a block definition will be erased. They can be recovered by typing **oops** ↵.

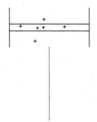

FIGURE 7.35: Zooming in to the window in the middle of the living room (a) and the result of the modifications to the Win-1 block (b)

14. Zoom into a closer look at part of the floor plan (Figure 7.36).

15. This is a good time to turn off the blips if you find them more a nuisance than an aid. To turn them off, pick Tools ➤ Drawing Aids, then click in the checkbox next to Blips to make the checkmark disappear. Click OK.

16. Zoom Previous. Save this drawing as Cabin7b.

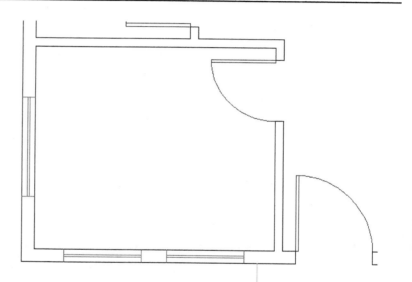

FIGURE 7.36: Zooming in to see the revised window blocks with double glazing

Wblocking

Blocks can be copied out of one drawing and inserted into another one. This feature allows blocks generated during the course of one job to be used in future jobs. Usually a folder is set up on the hard drive to contain these blocks. This folder is often called a *Symbols Library* and may have sub-folders for kitchen fixtures, bathroom fixtures, doors, etc. You'll create a Symbols

Skill 7

folder below. Sets of standard, pre-drawn blocks are often purchased from software vendors and loaded into your Symbols Library.

When a block is copied from a drawing to a Symbols Library, the Wblock command is used and two things happen to the copy of the block as it leaves the drawing: It is unblocked, and it is made into a .dwg file. So blocks stored in the Symbols Library are actually little drawing files. When they are inserted into another drawing, they get reblocked in the insertion process.

To see how this works, you will wblock the Win-1 block out of your cabin drawing. Then you will insert it into another drawing.

1. Minimize AutoCAD and open Windows Explorer. Find the training folder where your cabin drawings are stored and highlight the folder. Create a sub-folder in this directory called "Symbols." Close Windows Explorer and restore AutoCAD.

2. Type **wblock** ↵ to start the Wblock command. The Create Drawing File dialog box comes up. Find the Symbols folder that you just created. Open this folder. You will store the win-1.dwg file here.

3. Click in the Filename text box, then type **win-1** ↵ to set the filename. You are returned to your drawing, and the prompt reads Block name:. AutoCAD is asking you to identify the block you want to make a drawing file from. Because you are naming the drawing file the same name as the block, you can use a shortcut.

4. Type = ↵. That's it. The wblock process is complete, and you have a new drawing file called win-1.dwg stored on your hard disk in the Symbols folder.

5. If you want to see if it's there, minimize AutoCAD and open up Windows Explorer or File Manager. Find and open the Symbols folder. There should be a win-1.dwg in the folder. Close Windows Explorer and restore AutoCAD.

Next you need to create a new drawing and put a couple of wall lines in it so you can insert this new win-1 drawing.

Inserting a DWG File into a DWG File

If you need more help setting up a new drawing than the following steps provide, refer to Skill 3. For a reminder on how to change layer properties, review Skill 6.

1. Click the New button on the Standard toolbar. Click Yes to save changes. Click the Start from Scratch button, then click OK. A new, blank drawing comes up.

2. Click Format ➤ Units, and select Architectural for the Units. Click OK.

3. Click the Layers button, and create two new layers: Walls and Windows. Leave the Windows layer its default color and make the Walls layer blue.

4. With the Walls layer highlighted, click the Current button to make the Walls layer current. Click OK to return to the drawing.

5. Start the Rectangle command. For the first corner, type **0,0** ↵. For the other corner, type **25',15'** ↵.

6. Zoom Extents, then use the Zoom Realtime button to zoom out just enough to create a border of blank space around the rectangle (Figure 7.37a).

7. Use the Offset command to offset this rectangle 6 inches to the inside (Figure 7.37b).

8. Use the Layers drop-down list to make the Windows layer current.

9. Pick the Insert command from the Draw menu. In the Insert dialog box, click File.

10. In the Select Drawing File dialog box, find and open the Symbols directory, highlight win-1.dwg and click Open.

11. In the Insert dialog box, win-1 will be displayed in the text box next to the Block button. It is now a new block in this new file. Win-1.dwg will be displayed along with its directory path in the text box next to the File button. Click OK.

12. In your drawing, pick the Midpoint Osnap and pick the bottom outside wall line. Type **6** ↵, then type **1** ↵, then press ↵ again. The Win-1 block is inserted in the wall (Figure 7.38). Save this drawing as Cabin-test.

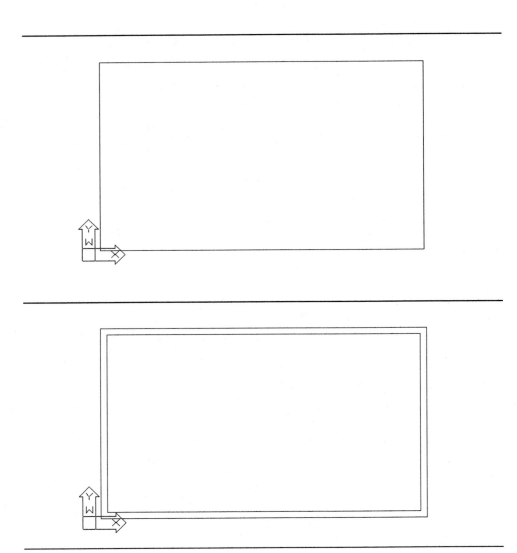

FIGURE 7.37: The rectangle after Zoom Realtime (a) and after Offsetting (b)

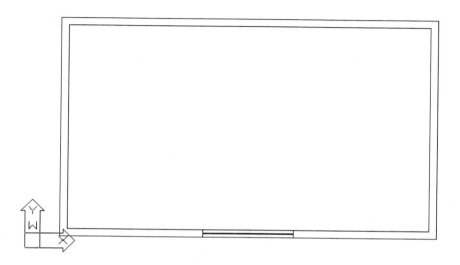

FIGURE 7.38: The win-1.dwg file is inserted into the new drawing.

You have completed the basic procedure for using a block created in one drawing, in another drawing. It will help to practice this routine. Make a couple of openings in the Cabin-test drawing, and repeat the steps for one or two of the door blocks. You won't have to create a new directory for the symbols this time. Here is an outline of the procedure:

- Explode the two rectangles.

- Create openings, then save Cabin-test.

- Open Cabin7b.

- Start the Wblock command.

- Open the Symbols folder and type in a filename identical to the name of the block to be wblocked. Click Save.

Skill 7

- When prompted for the block name, type =↵.

- Bring up Cabin-test. Don't save changes to Cabin7b.

- Start the Insert command and click File.

- Open the Symbols folder and select the dwg file named after the block.

- Place the insertion point and respond to the scale factor and rotation prompts.

If you want to practice creating blocks, open the Cabin7b drawing and make blocks out of any of the fixtures in the bathroom or kitchen. Try to decide on the best location to use for the insertion point of each fixture. Then insert them back into the Cabin7b drawing in their original locations. You can also wblock any of these new blocks into the Symbols folder, then insert them as dwg files into the Cabin-test drawing.

This skill has outlined the procedure for setting up and using blocks. Blocks follow a set of complex rules, some of which are beyond the scope of this book. For a more in-depth discussion on blocks, refer to *Mastering AutoCAD 14* by George Omura (Sybex, 1997).

Are You Experienced?

Now you can...

- ☑ create blocks out of existing objects in your drawing
- ☑ insert blocks into your drawing
- ☑ vary the size and rotation of blocks as they are inserted
- ☑ detect blocks in a drawing
- ☑ use point filters to locate an insertion point
- ☑ control the visibility of blips in your drawing
- ☑ use a partial insert to update a block
- ☑ use the Wblock command to put blocks in a Symbols folder
- ☑ insert blocks from the Symbols folder into a drawing

Skill 7

Generating Elevations

- ➔ Drawing an exterior elevation from a floor plan
- ➔ Using grips to copy objects
- ➔ Setting up, naming, and saving a User Coordinate System and a new view
- ➔ Transferring height lines from one elevation to another
- ➔ Moving and rotating elevations

Now that you have created all the building components that will be in the floor plan, it's a good time to draw the exterior elevations. *Elevations* are views of the building horizontally, as if you were standing facing the building, instead of looking down at it, as you do in the floor plan. The elevations view shows you how windows and doors fit into the walls, and gives you an idea of how the building will look from the outside. In most design projects at least four exterior elevations are included in the drawings: front, back, and one from each side. I'll go over how to create the front elevation first. Then I will discuss some of the considerations necessary to complete the other ones, and you will have the chance to draw these on your own. Finally, we will look at how interior elevations are set up. They are similar to exterior elevations, but usually of individual walls on the inside of a building, to show how objects such as doors, windows, cabinets, shelves, and finishes will look in and on the walls.

Drawing the Front Elevation

The front elevation is drawn using techniques very similar to those used on the traditional drafting board. You will draw the front elevation view of the cabin directly below the floor plan by dropping lines down from key points on the floor plan and intersecting them with horizontal lines representing the heights of the corresponding components in the elevation. Those heights are shown in Figure 8.1.

1. Open Cabin7b.

2. Create a new layer called F-elev, assign it color 42 and make it current. Here's a summary of the steps to do this:

   - Click the Layer button, then click New.
   - Type in the new layer's name (F-elev) and press ↵.
   - Click the colored square for the F-elev layer, type **42** ↵, then click OK.
   - Click Current, then click OK.

3. Thaw the Roof and Headers layers, then offset the bottom horizontal roof line 24 feet down. The offset line will be off the screen.

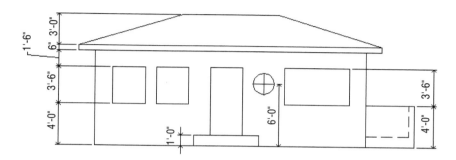

FIGURE 8.1: The front elevation with heights of components

4. Click the Zoom Extents button on the Zoom flyout toolbar.

5. Use Realtime Zoom to zoom out just enough to bring the offset roof line up off the bottom edge of the drawing area.

6. Erase this offset line. Your drawing should look like Figure 8.2.

Setting Up Lines for the Heights

You need to establish a base line to represent the ground. Then you can offset the other height lines from the base line or from other height lines.

1. With Ortho on, draw a horizontal ground line across the bottom of the screen using the Line command. Be sure the line extends a few feet beyond a point directly below the outside edge of the roof on the left and the balcony on the right (Figure 8.3).

2. Offset the ground line 1' up to mark the height of the step.

3. Offset the ground line 4' up to mark the top of the balcony wall and the bottom of the windows.

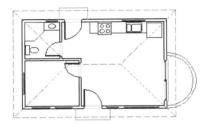

FIGURE 8.2: The floor plan with space below it for the front elevation

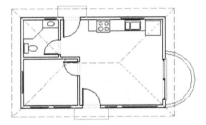

FIGURE 8.3: The floor plan with the ground line

4. Offset the bottom line for the windows 3'-6" up to mark the top of the door and windows.

5. Offset the top line for the windows and door 1'-6" up to mark the soffit of the roof.

 NOTE   A roof *soffit* is the underside of the roof overhang which extends from the outside edge of the roof, back to the wall.

6. Offset the soffit line 6" up to mark the lower edge of the roof's top surface.

7. Offset this lower edge of the roof's top surface 3' up to mark the roof's ridge (Figure 8.4).

8. Press ⏎ to end the Offset command.

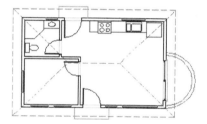

FIGURE 8.4: The horizontal height lines for the elevation in place

Each of these lines represent the height of one or more components of the cabin. Now you will drop lines down from the points in the floor plan which coincide with components that will be visible in the front elevation. The front elevation will consist of the balcony, front step, front door and windows, the front corners of the exterior walls, and parts of the roof.

Using Grips to Copy Lines

In the following steps, you will learn how to use grips to copy the dropped lines.

1. Be sure your Endpoint Osnap is running, and make sure Ortho is on. Start a line from the lower-left corner of the building, pick Perpendicular Osnap and click the ground line. Press ↵ to end the Line command (Figure 8.5a).

2. At the Command: prompt, select the line you just drew. The line is selected and small squares appear on the line's midpoint and endpoints (Figure 8.5b). These are *grips*.

3. Click the grip on the upper endpoint. The grip turns color and the prompt changes to <Stretch to point>/Base point/Copy/Undo/eXit:. This is the *Stretch command* activated by grips. Any time you start grips, the Stretch command starts first. If you don't want to use Stretch, press the space bar to get to the next command.

4. Press the space bar once. This begins cycling you through the five commands with which you can use grips: Stretch, Move, Rotate, Scale, and Mirror. The prompt changes to <Move to point>/Base point/Copy/Undo/eXit:. This is the *Move command* activated by grips. You'll use the Move command with its Copy option to copy the line you just selected.

5. Type c ↵ to select the Copy option of the Move command.

NOTE   Each of the commands that work with grips has a Copy option, which keeps the original object as is while you modify the copy. You can copy with grips in several ways you can't with the regular Copy command.

6. Select the lower-right corner of the building. The line is copied to this corner.

7. Select the Quadrant Osnap and click the right extremity of the outside wall line of the balcony. Another line is copied, this time to the balcony. It does not extend to the ground line, because it was directly copied and therefore is the same length as the other two lines. You will extend it later.

8. Type x ↵ to end the Move command. Press Esc twice to remove the grips. Your drawing will resemble Figure 8.5c.

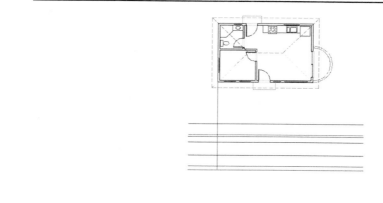

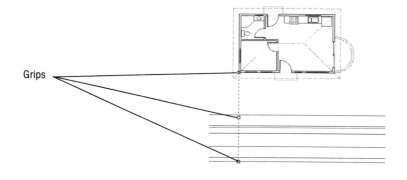

Grips

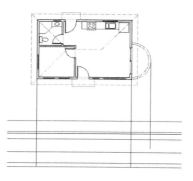

Skill 8

FIGURE 8.5: Dropping a line from the floor plan to the elevation (a), the dropped line with grips (b), and the copied lines (c)

In Skill 7, you saw how grips could be used to detect whether an object is a block or not, but they actually serve a larger function. The grips feature is a tool for editing objects quickly using one or more of the following five commands mentioned above: Stretch, Move, Rotate, Scale, or Mirror. These commands operate a little differently when using grips than when using them normally. There are a few more things the commands can do with the help of grips. Each command has a Copy option, so, for example, if you rotate an object with grips, you have the option of having the original object stay unchanged while you make multiple copies of the object in various angles of rotation. This can't be done using the Rotate command in the normal way, nor by using the regular Copy command.

The steps to use grips are summarized as follows:

- Click an object you wish to modify when no commands have been started.

- Click the grip that will be the base point for the command's execution.

- Watch the prompt and cycle through the five commands by pressing the space bar.

- When the command you need comes up, execute the necessary option.

- Type **x** ↵ when finished.

- Press Esc twice to delete the grips.

The key to being able to use grips efficiently is knowing which Grip to select to start the process. This requires a good understanding of the workings of the five commands that work with grips.

This book will not cover grips in much depth, but will introduce you to the basics. You will get a chance to use the Move command with grips in this skill, and we will use grips again when we get to Skill 11, *Dimensioning the Floor Plan*.

Trimming Lines in the Elevation

The next task is to trim the appropriate lines in the elevation, but first you need to extend the line dropped from the balcony down to the ground line.

1. Start the Extend command. Select the ground line. Press ↵. Pick the line dropped from the balcony anywhere on its bottom half. Press ↵ to end the Extend command.

2. Start the Trim command. For cutting edges for the two building lines, select the soffit line, then press ↵. The two lines to be trimmed are the ones that were dropped from the corners of the building. Pick them anywhere between the soffit line and the floor plan. The lines are trimmed (Figure 8.6).

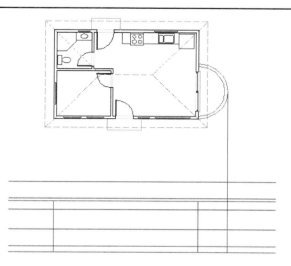

FIGURE 8.6: The building corner lines after being trimmed to the soffit line

3. Press ↵ twice to stop and re-start the Trim command. For the balcony, you need to trim a horizontal height line and a vertical dropped line. To select cutting edges, pick the line dropped from the balcony and the horizontal height line that represents the top of the balcony wall and the bottom of the windows (Figure 8.7a). The lines become ghosted (change to lines with small dashes) after they've been selected. Press ↵.

4. To trim the lines properly, click the line dropped from the balcony anywhere above the balcony in the elevation. To trim the horizontal line representing the top of the balcony wall, pick this line anywhere to the right of the line dropped from the balcony (Figure 8.7b). The lines are trimmed (Figure 8.7c). Press ↵ to end the Trim command.

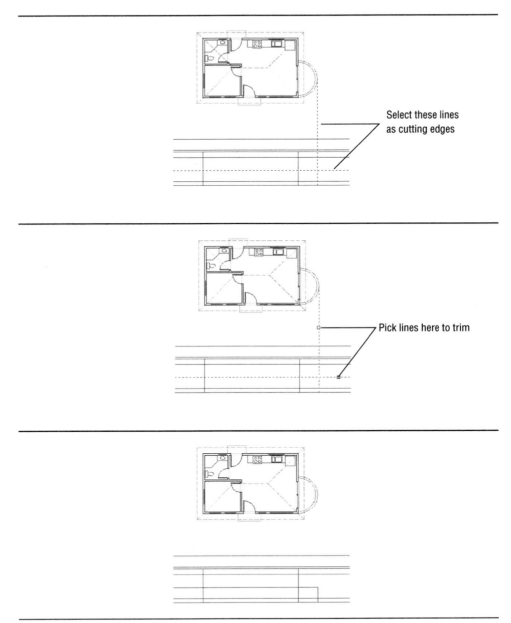

Select these lines
as cutting edges

Pick lines here to trim

FIGURE 8.7: Trimming the balcony lines: selecting cutting edges (a), picking lines to be trimmed (b), and the result (c)

This is the basic process for generating an elevation: Drop lines down from the floor plan and trim the lines that need to be trimmed. The trick is to learn to see the picture you want somewhere in all the crossed lines and then be able to perform the Trim command accurately to trim the appropriate lines away.

 TIP The Trim command is forgiving in that if you trim a line and are not happy with the results, you can type **u** ↵ right after you make a bad trim and the last trim will be undone. Then you can continue trimming.

We'll try the process a couple more times. First we'll make the roof.

Drawing the Roof in Elevation

Follow these steps:

1. Use the Line command with Ortho on and Endpoint Osnap running to draw a line from the right endpoint of the ridge line of the roof straight down past the soffit line (Figure 8.8a). End the Line command.

2. Click this line to activate grips, select the grip at its upper endpoint, and press the space bar once to access the Move command.

3. Type **c** ↵ and then click the lower-right and lower-left corners of the roof, and on the left endpoint of the ridge line. This will copy the dropped line to these three locations (Figure 8.8b).

4. Type **x** ↵ to end the Move command, then press Esc twice to delete the grips.

5. Start the Trim command and select the two lines dropped from the ridge line. Press ↵.

6. In the elevation, pick the ridge line to the left and right of these dropped lines (Figure 8.9a). The ridge line is trimmed back to its correct length (Figure 8.9b). Press ↵.

7. Erase the two dropped lines which were just used as cutting edges.

Skill 8

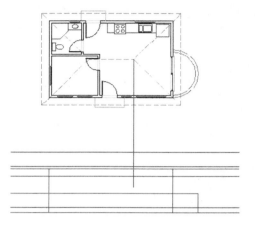

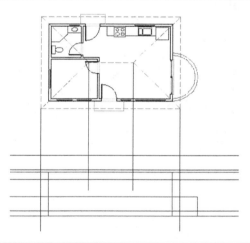

FIGURE 8.8: Dropping a line from the roof (a) and copying this line (b)

8. Type **tr** ↵ to restart the Trim command. Select the two lines dropped from the corners of the roof, the horizontal soffit line, and the line 6 inches above the soffit line to be cutting edges. Press ↵.

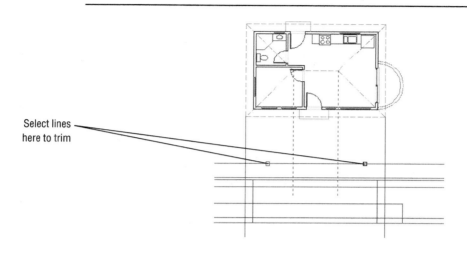

Select lines
here to trim

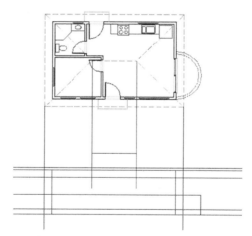

FIGURE 8.9: Selecting the lines to trim (a) and the result (b)

9. To do the trim, click the dropped lines above and below the two horizontal cutting edges, then click the two selected horizontal lines to the left and right of the dropped lines (Figure 8.10a). Press ↵. The roof edge is complete (Figure 8.10b).

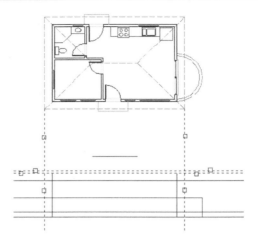

FIGURE 8.10: Trimming the lines to form the roof edge (a) and the result (b)

10. Use the Line command to draw the two hip lines from the roof edge to the ridge line. Zoom in to do this if you need to, then zoom previous when you're finished. The front elevation of the roof is complete (Figure 8.11).

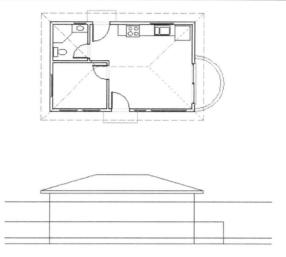

FIGURE 8.11: The completed roof in elevation

Putting in the Door, Step, and Windows

To finish the front elevation, all you need to put in it are the front door, windows, the front step, and a few finishing touches. We'll do the door, step, and all windows except the round one in one cycle.

1. With Ortho on, draw a line from the left end of the left-most window in the front wall, down to the ground line, using Endpoint and Perpendicular Osnaps.

2. Click this line at the Command: prompt to start the grips and follow the same process as you did above to copy this line to (a) each end of each window in the front wall except the 2-foot circular one to the right of the front door, (b) the lower-left and lower-right corners of the front step, and (c) each edge of the front door opening.

3. Type **x** ↵ to end the Move command and press ↵ twice to delete the grips (Figure 8.12).

Before we begin trimming all these lines, study the floor plan and elevation for a minute and try to visualize the three windows, the door, and the step in the middle of all the crossing lines.

We'll trim a few at a time, working from the top down.

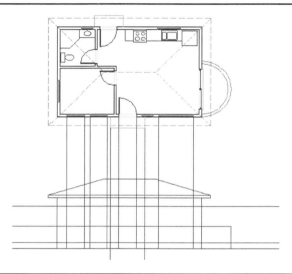

FIGURE 8.12: Dropping a line from a window and copying it to the edges of the windows, the front door, and the front step

4. Start the Trim command and, for cutting edges, select the horizontal line representing the top of the windows and doors, and all the lines dropped from the sides of the windows and door, but not the step (Figure 8.13a). Press ↵.

5. To trim, pick the horizontal line at each segment between windows and the door, and on the far left and right of the line (five places). Then pick each selected dropped line above the tops of the windows and door (eight places). This makes 13 places to pick. Then press ↵. The results of the trim are shown in Figure 8.13.

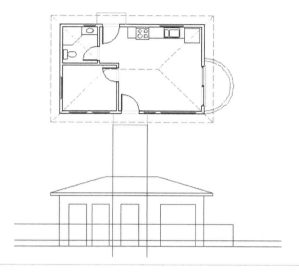

FIGURE 8.13: Trimming the top of the door and windows

Moving down, trim the lines that form the bottom of the windows.

1. Start the Trim command and select as cutting edges (a) the horizontal line representing in the bottom of the window and the top of the balcony wall, (b) the six vertical lines forming the sides of the windows, and (c) the vertical line representing the edge of the right wall. Press ↵.

2. To trim, pick the horizontal line at each segment between windows, and between the right edge of the 6' window and the right edge of the building. Then pick lines extending below the bottoms of the windows. This will be 10 places. Then press ↵. The results of the trim are shown in Figure 8.14.

3. Now trim the step and balcony floor, and the bottom of the door. Press ↵ to restart the Trim command. For cutting edges, pick the ground line, the horizontal line representing the top of the step and balcony floor, the two dropped lines forming the sides of the step, and the vertical lines serving as the right edge of the building and the right edge of the balcony. Press ↵.

4. To trim, pick each of the dropped lines both above the step and below the ground line. Then pick the two vertical door lines below the top of the step. Finally, pick the horizontal step line to the left and right of the step, and to the right of the balcony. Figure 8.15 shows the results.

Skill 8

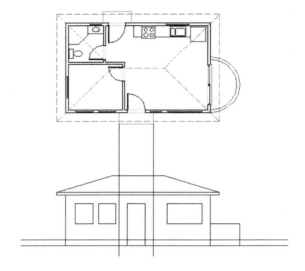

FIGURE 8.14: Trimming the bottom of the windows

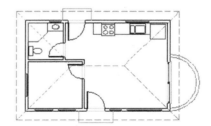

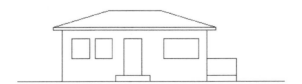

FIGURE 8.15: Trimming the step and balcony floor

The results show a nearly complete front elevation. To finish it off, you need to put in the round window and finish the balcony. Then we'll add some final touches. Take another look at Figure 7.1 and note that the center of the round window is 6 feet above the ground line.

1. Offset the ground line 6 feet up. Drop a line from the insertion point of the 2-foot window in the floor plan, down through the offset guideline. Then draw a circle using the intersection of these two lines as the center and give it a 12-inch radius (Figure 8.16a).

2. Start the Trim command and select the circle as a cutting edge, then press ↵.

3. Pick the intersecting lines in four places outside the circle. The round window is finished (Figure 8.16b).

4. Make a zoom window around the front elevation.

5. Offset the vertical line representing the balcony's right edge 6 inches to the left (Figure 8.17a).

6. Use the Fillet command with a radius of zero to fillet this line with the balcony floor line.

7. Click the Properties button and select these two lines, then press ↵.

8. In the Change Properties dialog box, click the Linetype button, then highlight Dashed and click OK. Click OK again. The lines are changed to dashed lines to indicate they are hidden in the elevation (Figure 8.17b).

9. Zoom Previous and save this drawing as Cabin8a.

Finishing Touches

You have gotten all the information you can from the floor plan to help you with the front elevation. You may, however, want to add some detail to enhance the appearance of the elevation.

1. Try zooming in and adding detail to the windows and door and place an extra step leading to the front step. Figure 8.18 shows an example. Yours can be different.

2. Zoom Previous when finished.

3. Save this drawing as Cabin8b.

Skill 8

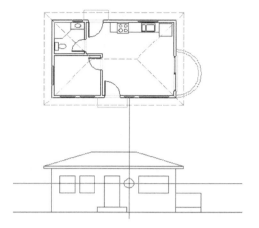

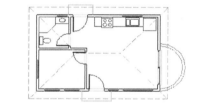

FIGURE 8.16: Drawing the round window (a) and the result of trimming back guidelines (b)

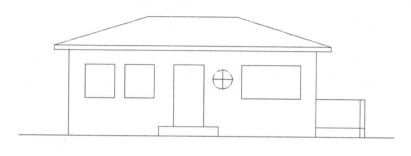

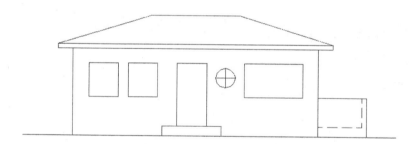

FIGURE 8.17: Completing the balcony: an offset line (a) and the two lines filleted and changed to dashed lines (b)

FIGURE 8.18: The Front Elevation with detail added

Generating the Other Elevations

In a full set of construction drawings for a building—drawings to be used by contractors to build the building—there will be an elevation for each side of the building. In traditional drafting, the elevations are usually drawn on a separate sheet. This would require transferring measurements from one drawing to another by taping drawings next to drawings, turning the floor plan around to orient it to each elevation and several other cumbersome techniques. You actually do about the same thing on the computer, but it is much easier to move the drawing around, and you can quickly borrow parts from one elevation that can be used in another.

Making the Rear Elevation

Because the rear elevation shares components and sizes with the front elevation, you can mirror the front elevation to the rear of the building and then make the necessary changes.

1. Open up Cabin8a. You need to change the view to include space behind the floor plan for the rear elevation.

2. Use Realtime Pan to move the floor plan to the middle of the screen, then use Realtime Zoom to zoom the view out enough to include the front elevation.

3. Start the Mirror command, and with a window, select the front elevation and press ↵.

4. For the mirror line, be sure Ortho is turned on, select the Midpoint Osnap and pick the right edge line of the roof in the floor plan.

5. Hold the cursor directly to the right of the point you just picked (Figure 8.19a) and pick another point. At the Delete old objects? <N> prompt, press ↵ to accept the default of No. The front elevation is mirrored to the rear of the cabin (Figure 8.19b). You can now make the necessary changes to the rear elevation so that it correctly describes the rear of the cabin, but you may find it easier to work if the view is right-side-up.

6. Click View ≻ Display ≻ UCS Icon ≻ On to make the User Coordinate System icon visible. (We turned it off in Skill 5.) The two arrows in the icon show the positive X and Y directions. This can be changed.

7. Type **ucs** ↵ **z** ↵ **180** ↵. This will rotate the icon to an upside-down position.

8. Type **plan** ↵ to activate the *Plan Command*. At the <Current UCS>/Ucs/World: prompt, press ↵. The entire drawing is rotated 180 degrees and the mirrored front elevation, which will eventually be the back elevation, is now right-side-up (Figure 8.20a). Note that the UCS icon is now oriented the way it used to be, but the W in the icon is gone.

9. Use Realtime Zoom to zoom out enough to bring the outermost lines of the drawing in a little from the edge of the drawing area, then use Zoom Window to zoom in so the floor plan and mirrored elevation fill the screen (Figure 8.20b). Now you can work on the rear elevation.

Skill 8

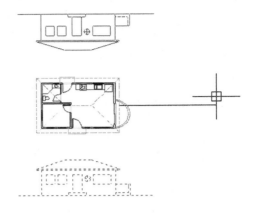

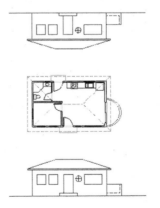

FIGURE 8.19: Specifying a mirror line (a) and the result (b)

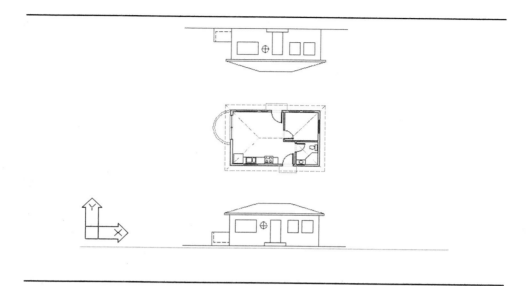

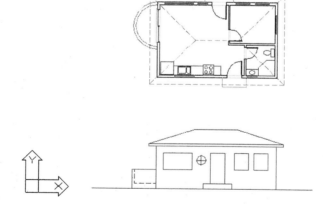

FIGURE 8.20: The cabin drawing rotated 180 degrees (a) and the results of zooming in (b)

Revising the Rear Elevation

A brief inspection will tell us that the roof, deck, and building wall lines need no changes. The windows, door, and step need revisions:

- The round window and one of the 3-foot windows need to be deleted.
- The two remaining windows need resizing and repositioning.
- The door and step need repositioning.
- The step needs resizing.

These tasks can be accomplished quickly with commands you are now familiar with.

1. Erase the round window and one of the 3-foot windows.

2. Erase the sides of the remaining windows (Figure 8.21a).

3. Drop lines down from the jambs of the two windows in the back wall of the floor plan, past the bottoms of the windows in elevation (Figure 8.21b).

4. Extend the horizontal window lines that need to meet the dropped lines, and trim all lines that need to be trimmed.

5. Use a similar strategy to relocate and resize the step. The door can be moved into position by using point filters or by dropping a guideline. The finished rear elevation looks like Figure 8.21c.

6. You need to save the User Coordinate System (UCS) you used to work on this elevation. Type **ucs ↵ s ↵**. For the UCS name, type **rear_elev ↵**. This will allow you to recall it if you need to work on this elevation again.

7. You also can save the view to be able to quickly recall it. Click **View ➤ Named Views**. The View Control dialog box comes up.

8. Click **New**. The Define New View dialog box appears.

9. In the New Name text box, type **rear_elev**, then, with the Current Display radio button selected, click Save View. Back in the View Control dialog box, REAR_ELEV appears in the list of views. Now you can restore the drawing to its original orientation with the front elevation below the floor plan and right-side-up.

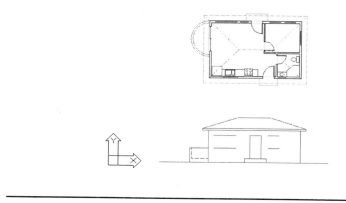

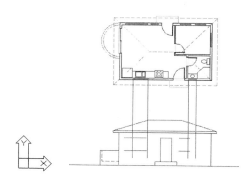

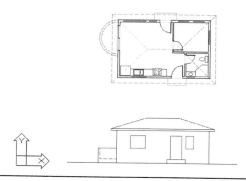

FIGURE 8.21: Erased lines (a), dropped lines (b), and the revised rear elevation (c)

NOTE By defining and saving a set of views, you can quickly restore a previously defined view of your drawing. You used the UCS command to create and save a new UCS that allows you to work on your drawing while it's upside down. The Plan command was used to rotate the drawing so it and the new UCS's positive X and Y directions would be to the right and up, just as the original, default UCS had been.

10. Type **ucs** ↵ ↵. This sets the original and default UCS—called the *World UCS*—as the current UCS. Now you need to re-orient the drawing to the plan view in the World UCS.

11. Type **plan** ↵ ↵. This zooms to extents and displays a plan view of the drawing with the X and Y positive directions in their default orientation.

The current UCS sets the positive directions for X and Y coordinates. The default UCS is called the *World Coordinate System* and sets the positive X direction to the right and positive Y straight up. When you set up and use several other UCS systems, you can always quickly return to the World Coordinate System. The UCS icon has a W in it when it is acting as the World Coordinate System icon.

TIP Any view of your drawing can be named and saved, then recalled later.

Making the Left and Right Elevations

The left and right elevations can be generated using techniques similar to those you have been using for the front and back elevations. You need to be able to transfer the heights of building components from the front elevation to one of the side elevations. There are several ways of doing this: One is almost identical to the traditional, hand-drafting way, and that may be the most efficient way. We'll use this method to create the right elevation.

1. Use Realtime Zoom to zoom out slightly. You need to transfer the height data from the front elevation to the right elevation. To insure that the right

elevation is the same distance from the floor plan as the front elevation, we'll use a 45° line extending down and to the right, from the right-most and lower-most lines in the floor plan.

2. With Ortho on and Endpoint Osnap running, start a line at the lower-right corner of the roof lines and extend it to the right until it goes past the balcony. Pick a second point and press ↵ twice. Select the Quadrant Osnap button and start a second line from the right extremity of the balcony arc. Pick Perpendicular Osnap and then pick on the line you just drew, then type **@35'<315** ↵. Press ↵. A line is drawn down and to the right at 45° (Figure 8.22a).

3. With Ortho on, draw a line from the right endpoint of the roof ridge in the front elevation to the right almost to the end of the drawing area (Figure 8.22b). Press ↵.

4. Copy this line to the endpoint of each object whose height needs to be transferred to the right elevation (Figure 8.22c). Use the zooming tools if you need to get a closer view.

5. Start the Trim command and select the 45° line as a cutting edge. Press ↵. You'll use a selection fence to select the height lines to trim.

6. Type **f** ↵ then click the Snap to None Osnap button and pick a point below the ground line and to the right of the 45° line. Click the Snap to None button again, then move the cursor up and to the left so a dashed line appears to the right of and approximately parallel to the 45° line, until it crosses all the height lines (Figure 8.23a), then pick a point.

NOTE   The *selection fence* is a line of one or more segments you draw through objects to select them. It is similar to the lines of a crossing window, in that any objects crossed by the fence line segments are selected.

7. Press ↵. All lines are trimmed (Figure 8.23b). Press ↵ to end the Trim command. If you zoomed in to perform this operation, zoom previous now.

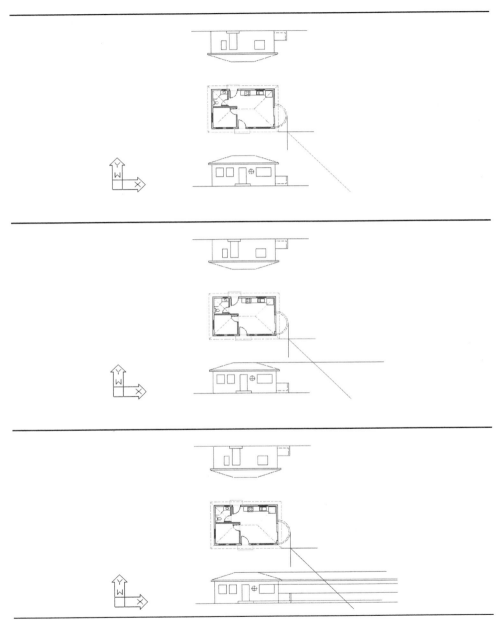

FIGURE 8.22: Drawing a 45° line as a guideline (a), drawing a height line across the guideline (b), and copying the height line down through the elevation (c)

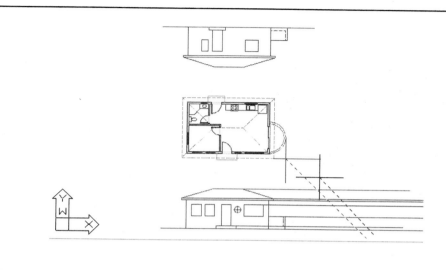

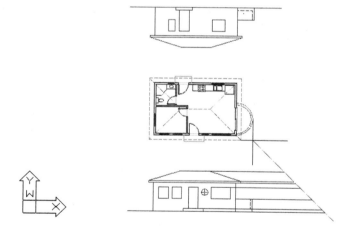

FIGURE 8.23: Using a fence to trim the height lines (a) and the results (b)

8. Erase the diagonal line and the two guidelines used to draw it, then draw a vertical line up from the right endpoint of the horizontal ground line, until it extends above the back edge of the roof in the floor plan (Figure 8.24a).

9. Copy this line, using the Multiple option, to each endpoint of the height lines (Figure 8.24b). This transfers the height lines "around the corner" where they can now be used to construct the right elevation.

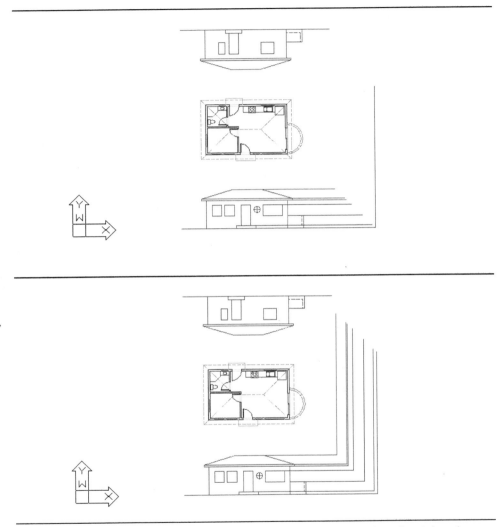

FIGURE 8.24: The ground line is drawn for the right elevation (a) and copied to make the other height lines (b)

TIP   If you're working on a small monitor, you may have to do some extra zooming in and out that isn't mentioned in these steps.

The rest of the process for creating the right elevation is straightforward and uses routines you have just learned. Here's a summary of the steps:

- Set up a new UCS for the right elevation and use the Plan command to rotate the drawing to the current UCS.

- Drop lines from the floor plan across the height lines in the right elevation.

- Trim as required and add any necessary lines.

- Name and save the UCS and view.

The left elevation can be created from a mirrored image of the right elevation. Here are the steps:

- Mirror the right elevation to the opposite side.

- Set up a UCS for the left elevation and use Plan to rotate the drawing to the current UCS.

- Revise the elevation to match the left side of the cabin.

- Name and save the UCS and view.

When you have completed all elevations:

1. Return to the World Coordinate System.

2. Call up the Plan view.

3. Zoom out slightly. The drawing will look like Figure 8.25.

4. Save the drawing as Cabin8c.

Once an elevation has been drawn, it may be rotated to the same orientation as the front elevation and moved to another area of the drawing. The four elevations for the cabin could all be displayed next to each other as in Figure 8.26.

Skill 8

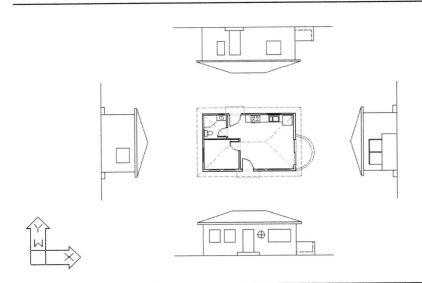

FIGURE 8.25: The finished elevations

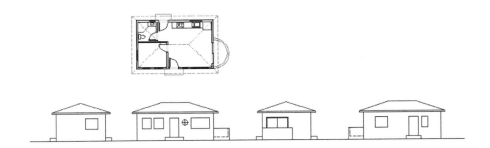

FIGURE 8.26: The elevations in line

Drawing Scale Considerations

This last view brings up several questions: How will these drawings best fit on a page? How many pages will it take to illustrate these drawings? What size sheet should be used? At what scale will the drawing be printed? In traditional hand drafting, the first line could not be drawn without answers to some of these questions. You have completed a great deal of the drawing on the computer without having to make decisions about scale and sheet size because in AutoCAD you draw in full scale. This means that when you tell AutoCAD to draw a 10-foot line, it draws it 10 feet long. If you inquire how long the line is, AutoCAD will tell you it is 10 feet long. Your current view of the line may be to a certain scale, but that changes every time you zoom in or out. The line is stored in the computer as 10 feet long.

Decisions about scale need to be made when you are choosing the sheet size, putting text and dimensions on the drawing, or using hatch patterns and non-continuous linetypes. Since we have a dashed linetype in the drawing, we had to make a choice about scale in Skill 6 when we assigned a linetype scale factor of 24 to the drawing. That number was chosen because when the drawing consisted of only the floor plan and you had it zoomed as large as you could while still having all objects visible, the scale of the drawing at that view was about 1/2" = 1'-0". That scale has a true ratio of 1:24, or a scale factor of 24. We will get further into scale factors and true ratios of scales in the next skill.

If you look at your Cabin8c drawing with all elevations visible on the screen, the dashes in the dashed lines look like they may be too small, so you may need to increase the linetype scale factor. Don't worry about that now. Beginning with Skill 9, and right on through the end of the book, we will need to make decisions about scale each step of the way.

Interior Elevations

Interior elevations are constructed using the same techniques you have learned for the exterior elevations. Lines are dropped from a floor plan through offset height lines and then trimmed away. Interior elevations usually include fixtures and built-in cabinets and shelves, and are used to show finishes. Each elevation will consist of one wall and may include a side view of items on an adjacent wall if the item extends into the corner. Not all walls are shown in elevation—usually just the ones that require special treatment or illustrate special building components. You might use one elevation to show a wall that has a window, to describe how the window is treated or finished, then assume that all other windows in the building will be treated in the same way, unless noted otherwise. A few examples of interior wall elevations are shown in Figure 8.27. Try to identify which walls of the cabin each one represents.

For some practice with interior elevations, try drawing one or two, using Figure 8.27 as a guide. Save what you draw as Cabin8d.

In the next skill, you will learn how to use hatch patterns and fills to enhance floor plans and elevations.

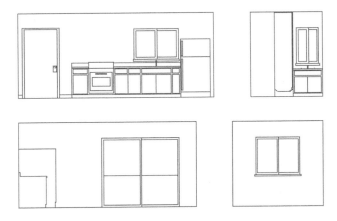

FIGURE 8.27: Samples of interior elevations of the cabin

Are You Experienced?

Now you can...

- ☑ draw an exterior elevation from a floor plan
- ☑ use grips to copy objects
- ☑ add detail to an elevation
- ☑ set up, name, and save a User Coordinate System and a new view
- ☑ transfer height lines from one elevation to another
- ☑ move and rotate elevations

Skill 8

Working with Hatches and Fills

- ➔ **Creating a predefined hatch pattern and applying it to a drawing**
- ➔ **Setting up and applying user-defined hatch patterns**
- ➔ **Modifying the scale and shape of a hatch pattern**
- ➔ **Specifying the origin of a hatch pattern**
- ➔ **Filling an enclosed area with a solid color**

*H*atches can be abstract patterns of lines, or they can resemble the building material that covers a surface. To give texture to an AutoCAD drawing, a drafter will hatch in areas or fill them in with a solid color. Solid *fills* in a drawing can give a shaded effect when printed using a half-screen, resulting in a look quite different from the solid appearance in the AutoCAD drawing on the screen.

In a floor plan, the inside of full-height walls are often hatched or filled to distinguish them from low walls. Wooden or tile floors can be hatched to a parquet or tile pattern, and, in a site plan, hatches are used to distinguish between areas with different ground covers, such as grass, gravel, or concrete. When working with elevations, almost any surface can be hatched to show shading and shadows, and realistic hatch patterns can be used to illustrate surface materials such as concrete, stucco, or shingles. Hatches and fills are widely used in details as a tool to aid in clear communication.

For the purposes of learning how to hatch and fill areas, you will start with some of the visible surfaces in the front elevation. Then you will move to the floor plan and hatch the floors, and put hatch patterns and fills in the walls. The *Hatch command* will be used for all hatching and filling. It is a complex command with many options.

A key part of a hatch pattern is the boundary of the pattern. The area being hatched is defined through a complex procedure in which AutoCAD searches the drawing for lines or objects to serve as the hatch boundary.

Hatching the Front Elevation

Hatches and fills generally need to be on their own layers so they can be frozen without making other objects also invisible. We will begin the exercise by creating new layers for the hatches and assigning colors to them.

1. Open the Cabin8a drawing. It should contain the floor plan and front elevation only. Turn off any running Object Snaps.

2. Set up three new layers as follows:

Layer Name	Color
Hatch-elev-42	42
Hatch-elev-gray	Dark gray (8)
Hatch-elev-black	Black (White) (7)

3. Make the Hatch-elev-gray layer current. Now, any new objects we create will be assigned to this current layer.

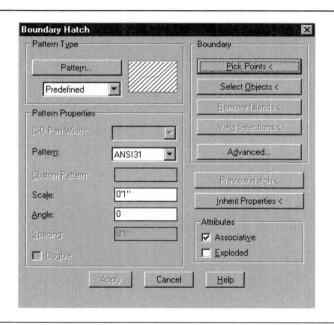

4. Start the Hatch command. You can select the Hatch button from the Draw toolbar, pick Draw ➤ Hatch, or type **h** ↲. The Boundary Hatch dialog box comes up (Figure 9.1). You will use this dialog box to choose a pattern, set up the pattern's properties, and determine the method of specifying the boundary of the area to be hatched.

FIGURE 9.1: The Boundary Hatch dialog box

5. At the upper-left corner, in the Pattern Type area, click the Pattern button. The Hatch pattern palette dialog box comes up (Figure 9.2). The scrolling list on the left includes all the pattern names. ANSI31 is highlighted, as is the third pattern icon in the top row.

6. Click AR-RROOF near the bottom of the list. The third pattern icon in the bottom row is highlighted.

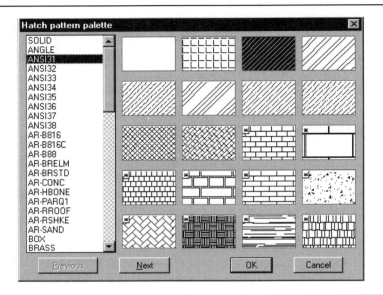

FIGURE 9.2: The Hatch pattern palette dialog box

7. Click OK. Back in the Boundary Hatch dialog box, the new pattern is dis-
    played in the viewing box next to the Pattern button and the name of the
    pattern is shown in the Pattern drop-down list in the Pattern Properties area
    (Figure 9.3). You can see in this area that the Scale and Angle settings can be
    changed. The default angle of 0 is fine, but you need to adjust the scale.

8. In the Scale box, delete 0'1" and type **6** ↵. The 0'1" is replaced by 0'6".

9. Move to the upper-right corner of the dialog box and click the Pick Points
    button. You will return to the drawing.

10. Click in the middle of the roof area in the elevation view. The lines forming
    the boundary of the roof area ghost, showing you an outline of the area to
    be hatched (Figure 9.4).

11. Press ↵. You are returned to the Boundary Hatch dialog box. Click Preview
    Hatch in the middle of the right side. In the preview drawing, take a look at
    how the hatch will appear, then click Continue in the little Boundary Hatch
    dialog box.

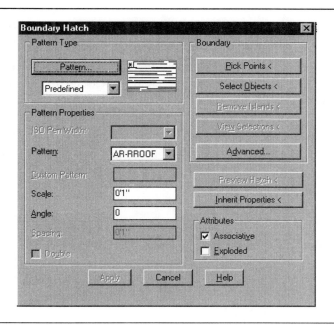

FIGURE 9.3: The Boundary Hatch dialog box with the AR-RROOF pattern selected

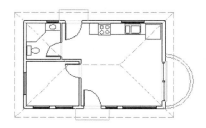

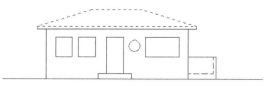

FIGURE 9.4: The roof's boundary is selected.

12. Back in the Boundary Hatch dialog box, click Apply near the lower-left corner. You are returned to the drawing and the hatch is now placed in the roof area (Figure 9.5).

13. Zoom in to a closer view of the front elevation, and note how the appearance of the hatch pattern changes with the new view.

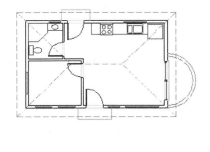

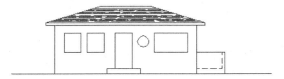

FIGURE 9.5: The finished hatch pattern in the roof area

Looking at Hatch Patterns

Let's take a short tour through the available patterns.

1. Type **h** ↵.

2. In the Boundary Hatch dialog box, click Pattern. The Hatch pattern palette dialog box comes up.

3. Look at the list of hatch pattern names. There are 11 names beginning with "AR-", including the one that we just used. These patterns have been designed to look like architectural and building materials, hence the AR prefix.

4. Click one or two of the AR patterns to see what they look like. In addition to the roof pattern we just used, there are several masonry wall patterns, a couple of floor patterns, and one for concrete, shakes, and sand.

5. Click a few of the ANSI patterns above the AR patterns. These are abstract line patterns developed by the American National Standards Institute and are widely used by public and private offices in the United States.

6. Click Next. There are 68 patterns in all, displayed on a little over three pages.

7. Click Cancel, then click Cancel again to close the dialog box.

As you work with hatch patterns, you will need to adjust the scale factor for each pattern so the patterns will have an appropriate appearance when the drawing is printed. The AR patterns are drawn to be used with the scale factor set approximately to the default of 0'1", and should only need minor adjustment. However, the pattern you just chose for the roof is an AR pattern, and its scale factor needed to be changed to 6". The AR-RROOF pattern is somewhat anomalous compared to the rest of the AR patterns and requires this unusually large adjustment.

 TIP   When using one of the AR patterns, leave the scale factor at 0'1" until you preview the hatch; then you can make changes. This rule also applies to the 14 ISO patterns displayed on the third page.

For the rest of the patterns, you will need to assign a scale factor which imitates the true ratio of the scale at which you expect to print the drawing. The table below gives the true ratios of some of the standard scales used in architecture and construction.

T A B L E   9 . 1 : Standard Scales and Their Corresponding Ratios

Scale	True Scale Factor
1"=1'-0"	12
½"=1'-0"	24
¼"=1'-0"	48
⅛"=1'-0"	96
¹⁄₁₆"=1'-0"	192

Some confusion arises from the fact that the scale is traditionally written by mixing inches with feet in the expression. For example, the third scale in the table, commonly called "quarter inch scale," shows that a quarter inch equals one foot. A True Ratio of this scale would have to express the relationship using the same units or as in ¼"=12". Simplifying this expression to have no fractions, you would translate it to say 1"=48". This is how you arrive at the True Scale Factor of 48, or True Ratio of 1:48.

Skill 9

As you continue through the skill, take special note of the various scale factors used for different hatch patterns.

Hatching the Rest of the Front Elevation

You will apply hatches to the foundation, front door, and front wall. Then we'll work with some special effects.

Using a Concrete Hatch on the Foundation

For the foundation hatch, you'll work on the same layer.

1. Draw lines from the upper-left and upper-right corners of the step out to the edge of the building to represent the top of the foundation (Figure 9.6a).

2. Start the Hatch command and click Pattern in the dialog box.

3. Select the AR-CONC pattern, then click OK.

4. To change the scale, delete 0'6" in the Scale box and type **1** ↵.

5. Click Pick Points, then, in the drawing, click once in each rectangle representing the foundation. The borders of these areas will ghost. Press ↵.

6. Click Preview Hatch, then click Continue. Now click Apply. The concrete hatch pattern is applied to the foundation surfaces (Figure 9.6b).

 NOTE When you select the Pick Points button in the Boundary Hatch dialog box, you then pick a point in the area to be hatched, and AutoCAD finds the boundary of that area and displays it in ghosted form.

Hatching the Front Door and Wall

For the front door, we'll use a standard hatch pattern: ANSI31. This is the default pattern when you first use the Hatch command, but now the default pattern is the last one used.

1. Start the Hatch command and select the Pattern button.

2. Select ANSI31 and click OK.

3. In the Scale text box, replace 0'1" with 18, then click Pick Points.

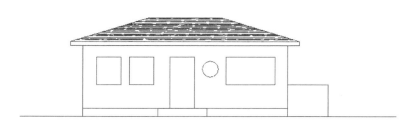

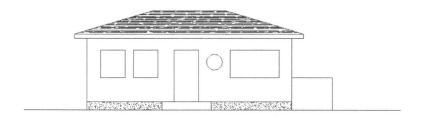

FIGURE 9.6: The front elevation with foundation lines drawn (a) and the resulting hatches in place (b)

4. Click in the middle of the door. The edges of the door and door sill ghost. Press ↵.

5. Click Preview Hatch, then click Continue, then Apply. The door is hatched (Figure 9.7).

6. Change the current layer to Hatch-elev-42.

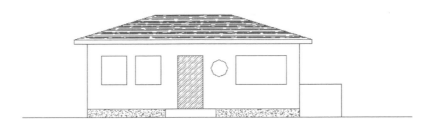

FIGURE 9.7: Hatching the door

7. Start the Hatch command and go through the same process to apply a hatch to the wall. This time you will use the AR-RSHKE pattern, which looks like wooden shingles (often called shakes). Here is a summary of the steps:

   - Click the Pattern button.
   - Select the AR-RSHKE pattern and click OK.
   - Set the Scale to 0'1" and click Pick Points.
   - Pick anywhere on the front wall that's not inside a window.
   - Press ↵, click Preview Hatch, click Continue, then click Apply.

The wall is hatched (Figure 9.8).

Using a Solid Fill Hatch

The windows will be hatched with a solid fill. It operates the same way as the other hatches you have been using except that you don't have a choice of scale or angle.

1. Make Hatch-elev-black the current layer.

2. Start the Hatch command, click Pattern and select the first pattern: SOLID. Press OK. Back in the Hatch Boundary dialog box, note that the text boxes for Scale and Angle are not available. These don't apply to solid fills.

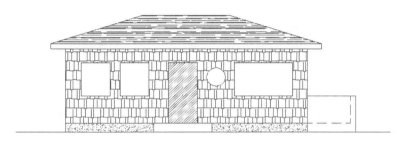

FIGURE 9.8: The hatching of the front wall is completed.

3. Click Pick Points and, in the drawing, select a point in the middle of each of the four windows. The round window will have to be clicked in four times because of the mullions (the separators between the panes). Press ↵.

4. Click Preview Hatch, then Continue, then Apply. The windows have a solid black fill (Figure 9.9).

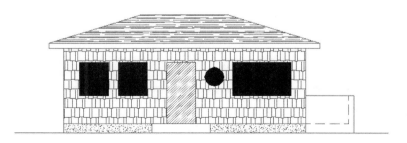

FIGURE 9.9: The windows with a solid fill hatch

Special Effects

To finish the Front Elevation, you will learn how to show shading and work a little with a curved surface.

Applying Shading to a Surface

When shaded surfaces are illustrated on an exterior elevation, they give a three-dimensional quality to the surface. We'll put some additional hatching at the top portion of the wall to illustrate the shading caused by the roof overhang.

You need to hatch the top 2'-6" of the wall with the same hatch that was put on the front door. To determine the boundary line of the hatch, you need to freeze the layer that has the shake pattern. Then you will create a guideline to serve as the lower boundary of the hatch.

1. Be sure The Hatch-elev-black layer is still current, then freeze the Hatch-elev-42 layer.

2. Offset the soffit line of the roof down 2'-6" (Figure 9.10a).

3. Start the Hatch command. In the Boundary Hatch dialog box, click Inherit Properties. You are returned to the drawing and the cursor is now a pickbox, telling you that AutoCAD is in Select Mode.

4. Pick the hatch pattern on the door. You are returned to the Boundary Hatch dialog box, and the ANSI31 pattern and scale used for the door has become the current pattern and scale.

5. Click Pick Points. In the drawing, pick a point on the wall above the offset line but not inside the door or windows. The boundary lines ghost (Figure 9.10b). Press ↵.

6. Click Preview, then Continue, and finally Apply. The pattern is applied to the upper part of the wall.

7. Thaw the Hatch-elev-42 layer and erase the offset guideline. The drawing will look like Figure 9.10c.

You erased the offset guideline because there is no edge on the wall at the bottom of the shaded area. And you used the Inherit Properties button to set up a hatch pattern exactly like one that was already existing in the drawing. You can also use the List command on hatch patterns to find out the name, scale, and rotation of an existing pattern, as well as the layer the hatch is on.

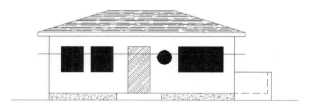

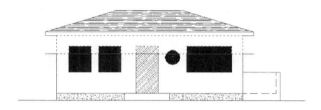

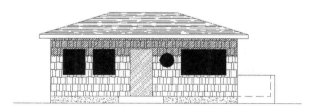

FIGURE 9.10: Applying a hatch to a shaded area: drawing a guideline (a), finding the hatch boundary (b), and the resulting effect (c)

Indicating a Curved Surface

The curved outside wall of the balcony appears as a rectangle in the front elevation. We need to use a pattern that will increase in density in the X direction as we move around the curve. Vertical straight lines will do this job if we space them properly. We'll use the floor plan to help us do that.

1. Use Realtime Zoom to zoom the view out until you can see the balcony in the floor plan.

2. Use the Line command with Quadrant Osnap to start a line from the right extremity of the outside balcony wall, and Endpoint Osnap to end it at the top-right corner of the balcony in elevation (Figure 9.11).

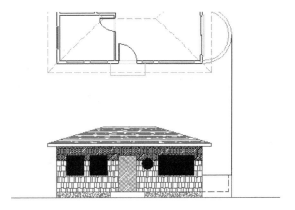

FIGURE 9.11: Drop a line from the balcony in the floor plan to the elevation.

3. Freeze the Headers, Roof, and Steps layers. Use Zoom Window to zoom into the lower half of the balcony in the floor plan. Then use Center Osnap to draw a line from the center point of the balcony arc, down to the lower-right corner of the building (Figure 9.12a).

4. At the Command: prompt, select the line you just drew. Grips will appear.

5. Click the grip at the line's upper endpoint. It will change color.

6. Press the space bar twice. The Rotate command is shown in the Command window.

7. Type **c** ↵. This activates the Copy option for the Rotate command.

8. Turn Ortho off and move the cursor to the right of the balcony (Figure 9.12b).

9. Type **10** ↵ **20** ↵ **30** ↵ **40** ↵ **50** ↵ **60** ↵ **70** ↵ **80** ↵ **x** ↵, then press Esc twice to delete the grips (Figure 9.12c).

10. Set Endpoint Osnap to running, then use grips again to copy/move the dropped line to the endpoint of each line that was just copied/rotated. Here is a summary of the steps:

    - Click the dropped line to activate grips.

    - Click the grip on the upper endpoint.

    - Press the space bar once. This switches from the default Stretch command to the Move command.

    - Type **c** ↵. This activates the Copy options for the move command.

    - Click each spoke line (like the spoke of a wheel) near its outer endpoint, but before the point where the spoke line crosses the inside balcony arc. Don't copy the line to the vertical spoke line you first drew.

    - Type **x** ↵, then press Esc twice.

    The results will look like Figure 9.13a.

11. Erase all the spoke lines and the original dropped line (Figure 9.13b).

12. Thaw the Headers, Roof, and Steps layers. Zoom Previous, then zoom in close to the elevation of the balcony.

Skill 9

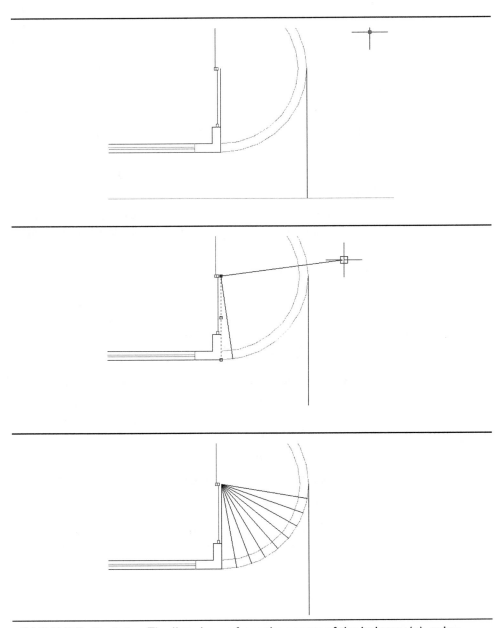

FIGURE 9.12: The line drawn from the center of the balcony (a), using grips to copy/rotate this line around (b), and the results (c)

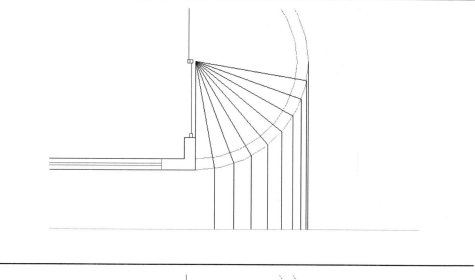

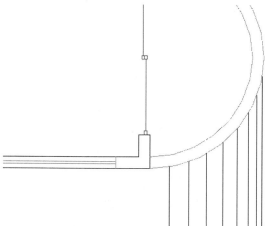

FIGURE 9.13: The drop line is copied to the ends of the spoke lines (a) and the spoke lines and first dropped line are erased (b)

13. Erase the two dashed lines that represent the floor and inside wall of the balcony. Extend the five dropped lines which don't yet reach down to the ground line, then trim all dropped lines to the top line of the balcony and the ground line (Figure 9.14).

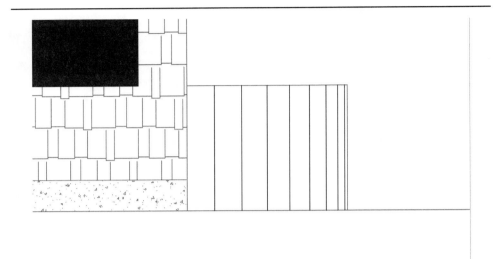

FIGURE 9.14: The balcony in elevation after erasing, extending, and trimming lines

Modifying a Hatch Pattern

You won't know for sure if the hatch patterns will look right until you print the drawing, but you can at least see how they look together now that you've finished hatching the elevation.

1. Zoom Previous and use Realtime Pan to have both the floor plan and elevation on the screen (Figure 9.15a). The roof hatch could be a little denser. You can use the *Modify Hatch command* to change the hatch scale.

2. Click Modify ➢ Object ➢ Hatch.

3. Select the roof hatch pattern.

4. In the Hatchedit dialog box, change the scale from 0'6" to 0'4".

5. Click Apply. The roof hatch pattern is denser now (Figure 9.15b).

6. Save this drawing as Cabin9a.

 NOTE   You can use the Modify Hatch command to change the pattern, scale, or angle of an existing hatch.

FIGURE 9.15: Full view of the drawing with the hatching completed for the front elevation (a) and the same view with the roof hatch modified (b)

If you worked on putting more detail in the front elevation in Skill 8, and saved this as Cabin8b, you can go through the exercise again with that drawing. Then you can see how more detail and hatch patterns enhance the way the elevations appear. Figure 9.16 shows the front elevation with hatch patterns and more detail in the door and windows. If you have the time to do any hatching on this drawing, save your work as Cabin9b.

FIGURE 9.16: Cabin9b with the front elevation hatched

Using Hatches in the Floor Plan

In the floor plan, hatches can be used to fill in the walls or to indicate various kinds of floor surfaces. We'll start with the floors.

Hatching the Floors

So far you have used only predefined hatch patterns—the 68 patterns that come with AutoCAD. There is also a *user-defined pattern* that is a series of parallel lines which can be set at any spacing and angle. If you want to illustrate square floor tile, the user defined pattern also has a Double option which uses two sets of parallel lines, one perpendicular to the other, resulting in a tiled effect.

The User-Defined Hatch Pattern

You'll use the user-defined pattern for a couple of rooms, then return to the pre-defined patterns.

1. With Cabin9a open, zoom in to the floor plan and be sure the Headers and Doors layers are thawed and visible. The header lines can be used to help form a boundary line across an entryway to a room and keep the hatch pattern from extending to another room.

2. With the floor plan in full view, zoom into the bathroom and freeze the Roof layer. Even if the roof lines are dashed, they will still form a boundary to a hatch.

3. Create a new layer called Hatch-plan-floor, assign it the color 140 and make it current.

4. Type **h** ↵ to start the Hatch command. In the Boundary Hatch dialog box, click Predefined in the upper-left corner. The Pattern Types drop-down list comes up.

5. Click User-defined. The list closes and User-defined replaces Predefined as the current Pattern Type. The pattern icon box says "No icon," and below that, the Scale text box is not available but the Spacing text box is.

6. In the Spacing text box, change 0'1" to 0'9", and click in the checkbox next to Double to put a check in it. Then click Pick Points.

7. Back in the drawing, be sure no Osnaps are running, then click a point in the bathroom floor, not touching the fixture lines or the door. Click again on the floor between the door swing and the door, being careful to not touch the door. Press ↵.

8. Click Preview Hatch. The tiled hatch pattern should fill the bathroom floor and stop at the header, while not going onto the door or fixtures. You can move the little Boundary Hatch dialog box out of the way if it's blocking your view of the bathroom. If the tile pattern looks OK, click Continue, then click Apply (Figure 9.17).

Skill 9

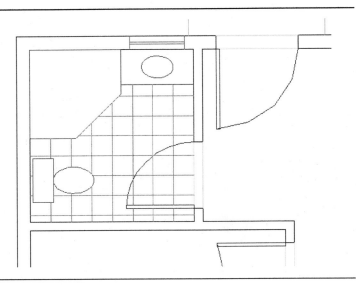

FIGURE 9.17: The tiled hatch pattern in place

Note that in the User-defined pattern, there is no scale factor to worry about. You simply set the distance you need between lines in the Spacing text box.

> If you can't get the Hatch command to hatch the area you want hatched, some of the lines serving as the hatch boundary may not have been drawn accurately. This may prevent AutoCAD from being able to find the boundary you intend to use. Zoom in to the areas where objects meet to check to see if they really do meet where they should.

Controlling the Origin of the Hatch Pattern

Often a designer will want to lay out the tile pattern such that the pattern is centered in the room. In this case the tiles would be set starting in the center of the room and move out to the edges, where tiles would be cut to fit. We'll use the *Snapbase* setting to set this up in the bedroom.

1. Use Realtime Pan to slide the drawing up until the bedroom occupies the screen. Use Realtime Zoom to zoom out if you need to.

2. Draw a diagonal line from one corner of the room to the opposite corner (Figure 9.18a). Use Endpoint Osnap to be accurate.

3. Type **snapbase** ↵, then activate Midpoint Osnap and select the diagonal line. This sets the origin of any subsequently created hatch patterns to be at the center of the room.

4. Erase the diagonal line and start the Hatch command. The User-defined Pattern Type is still current and the spacing is set to 9".

5. Change the spacing to 12", be sure Double is still checked, then click Pick Points.

6. In the drawing, pick a point anywhere in the middle of bedroom and between the door swing and the door, similar to how you did it in the bathroom. Press ↵.

7. Click Preview Hatch, inspect the drawing to see if the hatch looks all right, click Continue, then Apply. The hatch of 12" tiles is placed in the bedroom (Figure 9.18b). Note how the pattern is centered left-to-right and top-to-bottom.

The default setting for Snapbase is 0,0 or the origin of the drawing. Each time you change this setting, all subsequent hatch patterns will use the new setting as their origin. For most hatches, the origin isn't important, but if you need to control the location of tiles or specific points of other hatch patterns, you can reset the Snapbase setting before you create the hatch.

Finishing the Hatches for the Floors

To finish hatching the floors, you'll use a parquet pattern—from the set of pre-defined patterns—in the living room and kitchen, and another user-defined pattern on the balcony.

1. Use Realtime Pan and Zoom to readjust the view so it includes the living room, kitchen, and balcony.

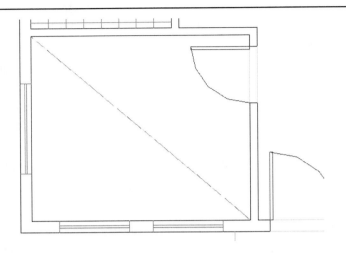

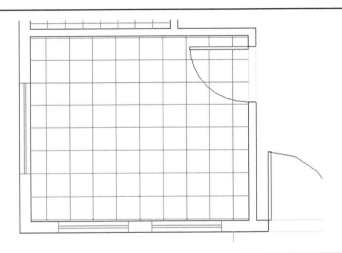

FIGURE 9.18: Hatching the bedroom: the diagonal line (a) and the finished, centered hatch (b)

2. Start the Hatch command and set the current Pattern Type to Predefined.

3. Set the Pattern to AR-PARQ1. Be sure the scale is set to 0'1" and the angle to 0, then click Pick Points.

4. Pick anywhere in the living room, then pick in between each of the door swings and doors, for the front and back doors. Check the ghosted boundary line to be sure it follows the outline of the floor. Press ↵.

5. Click Preview Hatch. The squares look a little small.

6. Click Continue. Reset the scale by entering **1.33** ↵ in the Scale text box.

7. Click Preview again. This looks better. Click Continue and click Apply. The parquet pattern is placed in the living room and kitchen (Figure 9.19).

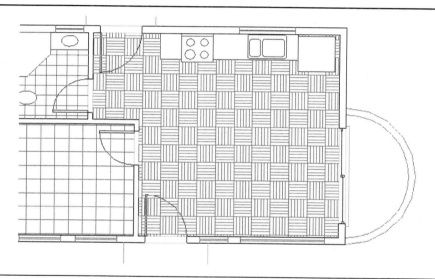

FIGURE 9.19: The parquet hatch in the kitchen

Skill 9

8. Type **snapbase** ↵, pick Midpoint Osnap and select the threshold line which extends across the sliding glass door opening.

9. Restart the Hatch command and set user-defined to be the Pattern Type.

10. Click the checkmark in Double to deactivate it, and set the spacing to 0'6". Click Pick Points.

11. Click anywhere on the balcony floor. Press ↵.

12. Click Preview Hatch, click Continue, and click Apply. The balcony floor is hatched with parallel lines 6" apart (Figure 9.20).

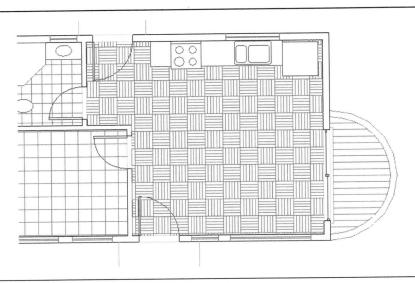

FIGURE 9.20: The user-defined hatch on the balcony floor

With the floors complete, the only components left to hatch are the walls.

Hatching the Walls in the Floor Plan

A solid fill is often used for full-height walls but not for low walls. The interior and exterior walls of the cabin are all full-height and will be hatched with a solid fill. Then you'll use a regular predefined pattern for the low balcony wall.

1. Zoom and pan to a full view of the floor plan.

2. Create a new layer called Hatch-plan-wall, assign it the color blue (same as the color for the Walls layer) and make it current.

3. Start the Hatch command, select the Pattern Type to Predefined, and select the Solid pattern.

4. Click Pick Points, and, in the drawing, pick in the 10 areas inside the wall between the door and window jamb lines (Figure 9.21a). Then press ↵.

5. Click Preview Hatch and look at the drawing. The fill will look a little odd because the blue boundaries of the wall line are ghosted. Check to be sure all 10 areas in the wall are properly filled, then click Continue.

6. Click Apply. The walls now have a solid fill (Figure 9.21b).

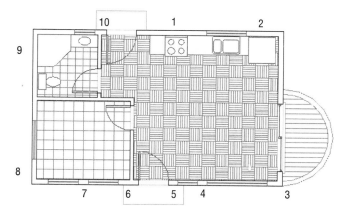

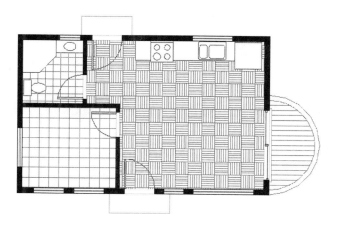

FIGURE 9.21: Areas to pick in the building walls (a) and the solid fill in the walls (b)

7. Restart the Hatch command and click Pattern.

8. Select ANSI37 for the pattern and enter a scale of 24.

9. Select Pick Points and pick a point between the two balcony arcs, then press ↵.

10. Click Preview, click Continue and then click Apply. A diagonal crosshatch pattern is placed on the balcony wall (Figure 9.22).

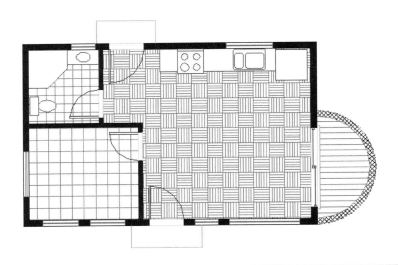

FIGURE 9.22: The hatched balcony wall

This completes the exercises for setting up and placing hatch patterns.

Modifying the Shape of Hatch Patterns

The final exercise in this chapter will be a demonstration of how hatches will automatically update when you modify a drawing containing hatches. You will be changing the current drawing, so before you begin making those changes, save the drawing as it is.

1. Zoom out and pan to get the floor plan and front elevation in the view. Thaw the Roof layer.

2. Save this drawing as Cabin9c. You'll use the Stretch command to modify this drawing.

3. Click the Stretch button on the Modify toolbar.

4. Pick a point above and to the right of the ridge of the roof in elevation. Drag a window down and to the left until a crossing selection window encloses the ridge line of the roof (Figure 9.23a). Click to complete the window, then press ↵ to finish the selection process.

5. For the base point, pick a point in the blank area to the right of the elevation.

6. Be sure Ortho is on, then hold the cursor directly above the point you picked and type **3'**↵. The roof is now steeper and the hatch pattern has expanded to fill the new roof area (Figure 9.23b).

7. Save this drawing as Cabin9d.

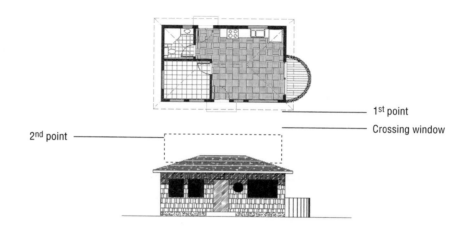

1st point

Crossing window

2nd point

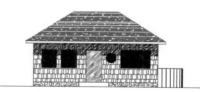

FIGURE 9.23: The crossing selection window (a) and the modified roof (b)

Hatches are a necessary part of many drawings. You have seen a few of the possibilities AutoCAD offers for using them in plans and elevations. For a more in-depth treatment on how they can be created and controlled, see *Mastering AutoCAD 14* by George Omura (Sybex, 1997).

Are You Experienced?

Now you can...

- ☑ create a predefined hatch pattern and apply it to a drawing
- ☑ set up and apply user-defined hatch patterns
- ☑ use grips to rotate and copy a line
- ☑ use lines to indicate a curved surface
- ☑ modify the scale of a hatch pattern
- ☑ modify the shape of a hatch pattern
- ☑ control the origin of a hatch pattern

Controlling Text in a Drawing

- ➔ Using text styles
- ➔ Inserting titles of views and labels
- ➔ Working with grid lines
- ➔ Dealing with several lines of text

You will have many uses for text in your drawings. Titles of views, notes, and dimensions are a few of the components of a drawing that require text, with each use possibly requiring a different height, orientation, and style of lettering. In order to control the text in your drawing, you will need to learn three basic operations:

- determine how the text will look by setting up text styles

- specify where the text will be located and enter it into the drawing

- modify the text already in your drawing

AutoCAD offers two types of text objects: single line and multiline text. Single line text makes a distinct object of each line of text whether the line is one letter or many words. This type of text is useful for titles of drawings, titles of views within a drawing, room labels, and short notes. Dimensions and longer notes are done with multiline text. AutoCAD treats a whole body of multiline text as one object, whether the text consists of one letter or many paragraphs.

The two types of text share the same text styles, but each have their own command for placing text in the drawing. When you modify text, you can use the same commands for either type of text, but the commands operate differently for multiline than for single line text. Dimension text is handled slightly differently than other text, and will be covered in Skill 11, *Dimensioning the Floor Plan*.

We will progress through this skill by first looking at the process of setting up text styles. Then you will start placing and modifying single line text in the cabin drawing. Finally we'll have a look at the methods of controlling multiline text.

Setting Up Text Styles

In AutoCAD, a text style consists of a combination of a style name, text font, height, width factor, oblique angle, and a few mostly static settings. Each of these text style properties will be specified with the help of a dialog box which comes up when you start the *Style command*. You will begin by setting up two text styles—one for labeling the rooms in the floor plan and the other for putting titles on the two views. You will need a new layer for text.

1. Open the Cabin9c drawing.

2. Create a new layer named Text1, assign it a color and make it current.

3. Freeze the Hatch-plan-floor and Hatch-plan-walls layers. Your drawing should look like Figure 10.1.

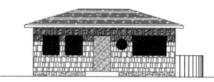

FIGURE 10.1: The Cabin9c drawing with the Hatch-plan-floor and Hatch-plan-walls layers frozen

Text and Drawing Scale

Before you set up text styles for this drawing, you have to determine how high the text letters need to be. To make this determination, you first need to decide the scale at which the final drawing will be printed.

In traditional drafting, you could ignore the drawing scale and set the actual height each kind of text needed to be. This was possible because the drawing was drawn to a scale and the text didn't have to conform to that scale, because the text was drawn actual size. In the cabin drawing, the drawing is actual size but the text has to be much larger than actual size because both the drawing and its text will be scaled down by the same factor in the process of printing the drawing. (You will learn about an alternate way of handling text height in Skill 13, *Getting Familiar with Paper Space*.)

We will use a final scale of this drawing of ⅛"=1'-0". This scale has a true ratio of 1:96 and a scale factor of 96 (see Table 9.1 in Skill 9, *Working with Hatches and Fills*). If you want the room label text to be ⅛" high when you print the drawing at eighth-inch scale, multiply ⅛" by the scale factor of 96 to get 12" for the text height. You can check that calculated text height by studying the floor plan for a moment and noting the sizes of the building components represented in the drawing. You can estimate that the room label text should be about half as high as the front step is wide, or 1 foot high.

Defining a Text Style for Room Labels

Now that you have a good idea of the text height you need, it's time to define a new text style. Each new AutoCAD dwg file comes with one predefined text style named Standard. You will add two more.

1. Type **st** ↵ or select Format ➣ Text Style. This starts the Style command and brings up the Text Style dialog box (Figure 10.2). In the Style Name area, you will see the default Standard text style.

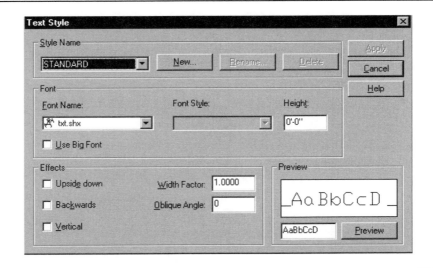

FIGURE 10.2: The Text Style dialog box allows you to modify text properties.

NOTE   All dwg files by default have the Standard text style as the current text style.

2. Click New. The New Text Style dialog box comes up. There is a Style Name text box with Style1 in it, highlighted. When you enter a new style name, it will replace Style 1.

3. Type **label** ↵. The New Text Style dialog box closes and, in the Text style dialog box, Label appears in the Style Names drop-down list. You have created a new text style named Label. It has settings identical to those of the Standard text style, and it is now the current text style. Now you will change some of the settings for this new style.

4. Move down to the Font area and click the Font Names drop-down list to open it. A list of approximately 100 fonts appears.

5. Scroll through the list until you find romans.shx, then click on it. The list closes and the romans.shx font replaces the txt.shx font that was previously in the Font Name text box. In the Preview area in the lower-right corner, a sample of the romans.shx font replaces that of the txt.shx font.

NOTE A font is a collection of text characters and symbols that all follow a characteristic style of design and proportion.

6. Press the Tab key to jump to the next text box. The Height setting is highlighted, at the default of 0'0".

7. Type **12**, then press Tab again. A height of 1'-0" replaces the default height of 0'-0" (Figure 10.3).

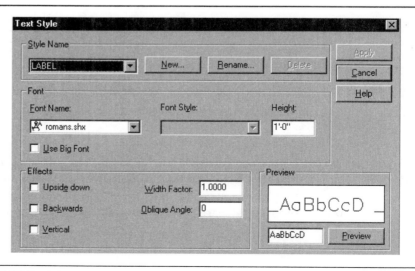

FIGURE 10.3: The Text Style dialog box, with the new Label text style defined

Skill 10

8. You won't need to change any of the other parameters that define the new Text Style. They can all stay at their default settings.

9. Click Apply in the upper-right corner of the dialog box. The Label text style is saved with the current drawing, and becomes the current text style.

 NOTE   The current text style is similar to the current layer. All text created while a text style is current will follow the parameters or settings of this text style.

When you define a new text style, you first name the new style. This has the effect of making a copy of the current text style settings, giving them the new name and making the new text style current. Then you change the settings for this new style and save the changes by clicking Apply.

Defining a Second Text Style

Before you close the dialog box, define another text style.

1. Click New.

2. In the New Text Style dialog box, type **title** and click OK. A new text style called Title has been created and is now the current text style. Its font, height, and other settings are a copy of the Label text style. Now you will make changes to these settings to define the Title text style.

3. Click the current font, romans.shx. The drop-down list of fonts opens. Scroll up just one font and click romand.shx, then click OK.

4. Tab once to move to the Height text box and type **18,** then Tab once more. The height is converted to 1'-6".

5. Click Apply, then click Close.

As you will soon see, the romans.shx font is a very simple font, often used for notes in a drawing. The romand.shx font is very similar, although it is boldface. More complex fonts are used for titles of drawing sheets and other larger text.

Of the many fonts available in AutoCAD, you will only use a few of them for your drawings. Some are set up for foreign languages or mapping symbols.

Others would appear out of place on architectural or technical drawings. Later on in the chapter, you'll have a chance to experiment with the available fonts.

Look back at Figure 10.2 for a moment, and note that the Standard text style has a height of 0'-0". When a text style has a height set to 0, you can make the text any height and are prompted to enter a height each time you begin to place text in the drawing.

Now that you have two new text styles, you can start working with single line text.

Using Single Line Text

Your first task is to put titles in for the floor plan and front elevation, using the new Title text style.

Placing Titles of Views in the Drawing

The titles need to be centered under each view. If we establish a vertical guideline through the middle of the drawing, we can use it to position the text.

1. Pan the drawing up to create a little more room under the front elevation.

2. With Ortho on, drop a line from the midpoint of the ridge line in the floor plan, down through the front elevation to a point near the bottom of the screen.

3. Offset the bottom line of the front step in plan down 4 feet.

4. Type **dt ↵** or pick Draw ➤ Text ➤ Single Line Text. This will start the *Dtext command*—the command used for single line text.

5. The prompt in the Command window reads
   `_dtext Justify/Style/<Start Point>:`.
   The _dtext portion tells you that the Dtext command has been started. The other part is the actual prompt, with three options.

6. Type **s ↵** to check that the Title text style is current. The prompt now reads `Style name (or ?) <TITLE>:`, which tells you that Title is the current text style.

7. Press ↵ to return to the original prompt. The Justification point is set to the lower-left corner of the text by default and you need to change it to the middle of the text to be able to center it on the guideline.

8. Type j ↵. All the possible justification points appear in the prompt.

9. Type c ↵ to choose Center as the justification.

10. Hold down the Shift key and click the right mouse button. The Cursor menu appears on the screen where the cursor had just been positioned.

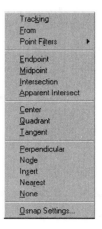

Click Intersection Osnap and pick the intersection of the guideline and the offset line.

NOTE   The Cursor menu (Shift+right-click) contains all the Object Snap options, an Osnap Settings option which opens the Osnap Settings dialog box to allow you to set running Osnaps, and a Point Filters menu.

11. For the rotation, press ⏎ to accept the default angle of 0. An "I" cursor will replace the cross and be positioned at the intersection (Figure 10.4).

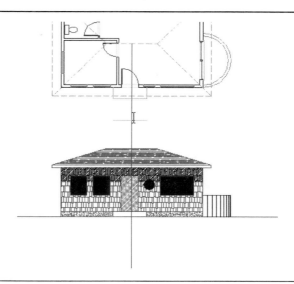

FIGURE 10.4: Guidelines have been set up to locate the text.

12. With Caps Lock on, type **floor plan** ⏎. The text is at the intersection as you type it (but not centered yet) and the cursor jumps down to allow you to type another line (Figure 10.5a).

13. Press ⏎ again to end the Dtext command. The text is centered relative to the vertical guideline and sits on the offset line (Figure 10.5b).

14. Offset the ground line of the elevation 4 feet down. Start the Dtext command again and follow the same steps as above, this time entering **front elevation** (again with Caps Lock on). When finished, erase the offset lines and the guideline. Your drawing will look like Figure 10.6.

Skill 10

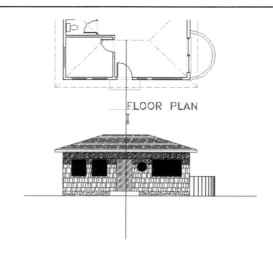

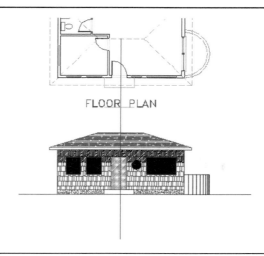

FIGURE 10.5: The first line of text is entered (a) and placed (b).

You specified a location for the text in two steps: First, you set the justification point of each line of text to be centered horizontally; then you used the Intersection Osnap to position the justification point at the intersection of the two guidelines. We will discuss justification in more depth a little later in the chapter.

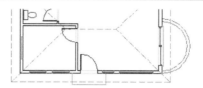

FLOOR PLAN

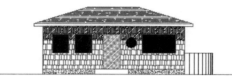

FRONT ELEVATION

FIGURE 10.6: The drawing with the titles complete

Next you will move to the interior of the cabin floor plan and place the room labels in their respective rooms.

Placing Room Labels in the Floor Plan

Text for the room labels will use the Label text style, so you need to make that style current before you start placing text. You can accomplish this from within the Dtext command by using the *Style option*.

1. Pan the drawing down and zoom into the floor plan. Turn off any running Osnaps.

2. Type **dt** ↵ to start the Dtext command. At the prompt, type **s** ↵ to choose the Style option. The prompt reads Style name (or ?) <TITLE>:. You saw this prompt above in step 6 when you were checking to see if Title was current.

3. Type **?** ↵ ↵ to see a list of defined text styles. In the text screen, you see Label, Standard, and Title listed along with information about the parameters of each style (Figure 10.7). At the bottom of the list you can see the Dtext prompt again.

FIGURE 10.7: The text screen listing the defined text styles

4. Type **s** ↵ again. Then type **label** ↵ to make Label the current text style.

5. Press F2 to return to the drawing.

6. Pick a point in the kitchen a couple of feet below and to the left of the oven.

7. Press ↵ at the Rotation prompt. The text cursor appears at the point you picked.

8. With Caps Lock on, type **kitchen** ↵ **living room** ↵ **bedroom** ↵ **bath** ↵ ↵. The Dtext command ends and you will have four lines of text in the kitchen and living room area (Figure 10.8).

For this text, you used the default Left justification and each line of text was positioned directly below the previous line at a spacing set by AutoCAD. In many cases it is more efficient to type in a list of words or phrases first, and then move the text to its appropriate location. That's what we are doing for this text.

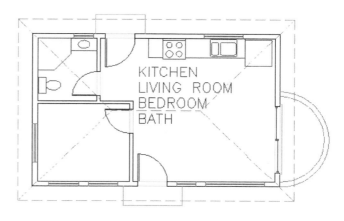

FLOOR PLAN

FIGURE 10.8: The four room labels placed in the cabin

Moving Text

We will "eyeball" the final position of this text because it doesn't have to be exactly centered or line up precisely with anything—it should just sit in the rooms in such a way that it is easily readable.

1. Start the Move command and pick anywhere on the text that says BATH, then press ↵.

2. Move the cursor to a place near the middle of the word BATH and pick that point. BATH is attached to the cursor (Figure 10.9a).

3. Be sure that Ortho is turned off, move the cursor to the bathroom and click a location to place the word in such a way that the letters, while they may be on top of the door swing and the roof line, don't touch any fixtures or walls (Figure 10.9b). The Move command automatically ends when you complete a move.

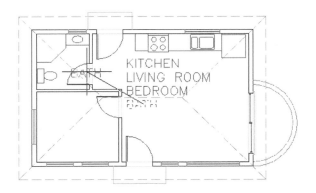

FLOOR PLAN

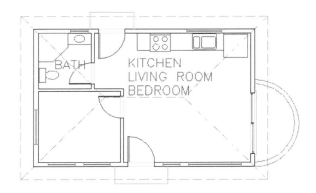

FLOOR PLAN

FIGURE 10.9: Selecting a base point for the BATH text (a) and the new location (b)

4. Press ⏎ to restart the Move command. Select the BEDROOM text and press ⏎.

5. Pick a point in the middle of the selected text.

6. Pick a point in the bedroom so that the BEDROOM text is positioned approximately at the center of the bedroom and only crossing the roof line (Figure 10.10a).

7. Repeat this process to move the LIVING ROOM and KITCHEN text into their appropriate locations (Figure 10.10b). You may not have to move the KITCHEN text.

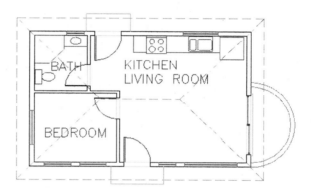

FLOOR   PLAN

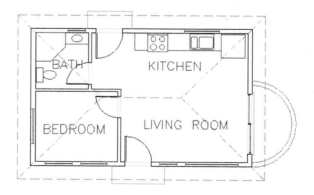

FLOOR   PLAN

FIGURE 10.10: The BEDROOM text moved to the bedroom (a) and the LIVING ROOM and KITCHEN text moved to their positions (b)

As you have seen, text is easily moved around the drawing. Often, however, you will be unable to position it without it sitting on top of a line or other object. In the cabin, three of the room labels are crossing the roof line and BATH is crossing a door swing. You need to erase parts of these lines around the text. To do this, you'll use the Break command.

Breaking Lines

The *Break command* separates a line into two lines. When working with text which is sitting on a line, you will usually want a gap left between the lines after the break. You can start the Break command in three ways.

1. Be sure no Osnaps are running, then click the Break button on the Modify toolbar, pick Modify ➤ Break, or type **br** ↵. Each of these actions start the Break command.

2. Move the cursor near the roof line which crosses through the LIVING ROOM text. Place the pickbox on the roof line just above the text, and click. The line ghosts and the cursor changes to the crosshair cursor.

3. Put the crosshair cursor on the roof line just below the text and pick that point. The line is broken around the text and the Break command ends.

4. Press ↵ to restart the Break command and do the same operation on the roof line that crosses the BEDROOM text.

5. Press ↵ again and break the roof line around the BATH text. The arc representing the door swing is part of the Door2_6 block, and, as such, cannot be broken. You must explode the block to be able to break the arc.

6. Select the Explode button on the Modify toolbar and select the bathroom door, then press ↵. The Door2_6 block is exploded.

7. Zoom in closer to the bathroom, then start the Break command and pick two points on the arc to break it around the BATH text (Figure 10.11). Zoom previous.

You should use your own judgement to determine how far away from the text a line has to be broken back. You have to strike a balance between making the text easier to read and keeping it clear what the broken line represents. In the bathroom, you were directed to keep the text away from any fixtures because if any lines of the fixtures had to be broken to accommodate the text, this might have made it difficult for a viewer to recognize that those lines represent a shower or a toilet.

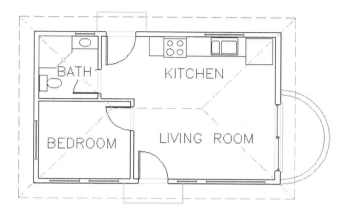

FLOOR PLAN

FIGURE 10.11: Lines are broken around the room labels.

 NOTE

Just now, after starting the Break command, when you selected the line to break, the point at which you picked the line became the beginning of the break. If the point where the break needs to start is at the intersection of two lines, you must select the line to be broken somewhere else than at a break point. Otherwise, AutoCAD won't know which line you want to break. Then type **f** ⏎. You will be prompted to pick the first point of the break, and the command continues.

The Break command can also be used to break a line into two segments without leaving a gap. You might want to do this to place one part of a line on a different layer from the rest of the line. To break the line this way, after picking the first point to break, type @ ⏎. This will force the second break point to be at the same place as the first one.

Using Text in a Grid

AutoCAD provides a grid of dots which you worked with in Skill 3. It is a tool for visualizing the size of the drawing area and for drawing lines whose geometry conforms to the spacing of the dots in the grid. Many floor plans have

Skill 10

a separate grid, created specifically for the project, and made up of lines running vertically and horizontally through key structural parts of the building. At one end of each grid line a circle or hexagon is placed and a letter or number is centered in the shape to identify it. This kind of grid is usually reserved for large, complex drawings, but we will put a small grid on the cabin floor plan to learn the basic method for laying one out.

1. Create a new layer called Grid, assign it a color and make it current.

2. Type z ↵ .6x ↵ to make more room around the floor plan.

3. Offset the upper roof line 10' up and the left roof line 10' to the left. Then offset the lower roof line 2' down and the right roof line 4' to the right.

4. Set Endpoint and Perpendicular Osnaps to running, then start the Line command.

5. Draw lines from the upper-left and upper-right corners of the building up to the horizontal offset line. Then draw lines from the left upper and lower corners of the building to the vertical offset line on the left (Figure 10.12).

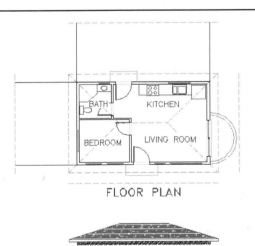

FLOOR PLAN

FIGURE 10.12: The first grid lines

6. Now you need to draw grid lines through the middle of the interior walls. Zoom into the bathroom area and draw a short guideline across the

interior wall between the bathroom and bedroom where this wall meets the exterior wall (Figure 10.13).

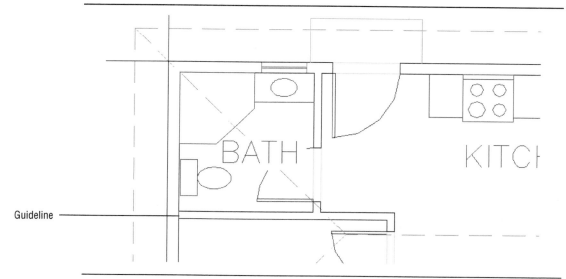

FIGURE 10.13: A guideline for drawing a grid line through one of the interior walls

7. Use Realtime Zoom and Pan to set up the view so it contains the bathroom and the offset roof line above and to the left of the plan.

8. Draw three lines from the middle of the interior walls out to the offset roof lines. Use Midpoint Osnap and pick one of the jamb lines or the guideline to start each line from the middle of a wall (Figure 10.14).

9. Erase the guideline you drew in step 6, then zoom out to a view that includes the floor plan, the grid lines and all the offset roof lines (Figure 10.15a).

 TIP   Use a regular selection window to select the guideline.

10. Use the Extend command to extend the seven grid lines to the right or down, using the offset roof lines on those sides of the floor plan as boundary edges (Figure 10.15b).

Skill 10

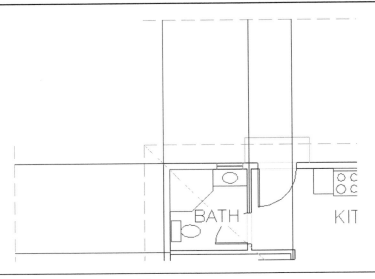

FIGURE 10.14: Drawing the grid lines

This completes the grid lines. To finish the grid, you need to add a circle with a letter or number in it, to the left or upper end of the lines. We'll use letters across the top and numbers running down the side.

1. Erase the four offset roof lines.

2. Type **c** ↵ **2p** ↵, then pick the upper end of the left most vertical grid line.

3. Type **@2'<90** ↵. A 2-foot diameter circle is placed at the top of the grid line (Figure 10.16a).

4. Start the Copy command, select the word KITCHEN, then press ↵.

5. For the base point, pick the Insert Osnap on the Object Snap toolbar, then click anywhere on the KITCHEN text.

6. For the second displacement point, pick the Center Osnap and click the circle on the grid. The KITCHEN text is placed on the circle with its lower-left corner at the center of the circle (Figure 10.16b).

FIGURE 10.15: Zoomed view for completing the grid lines (a) and the completed grid lines (b)

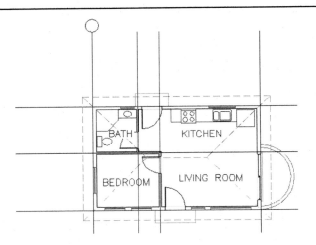

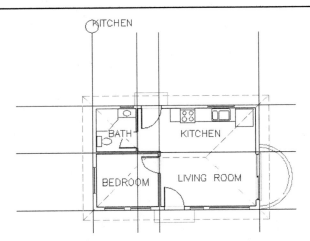

FIGURE 10.16: The circle on the grid line (a) and the KITCHEN text copied to the circle (b)

7. Click the Properties button on the Object Properties toolbar, then click the copy of the KITCHEN text that's now on the grid. Press ↵. The Modify Text dialog box comes up.

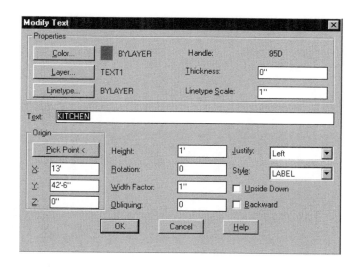

8. Use this dialog box to change the KITCHEN text as follows:

    • Change the layer from Text1 to Grid.

    • Change the word *KITCHEN* to the letter *A*.

    • Click the Justify drop-down list and select Middle.

9. Click OK. The KITCHEN text changes to the letter *A*, is centered in the grid circle and moves to the Grid layer (Figure 10.17).

This may at first seem like a round-about method for generating letters for the grid symbols, but the exercise is meant to show you how easy it is to use text from one part of the drawing for a completely different purpose. It's a handy technique as long you want to use a font that has been chosen for a previously defined text style.

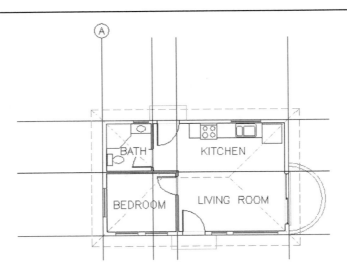

FIGURE 10.17: The grid circle with the letter A

You used the Insertion Osnap on the KITCHEN text to position its justification point at the center of the circle. Then you modified the justification point from the Left position (which is actually short for Lower Left) to Middle—short for Center Middle—which is the middle, horizontally and vertically, of the line of text. Let's look at Text Justification briefly.

Text Justification

Each line of single line text is an object. It has a justification point that is similar to insertion points on blocks, and can be snapped to with the Insertion Osnap. When you use the Dtext command, the default justification is the lower-left corner of the line of text. At the Dtext prompt (`Justify/Style/<Start point>:`), if you type **j** ↵, you get the prompt `Align/Fit/Center/Middle/Right/TL/TC/TR/ML/MC/MR/BL/BC/BR:`. These are your justification options. Most of these options are represented in Figure 10.18. The dots are in three columns—left, center, and right—and four rows—top, middle, lower, and base. The names of the justification locations are based on these columns and rows, so you have, for example, TL for Top Left, MR for Middle Right, etc. The lower row of positions doesn't use the name "lower" and simply goes by left, center, and right, with left being the default justification position (so it's not in the list of options). The Middle position will sometimes coincide with the Middle Center position, but not always. For example, if a line of text has descenders—lower case letters that drop below the base line—the Middle position will drop below the Middle Center position.

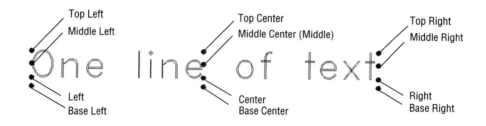

FIGURE 10.18: The justification points on a line of text

Finishing the Grid

To finish the grid, you need to copy the grid circle with its text to each grid line, then change the text.

1. Be sure Endpoint Osnap is still running. Then, at the Command: prompt, click the letter *A*, then click the circle. Grips appear (Figure 10.19a).

2. Click the grip at the bottom of the circle to activate it.

3. Press the space bar once to get to the Move command, then type **c** ↵ to copy (Figure 10.19b).

4. Pick the top end of each vertical grid line, then type **x** ↵ (Figure 10.19c).

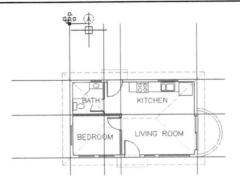

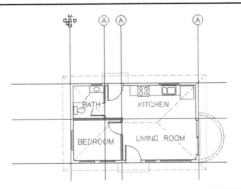

FIGURE 10.19: Grips appear on the grid circle and text (a), the Move/Copy command is started (b), and the letter is copied to all three points (c).

5. Select the grip on the right side of the circle to activate it.

6. Press the space bar once, then type **c** ↵.

7. Pick the left end of each horizontal grid line, then type **x** ↵ and press Esc twice to delete the grips. Now you'll use the *Change command* to change the text in each circle.

8. Be sure Caps Lock is on. Type **change** ↵, then select each letter *A* except the original one. Start at the top and move from left to right, then move to the left and pick them top to bottom. Press ↵. The prompt becomes `Properties/<Change point>:`.

9. Press ↵ four times, then type **b** ↵.

10. Press ↵ three times, then type **c** ↵.

11. Press ↵ three times, then type **d** ↵ ↵ ↵ ↵ **1** ↵ ↵ ↵ ↵ **2** ↵ ↵ ↵ ↵ **3** ↵. The letters and numbers are all in place and the grid is complete (Figure 10.20).

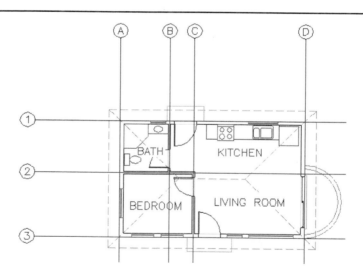

FIGURE 10.20: The completed grid

12. Zoom to extents, then zoom out a little (Figure 10.21).

13. Save this drawing as Cabin10a.

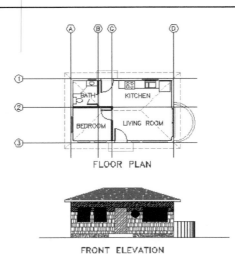

FLOOR PLAN

FRONT ELEVATION

FIGURE 10.21: The Cabin10a drawing

Often it is easier to copy existing text and modify it, than to create new text, and grips are a handy way to copy text. The Change command is a quick way to modify short lines of text consisting of a word or a few letters. When you were changing the *A* to the appropriate letter or number, you were hitting the ↵ key four times to cycle through the other aspects of the text you could change—in addition to the actual text content—by using the Change command. The Properties button is very useful for changing all aspects of a line of text, but it operates on only one line at a time.

For the final exercise with text, you get a chance to set up some more new text styles, place text precisely and use another handy command for modifying text content: the Ddedit command. Also, you'll get to work with the other kind of text: multiline text. This will all be done as you develop a title block for your drawing.

Creating a Title Block and Border

The first step in creating a title block and border for the cabin drawing is deciding on a sheet size for printing the final drawing. Because many people have access to a 8 ½"×11" format printer, we will use that sheet size. If we print the drawing at a scale of 1"=8'-0", will it fit on the sheet?

To answer that question, we have to ask ourselves: How big of an area will fit on a 8 ½"×11' sheet at 1"=8'-0" scale? The answer is really quite simple: If every inch on the sheet represents eight feet, then you multiply each dimension of the sheet in inches by eight feet per inch. For this sheet you multiply 8 ½"×8'per inch to get 68', and you multiply 11"×8'per inch to get 88'. So the 8 ½"×11" sheet represents a rectangle with dimensions of 68'×88'. That should be plenty of room for your cabin drawing. This is the information we need to start the title block.

Drawing the Border

The border of the drawing will be set in from the edge of the sheet.

1. Create a new layer called Tblk1, leave the default color assigned and make this layer current.

2. Start the Rectangle command (it was used in Skill 4 to make the doors).

3. At the prompt, type 0,0 ↵, then type 68',88' ↵. A rectangle is drawn that extends off the top of the screen (Figure 10.22a).

4. Use Realtime Zoom to zoom out until the entire rectangle is visible in the drawing area (Figure 10.22b). You need to fit the drawing into the rectangle as if you were fitting it on a sheet of paper—the easiest and safest way to do this is to move the rectangle over to the drawing.

5. At the Command: prompt, click the rectangle to turn on grips. Grips appear at the corners of the rectangle.

6. Click the lower-left grip, press the space bar once, then move the rectangle over the drawing (Figure 10.23a).

7. When the rectangle is approximately in the position shown in Figure 10.23b, click and press Esc twice to turn off the grips. The rectangle is positioned around the drawing and represents the edge of the sheet.

Skill 10

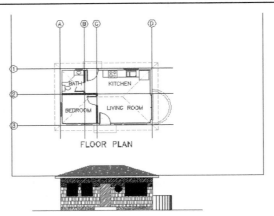

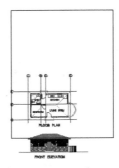

FIGURE 10.22: Creating the rectangle (a) and zooming out to include the entire rectangle (b)

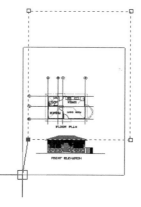

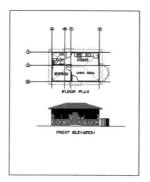

FIGURE 10.23: Moving the rectangle with grips (a) and the results (b)

8. You need a border set in from the edge. Offset the rectangle 3' to the inside. (With a scale of 8'-0"=1", each 1'-0" on the drawing will represented by ⅛" on the sheet, so a 3' offset distance will create an offset of ⅜" on the printed sheet.)

9. Type **pe** ↵ to start the *Polyline Edit command*. Select the inside rectangle.

10. Type **w** ↵ **3** ↵. This will set the width of the rectangle lines to 3". Type **x** ↵ to end the Polyline Edit command.

11. Erase the outside rectangle. Zoom to extents, then zoom out a little. You now have a border for the drawing (Figure 10.24).

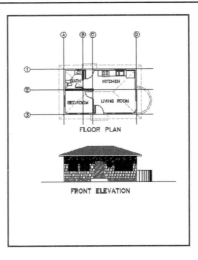

FIGURE 10.24: The drawing with its border

Constructing a Title Block

The title block is a box that contains general information about the drawing, such as the name of the project, the design company, the date of the drawing, and so on. It will be set up in the lower-right corner of the border and use the same special line—the polyline—that was used in the Rectangle command.

Polylines

We first used the Rectangle command in Skill 4 for drawing the doors. At that time, it was mentioned that rectangles created with the Rectangle command were made up of a polyline whose four segments were grouped as one object. In step 10 above, you saw that these segments can have varying widths.

There is also a *Polyline command*, nicknamed the ~~Pline~~ command, which allows you to draw straight and curved line segments of varying width, with all segments behaving as if they were one object.

When you explode a polyline using the Explode command, the segments lose any width they had and become independent lines. The ability of a polyline to have a width makes them useful in constructing title blocks.

1. Zoom into a view of the lower part of your drawing, including the bottom of the border. Be sure Endpoint and Perpendicular Osnaps are running.

2. Start the Polyline command. To do this, type **pl** ↵, pick the Polyline button on the Draw toolbar, or select Draw ➤ Polyline. The `From point:` prompt is identical to that for the Line command.

3. Be sure Ortho is on, then select From Osnap, click the lower-left corner of the border, click the None Osnap button on the Object Snap toolbar, and type **@12'<90** ↵. This starts a polyline on the left side of the border 12 feet above the lower-left corner (Figure 10.25a).

4. Notice the bottom two lines in the Command window. The upper one tells you the current width set for polylines, and the lower displays the options for the Polyline command with the default option being to pick a second point. You need to set the line width.

5. Type **w** ↵, then type **3** ↵ ↵. This sets the starting and ending width of polyline segments to 3 inches. The original Polyline command prompt returns and you can pick a point to define the line segment.

6. Hold the crosshair cursor with its target box on the right side of the border and, when the perpendicular icon appears, click. Then press ↵. The first polyline segment is drawn (Figure 10.25b). The 3" width setting will stay until you change it and will be saved with the drawing file.

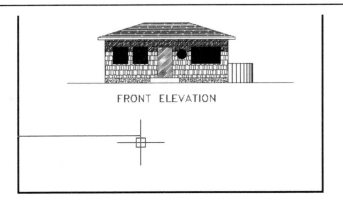

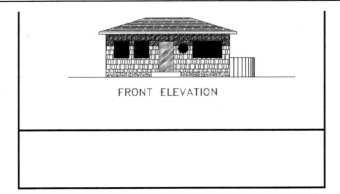

FIGURE 10.25: Starting a polyline (a) and completing the segment (b)

7. Restart the Polyline command, choose the Midpoint Osnap and start a new segment at the midpoint of the line you just drew.

8. Click the bottom of the border near its midpoint. The running Perpendicular Osnap will activate and the left edge of the title block will be drawn (Figure 10.26a). Press ⏎ to end the Polyline—or Pline—command.

9. Trim the left half of the first Pline drawn, back to the Pline just drawn.

10. Offset the horizontal Pline down 4', then offset this line down 3', then offset this line down 2'-6" (Figure 10.26b).

11. Start the Pline command and, using Midpoint Osnap, start a Pline at the midpoint of the third horizontal line down. Then end the segment at the bottom of the border, taking advantage of the Running Perpendicular Osnap. Press ⏎ to end the Pline command.

12. Trim the right side of the line just above the bottom of the border, back to the line you just drew (Figure 10.26c).

The lines for the title block are almost done. Some of the Plines may look wider than others. This almost certainly is caused by the monitor distorting the picture at the current view. By zooming in, you can assure yourself that everything is correct.

1. Zoom into a close view of the title block. Notice that the intersection of the outer lines in the upper-left corner doesn't seem clean.

2. Zoom into that corner using a zoom window (Figure 10.27a). The lines don't intersect in a clean corner. They need to be joined.

3. Type **pe** ⏎ to start the Polyline Edit command and select one of the two lines. You must place the pickbox on the edge of the polyline to select it—not in the middle of it.

4. Type **j** ⏎, then pick the other Pline and press ⏎. The corner is corrected (Figure 10.27b). Type **x** ⏎ to end the Pedit command.

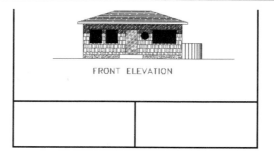

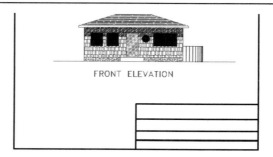

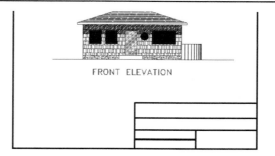

FIGURE 25: Building the title block: the left edge (a), the horizontal lines (b), and the last line trimmed (c)

FIGURE 10.27: Zoomed into the upper-left corner (a) and the corner corrected (b)

5. Zoom previous then use Realtime Zoom to zoom out just enough to see the Front Elevation text at the top of the screen (Figure 10.28).

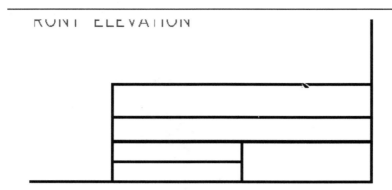

FIGURE 10.28: The completed lines of the title block, after zooming out

Putting Text in the Title Block

The title block has five boxes that will contain distinct pieces of information. The large one at the top will contain the name of the project. Below that will be the name of the company producing the drawing—your company. Below that, on the left, will be the name of the person who drew this drawing—you—and below that, the date. In the lower-right corner will be the sheet number, in case more than one sheet is required for this project. This follows a standard format, but many title block layouts will contain this and more information as well, depending on the complexity of the job.

You need to put labels in some of the boxes to identify what information will be shown there. For this, you need to set up a new text style.

1. Type **st** ↵. The Text Style dialog box appears. The Label text style should still be current.

2. Click New and type **tblk-label** and click OK. Leave the font set to romans.shx, but change the height to 8 inches. Then click Apply and Close. Tblk-Label is the current text style.

If you press Enter after changing the height, the Apply button ghosts out. Pressing Enter has the same effect as clicking the Apply button.

3. Be sure Caps Lock is on, then type **dt** ↵ to start the Dtext command. Click the None Osnap button, then pick a point in the upper-left corner of the upper box of the title block. It doesn't have to be the perfect location, as you can change it after you see the text.

4. Press ↵ at the rotation prompt, then type **project:** ↵ ↵. The word PROJECT: will be placed in the upper box (Figure 10.29a).

5. If necessary, move this text to the upper-left corner as far as possible while still allowing it to be readable. It will help if Ortho is turned off.

6. Use the Copy command to copy this text to the bottom two boxes on the left, using the Multiple option and the endpoint of the horizontal lines above each of the boxes as the base and displacement points. This will keep each piece of text in the same position relative to the upper-left corner of each box.

7. Pick Modify ➢ Object ➢ Text to start the Ddedit command, then click the upper copy of text. The Edit Text dialog box appears with PROJECT: highlighted.

8. Type **drawn by:** and click OK, then pick the lower copy of text. The Edit Text dialog box returns.

9. Type **date:** and click OK. Press ↵ to end the Ddedit command. The text is changed and three of the boxes have their proper label (Figure 10.29b).

The Ddedit command is a quick way to change the wording of text and make spelling corrections. You have to change one line at a time, but the command keeps running until you stop it.

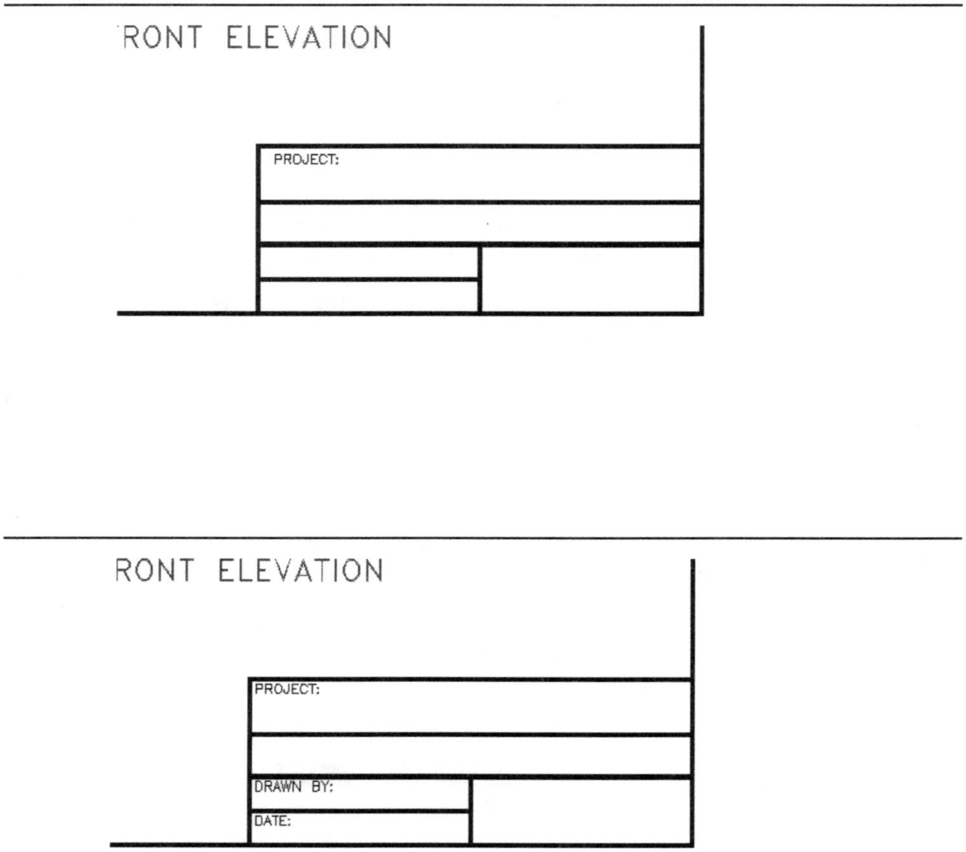

RONT ELEVATION

PROJECT:

RONT ELEVATION

PROJECT:

DRAWN BY:

DATE:

FIGURE 10.29: One line of text placed (a) and the text changed to the correct wording (b)

The next area to work on is the lower-right box. This is where the sheet number is located and it is usually displayed in such a way that the person reading the drawing can tell not only the page number of the current sheet, but also the number of sheets being used for the project. We will create a new text style for this box.

1. Start the Style command and in the Text Style dialog box click New.

2. Type **sheet_no** and click OK. For the font, select romand.shx, and change the height to 1'-3". Click Apply, then click Close. Sheet_No is now the current text style.

3. You will need to center the text horizontally in the box. To do this, break the horizontal line running across the top of the box at the upper-left corner of the box. Click the Break button on the Modify toolbar. Then select the line to break somewhere on the line where no other lines are touching it.

4. Type **f** ↵ to select the first point of the break, then use the running Osnap to pick the upper-left corner of the box.

5. At the Enter second point: prompt, type @ ↵. This forces the second point to coincide with the first point, and the line is broken without leaving a gap.

6. Start the Dtext command and type **j** ↵, then type **tc** ↵, then pick Midpoint Osnap and pick a point on the line across the top of the box.

7. Press ↵ at the rotation prompt and, with Caps Lock on, type **sheet no.:** ↵ **1 of 1** ↵ ↵. (When you get to the "of", turn Caps Lock off.) For clarity, leave a double space after the first 1, and before the second 1. The text is inserted into the box and is centered horizontally (Figure 10.30a).

8. Use the Move command with Ortho on to move the text down and center it vertically in the box (Figure 10.30b). Remember, when you select the text to move it, you have to pick each line because they are two separate objects.

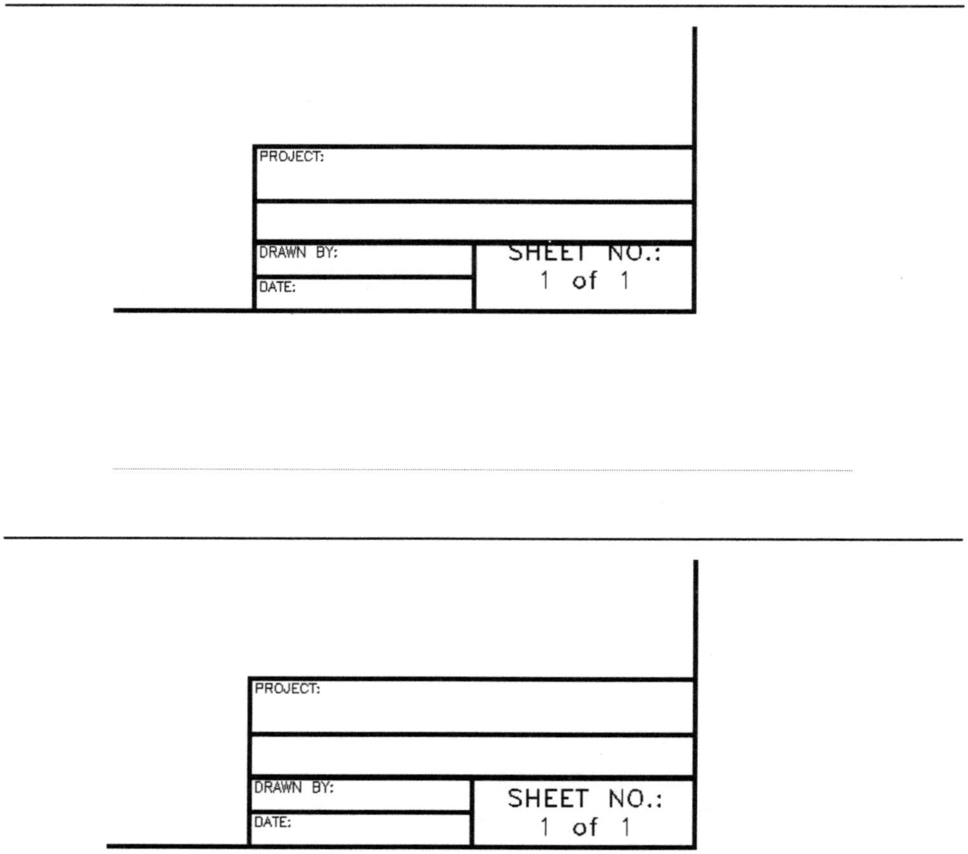

FIGURE 10.30: The text after being inserted (a) and after centering vertically (b)

Now it's time for you to experiment. Use the same techniques you just went through to fill in the text for the other four boxes. Feel free to try other fonts, but you will have to be sure the height for each text style is set up for the text to fit in the box. Here are some guidelines for height:

Box	Recommended Height of Text
Project:	2'-6"
Company:	1'-3"
Drawn By:	1'-0"
Date:	1'-0"

If you don't have a company name, make one up.

You will have to set up a new style for each new font or height you choose, unless you set up a style with a height of 0'-0". In that case, you will be prompted for the height each time you start to place text in the drawing. This is the recommended way to operate for the top two boxes, because it will give consistency to the text even when heights vary. You might try several fonts, then come back to this technique at the end. I also recommend that you use a relatively simple font for the text in the Drawn By and Date boxes—something a little larger and possibly bolder than the labels in those boxes.

Try these fonts:

- **romant.shx** or **romanc.shx**

- any of the **swis721** series

- **Times New Roman**

- **Technic**

- **SansSerif**

- **CityBlueprint** or **CountryBlueprint**

- **Arial**

In the top two boxes, the text can be centered vertically and horizontally if you draw a line diagonally across the box, choose Middle as a justification for the text, and use Midpoint Osnap to snap to the diagonal line when you start the text. For the Drawn By and Date boxes, centering the text horizontally is not advisable because the label text already in the boxes takes up too much space. You can use the same technique with the diagonal line to center it, however, then put Ortho on and move the text to the right until it makes a good fit. This will keep it vertically centered.

Be careful in your use of running Osnaps as you position text. If you are eyeballing the final location, it is best to have no running Osnaps. On the other hand, if you are precisely locating justification points by snapping to lines and other objects, you might try having the following Osnaps running: Endpoint, Intersection, Perpendicular, and Insertion.

When you finish, your title block should look something like Figure 10.31. In this sample, romant.shx font was used for a style that was set to 0 height, then applied to the top two boxes at the recommended heights. The romand.shx font was used for the Drawn By and Date boxes, also at the recommended height.

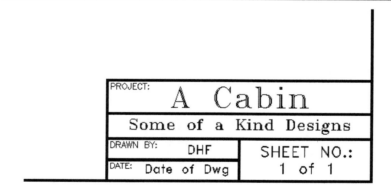

FIGURE 10.31: The completed title block

If you are going to design your own company title block, be ready to spend a little time setting it up and deciding which fonts will give the look that best reflects the image you want to project.

Zoom to extents, then zoom out a little. Save this drawing as `Cabin10b` (Figure 10.32).

The final part of the skill will introduce you to multiline text, which you will also work with as you learn about dimensions in the next skill.

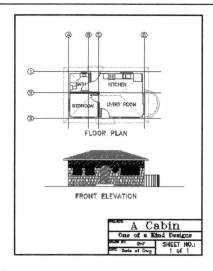

FIGURE 10.32: The latest version of the cabin drawing

Using Multiline Text

Multiline text (often referred to as MText) is a more complex form of text than single line text. It can be used the same way single line text has been used in this chapter, and it can do more. If you have several lines of text, or if you need certain words within a line of text to appear differently than the adjacent words, multiline text is the best thing to use.

A paragraph of multiline text is a single entity. The text will wrap around and the length of a line can be easily modified after the text has been placed in the drawing. Within the multiline text entity, all text is fully editable and behaves as if it were in a word processor. A special word or letter of the text can be given its own text style or color. Everything you have learned about defining a new text style also applies to multiline text, as both kinds of text use the same text styles, saved with the drawing file. Just as polylines become lines when exploded, multi-line text is reduced to single line text when exploded.

  Dimensions use multiline text, and any text that is imported into an AutoCAD drawing from a word processing document or text editor will become multiline text in the drawing. In this section, you will learn how to place a paragraph of multiline text in the cabin drawing and then modify it. In Skill 11, *Dimensioning a Drawing*, you will work with dimension text and text with leader lines, both of which use multiline text.

1. Click the Make Object's Layer Current button on the left end of the Object Properties toolbar, and click the FRONT ELEVATION text to make the Text1 layer current. Zoom into the blank area to the left of the title block, in the lower-left corner of the cabin drawing.

2. Type **t** ↵, or click the Text button on the Draw toolbar, or pick Draw ➢ Text ➢ Multiline Text. Any of these will start the Multiline Text Command. At the Command window, you are shown the name of the current text style and height, and are prompted to specify a first corner.

3. Pick a point near the left border line in line with the top of the title block. The prompt now reads
    `Specify opposite corner or Height/Justify/Rotation/Style/Width]:`
    which are all the options for the Multiline Text command.

4. If the current style is Label go on to step 5. Otherwise type **s** ↵ for the style option and type **label** ↵.

5. Drag open a window to define the length of line for the multiline text (Figure 10.33), and click to finish the window.

6. The Multiline Text Editor dialog box opens, and you can see a long blank area with a flashing cursor in it. This is where you will type in the text. In the drop-down lists at the top, you can see the font and height of the current text style.

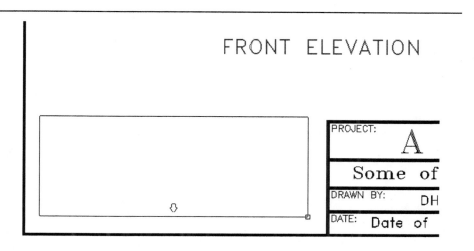

FRONT ELEVATION

PROJECT:

A

Some of

DRAWN BY: DH

DATE: Date of

FIGURE 10.33: Making a Multiline text window

FIGURE 10.33: Making a Multiline text window

7. Type in the following text, using single spacing and pressing Enter only at the end of each note:

GENERAL NOTES:

1. **All work shall be in accordance with the 1990 Ed. Uniform Building Code and all local ordinances.**

2. **Roof can be built to be steeper for climates with heavy snowfall.**

3. **Solar panels available for installation on roof.**

4. **All windows to be double-paned.**

When finished, press OK. The text is placed in the drawing (Figure 10.34a). The window you specified was only used to define the line length. Its height does not control how far down the text will come, as that is determined by how much text you enter.

8. Click the Properties button on the Object Properties toolbar, then pick anywhere on the new text and press ↵. The Modify MText dialog box comes up.

9. Change the Text Height to 9 and click OK. The text is redrawn smaller and now fits better in the space available (Figure 10.34b).

Skill 10

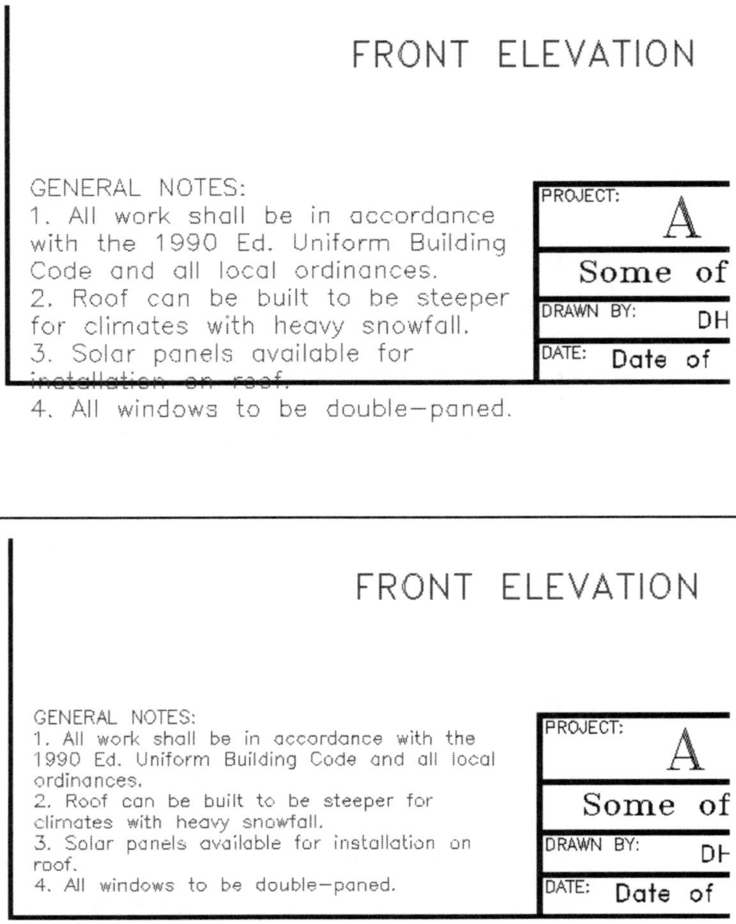

FRONT ELEVATION

GENERAL NOTES:
1. All work shall be in accordance
with the 1990 Ed. Uniform Building
Code and all local ordinances.
2. Roof can be built to be steeper
for climates with heavy snowfall.
3. Solar panels available for
installation on roof.
4. All windows to be double-paned.

PROJECT:	A
Some of	
DRAWN BY:	DH
DATE:	Date of

FRONT ELEVATION

GENERAL NOTES:
1. All work shall be in accordance with the
1990 Ed. Uniform Building Code and all local
ordinances.
2. Roof can be built to be steeper for
climates with heavy snowfall.
3. Solar panels available for installation on
roof.
4. All windows to be double-paned.

PROJECT:	A
Some of	
DRAWN BY:	DH
DATE:	Date of

FIGURE 10.34: MText in the drawing (a) and modified to be smaller (b)

10. Restart the Properties command and select the text again and press ⏎. In the
     Modify MText dialog box, click Full Editor. The Multiline Text Editor dialog
     box comes up.

11. Move the cursor to the upper-left corner of the window containing the text, in front of the *G* in the first word, and hold down the left mouse button and drag to the right and down until all text is highlighted. Then release the mouse button.

12. In the fonts drop-down list, select SansSerif to be the current font. The selected text will change to the new font.

13. Click OK, and, in the Modify MText dialog box, click OK again. The MText in the drawing has become more compact and there is room for more notes (Figure 10.35).

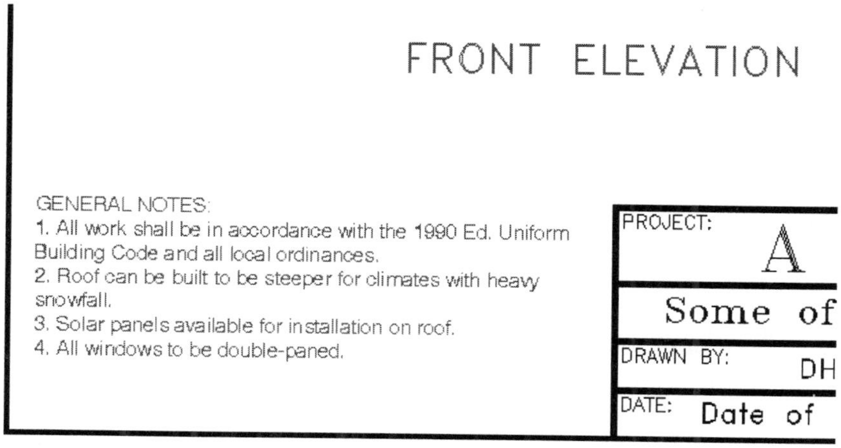

FRONT ELEVATION

GENERAL NOTES:
1. All work shall be in accordance with the 1990 Ed. Uniform Building Code and all local ordinances.
2. Roof can be built to be steeper for climates with heavy snowfall.
3. Solar panels available for installation on roof.
4. All windows to be double-paned.

PROJECT: A

Some of

DRAWN BY: DH

DATE: Date of

FIGURE 10.35: The results of a font modification

The SansSerif is a TrueType font supported by Windows, and, when used in AutoCAD drawings, can be italicized or boldface. To see how to change individual words within the text, we will underline and boldface "Uniform Building Code."

1. Restart the Properties command, select the MText again and press ↵. The Modify MText dialog box appears again. Click Full Editor to bring up the Multiline Text Editor dialog box.

2. Use the same technique used earlier to highlight "Uniform Building Code," then click the Bold and Underline buttons at the top of the Modify MText dialog box. The selected text is underlined and boldfaced.

3. Click OK, then click OK again. The text is redrawn with the changes (Figure 10.36).

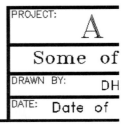

FRONT ELEVATION

GENERAL NOTES:
1. All work shall be in accordance with the 1990 Ed. **Uniform Building Code** and all local ordinances.
2. Roof can be built to be steeper for climates with heavy snowfall.
3. Solar panels available for installation on roof.
4. All windows to be double-paned.

PROJECT: A
Some of
DRAWN BY: DH
DATE: Date of

FIGURE 10.36: The MText with individual words modified

Individual words can also be italicized and given a different color or height than the rest of the MText, by using the other tools at the top of the Multiline Text Editor dialog box. You are encouraged to experiment with all these tools to become familiar with them.

The length of a line can be easily altered to make the MText fit more conveniently on the drawing. Let's say you've decided to put your company logo to the left of the title block. You need to squeeze the text into a narrower space. You have some extra room at the bottom, so you should be able to do it.

1. At the Command: prompt, select the text. Four grips appear at the corners of the body of MText.

2. Click the upper-right grip to activate it.

3. Slowly move the cursor to the left, stopping periodically until the defining rectangle appears. When the bottom of the rectangle gets close to the bottom line of the border, you will have moved about ⅓ of the way to the left border line (Figure 10.37a).

4. Click the mouse button, then press Esc twice. The text is squeezed into a narrower space but still fits on the page (Figure 10.37b).

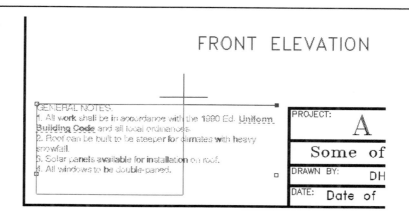

FIGURE 10.37: Modifying the MText line length with grips (a) and the results (b)

5. Zoom to extents, then zoom out a little (Figure 10.38). You won't be able to read the MText at this magnification, but it will look fine when you print your drawing.

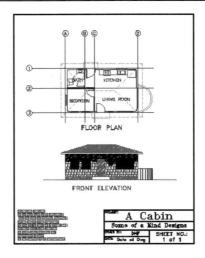

FLOOR PLAN

FRONT ELEVATION

A Cabin
Some of a Kind Designs
SHEET NO.:
1 of 1

FIGURE 10.38: The full drawing

6. Save this drawing as Cabin10c.

MText has justification points similar to those of single line text, and they behave the same way. The default justification point for MText, however, is the upper-left corner of the body of text, and the available options are for nine points distributed around the perimeter of the body of text and at the center (Figure 10.39).

This completes the exercises for this skill. If you want to play around with the MText, it can be edited with the Multiline Text Edit dialog box by picking Modify ➤ Object ➤ Text and selecting the text you need to edit.

With both MText and single line text, you can add special characters—degree symbol, diameter symbol, etc.—which are not included in most font character packages. You will have a chance to do this in the next skill.

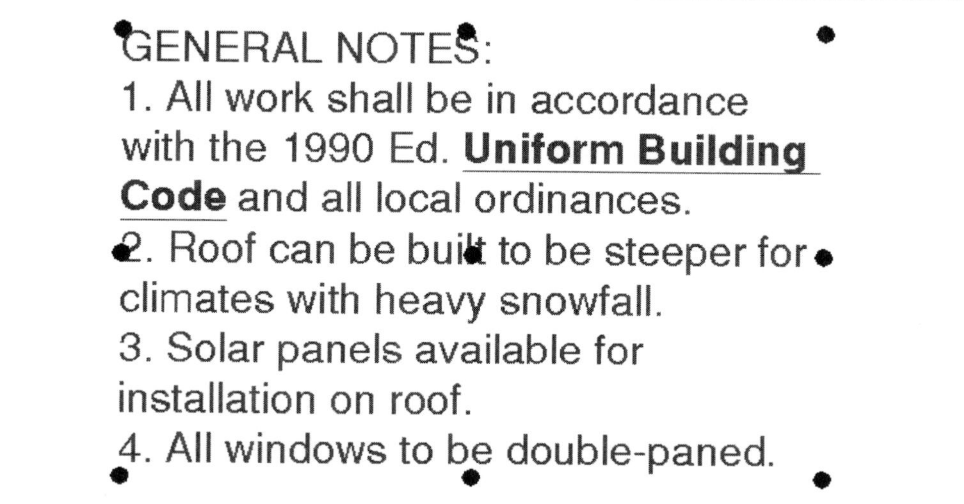

GENERAL NOTES:
1. All work shall be in accordance
with the 1990 Ed. **Uniform Building
Code** and all local ordinances.
2. Roof can be built to be steeper for
climates with heavy snowfall.
3. Solar panels available for
installation on roof.
4. All windows to be double-paned.

FIGURE 10.39: Justification points for MText

Are You Experienced?

Now you can...

- ☑ set up text styles
- ☑ place single line text in a drawing for titles and room labels
- ☑ create a grid for a drawing
- ☑ modify single line text
- ☑ construct a title block and place text in it
- ☑ place MText in a drawing
- ☑ modify MText in several ways

Dimensioning a Drawing

- ➔ Setting up a dimension style
- ➔ Dimensioning the floor plan of the cabin
- ➔ Modifying existing dimensions
- ➔ Modifying existing dimension styles

Dimensions are the final ingredient to be added to your drawing. To introduce you to dimensioning, we are going to follow a pattern similar to the one we used in the previous skill on text.

Dimension Styles

Dimension styles are similar to text styles, but are more complex. They are set up the same way, but there are many parameters controlling the various parts of dimensions, including the dimension text.

Before you start setting up a dimension style, you need to make a few changes to your drawing to prepare it for dimensioning.

1. Open up Cabin10c and zoom into the upper half of the drawing.

2. Create a new layer called Dim1, assign it a color, and make it current.

3. Create a new text style called Dim using the following criteria:

    -   romand.shx font
    -   0'-0" height
    -   0.8000 width factor
    -   leave all other settings as the default

If you need a reminder on creating text styles, refer to Skill 10, *Controlling Text in a Drawing*.

4. Apply this text style to make it current, then close the Text Style dialog box.

5. Freeze the Grid layer.

6. Set Endpoint Osnap to be running.

7. Select View ➢ Toolbars and enable the Dimension toolbar. The toolbar will appear on the drawing area. Close the Toolbar dialog box.

8. Move the Dimension toolbar to the top center of the drawing area, being careful to avoid docking it. (In Skill 1, *Getting to Know AutoCAD*, you learned about moving toolbars around on the screen.) Your drawing will look like Figure 11.1.

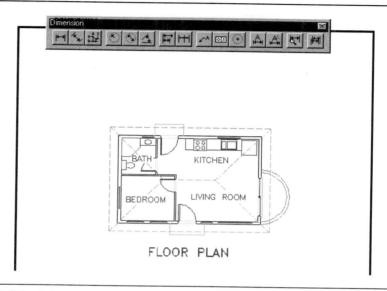

FIGURE 11.1: The floor plan of Cabin10c with the Dimension toolbar centered at the top of the drawing area

Making a New Dimension Style

Each dimension has several components: the dimension line, arrows or tick marks, extension lines, and dimension text (Figure 11.2). The appearance and location of each of these components is controlled by an extensive set of variables that is stored with each drawing file. You will work with these variables through a series of dialog boxes that have been designed to make setting up a dimension style as easy and trouble-free as possible. Remember that AutoCAD has been designed to be useable by drafters from many trades and professions, each of which has its own standards for drafting. To satisfy the widely varied dimensioning needs of these folks, AutoCAD dimensioning features have many options and settings for controlling the appearance and placement of the dimensions in your drawings.

Skill 11

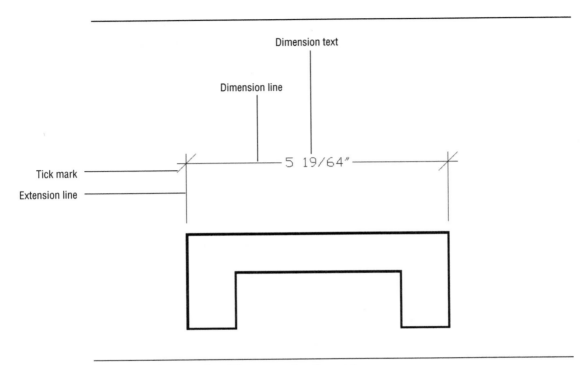

FIGURE 11.2: The parts of a dimension

Naming a Dimension Style

Every dimension variable has a default setting, and these as a group comprise the default Standard dimension style. As in defining text styles, the procedure is to make a copy of the Standard dimension style and rename the copy—in effect, making a new style which is a copy of the default style. Then you make changes to this new style so it has the settings you need to dimension your drawing.

1. Click the Dimension Style button on the Dimension toolbar. The Dimension Styles dialog box comes up. At the top, in the Dimension Style area, Standard is in both the Current and the Name text boxes.

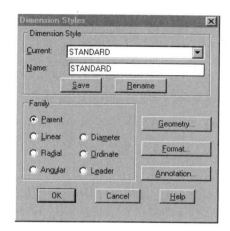

2. Click and drag the cursor across Standard in the Name text box to highlight it, then type **plan1** and click Save. Plan1 replaces Standard in the Current text box, and at the bottom of the dialog box, a message says "Created Plan1 from Standard." You have created a new dimension style for this drawing called Plan1. It is identical to the default Standard style. Now you will make some changes to this style.

Using the Geometry Dialog Box

You will use the Geometry dialog box to control the appearance of several dimensioning features.

1. Click the Geometry button on the Dimension Styles dialog box. The Geometry dialog box appears. This is where you control the appearance of the dimension lines, extension lines, arrowheads, and center marks. Also, in the Scale area at the bottom, you set the overall scale.

2. In the Arrowheads area, click Closed Filled in the first text box to activate the drop-down list of arrowheads.

3. Click Architectural Tick. The drop-down list closes with Architectural Tick displayed in the text box and a graphic of the new arrowhead type displayed above.

4. In the Size text box, change 0'-0 ³⁄₁₆" to 0'-⅛".

5. In the Dimension Line area, change the Extension distance from 0" to ³⁄₃₂". This will extend the dimension line past the tick mark a short distance.

6. In the Extension Line area, change the Extension distance from 0'-0 ³⁄₁₆" to ⅛". This controls how far the extension line will extend beyond the dimension line.

7. At the bottom, change the Overall Scale to 96.0. This will adjust all settings by the scale factor of the scale at which we will ultimately be plotting: ⅛"=1'-0". The settings in the Geometry dialog box will look like Figure 11.3.

8. Click OK to close the Geometry dialog box.

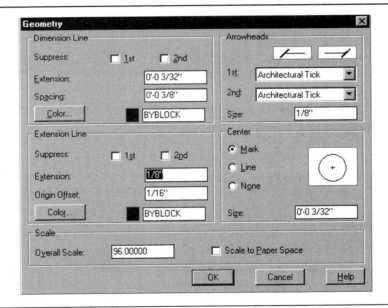

FIGURE 11.3: The Geometry dialog box with setting changes

Before saving these changes, make some more modifications to the Plan1 style.

Using the Format Dialog Box

The settings in the Format dialog box control how the dimension text is located relative to the dimension and extension lines.

1. Click the Format button on the Dimension Styles dialog box. The Format dialog box opens. There are three areas with icon graphics that illustrate how particular settings affect the location of dimension text. The icons themselves can be clicked to change the settings. In the upper-right corner of the dialog box is the Text area, where there is an icon and two checkboxes. This controls whether dimension text is always oriented horizontally or will follow the direction of the dimension line.

2. Click the icon in the Text area. Both checkmarks are cleared, and the icon changes to show that dimension text orientation will always be parallel to the dimension line. Below the Text area is the Vertical Justification area, again with an icon, as well as a drop-down list. It controls whether the dimension text is placed in the middle of the dimension line or above it.

3. Open the drop-down list in the Vertical Justification area to see the options, then select Above. The icon changes to show that text will always be above the dimension line, and the drop-down list now has Above in its text box. These are all the changes you need to make in this dialog box for now. It should look like Figure 11.4.

4. Click OK to close the Format dialog box. You need to make a few more changes.

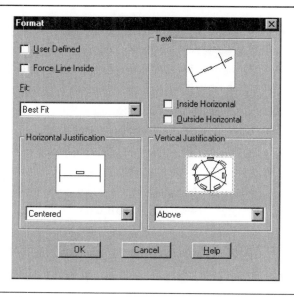

FIGURE 11.4: The Format dialog box with settings changed

Using the Annotation Dialog Box

The last few setting changes you need to make for the Plan1 dimension style are made in the Annotation dialog box and, from within it, the Primary Units dialog box. These two dialog boxes contain a few settings for controlling dimension text appearance that we need to change, and also several settings for tolerances and alternate units that we won't be working with in this book. There's only a few changes to make here.

1. Click the Annotation button on the Dimension Styles dialog box. The Annotation dialog box appears.

2. In the upper-left corner—in the Primary Units area—click the Units button. The Primary Units dialog box is displayed. Even though you have set the units for your drawing to Architectural (feet and inches), dimension units operate independently and must be set separately, in this dialog box.

3. Click the Units drop-down list to open it, and select Architectural.

4. Directly below, in the Zero Suppression area, clear the checkmark next to 0 Inches. This will direct AutoCAD to display 0" along with the feet when the distance is an even number of feet, as in 16'-0". Leave the 0 Feet box checked so that a distance less than 1' will have only inches and *not* be expressed as, for example, 0'-6". (These are Architectural standards widely accepted in the profession.)

5. These are the only changes necessary in this dialog box. It should look like Figure 11.5. Click OK to close this dialog box and return to the Annotation dialog box. The changes you need to make here are all in the Text area in the lower-right corner.

6. Open the Style drop-down list in the Text area, and select Dim to be the text style for dimensions.

7. Change the height from 0'-0 ³⁄₁₆" to 0'-0 ³⁄₃₂".

8. Change the Gap setting from ³⁄₃₂" to ¹⁄₁₆". When dimension text is placed above the dimension line, this setting controls the distance between the dimension text and the dimension line.

9. The dialog box will look like Figure 11.6. Click OK to close the dialog box and return to the Dimension Styles dialog box.

10. Click Save. At the bottom of the dialog box, a message is displayed telling you that the changes have been saved to the Plan1 dimension style.

11. Click OK to close the Dimension Styles dialog box. You are ready to begin dimensioning your drawing.

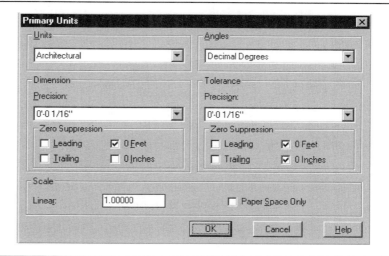

FIGURE 11.5: The Units dialog box with settings changed

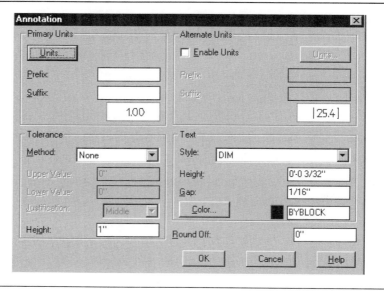

FIGURE 11.6: The Annotation dialog box with settings changed

You have made changes to 14 settings that control dimensions. This is not too many, considering that there are over 50 dimension settings. Here is a summary of the changes you've made to make the dimensions work with the cabin drawing:

Dialog Box	Setting	Default Setting	Plan1 Setting
Geometry	Arrowheads	Closed Filled	Architectural Tick
	Arrow size	³⁄₁₆"	⅛"
	Dim Line Extension	0"	³⁄₃₂"
	Ext. Line Extension	³⁄₁₆"	⅛"
	Overall Scale	1.0	96.0
Format	Text Horiz. Inside	On	Off
	Text Horiz. Outside	On	Off
	Text Vert. Justification	Centered	Above
Units	Primary Units	Decimal	Architectural
	Zero Suppression Units	On	Off
Annotation	Text Style	Standard	Dim
	Height	³⁄₁₆"	³⁄₃₂"
	Gap	³⁄₃₂"	¹⁄₁₆"

You will change a few more settings as you begin to dimension the cabin in the next set of exercises.

Placing Dimensions on the Drawing

Upon returning to your drawing, it should still look like Figure 11.1, and it should have the following:

- A new layer called Dim1 which is current
- A new text style called Dim which is current
- The Grid layer frozen
- Endpoint Osnap running

Horizontal Dimensions

You will dimension first across the top of the plan, from the corner of the building to the center of the interior wall, then to the other corner. Then you'll dimension the roof.

1. Click the Linear button at the left end of the Dimension toolbar to activate the *Linear command*. The prompt reads First extension line origin or press ENTER to select:.

2. Pick the upper-left corner of the cabin walls. The prompt changes to Second extension line origin:. At this point, zoom into the bathroom area where you can see the wall between the bathroom and kitchen close up.

3. Type x ↵ to start point filters.

4. Activate Midpoint Osnap and click the upper jamb line of the bathroom door opening when the triangle appears at the jamb's midpoint (Figure 11.7).

5. Click the upper-left corner of the cabin walls again. The dimension appears in ghosted form attached to and moving with the cursor (Figure 11.8a). Notice that the right extension line starts just outside the outer wall line, the result of using the point filters.

6. Pan the drawing down until there's room to place the dimension, then move the cursor until the dimension line is about 3' above the back step, then click to place it (Figure 11.8b).

Your first dimension has been completed.

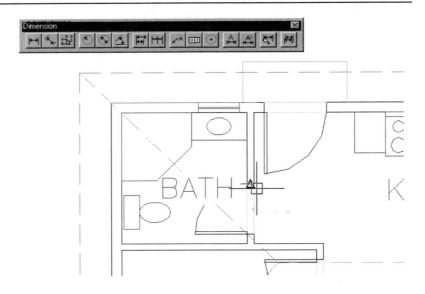

FIGURE 11.7: Selecting the jamb with Midpoint Osnap

When dimensioning walls, you usually dimension to the outside of the exterior ones and to the center of the interior ones. The next dimension will run from the right side of the first one, to the right corner.

 NOTE When dimensioning buildings which have 2x4 or 2x6 stud walls, architects usually make the dimensions show the distance to the face of the stud for the outside walls, but we are not able to go into that level of detail in this book. (Studs are the small, upright members in the framing of a wall.)

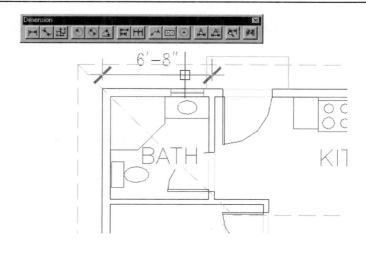

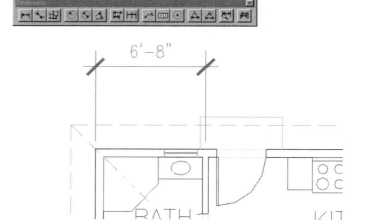

FIGURE 11.8: The dimension attached to the cursor (a) and placed (b)

The Continue Command

AutoCAD has an automatic way of placing adjacent dimensions in line—the *Continue command*.

1. Zoom out and pan until you have a view of the upper wall and roof line, with space above them for dimensions (Figure 11.9).

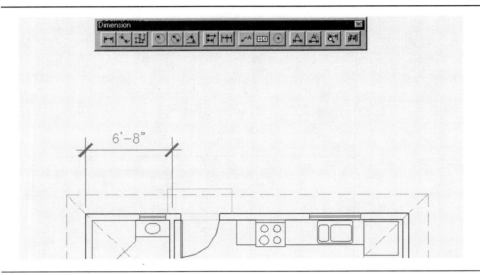

FIGURE 11.9: The result of zooming and panning for a view of the top of the floor plan

2. Select the Continue button of the Dimension toolbar. The prompt reads `Specify a second extension line origin or (Undo/<Select>):`. All you need to do here is pick a point for the right end of the dimension—in this case, the upper-right corner of the walls.

3. Click the upper-right corner of the house. The second dimension is drawn in line with the first (Figure 11.10). Note that the same prompt has returned to the Command window. You could keep picking points to place the next adjacent dimension in line. Press Esc to cancel the Continue command.

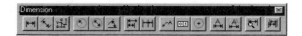

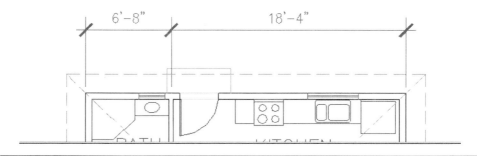

FIGURE 11.10: The completion of the Continue command

With the Continue command, you can dimension along a wall of a building very quickly just by picking points. AutoCAD assumes that the last extension line specified for the previous dimension will coincide with the first extension line of the next dimension. If the extension line you need to continue from is not the last one specified, press ↵ at the prompt, then pick the extension line you want to continue from, and continue the command.

Another automatic routine that can be used with linear dimensions is called Baseline.

The Baseline Command

The *Baseline command* gets its name from a style of dimensioning called baseline, in which all dimensions begin at the same point (Figure 11.11). Each dimension is stacked above the previous one. You can use the Baseline command for overall dimensions. AutoCAD will stack the overall dimension a set height above the incremental ones.

Skill 11

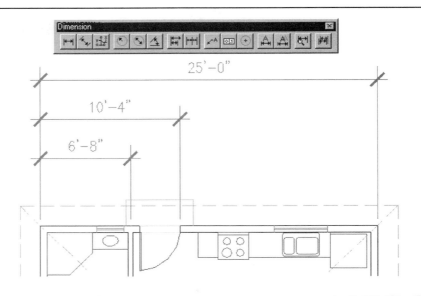

FIGURE 11.11: Example of baseline dimensions

1. Pick the Baseline button on the Dimension toolbar. The prompt reads
   Specify a second extension line origin or (Undo/<Select>):, just
   like the first prompt for the Continue command.

2. Press ↵ to choose the Select option.

3. Pick the extension line that extends to the upper-left corner—the first
   extension line of the first dimension.

4. Pick the upper-right corner of the walls. The overall dimension is drawn
   over the first two dimensions (Figure 11.12). Press Esc to cancel the Baseline
   command. (The Baseline command will keep running until you cancel it,
   just like the Continue command.)

The Baseline command assumes the baseline is the first extension line of the
last dimension. For the cabin, that would be the extension line that extends
to the center of the interior wall. You want the baseline to be the upper-left
corner, so you pressed ↵ to select another extension line to be the baseline.

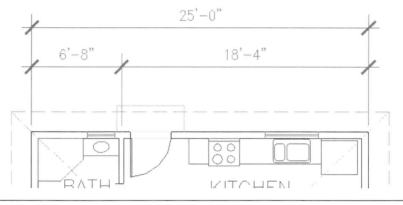

FIGURE 11.12: The completion of the overall dimension with the Baseline command

It would be nice to have a dimension for the roof spaced the same distance above the overall dimension, as the overall dimension is spaced above the incremental dimensions. The Baseline command can help you do this.

1. Start the Baseline command again and press ↵ for the Select option.

2. Pick the extension line for the upper-left corner of the walls as the baseline.

3. Pick the upper-right corner of the roof. A dimension is placed above the overall dimension (Figure 11.13a). Press Esc to cancel the Baseline command. To finish it, you need to move the left extension line of this last dimension to the upper-left corner of the roof.

4. Click the text of the roof dimension. Grips appear in five places on the dimension, and the dimension ghosts (Figure 11.13b).

5. Click the grip at the bottom of the left extension line to activate it.

6. Click the upper-left corner of the roof, then press ↵ twice. The extension line moves, and the dimension text is updated to display the full length of the roof (Figure 11.13c).

This completes the horizontal dimensions for the floor plan.

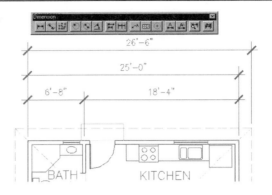

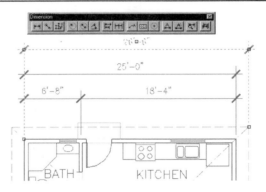

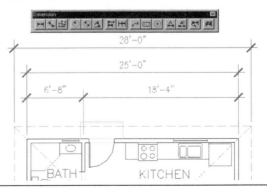

FIGURE 11.13: The result of the second use of the Baseline command (a), starting grips to modify the dimension (b), and the results (c)

Vertical Dimensions

Because the Linear command can be used for vertical and horizontal dimensions, you can follow the same steps as above to do the vertical dimensions on the left side of the floor plan. The only difference here from the horizontal dimensioning is that there is no jamb line which can be used with point filters to establish the center of the interior wall between the bedroom and bathroom. You will have to draw a guideline—the same one you drew in the last skill to help make the grid. The following steps will take you through the process of placing the first vertical dimension. Then you'll be able to finish the rest of them by yourself.

1. Pan and zoom to get a good view of the left side of the floor plan, including the space between the roof and the border (Figure 11.14).

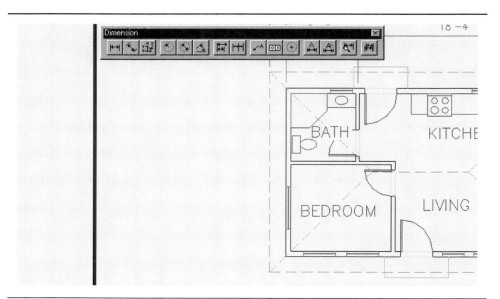

FIGURE 11.14: The result of zooming and panning for a view of the left side of the floor plan

Skill 11

2. Draw a guideline between the two horizontal interior wall lines where they meet the exterior wall (Figure 11.15a). Endpoint Osnap should be running, and you should be able to do this without having to zoom in.

3. Click the Linear button. Then pick the upper-left corner of the walls.

4. Type .y ↵ to start the point filters, pick Midpoint Osnap, and move the cursor to the short guideline you just drew. When the triangle appears on the line, click the mouse.

5. Click again on the upper-left corner of the walls to complete the point filter process. The vertical dimension appears in ghosted form, attached to the cursor.

6. Move the dimension line to a point about 3' to the left of the roof line and click. The first vertical dimension is drawn (Figure 11.15b).

7. Erase the short guideline from between the interior walls.

Finishing the Vertical Dimensions

The rest of the vertical dimensions are placed using the same procedure as was used to complete the horizontal dimensions. Here is a summary of the steps:

- Use the Continue command to dimension the bedroom.

- Use the Baseline command to place an overall dimension.

- Use the Baseline command to place a roof dimension to the left of the overall dimension.

- Use grips to move the first extension line of the roof dimension to its corner.

Refer back through this section if you need more detailed instructions. The completed vertical dimensions will look like Figure 11.16.

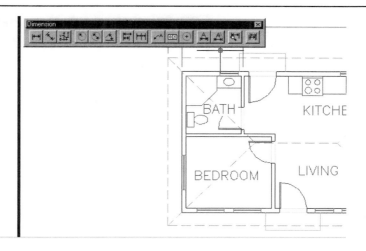

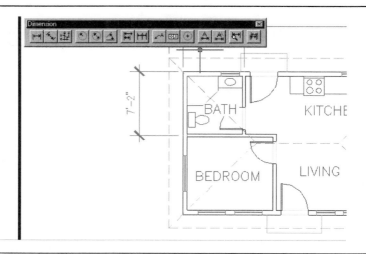

FIGURE 11.15: A guideline is drawn to help find the center of an interior wall (a) and the first vertical dimension is placed (b).

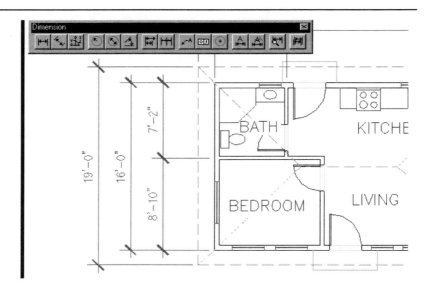

FIGURE 11.16: The completed vertical dimensions

The next area to dimension will be the balcony.

1. Pan to a view of the balcony and the space to the right of it.

2. Start the Linear command and pick the lower-right corner of the building walls.

3. Use Quadrant Osnap and pick near the right-most edge of the outside balcony wall.

4. When the dimension appears, move it down below the roof line and place it there (Figure 11.17).

This will be enough vertical and horizontal linear dimensions for now. Take a look at some other kinds of dimensions.

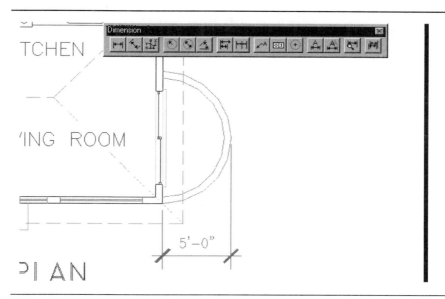

FIGURE 11.17: The horizontal balcony dimension

Other Types of Dimensions

AutoCAD provides tools for placing linear dimensions which are neither vertical nor horizontal, as well as radial and angular dimensions. You'll use the *Radial command* to dimension the inside radius of the balcony.

Radial Dimensions

On the Dimension toolbar, there are buttons for Radius and Diameter dimensions. They both operate the same way and are controlled by the same settings.

1. Double-click the Osnap button on the status bar to temporarily disable any running Osnaps.

2. Click the Radius Dimension button to start the Dimradius command.

 NOTE   Most of the commands used for dimensioning are prefaced with a "dim" when you enter them at the command line, and that is the actual name of the command. For example, when you click the Radius Dimension button on the Dimension toolbar or pick Dimension ➤ Radius on the menu bar, you will see _dimradius in the Command window to let you know that you have started the Dimradius command. The same command can be started by typing **dimradius** ↵ or **dra** ↵ (the shortcut alias).

3. Click the inside arc of the balcony. The radius dimension appears in ghosted form, and its angle of orientation is controlled by the cursor. The radial line changes as you move the cursor from inside the arc to outside it (Figure 11.18a, b).

4. Notice that the tick mark used for linear dimensions is used here also. We must have an arrowhead for the radial dimension. Press Esc to cancel the command.

We will have to alter the dimension style to specify an arrowhead for radial dimensions.

Parent and Child Dimensioning Styles

The Plan1 dimension style you set up at the beginning of this chapter applies to all dimensions and is called the *parent* dimension style, but you can change settings in this dimension style for particular types of dimensions, like, say, the radial type. This makes a *child* dimension style. The *child* version is based on the *parent* version, but has a few settings that are different. In this way, all your dimensions will be made using the Plan1 dimension style, but radial dimensions will be

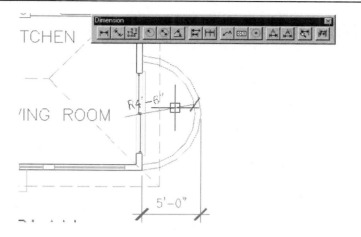

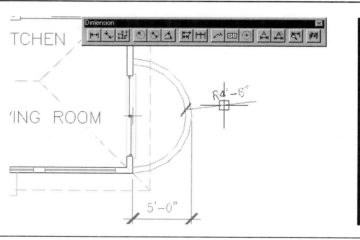

FIGURE 11.18: The radius dimension inside the arc (a) and outside it (b)

using a child version of the style, while most other dimensions will be using the parent version of the style. Once you create a child dimension style from the parent style, you then refer to both styles by the same name, but you call them a dimension style family.

1. Click the Dimension Style button on the Dimension toolbar to bring up the Dimension Styles dialog box. It will look like Figure 11.19.

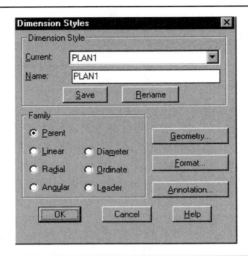

FIGURE 11.19: The Dimension Styles dialog box with Plan1 current

2. In the Family area, click the radio button next to Radial. Any changes you make to the dimension style settings will only affect radial dimensions (radius and diameter).

3. Click the Geometry button to bring up the Geometry dialog box.

4. In the upper-right corner, click the 1st Architectural Tick.

5. Select Right-Angle. Click OK to close the Geometry dialog box.

6. Click Save, then click OK to close the Dimension Styles dialog box.

7. Click the Radius button on the Dimension toolbar.

8. Click the inside arc of the balcony. The radius dimension appears in ghosted form, and it now has an arrow instead of a tick mark.

9. Move the cursor to the outside of the balcony, and place the dimension so it looks similar to Figure 11.20.

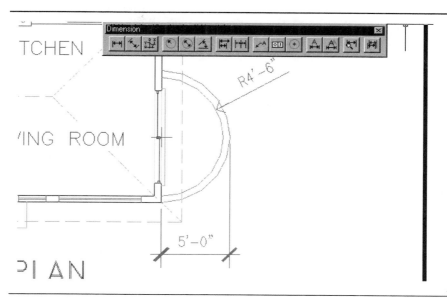

FIGURE 11.20: The radius dimension for the balcony

When the dimension text for a radius or diameter dimension is on the outside of the arc or circle, a cross is placed at the center of the arc or circle. When the text is inside, there is no cross. When placing the dimension, you have control over the angle of the dimension line and the location of the dimension text on that line.

The balcony also needs to be identified in the drawing as the rooms are.

Leader Lines

You can use the *Leader Line command* to draw an arrow to the balcony and place the text outside the arcs. The Leader Line dimension also requires an adjustment of a few dimension style settings.

1. Click the Dimension Styles button on the Dimension toolbar.

2. In the Family area, click Leader.

3. Click Geometry, then click Architectural Tick in the first Arrowhead text box. Select Right-Angle, then click OK.

4. Open the Format dialog box. In the Vertical Justification area, change Above to Centered, then click OK.

5. Click Save, then click OK. A child Plan1 dimension style has been created. It's identical to the regular Plan1 style except for the two settings you just changed.

6. Click the Leader button on the Dimension toolbar. Pick a point inside the balcony.

7. Turn Ortho off and drag the line to the outside of the balcony, making the line approximately parallel to the radius dimension line and pick a point (Figure 11.21a). The prompt now reads `To point (Format/Annotation/Undo) <Annotation>:`.This prompt is telling you that you can continue picking points to make a multi-segmented leader line, change the format to make a curved leader line, or press ↵ to begin entering the leader text.

8. Press ↵, then, with Caps Lock on, type **balcony** ↵. The prompt changes to read `Mtext:`, which gives you the opportunity to enter multiple lines of text for the leader. Press ↵. The leader line is completed and BALCONY is placed at the end of the line (Figure 11.21b).

 NOTE   If the angle of the leader line is steeper than 15°, a short horizontal line called a *dogleg* or *hook line* is added between the leader line and the text.

9. Zoom to extents, then zoom out a little and pan to view the whole drawing with dimensions.

10. Save this drawing as Cabin11a.

This exercise gets you started using the Leader command. In the section on modifying dimensions, later on in this skill, you will get another chance to work with leader lines and their text. Next, I have two more types of dimensions to introduce to you.

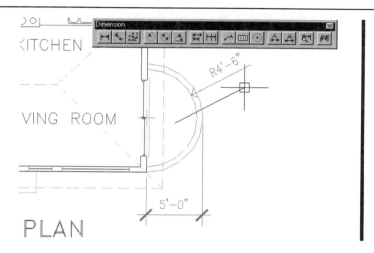

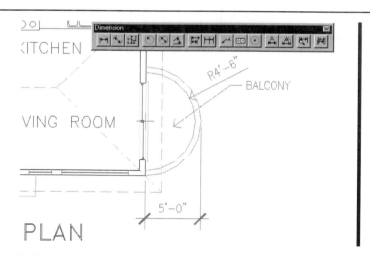

FIGURE 11.21: The leader line being drawn (a) and the completed leader (b)

Angular and Aligned Dimensions

To get you familiar with the Aligned and Angular dimension types, we'll set up a second dimension layer and make some changes to the appearance of the drawing.

1. Make the Roof layer current.

2. Freeze all other layers. Click the Layers button. In the Layer & Linetype Properties dialog box, click the left-most sun icon in the 0 layer row, then scroll down to the last layer on the list.

3. Hold down the Shift key and click the left-most sun icon in the row for the last layer.

4. Click OK in the warning box. The sun icon changes to a snowflake for all layers except the Roof layer (because it is the current layer).

5. Click OK to close the dialog box and return to the drawing. Everything has disappeared except the roof lines.

6. Zoom in to a closer view of the roof (Figure 11.22).

7. Create a new layer called Dim2, keep the black/white color, and make it current. Now you are ready to dimension.

Aligned Dimensions

Aligned dimensions are linear dimensions that are not horizontal or vertical. They are placed in the same way that horizontal or vertical dimensions are placed with the Linear command. You can also use the Baseline and Continue commands with aligned dimensions.

We'll use the *Aligned command* to dimension a hip line of the roof.

1. Double-click the Osnap button on the status bar to activate any running Osnaps (Endpoint should still be running). Then click the Aligned button on the Dimension toolbar.

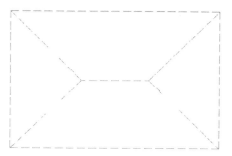

FIGURE 11.22: The zoomed-in view of the roof with all layers frozen except Roof and Dim2

2. Pick the right end of the roof's ridge line.

3. Be sure Ortho is off, then pick the upper-right corner of the roof. The dimension appears in ghosted form, and the cursor controls the position of the dimension line (Figure11.23a).

4. Move the cursor up and to the left. When the dimension line is a couple of feet above the hip line, click to place the dimension (Figure 11.23b).

The last type of dimension you need to learn about is the Angular dimension.

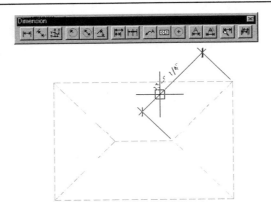

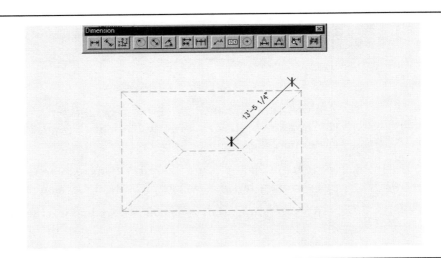

FIGURE 11.23: Placing an aligned dimension line (a) and the results (b)

Angular Dimensions

The angular dimension is the only basic dimension type that uses angles in the dimension text instead of linear measurements. Generally, tick marks are not used with angular dimensions, so we need to create another child dimension style for this type of dimension.

1. Open the Dimension Styles dialog box (click the Dimension Styles button on the Dimension toolbar).

2. In the Family area, click the Angular radio button.

3. Click the Geometry button, then, in the Arrowheads area, click the 1st Architectural Tick and select Right-Angle to replace it. Click OK.

4. Click Save, then click OK. Now angular dimensions will have arrows instead of tick marks.

5. Click the Angular button on the Dimension toolbar.

6. Pick the hip line you just dimensioned with the Aligned command, then pick the adjacent hip line below it. The angular dimension appears in ghosted form and the dimension line is attached to the cursor and moves with it.

7. Move the cursor around the point where the two hip lines intersect and, at the same time, move the cursor close to the hip line intersection, and then away from it (Figure 11.24a,b,c). The dimension can be placed in several different positions relative to the hip lines.

8. Position the cursor so the dimension line falls between the two hip lines but is far enough to the right for the dimension text to stay inside the hip lines, then click to fasten the dimension line to this location (Figure 11.25a).

The angular dimension is set, but the text is an angle with four decimal places. You need to adjust the dimension style so angles will display only two decimal places. To correct this, change the child dimension style for angular dimensions.

1. Open up the Dimension Styles dialog box. In the Family area, click the Angular radio button.

2. Click the Annotation button, then click the Units button. The Units area is deactivated because angular dimensions only use angular measurements. In the Dimension area on the left, click the Precision drop-down list and select 0.00. Click OK to close the dialog box.

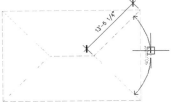

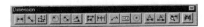

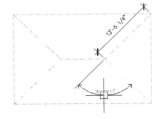

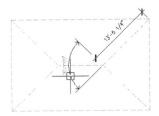

FIGURE 11.24: Various positions possible for the Angular dimension: between the hip lines (a), below the hip line intersection (b), and opposite the hip lines (c)

3. Click OK to close the Annotation dialog box. In the Dimension Styles dialog box, click Save, then click OK. In the drawing, the 90.0000° has been automatically revised to 90.00° (Figure 11.25b).

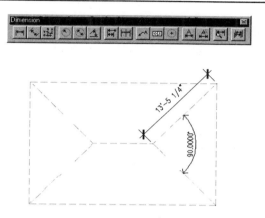

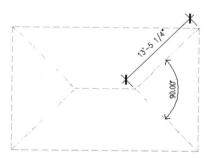

FIGURE 11.25: The completed angular dimension (a) and the same dimension with angular precision changed (b)

When settings for a dimension style are changed, dimensions created when that style was current will be automatically updated to reflect the changes. You'll do more modifications of dimensions in the next part of this skill.

You have been introduced to the basic types of dimensions—linear, radial, leader, and angular—and some auxiliary dimensions—baseline, continue, and aligned—that were special cases of the linear type. Baseline and continue can also be used with angular dimensions.

The final part of this skill will be devoted to teaching you a few methods for modifying various parts of dimensions.

Modifying Dimensions

Several commands, as well as grips, can be used to modify dimensions, depending on what the desired change is. You can:

- Change the dimension text content
- Move the dimension text
- Move the dimension or extension lines
- Change the dimension style settings for a dimension, or group of dimensions
- Revise a dimension style

The best way to understand how modifications of dimensions are achieved is by making a few yourself.

1. Thaw all layers and make the Dim1 layer current again.

2. Freeze the following layers:

   - Dim2
   - Grid
   - Hatch-plan-floor
   - Hatch-plan-walls

3. Zoom out and pan until your view of the floor plan is similar to Figure 11.26.

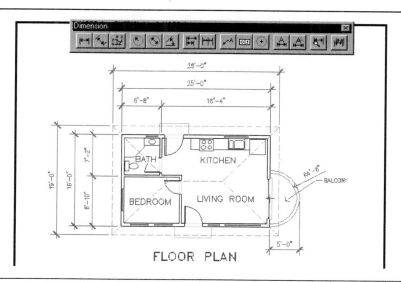

FIGURE 11.26: Modified view of the floor plan

Modifying Dimension Text

Any aspect of the dimension text can be modified. We'll look at how the content is changed first.

Editing Dimension Text Content

To change the content of text for one dimension, or to add text before or after the actual dimension, use the Ddedit command. (You used this command in Skill 10 to modify text.) We'll change the text in the horizontal dimensions for the roof and walls.

1. Type **ddedit ↵**, then select the horizontal roof dimension at the top of the drawing. The Multiline Text Editor dialog box appears. The angle brackets in the editing box represent the existing text in the dimension. You can highlight the brackets and enter a new dimension, or enter new text before or after the brackets.

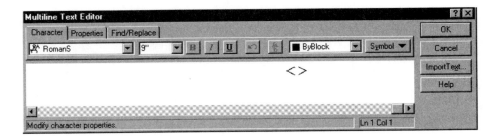

2. Click to the right of the brackets, then type (*space*)**verify in field** and click OK. The phrase is added to the dimension (Figure 11.27a). The prompt tells you that you can select another object to edit.

3. Click the dimension just below the last one.

4. In the Multiline Text Editor dialog box, click to the right of the angle brackets again, then click the Symbol button in the upper-right corner. A drop-down list gives three special characters and some other choices.

5. Select Plus/Minus. The ± symbol is now in the edit box.

6. Click OK. The dimension now has a ± after it (Figure 11.27b).

If you need to change the text of several dimensions at once, use the *Dimedit* *command*.

1. Click the Dimension Edit button on the Dimension toolbar.

2. At the `Dimension Edit (Home/New/Rotate/Oblique) <Home>`: prompt, type **n** ↵ to replace the existing text or add to it.

3. In the Multiline Text edit dialog box, highlight the angle brackets.

4. Type **Unknown** and click OK.

5. In the drawing, click on the 6'-8" and 18'-4" dimensions, then press ↵.

6. The two dimensions now read Unknown (Figure 11.28).

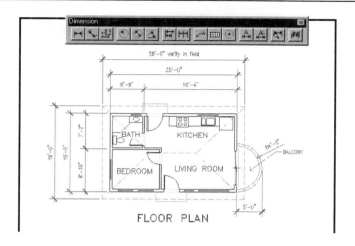

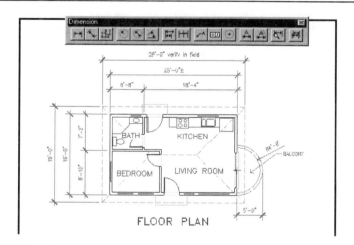

FIGURE 11.27: Adding a phrase to dimension text (a) and adding a special character (b)

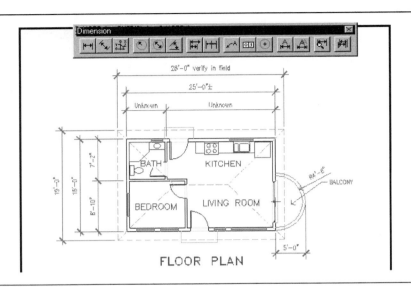

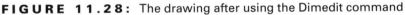

FIGURE 11.28: The drawing after using the Dimedit command

Next, you'll learn about moving the dimension text.

Moving Dimension Text Around

You can use grips to move dimension text and the dimension line.

1. Zoom in to the balcony area and set up a view that includes the entire balcony and its three dimensions.

2. At the Command: prompt, click the 5'-0" dimension. Grips appear.

3. Click the grip just below the dimension text to activate it.

4. Move the cursor up until the dimension text is above the balcony, then click again to fix it there (Figure 11.29). The dimension and line and text move to a new position, and the extension lines are redrawn to the new position. Press Esc twice.

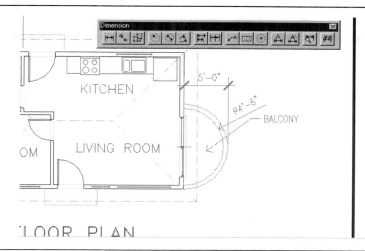

FIGURE 11.29: The linear dimension moved to a new position

5. Click the leader line, then click the word Balcony. Two grips appear on the leader line and one on the text (Figure 11.30a).

6. Hold down the Shift key and click the two grips near the text.

7. Click one of the two activated grips, then move the cursor down to reposition the leader and text as in Figure 11.30b, then click to fasten them there. Press Esc twice.

8. Click the 4'-6" radial dimension. Three grips appear.

9. Click the grip at the arrowhead.

10. Pick Nearest Osnap, then move the cursor to a position on the inside arc enough below the just relocated leader line to make the radial dimension line parallel to the leader line and pick that point (Figure 11.31a).

11. With grips still on the radial dimension, click the grip just under the dimension text.

12. Drag it down and to the right until it clears the leader line and its text. Then click again to fix it there. Press Esc twice (Figure 11.31b).

To finish the changes to the balcony, you need to suppress the left extension line of the 5'-0" dimension because it overlaps the wall and header lines.

Dimension Overrides

Suppression of the left extension line will be done with the Properties command, which allows you to change a setting in the dimension style for one dimension without altering the style settings.

1. Freeze the Headers layer.

2. Click the Properties button on the Object Properties toolbar.

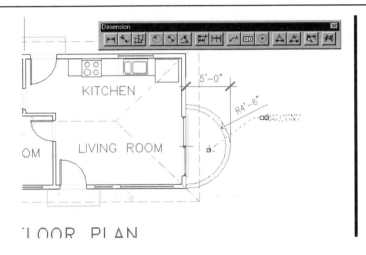

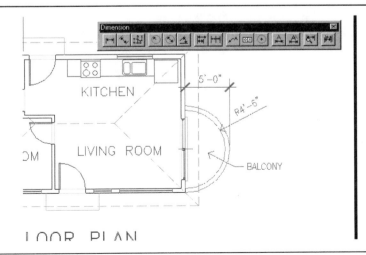

FIGURE 11.30: Moving the leader with grips (a) and the results (b)

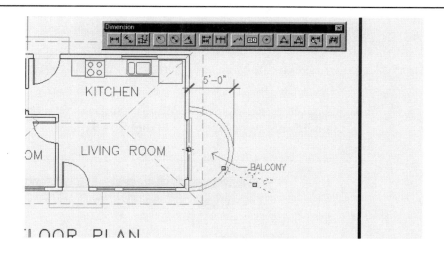

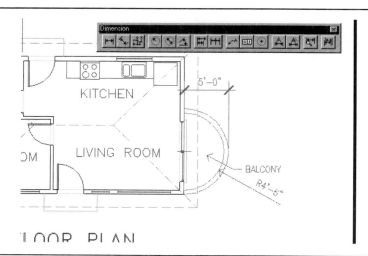

FIGURE 11.31: The radial dimension moved with grips (a) and the radial dimension text moved (b)

3. Click the 5'-0" dimension, then press ↵.

4. In the Modify Dimension dialog box, click the Geometry button on the right.

5. In the Extension Line area, put a checkmark in the Suppress 1st checkbox, then click OK.

6. Click OK again to close the Modify Dimension dialog box. The left extension line has been suppressed (Figure 11.32).

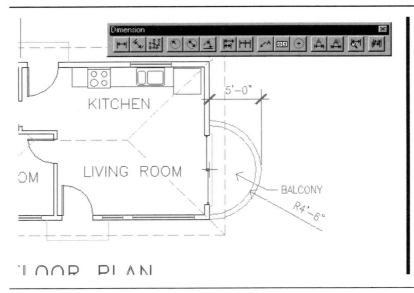

FIGURE 11.32: The 5'-0" dimension with the left extension line suppressed

The bedroom needs a horizontal dimension. Because of a shortage of space outside the floor plan, you'll place the dimension inside the bedroom and suppress both extension lines with an override to the current dimension style.

1. Pan the drawing over until the bedroom is fully in view.

2. Open the Dimension Styles dialog box and click the Geometry button.

3. In the Extensions area, put a checkmark in the Suppress 1st and 2nd checkboxes, then click OK.

4. In the Dimension Styles dialog box, do *not* click Save. Just click OK.

5. Click the Linear button on the Dimension toolbar.

6. Pick the lower-left inside corner, then pick the lower-right inside corner. The dimension appears in ghosted form, attached to the cursor.

7. Suppress the running Osnaps for one pick, then move the dimension up to a position below the BEDROOM text and above the lower wall, and click to fix it there. Move the dimension up to a position below the window and click to fix it there. The dimension is placed, and both extension lines have been suppressed (Figure 11.33).

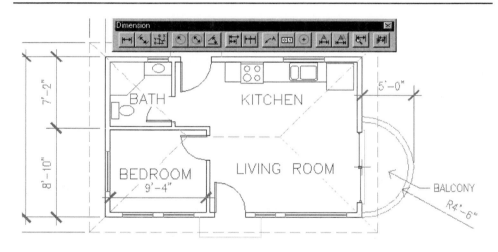

FIGURE 11.33: The completed bedroom dimension

8. Open the Dimension Styles dialog box. In the Current drop-down list, the current style is +Plan1. The + sign indicates the override style that was use to dimension the bedroom with suppressed extension lines. It needs to be deleted.

9. Click +Plan1 in the Current drop-down list to open it, then click Plan1. You are asked whether to save changes to the current style.

10. Click No. Plan1 replaces +Plan1 as the current dimension style and +Plan1 is deleted. Click OK to close the dialog box.

Extension lines are usually about the thinnest lines in a drawing, so it is usually not critical that they be suppressed in most cases. However, if a print were made with the Headers layer frozen, the left extension line of the 5'-0" dimension for the balcony would have to be suppressed or moved so it would not be visible spanning the sliding door opening.

Dimensioning Short Distances

When you have to dimension distances so short that the text and arrows (or tick marks) can't both fit between the extension line, a dimension style setting determines where they are placed. To see how this works, you'll redo the horizontal dimensions above the floor plan, this time dimensioning the distance between the roof line and wall line, as well as the thickness of the interior wall. By changing a dimension style setting, the text that won't fit between the extension lines will be placed above the dimension.

1. Zoom out to a view of the upper portion of the floor plan so the horizontal dimensions above the floor plan are visible (Figure 11.34).

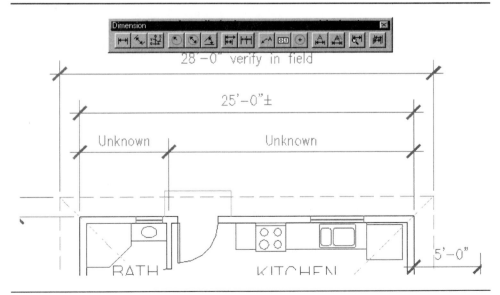

FIGURE 11.34: The new view of the upper floor plan and its dimensions

2. Use the Erase command to erase the four dimensions that are above the floor plan. Each dimension is a single object, so you can select them with four picks, or one crossing window.

3. Open the Dimension Styles dialog box and click Format.

4. Open the Fit drop-down menu in the upper-left corner and select No Leader. No Leader replaces Best Fit in the text box and the menu closes. Click OK to close the Format dialog box.

5. In the Dimension Styles dialog box, click Save, then click OK.

6. Select the Linear button and pick the upper-left corner of the roof, then pick the upper-left corner of the wall lines. Place the dimension line about 3' above the upper roof line (Figure 11.35a).

7. Select the Continue button and click the upper end of each interior wall line, then the upper-right corner of the wall lines, and finally the upper-right corner of the roof (Figure 11.35b). Press Esc to cancel the Continue command.

8. Click the Baseline button, press ↵, and then pick the left extension line of the 1'-6" dimension on the left end.

9. Click the upper-right corner of the roof. The overall dimension is placed a set distance above the lower dimensions (Figure 11.36a). Press Esc to cancel the Baseline command.

Because some of the text in the smaller of the lower dimensions was placed higher than normal, the overall dimension needs to be raised to clear that text.

1. Click the overall dimension. Grips appear. Click the grip at the intersection of the right extension line and the dimension line to activate it.

2. Move the cursor up until the dimension line clears the higher text on the lower dimensions. Press Esc twice (Figure 11.36b). The text of the two 1'-6" dimensions crosses over the outer extension lines.

3. You can move dimension text with grips. Click the right 1'-6" dimension. Grips appear. Click the grip right in the middle of the text, be sure Ortho is on, then move the text to the left until it clears the extension line, and click to place it.

4. Click the left 1'-6" dimension and repeat step 3, this time moving the text to the right.

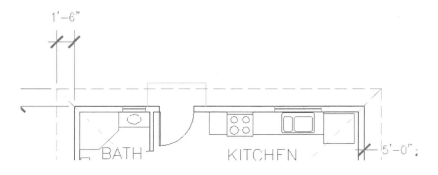

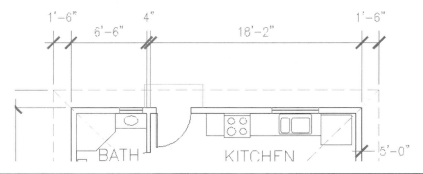

FIGURE 11.35: The first dimension is placed (a) and the other dimensions (b)

5. When the text is where you want it, press Esc twice to clear the grips (Figure 11.37).

When you use the No Leader option for the Fit setting in the Format dialog box, text that won't fit on its dimension line will be placed above the dimension and is moveable independent of the dimension line. This allows the flexibility to move the text to its optimum location.

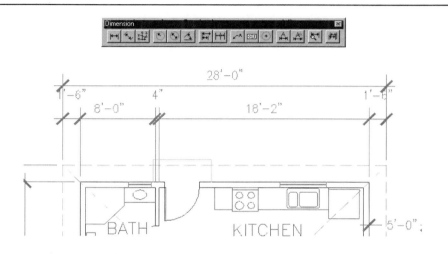

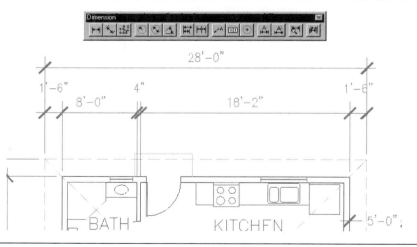

FIGURE 11.36: The overall dimension is placed using Baseline (a) and raised using grips (b).

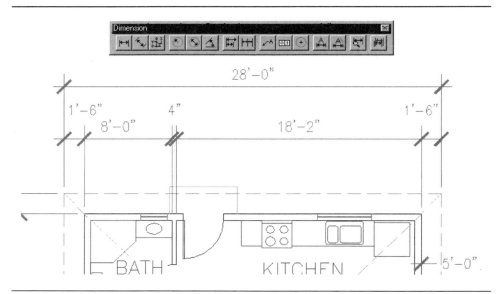

FIGURE 11.37: The 1'-6" dimensions are moved to clear the extension lines.

This concludes the exercises for dimensions in this skill. The current drawing won't be used in future skills, so feel free to experiment with the dimensioning commands you have just learned. When you finish a drawing session, before you save, it is a good habit to zoom to extents and then zoom out a little so all visible objects are on the screen. This way, the next time you bring up this drawing, you will have a full view of it at the beginning of your session.

1. Click the x in the upper right corner of the Dimension toolbar to close it.

2. Zoom to extents, then zoom out a little (Figure 11.38).

3. Save this drawing to your training folder as `Cabin11b`.

4. Take a break. You deserve one!

Working successfully with dimensions in your drawing requires an investment of time to become familiar with the commands and settings that control how dimensions appear, how they are placed in the drawing, and how they are modified. The exercises in this skill have led you through the basics of the dimension processes. For a thorough treatment of AutoCAD's dimensioning features, see *Mastering AutoCAD 14*, by George Omura, (Sybex, 1997).

The next skill will introduce you to external references, a tool for viewing a drawing from within another drawing.

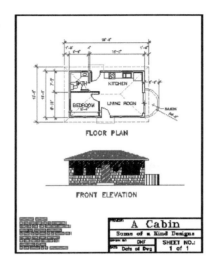

FIGURE 11.38: The full view of the cabin drawing with dimensions complete

Are You Experienced?

Now you can...

- ☑ create a new dimension style
- ☑ place vertical and horizontal dimensions in a drawing
- ☑ use radial, aligned, and angular dimensions
- ☑ create leader lines for notes
- ☑ modify dimension text
- ☑ override a dimension style
- ☑ modify a dimension style

Managing External References

- → **Understanding external references**
- → **Creating external references**
- → **Modifying external references**
- → **Converting external references into blocks**

*E*xternal references are dwg files which have been temporarily connected to the current drawing, and are used as information that anyone viewing the drawing may refer to. The externally referenced drawing is visible in the current drawing and its layers, colors, linetypes, and visibility can be manipulated, but its objects cannot be changed, and it is not a permanent part of the current drawing.

External references are similar to blocks in that they both behave as single objects, and they are inserted into a drawing in the same way. But blocks are part of the current drawing file and external references are not.

Blocks can be exploded and external references cannot. In Skill 7, you exploded the window block, changed it, and reblocked it, thereby updating all instances of the window block in the drawing. With an external reference—usually referred to as an *Xref*—the mechanism is different. Let's say Drawing A is current and Drawing B is the Xref file. To change Drawing B, you would make it current, change it, and save the changes. Then when you bring back up Drawing A, the changes you just made to Drawing B will show up automatically in Drawing A. In this example, Drawing A would be called the host drawing.

In order to be able to manage external references, you need to learn how to set up an Xref, manipulate its appearance in the host drawing, and update it. Before you set up the Xref, you will create a site plan for the cabin. Then you will Xref the cabin drawing into the site drawing (Figure 12.1). In this figure, the lines of the cabin floor plan comprise the Xref, and the rest of the objects are part of the host drawing.

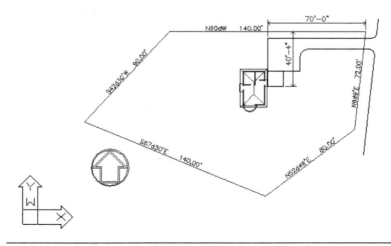

FIGURE 12.1: The site plan with the cabin as an external reference

Drawing a Site Plan

The site plan you will use has been simplified so that you can draw it with a minimum of steps and get on with the external referencing. These are the essential elements:

- Property lines
- Access road to the site
- North arrow
- Indication of where the building is located on the site

The first step is to draw in the property lines.

Using Surveyor Units

Property lines are drawn using surveyor units for angles and decimal feet for linear units. In laying out the property lines, you will use relative polar coordinates, so the form of the coordinates you enter will be *@distance<angle* where the distance is in feet and hundredths of a foot and the angle is in surveyor units to the nearest minute.

Surveyor Units

Surveyor units, called bearings in the civil engineering field, describe the direction of a line from its point of beginning. The direction, which is described as a deviation from the north or south to the east or west, is given as an angular measurement in degrees, minutes, and seconds. The angles used in a bearing can never be greater than 90°, so bearing lines must be headed in one of the 4 directional quadrants: north-easterly, north-westerly, south-easterly or south-westerly. If north is set to be at the top of a plot plan, then south is down, east is to the right and west is to the left. Thus, when a line from its beginning goes up and to the right, it will be headed in a north-easterly direction, and when a line from its beginning goes down and to the left, it is headed in a south-westerly direction etc. A line which is headed in a north-easterly direction with a deviation from true north of 30° and 30 minutes is shown as N30d30'E in AutoCAD notation.

Skill 12

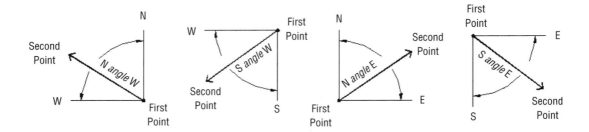

With the surveyor unit system, a sloping line which has an up-and-to-the-left direction would have a down-and-to-the-right direction if you started from the opposite end, so, for property lines, it is important to move in the same direction (clockwise or counter-clockwise) as you progress from one segment to the next.

Laying Out the Property Lines

You will set up a new drawing, and then start at the upper-right corner of the property and work your way around in a counter-clockwise direction.

1. Open Cabin11a from your training folder. Use File ➤ Save As to save the drawing as Cabin12a.

2. Click the New button on the Standard toolbar. In the Create New Drawing dialog box, click Start from Scratch, and then click OK.

3. From the menu bar, select Format ➤ Units. In the Units Control dialog box, change the Precision on the Units side to two decimal places (0.00).

4. On the Angles side, select Surveyor and change the precision to the nearest minute (N 0d00' E). Click OK. You will need an area of about 250' × 150' for the site plan.

5. Open the Format menu again and pick Drawing Limits. Press ↵ to accept the default 0.00,0.00 for the lower-left corner. Type **250,150** ↵. Don't use the foot sign.

6. From the menu bar, click Tools ➤ Drawing Aids. Change the Snap Spacing to 10.00 and the Grid to 0.00, then click in the Grid and Snap checkboxes to turn the grid and snap on. Click OK.

7. In the drawing, type z ↵ a ↵. Then zoom to .85× to see a blank space around the grid (Figure 12.2).

FIGURE 12.2:   The site drawing with the grid on

8. Create a new layer called Prop_line, assign it a color, and make it current.

9. Start the Line command and, for the first point, type **220,130** ↵. This will start a line near the upper-right corner of the grid.

10. Turn off Snap, then type:

   @140<n90dw ↵

   @90<s42d30'w ↵

   @140<s67d30′e ↵

   @80<n52d49'e ↵

   c ↵

The property lines are completed (Figure 12.3).

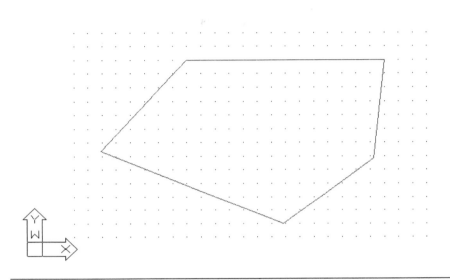

FIGURE 12.3: The property lines on the site drawing

Drawing the Driveway

The driveway is 8' wide and set 5' from the horizontal property line, and the access road is 8' from the parallel property line. The intersection of the access road line and the driveway lines form corners, each with a 3' radius. The driveway extends 70' in from the upper-right corner of the property. Let's lay this out now. First, switch to Architectural units and Decimal angular units.

1. Select Format ➤ Units from the menu bar, change the units to Architectural and the angular units to decimal. Then set the unit precision to $\frac{1}{16}$" and the angular precision to 0.00. Because of the way AutoCAD translates decimal units to inches, your drawing is now only $\frac{1}{2}$ the size it needs to be. (Use the Distance command to check it.) You will have to scale it up.

2. Click the Scale button on the Modify toolbar.

NOTE   The Scale command can also be started by selecting Modify ➤ Scale from the menu bar, or by typing **sc ↵**.

3. Type **all** ↵↵, then, for the base point, type **0,0** ↵.

4. At the <Scale factor>/Reference: prompt, type **12** ↵.

5. Zoom to extents, then zoom out a little. The drawing looks the same, but now it's the right size. Check it with the Distance command. (You were introduced to the Distance command in Skill 7, *Using Blocks and Wblocking*.)

6. Turn off the Grid, then offset the upper, horizontal property line 5' down, and offset the new line 8' down.

7. Offset the right-most property line 8' to the right (Figure 12.4a).

8. Create a new layer called Road, leave it assigned the default color, and make it current.

9. Use the Property button to move the driveway and road lines to the Road layer.

10. Extend the driveway lines to the access road line. Trim the access road line between the driveway lines.

11. Fillet the two corners where the driveway meets the road, using a 3' radius (Figure 12.4b).

Finishing the Driveway

A key element of any site plan is information that shows how the building is positioned on the site relative to the property lines. Property lines are staked out by surveyors. Then the building contractor will take measurements off the stakes to locate one or two corners of the building. In this site, you only need one corner because we are assuming the cabin is facing due west. A close look at Figure 12.1 will reveal that the end of the driveway lines up with the outer edge of the back step of the cabin. Below the driveway is a square patio, and its bottom edge lines up with the bottom edge of the back step. So the bottom corner of the back step coincides with the lower-left corner of the patio. This locates the cabin on the site (Figure 12.5).

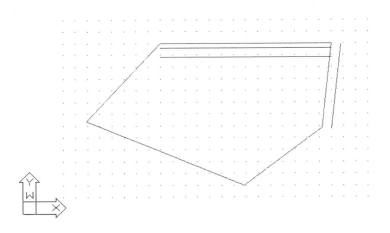

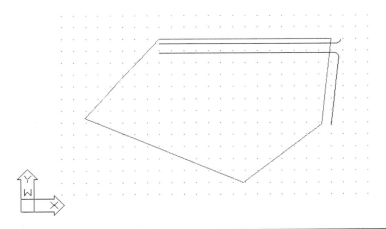

FIGURE 12.4: Offset property lines (a) and the completed intersection of the driveway and access road (b)

 NOTE   Imagine the site being on a bluff of a hill overlooking land which falls away to the south and west, offering a spectacular view in that direction. To accommodate this view, we will want to change the orientation of the cabin when we Xref it into the site drawing.

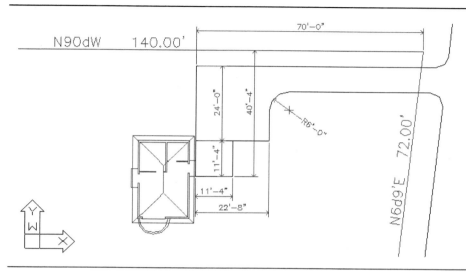

FIGURE 12.5: The driveway and patio lined up with the cabin

1. Be sure Ortho is on, then draw a line from the upper-right corner of the property lines straight up to a point near the top of the screen.

2. Offset this line 70' to the left. This will mark the end of the driveway.

3. Draw a line from the lower endpoint of this offset line down a distance of 40'-4", then, with Ortho on, continue this line to the right 11'-4".

4. Offset the 40'-4" line 11'4 to the right, and offset the new line 11'-4" to the right as well.

5. Offset the upper driveway line 24'-0" down. These are all the lines you need to finish the site plan (Figure 12.6a).

6. By using the Trim and Fillet commands as you have in several previous skills, you can finish the driveway and patio (Figure 12.6b).

7. Draw a north arrow and place it in the lower-left corner.

8. Open the Layer Control dialog box and change the linetype for the Prop_line layer to Phantom. (You will have to load it—see Skill 6, *Using Layers to Organize Your Drawing*.)

9. Type **ltscale** ↵, then type **100** ↵. You will see the phantom linetype for the property lines.

10. Save this drawing in your training folder as Site12a.

This completes the site plan. The next step is to create an external reference in the site plan to link it to the cabin drawing.

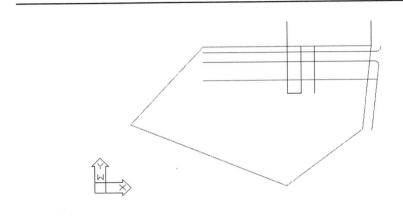

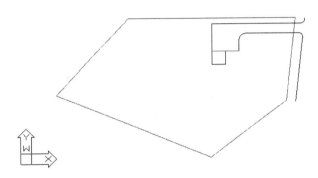

FIGURE 12.6: The offset lines (a) and the finished driveway and patio (b)

Setting Up External References

When you set up an external reference, you go through a process similar to that of inserting a drawing into another drawing, like you did in Skill 7. The Attach command is used to create the external reference. When using this command, you will name the drawing to be referenced and specify the location of its insertion point. There are options for X scale factor, Y scale factor and rotation angle—just as for inserting blocks—but here you can set the command up so that it uses the defaults for these options without prompting you for your approval.

The External Reference Dialog Box

All external reference operations are run through the External Reference dialog box, which is brought up by selecting Insert ➤ External Reference from the menu bar, or by typing **xr ↵.** There is also a Reference toolbar which has five command buttons related to Xrefs. You can bring it up the same way you brought up the Dimension toolbar in the last skill: Select View ➤ Toolbars on the menu bar, scroll to Reference and activate it. However, I don't recommend using the Reference toolbar while working through this skill unless you're an advanced user, for two reasons. First, there are seven other buttons on the toolbar used for Image commands, which allow you to import raster drawings into AutoCAD—an operation not covered in this book. Second, the toolbar does not include all of the Xref commands we will be covering. If you have already brought this toolbar up, click the × in the upper-right corner to delete it.

1. With Site12a as the current drawing, create a new layer called Cabin, select a color and make it current.

2. Pick Insert ➤ External Reference from the menu bar. The External Reference dialog box appears.

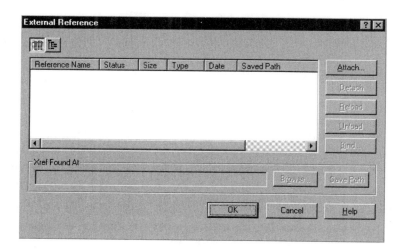

The blank area is where existing external references are listed. On the right side is a column of buttons, all of which are ghosted out except Attach. These are the commands you will use to set up and control the Xrefs. The ghosted ones will be useable after the first Xref is set up.

The Attach Command

The *Attach command* creates the link between the current, or host, drawing and the drawing to be externally referenced.

1. Click the Attach button. The Select File to Attach dialog box comes up. Find and open your training folder and highlight Cabin12a.

2. Click Open. The Attach Xref dialog box appears.

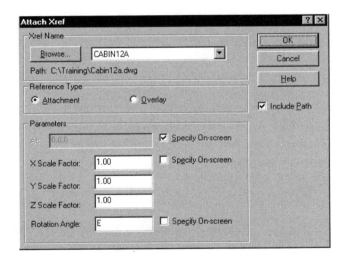

In the Xref Name area, Cabin12a is displayed in the drop-down list text box, and, just below that, the path of the file is shown. In Reference Type, Attachment should be chosen. In the Parameters area, you can specify the insertion point, scale factors, and rotation. You can also choose these parameters when you return to the drawing. By default only the insertion point is specified in the drawing. The other options are set to their defaults and you won't be prompted to specify them at the command line when you make the attachment.

3. Click OK. You return to your drawing and the cabin drawing appears and moves with the crosshair cursor.

4. Pick a point within the property line, to the left of the patio, to be the insertion point. The Xref drawing is attached and appears in the site plan (Figure 12.7).

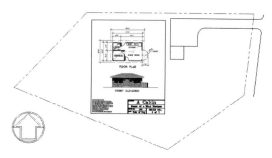

FIGURE 12.7: The Cabin12a drawing attached to the Site12a drawing

The attached Xref appears exactly as it did when it was the current drawing. As part of a site plan, we don't want all of the information in Cabin12a to be visible. In fact, we want most of the information invisible. We will accomplish this by freezing many of the layers in the Xref drawing.

Controlling the Appearance of an Xref

Xref layers will be part of the list of layers for the current, or host, drawing, but the name of the Xref file has been added to the front of the layer's previous name, separated from the layer's previous name by a vertical bar (|).

1. Click the Layer button on the Object Properties toolbar. The Layer Control dialog box comes up. Layers from the Xref drawing all have "Cabin12a" and a vertical bar before the name of the layer, as in Cabin12a | balcony.

2. Freeze all layers beginning with Cabin12a *except:*

   Cabin12a | balcony

   Cabin12a | roof

   Cabin12a | steps

   Cabin12a | walls

The drawing will now look like Figure 12.8. Because the color of objects controls their line weight when the drawing is printed, and because we will want all the lines making up the cabin to have the same line weight, we will make the color of the thawed cabin layers the same.

3. Click the Layer button again, and highlight the Cabin12a | balcony layer, then hold down the Ctrl key and click the other cabin layers listed in step 2 above, and change the color of one of the selected layers to a dark green. The rest of the selected layers will also change to a dark green. Click OK.

4. Finally, in the site plan, the roof should have a continuous line instead of the dashed line it currently has. Click the Layer button again. Highlight the Cabin12a | roof layer, and change its linetype to Continuous.

5. Click OK. The cabin is now all one color and the roof has continuous lines. Now the cabin needs to be moved and rotated to its position next to the patio.

6. Zoom into a view where the cabin and the left side of the patio are visible.

7. Start the Rotate command and click the cabin. The entire cabin is selected. Press ↵.

8. Click in the middle of the cabin, then type **-90** ↵. The cabin is rotated to the correct orientation (Figure 12.9a).

9. Be sure Endpoint Osnap is running, then use the Move command to move the lower-right corner of the back step to the lower-left corner of the patio (Figure 12.9b).

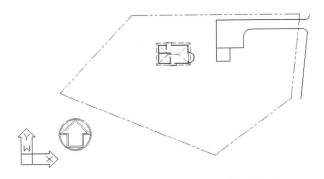

F I G U R E 1 2 . 8: The site plan with most cabin layers frozen

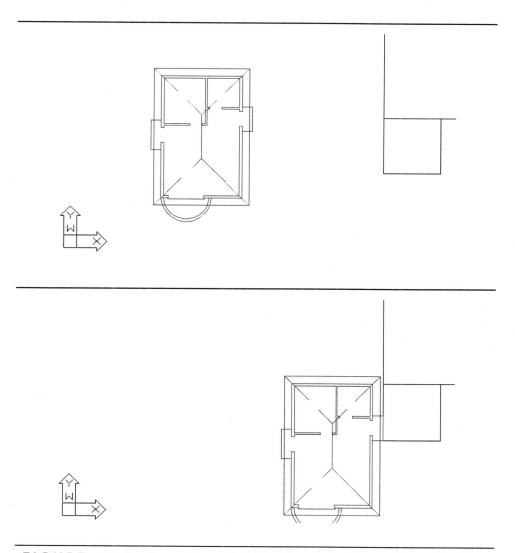

FIGURE 12.9: The cabin rotated (a) and positioned next to the patio (b)

10. Zoom previous. The cabin is oriented correctly on the site (Figure 12.10).

You have established Cabin12a as an external reference in this drawing and modified the appearance of some of the Xref's layers. The next step is to make some revisions to Cabin12a and see how this affects the Xref.

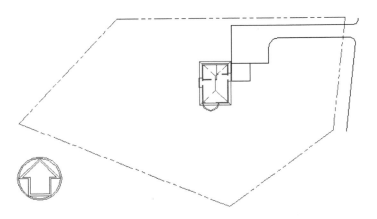

FIGURE 12.10: The cabin Xref is located on the site drawing.

Modifying an Xref Drawing

If you bring up Cabin12a and modify it, changes you make and save will be visible in the current file when you bring it back up, but the changes you have just made to the Cabin12a | layers will be lost unless you change a setting now.

1. Type **visretain** ↵. If the value in the angle brackets is set to 1, press ↵. Otherwise, type **1** ↵ to set the value to 1. This will allow you to save the layer settings of the Xref layers with the current file.

2. Use File ➤ Save As to save the current file as Site12b.

3. Open Cabin12a.

Because we found such a spectacular site for the cabin, we want to add a deck around what is now the west-facing entrance (previously the front entrance).

1. Zoom into the area that includes the floor plan and the area between it and the front elevation.

2.   Create a new layer called Deck, assign it a color and make it current. Next, give yourself some room to make this revision.

3.   Freeze the following layers:

Dim1

F-elev

any Hatch layers that aren't already frozen

Tblk1

Text1

The drawing will look like Figure 12.11. Use the Pline command to draw a deck across the front of the cabin that extends 10' down. (The Polyline command was introduced in Skill 10, *Controlling Text in a Drawing*.)

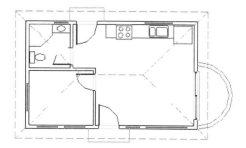

FIGURE 12.11: The view with selected layers frozen

4.   Make sure the Endpoint Osnap is running, then select the Polyline button from the Draw toolbar and pick the lower-left corner of the cabin to start the Pline.

5.   Type **w** ↵, then type **0** ↵ ↵ to reset the Pline width to 0.

6. Be sure Ortho is on, then hold the crosshair cursor straight down below the first point picked and type **10'** ↵.

7. Type **.x** ↵ to activate point filters and click the lower-right corner of the cabin walls. Then hold the cursor out to the right edge of the screen where the target box is not touching any object, and click. A horizontal line is drawn that parallels the front wall of the cabin, 10 feet below it.

8. Finally, pick the lower-right corner of the cabin to complete the outline of the deck (Figure 12.12a). Press ↵ to end the Pline command.

9. Offset this polyline 6 inches to the inside (Figure 12.12b). When a polyline is offset, all segments are automatically offset together and filleted to clean up the corners. (The fillet radius is 0 for this operation, even if it's currently set to a non-zero value.)

10. Save this file. Keep the name as Cabin12a—otherwise the Xref in the Site12b drawing would not be updated to include the deck. This is a revision to the Cabin12a drawing which has been externally referenced to the Site12b drawing. The revision should automatically show up when you open the Site12b drawing. Let's see how it looks.

11. Open the Site12b drawing. The cabin looks exactly the same—same layers visible with the same colors—as it was when you last saved the Site12b drawing, except the deck has been added (Figure 12.13).

12. Save this drawing. It's still called Site12b.

In this exercise, you have seen how a host drawing is automatically updated when the external reference is changed, and how the appearance of objects in the Xref drawing can be controlled from the host drawing by working with the Xref layers. This is a good example of the power of layers. They can be set up one way in the actual drawing and another way in the Xref of that drawing in another host file. In fact, you can Xref the same drawing into any number of host files and have the layer characteristics of visibility, color, and linetype be different in each host file, and saved as such with each host file.

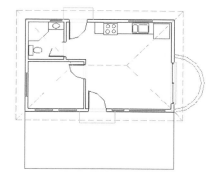

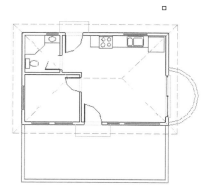

FIGURE 12.12: The outline of the deck (a) and the offset deck line (b)

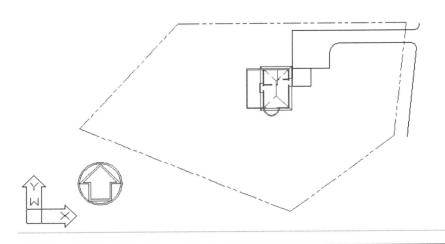

FIGURE 12.13: The Site12b drawing with the revised Xref of the cabin

This mechanism allows the host drawing to be a composite of several drawings, which are actually Xrefs. The Xrefs can be in various stages of completion and can be undergoing further refinement by other drafters while you are still developing the host drawing.

Applications for Xrefs

The applications for external references are diverse. A description of two common applications for Xrefs will illustrate the range of uses.

If you are working on a project as an interior designer and are a sub-contractor to the architect of the project, the architect can give you a drawing of a floor plan which is still undergoing changes. You would load this file onto your hard drive in a specially designated folder, then Xref it into your drawing as a background—a drawing to be used as a reference to draw over. Now you can proceed to do your work of laying out furniture, partitions, etc., while the architect is still refining the floor plan. At an agreed upon time, the architect will give you a revised version of the floor plan. You will delete the one you have on your computer and replace it with the latest one. Then you can reload the Xref into your furniture layout drawing and the newer version of the floor plan will now be the background. In this example, the architect may also be sending these same versions of the floor plan to the structural and mechanical engineers, and the landscape architect, all of whom are working on the project and using the architect's floor plan as Xrefs in their respective host drawings (Figure 12.14).

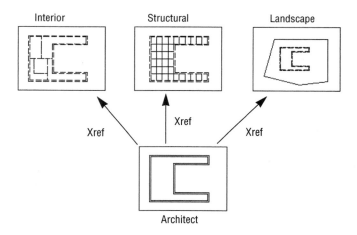

FIGURE 12.14: A single floor plan as an Xref to three sub-contractors

Another example of how Xrefs are often used takes place all in the same office where a network is in place. A project could involve work on several buildings all on the same site. Each building can be externally referenced to the site plan. This will keep the site plan drawing file from getting too large, and will allow the project work to be divided up to different work stations, while the project manager could have the site plan, or host, drawing on their computer and keep track of progress (Figure 12.15).

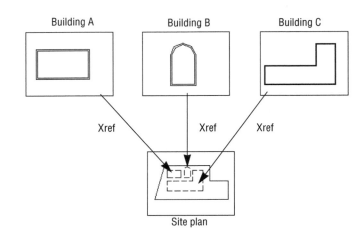

FIGURE 12.15: Three buildings as Xrefs to a single site plan

Additional Features of External References

You have seen how layers of an Xref can be changed and how modifications to an Xref can be updated in the host drawing. There are a few other features of external references that deserve mention.

The Xref Path

When you attach an Xref to the host drawing, AutoCAD stores the name of the Xref and its path.

 NOTE   The path of a drawing file is the name of the drive, folders and sub-folders where a file is stored, followed by the name of the drawing. C:\TRAINING\SITE12B.DWG is the path of the current drawing file.

Each time you bring up the host drawing, AutoCAD will be directed to search and find any Xrefs saved with the host file, and bring them up in the host drawing. If the Xref drawing is moved to a new folder after the Xref has been attached, AutoCAD won't be able to find the Xref and can't bring it up in the host drawing.

To correct this situation, you must update the host drawing with the new path to the Xref file. We'll go through a quick exercise to illustrate how this works.

1. Open a new drawing momentarily.

2. Use My Computer or Windows Explorer to create a new sub-folder called Xref within the Training folder you have previously set up. Move Cabin12a to this folder.

3. Bring up Site12b again. The Xref does not show up but there's a little line of information where the insertion point of the Xref was located in the host drawing. If you zoom in a couple of times, you will be able to read the information. It says Xref C:\Training\Cabin12a.dwg. This is the original path of the Xref.

4. Press F2 to switch to the AutoCAD text screen for a moment and note the line that says: Can't find C:\Training\Cabin12a.dwg. AutoCAD is unable to find the Xref because the path has changed. Press F2 again.

5. Type **xr** ⏎ to bring up the External References dialog box. In the large box where Xrefs are listed, the path is listed for each Xref under the heading Saved Path. You can slide the scroll bar to the right to see the full path.

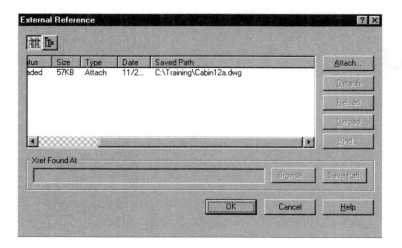

6. Click the Cabin12a Xref to highlight it.

7. Next to the Xref Found At text box, click Browse, and find Cabin12a in the new Xref folder. Highlight it and click Open.

8. Back in the External Reference dialog box, the path has been updated for Cabin12a. Click OK. The Xref is restored in your drawing.

TIP When you're working with a lot of Xrefs, it is important to be very careful where you store files that are acting as Xrefs to other files.

Binding Xrefs

There are occasions when you will want to permanently attach an Xref to the host drawing. If you send your drawing files to a printing service to be plotted, having to send a whole set of files that are Xrefs can make things complicated. Also, for archiving finished work, it's better to reduce the number of files. There will be occasions as well when the Xref has been revised for the last time and no longer needs to be a separate file. In all these situations, you will use the Bind command to convert an external reference into a block which can be inserted into the host drawing.

1. Type **xr** ↵ to open the External Reference dialog box and highlight the Cabin12a Xref.

2. Click the Bind button. The Bind Xrefs dialog box comes up.

The two options in the Bind Type area have to do with how layers are treated when an Xref is bound to the host drawing. The default is Bind. It will set the Xref layers to be maintained as separated layers in the host drawing. With the Insert option, layers that have the same name in the two drawings will be combined into one layer. None of the layers in Cabin12a have the same name as any layers in Site12b.

3. Leave the Bind Type set to Bind and click OK. The Xref disappears from the list of Xrefs.

4. Click OK. Your drawing looks unchanged.

5. Select the List button from the Inquiry flyout and select the cabin. Press ↵. The text screen shows that the cabin is now a block reference.

6. Press F2 and click the Layer button on the Object Properties toolbar. The names of the cabin's layers have changed slightly. The vertical bar separating Cabin12a from the layer name has been replaced by a 0. This form of name is used for layers that were in an Xref drawing that has since been bound to the host file.

7. Click OK, then pick Insert ➤ Block. In the Insert dialog box, click the Block button. In the Defined Blocks dialog box, Cabin12a is listed as a block, along with the window and two door blocks that you created in Skill 7, each with Cabin12a0 preceding their names. There are a couple of other blocks on the list. They are used by the dimensions in the drawing.

8. Click Cancel, then click Cancel again to return to your drawing. The cabin is now a permanent part of the Site12b drawing. If you need to make changes to the drawing, you can explode it and use the modify commands to make those changes.

9. Save this drawing as Site12c.

This has been a quick tour of the basic operations that are used to set up and control external references. There are more features and commands for working with Xrefs than have been covered here, but you now have enough to get you started working with them. What follows is a few additional operations and features that you may find useful when you delve more deeply into external references. Play around a little and see what you can do.

Other Features of Xrefs

- Externally referenced drawings can have drawings externally referenced to them. These are called *nested* Xrefs. There is no limit to the number of levels of nested Xrefs that a drawing can have.

- You can't explode an Xref, but you can detach it from the host. The Detach command is a button on the External Reference toolbar.

- You can bind Blocks, Layers, and Text and Dimension styles of an Xreffed drawing to the host drawing without binding the objects themselves. Use the *Xbind command* for this. Type **xbind** ↵ or pick the External Reference Bind button from the Reference toolbar to start this command.

- Large, complex drawings which are Xreferenced often have their insertion points coordinated in such a way that all Xreferences are attached at the 0,0 point of the host drawing. This helps keep drawings aligned properly. By default, any drawing which is Xreferenced into a host drawing uses 0,0 as its insertion point, but you can change the coordinates of the insertion point with the *Base command*. With the drawing you want to change current, type **base** ↵ and enter the coordinates for the new insertion point.

- You can limit which layers and, to some degree, which objects in a drawing are Xreferenced in the host drawing by using *Indexing* and *Demand*.

- A host drawing can be Xreferenced into the drawing that has been Xreferenced into the host. This is called an *overlay* and is an option in the Attach Xref dialog box. Overlays ignore nested Xreferences.

- If you freeze the layer that was current when an Xref was attached, the entire Xref is frozen.

- The Unload button in the External Reference dialog box allows you to deactivate Xrefs without detaching them from the host file. They stay on the list of Xrefs and can be reloaded at any time with the Reload button. This can be a time saver in complex drawings.

Are You Experienced?

Now you can...

- ☑ draw a basic site plan
- ☑ use Surveyor units to lay out property lines
- ☑ attach an external reference
- ☑ control the appearance of an external reference by modify layers
- ☑ use Visretain to save Xref layer changes
- ☑ revise a drawing that is externally referenced
- ☑ update an Xref path
- ☑ bind an Xref to a host file

Getting Familiar with Paper Space

- ➔ Putting a title block in Paper Space
- ➔ Setting up viewports in Paper Space
- ➔ Aligning viewports
- ➔ Controlling visibility in viewports
- ➔ Setting up a text style for Paper Space and adding text in Paper Space
- ➔ Working with tiled viewports

In the previous skill we introduced external references, a useful and powerful tool. Although the commands for Xrefs are a little tricky, the overall concept is fairly straightforward—in effect, you are viewing another drawing from within the current drawing. The concept of the *Paper Space* display mode is a little difficult to understand, but the commands are fairly simple. If you can understand this one, you are ready for advanced AutoCAD, because, essentially, this *is* advanced AutoCAD. Hang onto your mouse!

While external references help you combine several drawings into a composite, Paper Space allows you to set up and plot several views of the same file. As we go through the exercises to set up and control Paper Space, keep in mind that it was invented as a plotting tool, so its primary use is as a plotting aid. It can be used for other tasks as well, but the Paper Space features and commands are designed to set up a plot.

One way to visualize Paper Space is to think of it as a second drawing or a specialized layer that has been laid over the top of your current drawing. It starts out opaque so that you can't see your drawing underneath, but windows in the Paper Space layer are created that allow you to see your drawing. Paper Space has its own scale—usually 1"=1", or one-to-one, and is designed to contain in actual size the border and title block of the sheet on which you intend to plot your drawing.

Setting Up Paper Space

We will begin working with Cabin11a, which is the drawing we used for basic dimensioning in Skill 11. This drawing is essentially complete and ready to plot, and you will plot it in the next skill, just as it is right now (Figure 13.1). You will begin this skill by modifying this drawing and applying Paper Space to it to get a basic understanding of what Paper Space is and how it is activated and set up.

Drawing a Border in Paper Space

The first task in setting up Paper Space is to draw a border for the sheet you will plot to. We will use an 8 ½"×11" sheet to begin with.

1. Open Cabin11a. If you remember from Skill 10, *Controlling Text in a Drawing*, when you constructed the border and title block for this drawing, you had to make a calculation to determine that the size of the border for a scale of 1" = 8'-0" (one-eighth-inch scale) was based on a rectangle 68' wide × 88' high that was then offset 3' to make the border. With Paper Space you don't have to make this kind of calculation—you draw the border actual size.

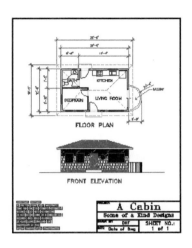

FIGURE 13.1: Cabin11a, ready to plot

2. Create a new layer called Tblk-ps, assign it a color and make it current.

3. Double-click the Tile button on the status bar. This activates Paper Space. Your drawing disappears momentarily and a triangle icon appears in the lower-left corner of the drawing area. Paper Space is now covering your cabin drawing. The first thing you need to do is to draw a rectangle to represent the 8 ½" × 11" sheet of paper you will be plotting the drawing on in the next skill.

4. Start the Rectangle command and type **0,0** ↵, then type **8.5,11** ↵. An 8 ½" × 11" rectangle is drawn.

5. Zoom to extents, then zoom out a little (Figure 13.2). You will construct a border and title block based on this rectangle, using the same procedure you used in Skill 10. We want a border that is set in from the edge of the sheet ⅜".

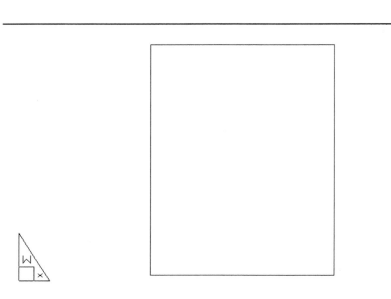

FIGURE 13.2: The 8 ½" × 11" rectangle in Paper Space

6. Offset the rectangle ⅜" to the inside. This border should be a line ½" wide.

7. Type **pe** ↵ to start the Pedit command. Select the inner rectangle, type **w** ↵, then type **1/32** ↵. The lines of the offset rectangle are now ½" wide and will serve as the new border (Figure 13.3). You'll be able to view your cabin within this border very soon, but first you need put a title block in Paper Space connected to this border. Let's look at the one you've already drawn. Type **x** ↵ to end the Pedit command.

8. Double-click the Tile button to deactivate Paper Space. The cabin drawing is now visible. Take note of the title block.

Designing a Title Block for Paper Space

The original title block was drawn to a size that could be plotted at eighth-inch scale so its dimensions are quite large (Figure 13.4a). You will need to make the size of the new title block much smaller to make it fit on a border that is 7 ¾" wide × 10 ¼" high. How much smaller? The dimensions of the new title block drawn at actual size are shown in Figure 13.4b.

FIGURE 13.3: The border, created from the rectangle

The text, too, has to be made smaller to fit in the new title block. Below is a chart showing the heights of the various text used in the two title blocks:

Text	Original Title Block	Paper Space Title Block
A Cabin	2'-6"	⁵⁄₁₆"
Some of a Kind Designs	1'-3"	⁵⁄₃₂"
DHF	1'-0"	⅛"
Date of Dwg	1'-0"	⅛"
SHEET NO.: 1 of 1	1'-3"	⁵⁄₃₂"
PROJ.:, DRAWN BY:, DATE	8"	¹⁄₁₂"

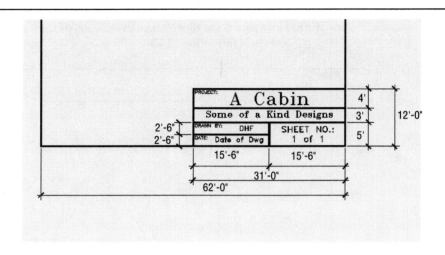

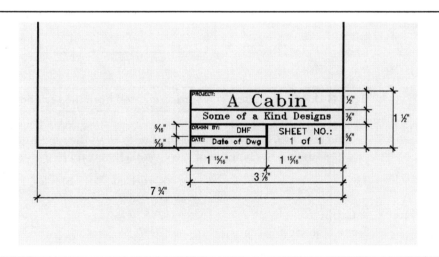

FIGURE 13.4: The original dimensions of the cabin title block (a) and the new, actual dimensions in Paper Space (b)

This may seem complicated at first, but think about the traditional way of drafting for a moment. On the drafting board, the drafter juggles two scales at the same time without thinking about it—one for text, border, and title block, and another for the lines that represent the actual building components. They use a scale to draw the building, say, at ⅛" = 1'-0". When it's time to draw the title block and fill it in with text, they don't keep using the eighth-inch scale. They use a ruler and make the text the actual height they want—one-eighth inch, one-quarter inch, ⁵⁄₁₆", etc.—and they will describe the title block as being three inches wide when it's right next to a building that maybe is six inches wide on the paper but in eighth-inch scale it's 48 feet wide. They'll put text in the building and call it ⅛" high, right next to a wall that is ⅛" wide on the paper but represents a wall that is 1'-0" wide. Paper Space allows you to do the same thing. You will put text, border, and title block in Paper Space at their actual size, and leave the rest of the drawing as it was, in what will now be called *Model Space*. Cabin11a is all drawn in Model Space, because Paper Space was not activated or set up when the drawing was made. Now that we have Paper Space set up, we can draw the title block, border, and text all at actual size in Paper Space.

NOTE Paper Space is named for the paper your drawing will eventually be printed on, and Model Space is named for your drawing in its capacity as a model of the building. All objects in the drawing are either in Paper Space or Model Space.

Traditional drafting has a scale for the lines which represent the building, and the text, title block, and border were drawn actual size. In CAD drafting without Paper Space, you have the convenience of being able to draw the building at full size, but you have to draw the text, title block, and border larger than they will eventually be in the finished plot, because there is only one scale for the drawing. With Paper Space, you can return to the method used by traditional drafters. Paper Space is the part of the drawing where everything that relates to the actual size of the sheet is put, and Model Space is where the building lines and objects representing building components reside. You'll see shortly how the two spaces work together to make a complete drawing.

Let's get back to this title block and finish making one in Paper Space. You need to look at the change of size of the title block and text from the original one to the new one. Because Cabin11a is set up to be printed at a scale of ⅛"=1'-0", the text, border, and title block have all been drawn larger than their actual size by the scale factor of eighth-inch scale. And what is the scale factor of eighth-inch scale? It's the true ratio of the scale and is found by dividing the smaller number on one side of the equation into the larger one. If you divide ⅛" into 1'-0" you will get the scale factor, or 96. The text border and title block are all 96 times larger in the original than they need to be in Paper Space, where they will be actual size.

After scaling the existing title block down by a factor of 96, you will have a new title block that will be actual size. Then you will need to put it into Paper Space, and attach it to the border. You can easily do both the scaling and the moving in one operation by using the Cut and Paste tools while in AutoCAD.

Cutting and Pasting in AutoCAD

When you use the Cut and Paste tools in AutoCAD, whatever is cut (or copied), becomes a block and can be inserted as a block back into the drawing, or into another drawing. With Paper Space deactivated, the Cabin11a drawing is visible on the screen.

1. Select Edit ➢ Cut from the menu bar and use either the crossing or regular selection window to select the title block and all of its text without the border. (Selection windows were described in Skill 6, *Using Layers to Organize Your Drawing*, when you were selecting the kitchen and bathroom fixtures to move them onto the Fixtures layer.) Press ↵.

2. Before activating Paper Space again, erase the border for the Cabin11a drawing.

3. Double-click the Tile button again (on the status bar) to reactivate Paper Space.

4. Select Edit ➢ Paste from the menu bar. The image of the title block is pasted into the Paper Space drawing: It's huge—you can see only the end of one line. Remember that we drew the original title block and border in a scaled-up fashion so they would fit with the drawing's scale. The original scale factor we used to scale it up was 96 for eighth-inch scale, so we'll use the reciprocal of that to scale it down.

5. Use Nearest Osnap and pick a point on the bottom line of the border for the insertion point. For the X scale factor, type **1/96** ↵. Press ↵ twice more to accept the other insertion option defaults. The title block is inserted onto the border at its proper size (Figure 13.5a).

6. Start the Move command and, using Endpoint and Perpendicular Osnaps, be sure Ortho is on and move the title block to the right until the right end of the top line in the title block (Endpoint) meets the right side of the border (Perpendicular). This will position the title block correctly on the border (Figure 13.5b).

7.   Use the Explode command to explode the title block, then use the Properties button to move the title block lines and text to the Tblk-layer. This completes the transfer of the title block from Model Space into Paper Space.

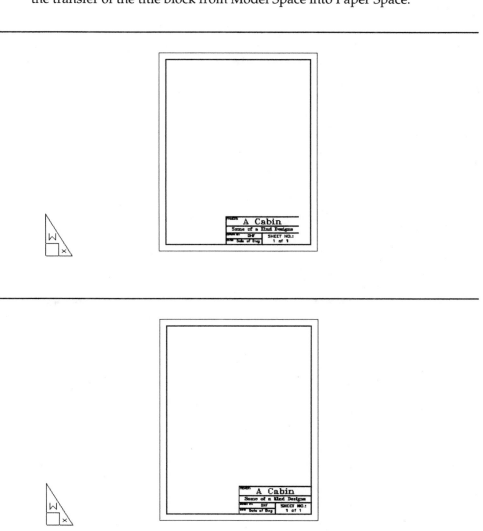

FIGURE 13.5: The title block inserted into the border in Paper Space (a) and positioned correctly (b)

Creating Floating Viewports

Now comes the amazing part. This will kind of be like magic in reverse: "Now you don't see it, now you do!" Remember that I originally advised you to think of Paper Space as a second drawing on top of your original drawing, initially opaque so you can't see your drawing. We will now create a window to see through Paper Space to see the Model Space drawing. The window is a new object called a *viewport*.

1. Create a new layer called Vport-ps, assign it a color that really stands out, like purple, and make this new layer current.

 TIP   It's useful to assign a color that will stand out in your drawing to the Vport-ps layer, so you are reminded that the viewports are not part of the building.

2. Pick View ➤ Floating Viewport ➤ 1 Viewport. This starts the *Mview command*, and the prompt becomes `ON/OFF/Hideplot/Fit/2/3/4/Restore/<First Point>:`.

 NOTE   The Mview command can also be started by typing **mv** ↵.

3. Double-click Osnap on the status bar to temporarily disable any running Osnaps, and pick a point in the lower-left corner just inside the border.

4. Move the cursor to the upper-right corner, still just inside the border, forming a window, as in Figure 13.6a.

5. Click to complete the window. Your cabin drawing appears in the window (Figure 13.6b).

 NOTE   You have just been introduced to a fourth AutoCAD feature which uses a window. Can you recall the first three? The zoom window, the selection window (regular and crossing) for selecting objects, and the Rectangle command. AutoCAD has several uses for windows.

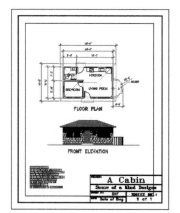

FIGURE 13.6: Forming a viewport (a) and the completed viewport (b)

6. Start the Erase command and pick the top dimension to erase. Try to pick something on the front elevation. You will find that you cannot pick anything in the cabin drawing. The only objects you can pick are the title block and the border lines which are in Paper Space. When Paper Space is current, only objects in Paper Space can be selected. The triangle icon in the lower-left corner of the drawing area is visible when Paper Space is current. Press Esc to cancel the Erase command.

7. Double-click Paper on the status bar. Paper changes to Model and the triangular Paper Space icon disappears.

 NOTE   On the status bar, the Tile button turns on a setting called *Tilemode*. When Tilemode is off, Paper Space is enabled. The Paper/Model button controls whether the Paper Space or Model Space portion of the drawing is active. If Paper Space is not enabled and you double-click on the Model button, Paper Space becomes enabled and also becomes the active portion of the drawing.

8. Move your cursor onto the cabin floor plan and then move it outside the border. As soon as the cursor moves past the viewport edge, the crosshair changes to an arrow. When you move back inside the viewport, the cursor becomes the crosshair again.

 NOTE   The cursor always resides in the active portion of the drawing. Work can be done only in one of the two portions (Model Space or Paper Space) at any one time.

9. Restart the Erase command and try to select objects in the cabin drawing again. This time you are able to select anything inside the viewport.

10. Try to select the viewport boundary line, the border, or the title block. You can't select anything in Paper Space when Model Space is current. Cancel the Erase command.

> **N) NOTE** The viewports in Paper Space are called *floating* viewports because they can be moved around. There is another kind of viewport in AutoCAD called *tiled* viewports which are fixed and exist only in Model Space. The "Tilemode Variable and Tiled Viewports" section later in this skill contains a brief discussion comparing the two. For brevity, in this skill, we will refer to floating viewports as viewports. Paper Space viewports always reside in the Paper Space portion of the drawing.

Picturing your drawing as two drawings in one is still a useful way to understand Paper Space, and will help you to understand how Paper Space and Model Space work together. The next task is to position the Model Space drawing correctly in the Paper Space border and adjust its magnification.

Zooming a Viewport to 1/xp

The real power of Paper Space will become apparent when you adjust the Model Space drawing's size in the Paper Space border so that the cabin will be plotted at eighth-inch scale.

1. Be sure the Model/Paper button reads Model on the status bar, then type **z** ↵. The prompt reads All/Center/Dynamic/Extents/Previous/ Scale(X/XP)/Window/<Realtime>:. Notice the options for scale: Scale (X/XP). Earlier in this book you learned about the X option when you zoomed to .6x or .85x. These zoom factors change the current magnification by the numerical value acting as a percentage, so .6x makes objects on the screen 60% of their previous size. The XP option changes the magnification of objects in Model Space by the ratio of one over the scale factor of the scale you want the drawing to be in when it's plotted. For eighth-inch scale, the zoom would be 1/96xp.

2. Type **1/96xp** ↵. The Model Space drawing enlarges slightly (Figure 13.7a).

3. Use Realtime Pan to move the Model Space drawing around in the viewport, much as you would slide a photograph around in a picture frame to position it (Figure 13.7b). Don't worry about the viewport's lower-right corner going through the title block. We'll fix that in a second. The viewport may need enlarging horizontally to accommodate the text in the lower-left corner. Press Esc when you're finished panning.

4. Double-click the Model button on the status bar. This puts you back in Paper Space. The viewports reside in Paper Space so you must be in Paper Space to create them or change them.

 NOTE   Viewports can be any size but they must always be rectangular.

5. At the Command: prompt, click the viewport boundary. Grips appear at the corners and the viewport boundary lines ghost.

6. Be sure running Osnaps are off, then click one of the two grips on the left corners to activate the grips editing mode. Move the cursor to the left but keep it inside the border. Click again. The viewport is widened enough to accommodate the text in the lower-left corner (Figure 13.8a). Press Esc twice. Now we need to make the viewport boundary invisible because we don't want it to print with the rest of the drawing.

7. Make the Tblk-ps layer current and freeze the Vport-ps layer. The viewport boundary disappears and the drawing is ready to print (Figure 13.8b). This drawing looks exactly like Cabin11a. In appearance, nothing has changed other than the color of the border and title block, but now you have an activated Paper Space which contains the title block and border at actual size.

8. Double-click the Tile button on the status bar. This deactivates Paper Space. The border and title block disappear and the triangular Paper Space icon disappears.

9. Zoom in to a close view of the front door in elevation.

10. Double-click the Tile button again. Paper Space is restored and the cabin sits in the border as it did previously.

11. Save this drawing in your training folder as Cabin13a.

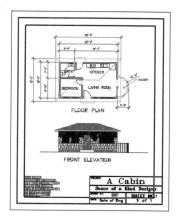

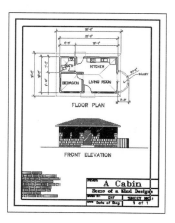

FIGURE 13.7: Adjusting the Model Space to the Paper Space: after zooming to 1/96xp (a) and after panning (b)

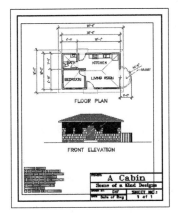

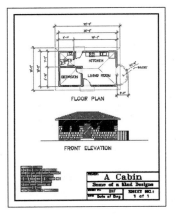

FIGURE 13.8: Adjusting the viewport in Paper Space: after stretching it with grips (a) and after freezing the Vport-ps layer (b)

Once you have set up a viewport in Paper Space, you can deactivate Paper Space and work on your drawing. Then, when you are ready to plot it out, reactivate Paper Space and the orientation and magnification of your drawing relative to the Paper Space border will be preserved. You can also work on your drawing while Paper Space is active by switching to Model Space, as you did above. You should not zoom while in Model Space, however, because that would change the relationship between Model Space and Paper Space that you set up by zooming to 1/*scale factor*xp. That zoom must be preserved for the drawing to plot at the right scale. So if you want to zoom in to your drawing at this point, zoom while in Paper Space. Then switch to Model Space to work on the drawing. When finished, switch back to Paper Space and zoom previous. This way, 1/*scale factor*xp zoom won't be affected.

NOTE   You can also switch back and forth between Paper Space and model space by typing **ps** ↵ **or ms** ↵.

This may seem like too much work to be worth the effort for a small drawing like this one, but be patient. As you start working on larger drawings, you will see what Paper Space is capable of doing for you.

Working with Multiple Viewports in Paper Space

The exercises above introduced you to Paper Space and taught you how it works. I used the example of a single viewport within a border and title block, all of which were in Paper Space. This is the way Paper Space is used most of the time, even in large projects. A title block is developed for a project. Each sheet in a set of drawings is a dwg file with a title block in Paper Space and one viewport that encompasses most of the area inside the border where you view the building components in model space. But this is certainly not the only way Paper Space is used. Often, more than one viewport will be used in a border. The rest of the exercises in this skill will lead you through an exploration of the advantages and techniques of using single and multiple viewports in Paper Space.

Setting Up Multiple Viewports

You'll start out by creating a new sheet size. Then you'll set up the views of the cabin to be viewed side by side.

1.   With Paper Space enabled and active, zoom out and use the Rectangle command to make a 11" × 17" rectangle in landscape orientation to the right of the existing drawing. Then pan over so both the drawing and the rectangle are visible (Figure 13.9a).

NOTE *Landscape orientation* means simply that the longer edge of the rectangle is horizontal. In *portrait orientation*, it is vertical.

2. Offset the rectangle ½" to the inside. Type **pe** ↵ to start the Polyline edit command and select the inner rectangle. Type **w** ↵ **1/32** ↵ **x** ↵. This changes the thickness of the lines of the offset rectangle to ½" and it is now a border for the new drawing (Figure 13.9b).

3. Start the Copy command and, using Endpoint Osnap and the lower-right corners of the two borders as base point and point of displacement, copy the title block over to this drawing (Figure 13.9c). It is now ready for a couple of viewports.

4. Thaw the Vport-ps layer and make it current.

5. Type **mv** ↵ to start the Mview command. Pick a point inside the new border near the left side about a quarter of the way up from the bottom. Move the cursor up to the ¾ point and to the right about half way across the rectangle (Figure 13.10a).

6. When the rectangular viewport looks like the one in Figure 13.10a, click to complete it. The entire cabin in Model Space is drawn in the new viewport (Figure 13.10b).

7. Double-click the Paper button on the Status bar to switch to Model Space. Note how the cursor is an arrow until you move it to the new viewport, where it should become the crosshair cursor. If it is still an arrow in the viewport, place the cursor in the viewport and click once. The outline of the viewport will darken and the cursor will become the crosshair cursor.

NOTE When Model Space is active, there can be only one active viewport at a time, and this is the one where the crosshair cursor appears. This is the viewport where you can manipulate objects. To make a viewport active, place the arrow cursor in the viewport and click.

FIGURE 13.9: Creating a new drawing: the rectangle (a), the border (b), and the title block (c)

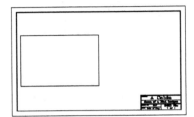

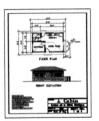
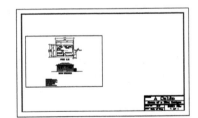

FIGURE 13.10: Forming a new viewport (a) and the completed viewport (b)

8. Type **z ↵ 1/96xp ↵** to adjust the scale of the viewport to eighth-inch scale (Figure 13.11a).

9. Pan the drawing in the viewport down until the floor plan is centered in the viewport (Figure 13.11b). Now, you will create a second viewport to the right of the first.

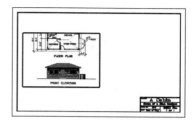

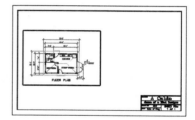

FIGURE 13.11: The new viewport set to eighth-inch scale (a) and panned to show the floor plan (b)

10. Double-click the Model button on the status bar to switch back to Paper Space. If necessary, use grips to resize the viewport you just created.

11. Be sure Ortho is on and start the Copy command. Select the first viewport to copy and place the copy to the right of the first one (Figure 13.12a). The new viewport has the same view of the cabin Model Space drawing as the first one, so its view does not need adjustment by zooming.

NOTE You may find this difficult to do if you have running Osnaps. You know by now that you can deactivate them for one pick (select the None button on the Object Properties toolbar) or disable them temporarily (double-click Osnap on the status bar).

12. Double-click the Paper button and move the cursor into the second viewport. Click in this viewport to make it the current viewport. Then pan the drawing in this viewport up until the front elevation is centered in the viewport (Figure 13.12b).

Aligning Viewports

The front elevation is not tall enough to fill the second viewport, so part of the floor plan is visible above and the note text is visible below. You can correct this by the same technique you used for the 8 ½" × 11" drawing: Make Paper Space active and use grips to stretch the viewport. But before you do that, you need to line up the front elevation with the floor plan, horizontally. Multiple elevations are lined up by their ground line, but there is no hard-and-fast rule for lining up these two views. In this case, lining up the title of each view horizontally will work fine.

1. Double-click the Model button on the status bar to switch to Paper Space.

2. Zoom in so the 11" × 17" drawing nearly fills the drawing area.

3. Type **mvsetup** ↵ to start the Mvsetup command. The prompt reads `Align/Create/Scale viewports/Options/Title block/Undo:`.

4. Type **a** ↵ to choose the align option. The prompt changes to read `Angled/Horizontal/Vertical alignment/Rotate view/Undo:`.

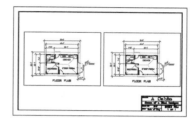

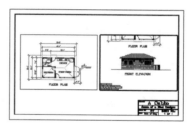

FIGURE 13.12: A second viewport copied from the first one (a) and the adjusted view in the new viewport (b)

5. Type **h** ↵ to choose horizontal. The prompt now reads `Basepoint:`. You need to select a point in one viewport that a point in the second viewport can be aligned to. We'll use the justification point for the FLOOR PLAN text in the first viewport for the basepoint.

6. Click in the left viewport to make it active, then select Insertion Osnap and click the FLOOR PLAN text. The prompt changes to read `Other point:`.

7. Pick Insertion Osnap again, click in the right viewport to make it active and click the FRONT ELEVATION text. The front elevation is moved down in the right viewport so the title text in the two viewports is aligned horizontally (Figure 13.13a). Press ↵ twice to end the Mvsetup command.

8. Double-click the Model button to switch to Paper Space.

9. Click the right viewport. Grips appear at the corners. Click the upper-right grip to activate it.

10. Be sure no running Osnaps are active, then move the cursor down until the top of the viewport is below the FLOOR PLAN text and above the front elevation, then click to set the top of the viewport in this position (Figure 13.13b). Press Esc twice to cancel the grips.

Finishing the 11" x 17" Drawing

To finish this drawing, you need to place the note text in the lower-left corner. You will accomplish this by creating a third viewport.

1. Type **mv** ↵ to start the Mview command.

2. Pick two points in the lower-left corner to create a square viewport. The entire Model Space drawing appears in the viewport (Figure 13.14a).

3. Double-click the Paper button to switch to Model Space.

4. Be sure the new viewport is active. If not, click in it, then pan the drawing in the new viewport until the note text is in the middle of the viewport. Press Esc to cancel Realtime Pan.

5. Type **z** ↵, then type **1/96xp** ↵. The text is now the right size.

6. Do any additional panning necessary to get the text centered vertically in the viewport and lined up near the left edge of the viewport.

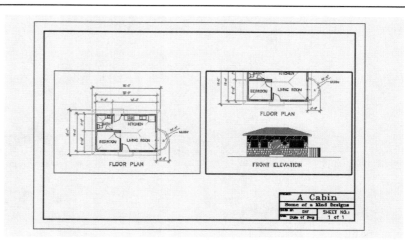

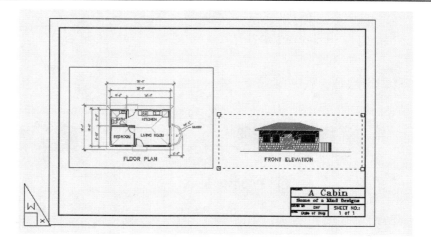

FIGURE 13.13: The two viewports horizontally aligned (a) and the right viewport resized (b)

7. Double-click the Model button to switch to Paper Space.

8. Use grips to stretch the viewport to the right until all the text is visible (Figure 13.14b). When finished, press Esc twice to remove grips.

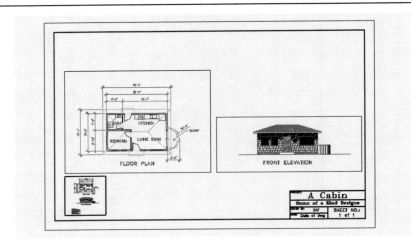

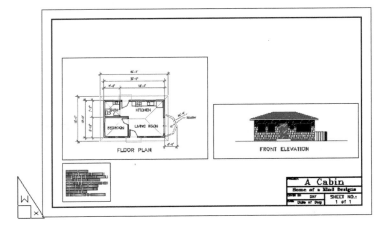

FIGURE 13.14: A third viewport is created (a) and the results of panning the view and stretching the viewport (b)

9. Make the Tblk-ps layer current and freeze the Vport-ps layer.

10. Zoom to extents, then zoom out a little to compare the two drawings (Figure 13.15).

11. Save this drawing to your training folder as `Cabin13b`.

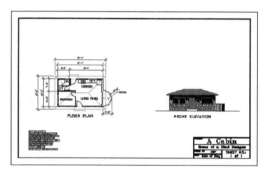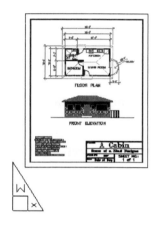

FIGURE 13.15: The completed 11" × 17" drawing next to the 8 ½" × 11" drawing

Now you have two drawings set up in Paper Space, both based on the same drawing in Model Space. There is room for more views in the larger of the two, possibly another elevation or a detail. We're going to move on to a larger drawing.

Setting Up Viewports to Different Scales

In the next set of exercises, you will create a 30" × 42" sheet for the site plan you created in Skill 12. Then you will use Paper Space to create several viewports that have drawings of different scales. Because the site plan has the cabin drawing Xreferenced into it, you will also have a chance to see how external references are handled in a drawing that is using Paper Space.

Setting Up a 30" x 42" Drawing with a Border and Title Block

To set up a 30" × 42" drawing, you will use almost the same procedure you used earlier. The title block will be different, but you won't take the time to fill in a complete title block—just indicate its location in the drawing.

1. Open Site12b.

2. Create new layers called Tblk-ps and Vport-ps, assign them the same colors you used for these layers in the cabin drawing, then make the Tblk-ps layer current.

3. Double-click the Tile button on the status bar to activate Paper Space. Paper Space is activated and the site drawing momentarily disappears.

4. Use the Rectangle command to draw a rectangle from the point 0,0 to the point 42,30. Zoom to extents, then zoom out a little (Figure 13.16a).

5. Offset the rectangle 1" to the inside.

6. Click the inner rectangle to start grips. Hold down the Shift key and select the two grips on the left side to activate them. Be sure Ortho is on and running Osnaps are off, then click one of the two active grips. Hold the cursor directly to the right of the selected grips and type **1** ⏎. The left side of the border is moved to the right 1", leaving room for a binding on the left edge of the sheet. Press Esc twice. The large sheet sizes usually have their title block on the right side, turned at 90°. We will draw a guideline to indicate the title block.

7. Offset the inner rectangle 4" to the inside, then explode the new rectangle. Erase the top, bottom, and left lines of this new rectangle, then use the Extend command to extend the remaining line up and down to the rectangle that will serve as the border (Figure 13.16b).

8. Start the Pedit command (type **pe** ⏎) and use the Width option to change the width of the border line to $\frac{3}{32}$". Type **x** ⏎ ⏎ to stop and restart the Pedit command, then pick the new line that represents the left side of the title block and press ⏎. Use Width again and set this line to the same width as you used for the border. You now have a border and title block area set up in Paper Space and are ready to create some viewports (Figure 13.16c).

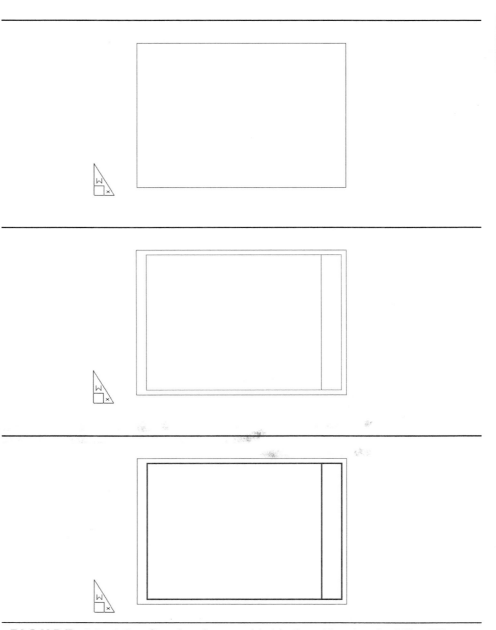

FIGURE 13.16: Creating the new title block and border: the 30" × 42" rectangle (a), the offset rectangle with title block (b), and the finished title block (c)

Making Viewports for the Site Plan and Floor Plan

On this 30" × 42" sheet, we will create a large viewport in the upper two-thirds of the area to view the site plan at eighth-inch scale. Then you'll make smaller viewports across the bottom for viewing the floor plan and front elevation at quarter-inch scale, and a closeup view of the bathroom.

1. Make Vport-ps the current layer.

2. Type **mv** ↵ to start the Mview command, and pick two points to make a viewport in the upper two thirds of the area inside the border. The site plan appears in the viewport (Figure 13.17a). The first thing you need to do is to zoom the view to eighth-inch scale to see if the drawing will fit in the viewport.

3. Type **ms** ↵ to switch to Model Space, then type **z** ↵ **1/96xp** ↵ to zoom the site drawing to eighth-inch scale. It should fit pretty well (Figure 13.17b). Pan in the viewport if necessary. If you need to adjust the size of the viewport, switch to Paper Space and use grips to stretch the viewport to the size you want. The view of the site plan is just like the drawing before Paper Space was activated. Remember that the cabin in this drawing is an external reference. Many of the cabin layers are frozen and the visible ones are all the same color, except the new deck. This will have to change when we set up other viewports for the floor plan and front elevation.

 **WARNING**   You always need to zoom to the 1/*scale factor*xp in a new viewport, even if the view looks perfect. This is the only way you can be sure the viewport is zoomed to the right scale.

4. Be sure that Paper Space is current and create a smaller viewport in the lower-left open area of the drawing. Switch to Model Space (type **ms** ↵) and pan the view to center the floor plan in the viewport.

5. Now zoom it to quarter-inch scale. Type **z** ↵ **1/48xp** ↵. The floor plan fills the viewport and the cabin is oriented and appears just as it was in the site plan (Figure 13.18a). Note how each of the two viewports have the User Coordinate System (UCS) icon in their lower-left corners. You will now rotate the floor plan so that it sits in the viewport oriented the way it was in the Cabin12a drawing.

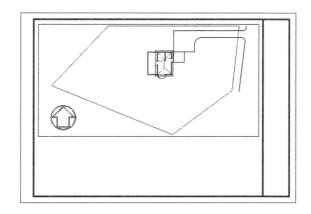

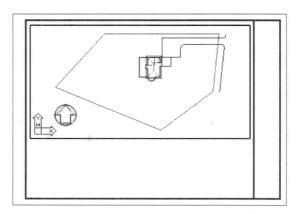

FIGURE 13.17: The new viewport completed (a) and the site plan zoomed to eighth-inch scale (b)

6. Type **mvsetup** ↵ to start the Mvsetup command, type **a** ↵ for the Align option, then type **r** ↵ for the Rotate option.

7. At the Basepoint: prompt, be sure there are no running Osnaps, then pick a point in the middle of the viewport.

8. At the Angle from basepoint: prompt, type 90 ↵. Then press ↵ twice more to end the Mvsetup command. The floor plan is rotated to the original orientation (Figure 13.18b). Note how the UCS icon has been rotated in the smaller viewport.

NOTE The visibility of the UCS icon can be controlled in each viewport, and in Paper Space, by picking View ➤ Display ➤ UCS Icon, and then clicking On. When the checkmark is visible, the UCS icon is displayed. When Paper Space is active, the icon is a triangle.

There are a couple of things that need to be done to this view to complete it. You'll need to resize the viewport and pan the view to get everything that you want to see visible. You also need to determine which layers you want visible in this viewport and freeze the ones whose objects you don't want to see. We'll work with the layers first because we need to make visible all objects to be displayed to be able to tell how big the viewport needs to be.

Controlling Layers in Viewports

You can control which layers are visible in each viewport, so two viewports can have a different combination of layers visible. The way this is done is to first thaw all frozen layers. Then, with Model Space current, you make a viewport active and freeze the layers you don't want visible in that viewport. When finished, you move to the next viewport and freeze layers you don't want visible. In this situation, you'll have to reset the visibility of the layers in both viewports.

1. Be sure Model Space is active and the lower-left viewport is current, then click the Layers button on the Object Properties toolbar. In the Layer & Linetype Properties dialog box, look at the list of layers and note the three columns of suns under three F headings.

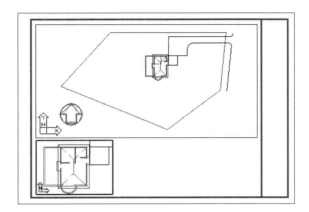

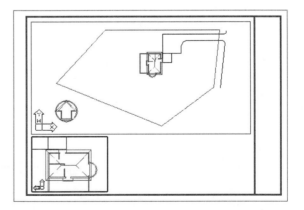

FIGURE 13.18: The floor plan zoomed to quarter-inch scale (a) and the view rotated 90° (b)

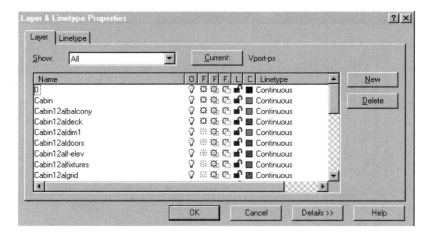

2. Hold the cursor on the headings bar between the middle F and the one to its right. A vertical bar with opposite horizontal arrows will appear when the cursor is right between the two buttons.

3. When the arrows and bar appear, hold down the left mouse button and drag the cursor directly to the right, to a point near the right edge of the layer list box, where the scroll bars are, and release the mouse button. The columns of suns and other icons to the right of the middle column of suns are moved out of visibility and the middle F column has more space around it. The title of the enlarged column is now visible: Freeze in Current Viewport.

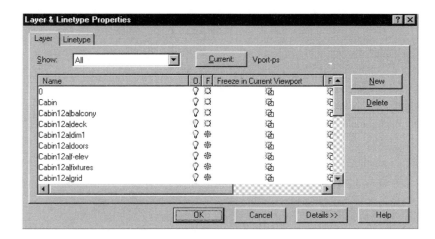

4. Thaw all currently frozen layers. (Click the first layer, scroll to the bottom, hold down the Shift key and click the last layer so that they are all highlighted, then click a snowflake. All layers are thawed. Scroll back to the top and click the Cabin layer. The rest of the layers are de-selected.) Now that all layers are visible, you need to go down the list of layers, and, when you see a layer that needs to be frozen in the current viewport, click the sun in the Freeze in Current Viewport column for that layer. The smaller viewport is current so let's start with the layers for that one.

5. Move down the list and click the sun in the Freeze in Current Viewport column for the following layers:

    - The Cabin12a | layers as follows: dim1, f-elev, roof, tblk1, text1, and all the hatch layers *except* hatch-plan-walls

    - Prop-line and Road layers

      Click OK when finished. You are returned to your drawing (Figure 13.19a). The smaller viewport looks OK except that it needs resizing, but all the layers are visible in the larger one. Let's set the layers for this viewport now.

6. Click in the larger viewport to make it active, then click the Layers button again. In the Layer & Linetype Properties dialog box, go down the list again, clicking the suns in the same column you did before to freeze the following layers for this viewport: all Cabin12a | layers except balcony, deck, roof, steps, and walls. Click OK when finished. The drawing in this viewport is what we want (Figure 13.19b). Now you need to adjust the size and view of the smaller viewport. You're going to stretch it up to a point where it will overlap the larger viewport, so, while the larger viewport is active, move the north arrow to the other side of the site plan.

7. Start the Move command and click the north arrow. Press ↵, then click in the middle of the arrow and click again to place it in a clear space in the lower-right corner of the larger viewport.

8. Type **ps** ↵ to switch to Paper Space and click the smaller viewport to make grips appear.

9. Click the upper-right grip, then, with Ortho off, move the cursor up and to the right at about a 45° angle and pick a point just below the property line (Figure 13.20a). Press Esc twice to cancel the grips.

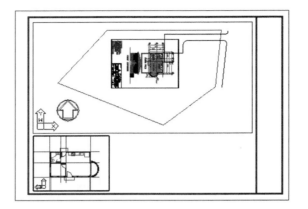

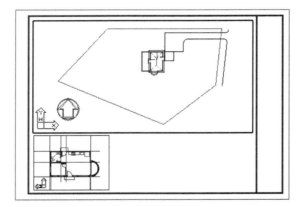

FIGURE 13.19: Layer changes made in the smaller viewport (a) and in the larger viewport (b)

10. Type **ms** ↵ to switch to Model Space, then click in the smaller viewport to make it active, and use the Pan command to move the floor plan around in the viewport until the deck and the grid are completely visible. Press Esc to

cancel the Pan command. Switch back to Paper Space and do a final adjustment of the size with grips, making the viewport as small as possible while still showing everything (Figure 13.20b). Press Esc twice to cancel grips.

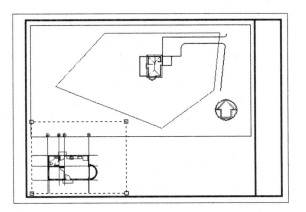

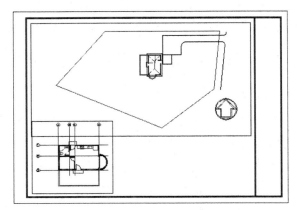

FIGURE 13.20: Stretching the viewport with grips in Paper Space (a) and panning the view in Model Space (b)

The layers are now set up so they are visible in all viewports except where frozen in particular viewports. When we create a new viewport, all layers will be visible at first. Then, with the new viewport current, you can click the sun icons in the Freeze in Current Viewport column for each layer you want to be invisible. AutoCAD will save these layer settings for each individual viewport with the drawing file.

When you copy a viewport, the layers settings for the original viewport will apply to the copy until you change them.

Copying Viewports

Create a new viewport the same size as the smaller one by copying it to the right. You will need to adjust the view to show the front elevation.

1. Be sure Paper Space is active, Ortho on and no Osnaps running, then start the Copy command and select the smaller viewport. Press ⌐. Pick a point in the middle of the small viewport, move the cursor to the right and position the copy just to the right of the original. The viewport is copied and the view is identical to that of the original (Figure 13.21a). The layers containing objects in the front elevation are frozen in both the smaller viewports.

2. Type **ms** ⌐ to switch to Model Space. Click in the new viewport to make it active, then click the Layers button.

3. In the Layer & Linetype Properties dialog box, click the snowflakes in the Freeze in Current Viewport column for the following Cabin12a l layers, to thaw them in the current viewport: f-elev, hatch-elev-42, hatch-elev-black, hatch-elev-gray, and Text1. Click OK, then pan the drawing up in the viewport until the FRONT ELEVATION text is sitting just above the lower border line (Figure 13.21b).

4. Type **ps** ⌐ to switch to Paper Space. Click the new viewport to start grips, then click one of the upper grips and stretch the top of the viewport down until nothing from the floor plan can be seen, then click again to set it. Press Esc twice to cancel the grips. The front elevation sits in the viewport correctly (Figure 13.21c).

5. Create one more viewport in the lower-right corner to display the bathroom. Follow these steps:

   - Start the Mview command and pick two points to create an approximately square viewport. The site plan appears. All layers are visible but the drawing is rotated to the same orientation as the front elevation viewport.

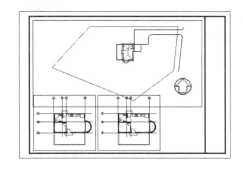

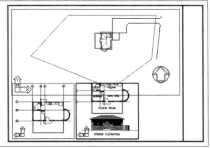

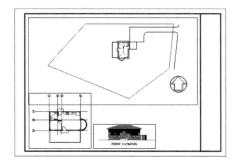

FIGURE 13.21: A copy of the smaller viewport (a), the new viewport with layer settings changed (b), and the viewport size adjusted (c)

NOTE   When a new viewport is created, the orientation of the drawing in the viewport will be the same as that of the last viewport that was active.

- Switch to Model Space, be sure the new viewport is current, and freeze the following layers: Cabin and all the Cabin12a | layers except for doors, fixtures, hatch-plan-floor, hatch-plan-walls, headers, walls, and windows.

- Zoom to 1/12xp.

- Pan the drawing until the bathroom is centered in the viewport. Try to line up the bottom bathroom wall to the ground line in the front elevation.

- Switch to Paper Space and adjust the size and position of the viewport, if necessary. Try to make the right and bottom boundary lines of the viewport coincide with the right and bottom edges of the wall lines.

NOTE   Once a viewport is zoomed to a scale with 1/xp, the final adjustment has two steps: panning the drawing in Model Space and adjusting the size and location of the viewport with grips in Paper Space.

- While in Paper Space, make the Tblk-ps layer current, then zoom into the bathroom door and draw an arc to fill in the blank space in the door swing which you broke out in Skill 10 to make room for text. Zoom previous when finished.

NOTE   You can draw lines in Paper Space to represent building components, but they stay in Paper Space.

The results should look something like Figure 13.22. For finishing touches you can adjust the floor plan so the bottom of the deck aligns horizontally with the ground line in the floor plan. We'll use the Mvsetup command.

6. At the Command: prompt, type **mvsetup** ↵ **a** ↵ **h** ↵. Pick Endpoint Osnap and click the ground line in the front elevation. (If the front elevation viewport is not active, click in it first, then click the ground line.)

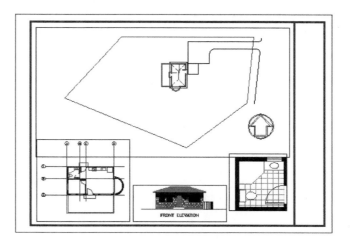

FIGURE 13.22: The completed bathroom viewport

NOTE   The Mvsetup command can be started while either Paper Space or Model Space is active. The command will automatically switch to the space mode it needs as the command progresses.

7.   Click in the floor plan viewport to make it active, use Endpoint Osnap and pick the lower-right corner of the deck.

8.   If necessary, switch to Paper Space and use grips to stretch the top of the floor plan viewport up slightly to make the grid fully visible.

TIP   Since viewports are usually made invisible, it isn't important to line them up evenly. They can overlap each other as long as the objects in the viewports do not overlap each other.

Adding Text to Paper Space

Now you'll add titles to the views in a style that matches the style of the title of the front elevation. Underneath each title we want to put the scale of the view.

1. Create a new text style called Title-ps. (Recall that the Style command is started by picking Format ➤ Text Style on the menu bar.) We want the new style to be identical to the Title text style we used in Model Space, but the height has to be adjusted for Paper Space. It was 1'-6" high in Model Space and the front elevation is now at quarter-inch scale, so if you divide 1'-6" by 48, you have the Paper Space text height: ⅜". Assign the romand.shx font and the ⅜" height. Click Apply, then click Close.

2. Type **ps** ↵, then select Draw ➤ Text ➤ Single Line Text from the menu bar. Type **j** ↵, then type **c** ↵, then type **.y** ↵ to activate point filters.

3. Pick the Insertion Osnap and click the FRONT ELEVATION text. Pick Midpoint Osnap and click one of the horizontal deck lines.

4. Press ↵ for the Rotation prompt and, with Caps Lock on, type **floor plan** ↵ ↵. The floor plan title is placed on the drawing. Zoom in to see it better (Figure 13.23a).

5. With Ortho on, copy this text down ¾", then use the Properties button to change this text to be ¼" high and to read "SCALE: ¼" = 1'-0" (Figure 13.23b). Leave an extra space before and after the = sign.

6. Zoom previous. Use the Insertion Osnap and copy the scale to the front elevation.

7. Use the Copy command with the Multiple option with Ortho on, to copy both the view title and the scale from the floor plan to the bathroom viewport, and then to the site plan, with Ortho off.

8. Select Modify ➤ Objects ➤ Text to start the Ddedit command and change the titles to read BATHROOM and SITE PLAN, and the scales to read 1" = 1'-0" and ⅛" = 1'-0", respectively.

9. Freeze the Vport-ps layer. The results should look like Figure 13.24a. The drawing looks complete except the property line in the site plan looks continuous. With Paper Space, you need to set the global linetype scale setting to 1. Then AutoCAD will adjust the linetype scale for each viewport, depending on the scale it's zoomed to.

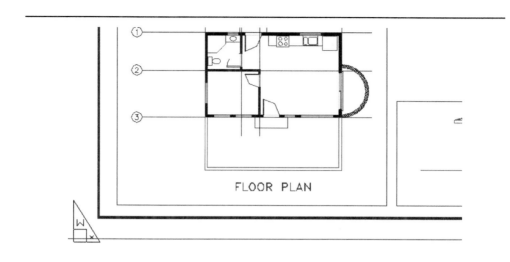

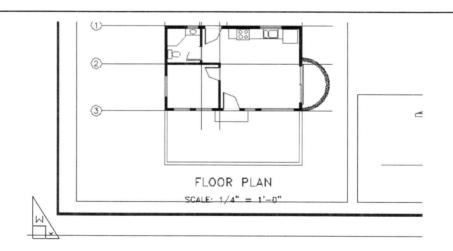

FIGURE 13.23: A title is placed on the floor plan (a) and a scale is added (b)

10. Type **ltscale** ⏎ **1** ⏎. The phantom linetype is now visible (Figure 13.24b).

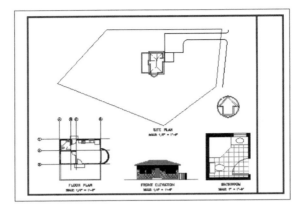

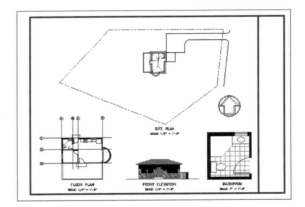

FIGURE 13.24: The 30" × 42" drawing complete with titles and scales of views (a) and with the ltscale setting adjusted for Paper Space (b)

You added one line of text in Paper Space to the drawing, then copied and changed it to make six more lines of the text.

As you have just seen, text and lines in Paper Space can be put on top of viewports. The viewport is like a window through which you can view the Model Space drawing, but the window has a transparent surface, like glass or cellophane, on which you can place text or other AutoCAD objects in Paper Space.

A layer can have some objects in Paper Space and some in Model Space, but this is not a good practice to get into because it can make the drawing harder to manage.

Turning Off Viewports

Beyond just controlling the visibility of layers in each viewport, you can turn off a viewport so all Model Space objects are invisible.

1. Thaw the Vport-ps layer for a moment.

2. Select View ➤ Floating Viewports ➤ Viewports Off from the menu bar.

3. Click each of the four viewports in the drawing, then press ↵. You will get a prompt that reads `Really want to turn off all active viewports? <N>`.

4. Type **y** ↵. All viewports go blank and all that's visible is the border, title block, the text, the viewport boundaries, and the arc in the bathroom, which are all in Paper Space (Figure 13.25).

5. Select View ➤ Floating Viewports ➤ Viewports On and pick the viewports for the site plan and bathroom, then press ↵. These two views are restored.

6. Repeat the command and restore the other two views, then freeze the Vport-ps layer.

Being able to turn viewports off can be an advantage for a complex drawing with many viewports, or a lot of information in each viewport. Remember that, even though all four views in this drawing are based on one drawing, AutoCAD is drawing at least part of that drawing in each viewport. In a complex drawing, this can slow down the computer, so it's handy to be able to temporarily turn off any viewports you are not working on.

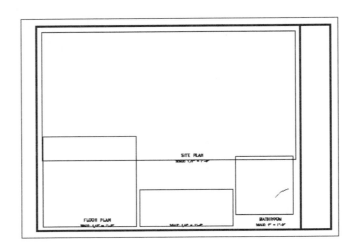

FIGURE 13.25: The 30" × 42" drawing with all viewports turned off

The Tilemode Variable and Tiled Viewports

The Tile button on the status bar controls whether Paper Space is enabled or not. When Tilemode is off, Paper Space is enabled. There is no reason for the average AutoCAD user to dig deeper into the Tilemode variable except for the fact that there is another kind of viewport in AutoCAD that works only when Paper Space is disabled. These viewports have some of the characteristics of floating Paper Space viewports, but not all of them. Only one kind of viewport can be used at a time but both can be set up in your drawing and saved with it.

1. Double-click the Tile button on the status bar to disable Paper Space. The site plan appears with all layers visible except those that had objects in Paper Space (Figure 13.26).

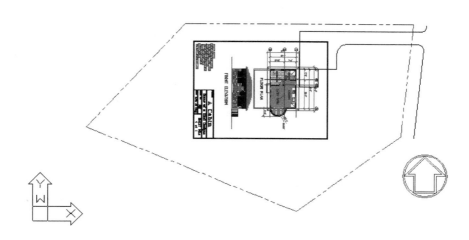

FIGURE 13.26: The site plan with Paper Space disabled

2. Select View ➤ Tiled Viewports ➤ 3 Viewports from the menu bar.

3. At the prompt, press ↵ to accept the default. The screen is redrawn with three tiled viewports and the site plan in each one (Figure 13.27a). The larger viewport on the right is the current viewport and has a dark border around it, and the cursor becomes the crosshair cursor when it is inside this viewport.

 NOTE   Tiled viewports get their name from the fact that their edges must always abut each other with no extra space between, i.e., they must be "tiled."

4. Make a zoom window to zoom into the floor plan of the cabin in the right viewport.

5. Click in the upper-left viewport to make it active, then use a zoom window again to zoom into the driveway area in this viewport (Figure 13.27b).

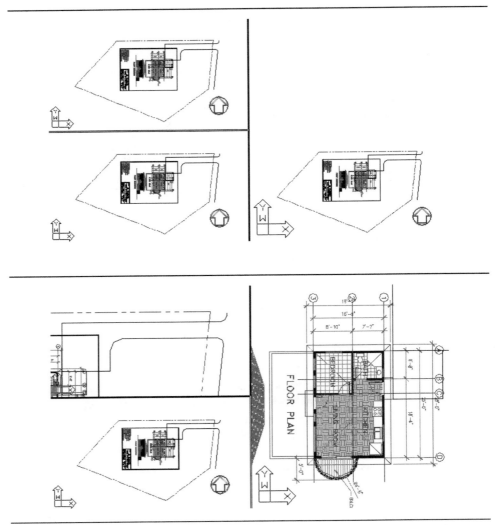

FIGURE 13.27: Tiled viewports with the site plan (a) and with the viewports zoomed to different magnification (b)

6. Double-click the Tile button to disable Tile mode and enable Paper Space. Your Paper Space setup is still there.

7. Double-click Tile again to disable Paper Space and enable Tile mode.

8. Click in the lower-left viewport to make it active.

9. Type **vports** ↵, then type **si** ↵. The tiled viewports are deleted and the full view of the site plan is restored.

10. Feel free to experiment with other tiled viewport arrangements, then, when you are finished, double-click the Tile button one more time to disable Tilemode and enable Paper Space.

11. Save this drawing as Site13.

Before Paper Space and floating viewports were implemented, tiled viewports were a feature of AutoCAD. They are a useful tool for working on your drawing, as certain tasks are difficult to accomplish without simultaneously having multiple views of your building, but they are not a plotting tool. You cannot plot more than one tiled viewport at a time.

The following are characteristics that distinguish tiled viewports from Paper Space floating viewports:

- Tiled viewports can be subdivided, but cannot be moved.

- They cannot overlap and must be tiled.

- Visibility of layers cannot be controlled for individual viewports.

In summary, Paper Space viewports can do anything tiled viewports can, and a lot more, but tiled viewports are still a useful tool in AutoCAD because they are easy to use and they can help you draw.

We will stay with the Paper Space viewports for the next skill, where you will round out your knowledge of AutoCAD by learning the principles of plotting and printing AutoCAD drawings.

Are You Experienced?

Now you can...

- ☑ enable Paper Space
- ☑ draw a border and title block in Paper Space
- ☑ set up viewports in Paper Space
- ☑ cut and paste in AutoCAD
- ☑ zoom to a scale in a viewport
- ☑ align viewports
- ☑ control layer visibility in individual viewports
- ☑ control the visibility of viewport boundaries
- ☑ copy viewports
- ☑ set up a text style for Paper Space and add text in Paper Space
- ☑ turn viewports off and on
- ☑ work with tiled viewports

Printing an AutoCAD Drawing

- ⊖ **Setting up a drawing to be printed**
- ⊖ **Configuring AutoCAD to a new printer**
- ⊖ **Assigning line weights to colors in your drawing**
- ⊖ **Setting up a user-defined sheet size**
- ⊖ **Previewing a print**
- ⊖ **Printing from Paper Space**

First of all, with today's equipment, there is no difference between printing and plotting. Printing used to refer to the smaller format printers, and plotting used to refer to the pen plotters, most of which were for plotting large sheets. But the terms are now used almost interchangeably. Pen plotters have a few extra settings that other printing devices do not have. Otherwise, the differences between them and laser jet, ink jet, dot matrix, and electrostatic printers, as far as AutoCAD is concerned, are minimal. So I'll refer to all printing and plotting processes as printing.

Getting your drawing onto paper can be very easy or very hard, depending on whether your computer is connected to a printer that has been set up to print AutoCAD drawings, and whether AutoCAD has been configured to work with the printer to which you have access. If these initial conditions are met, printing can be handily managed with the tools you will learn in this skill. If you do not have the initial setup, you will need to get some help to either set up your system to make AutoCAD work properly with your printer, or to find out how your system is already set up to print AutoCAD drawings. Then dive into this skill.

We will be using a couple of standard setup configurations between AutoCAD and printers to move through the exercises. You may or may not be able to follow through each step to completion, depending on whether you have access to an 8 ½" × 11" laser jet or desk jet printer, or a larger format printer, or both.

We have four drawings to print:

- Cabin11a—a drawing with Model Space only, to be printed on an 8 ½" × 11" sheet at eighth-inch scale

- Cabin13a—the same drawing as Cabin11a, except with the title block and border in Paper Space, to be printed from Paper Space on an 8 ½" × 11" sheet at a scale of one to one

- The 11" × 17" drawing in Cabin13b to be printed on an 11" × 17" sheet, using Paper Space

- Site13, printed on a 30" × 42" sheet, using Paper Space

If your printer won't allow you to print in all these formats, I would advise you to follow along through the text anyway. You'll at least get to preview how your drawing would have looked when printed in these formats, and you will be taking large strides towards learning how to set up and run a plot for your drawing. The skill is written to give you the basic principals for printing whether or not you have access to a printer.

The Print/Plot Configuration Dialog Box

The job of getting your AutoCAD file onto hard copy can be broken down into five tasks. You will need to specify to AutoCAD:

- The printing device you will use
- The line weight assigned to each color in your drawing
- The portion of your drawing you are printing
- The sheet size you are printing onto
- The scale, orientation, and placement of the print on the sheet

All of these tasks will be handled through the Print/Plot Configuration dialog box and other dialog boxes that open from it.

1. Open Cabin11a. Zoom to extents, then zoom out a little (Figure 14.1). This drawing is not quite ready to print.

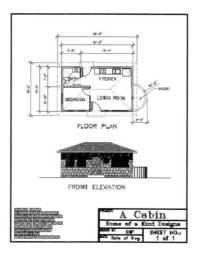

FIGURE 14.1: Cabin11a zoomed to extents, then zoomed out a little

2. Click the Print button on the Standard toolbar. The Print/Plot Configuration dialog box appears (Figure 14.2). We'll take a quick tour of this dialog box and then start setting up to print.

 NOTE The Print / Plot Configuration dialog box can also be brought up by selecting File ➤ Print, by typing Ctrl+P, or by typing **plot** ↵ or **print** ↵.

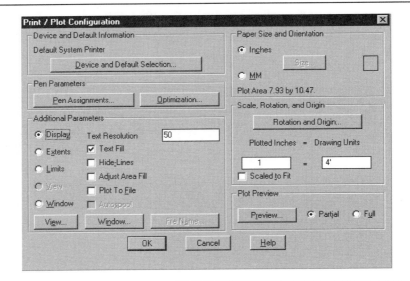

FIGURE 14.2: The Print/Plot Configuration dialog box

There are five areas in the dialog box which correspond to the five tasks listed above, and a Plot Preview area. Some of the buttons and boxes won't be activated. Others will be mentioned only in passing, as their functions are for more advanced techniques than those covered in this book.

Device and Default Information

In the Device and Default Information area, the current printing device is displayed above the Device and Default Selection button (in this case it's the Default System Printer). The fact that the Print/Plot Configuration dialog box has appeared means that AutoCAD has been configured to at least one printing device. If you are working with AutoCAD at a computer where a printer has not been configured, you will not be able to bring up the Print/Plot Configuration dialog box. Page forward in this skill to the section titled "Configuring AutoCAD for a Printer" and configure the system printer, or get some help to set up a printer configuration.

1. Click the Device and Default Selection button. A dialog box by that name appears.

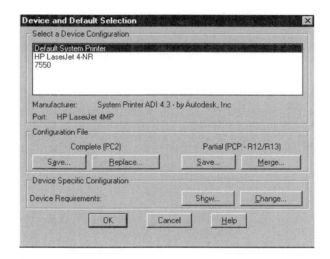

The Select a Device Configuration area at the top of the dialog box lists the various printing devices to which AutoCAD has been configured, with the current one—in this case, the Default System Printer—highlighted. Just below the list, the name of the driver and port are displayed for the selected printer in the list above.

2. If you have more than one printing device listed, click one that is not current and note how the name of the driver, and possibly the port, change.

The Configuration File area contains buttons for saving the settings for printing a specific way with a particular printer. We won't be saving any settings for these exercises, but if you find yourself repeatedly using the same setup for the same printer, using the buttons in this area will allow you to save the print settings for future use.

The Device Specific Configuration area has buttons that open other dialog boxes which allow you to see and change—or display information about how you can change—configuration settings specific to the current printer. The settings will vary, depending on which printer you have selected above in the list.

Pen Parameters

You should be generally familiar with this area, but we won't be making changes to the pen parameters until later in the skill.

1. In the Device and Default Selection dialog box, click the Default System Printer to select it, then click OK. If you don't have the Default System Printer in the list of choices of printers, click Cancel to close the Device and Default Selection dialog box without saving any changes you may have made. This will leave the printer which had been previously selected to be the current printer. The next area to look at is the Pen Parameters area.

2. Click the Pen Assignments button in the Pen Parameters area of the Print/Plot Configuration dialog box. The Pen Assignments dialog box appears.

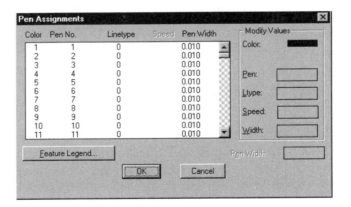

The left-most column is marked Color. The colors are listed in numerical order. These are the colors that have been assigned to layers in your drawing, with the first seven assigned names: red, yellow, green, cyan, blue, magenta, and white/black, respectively. Each color may have an assigned pen number, linetype, speed, and pen width. Note that the pen width for all colors is 0.010 by default and the speed setting is ghosted, because it is not available for this printer.

As was mentioned in Skill 6, *Using Layers to Organize Your Drawing*, colors control the line weight of objects in your drawing. When we assigned specific colors to layers in Skill 6, we didn't pay much attention to what line weight should be assigned to lines for particular building components. In a drawing on the computer screen, the different colors assigned to layers help you distinguish between objects which represent different building components. There is no difference in line weight on the screen, other than an occasional polyline used for a border or for special emphasis. But printed drawings usually consist of lines in one color, so line weight becomes important to help you read the drawing accurately.

The Modify Values area on the right side contains boxes where you can change any of the four parameters assigned to a color.

3.   Click color number 4 in the Color column. In the Modify Values area, the color box changes to cyan and 4 (cyan) is displayed just below. Further down, in the text boxes, the values for pen number, linetype, and width for color number 4 are displayed. You can change any of these and the new values will be visible in the list. By holding down Ctrl when you select color numbers, you can select any number of colors at the same time. We will leave all settings as they are for this plot. This will result in all lines being printed at the same weight.

 NOTE   The speed setting controls the speed at which a pen moves across the paper in a pen plotter. Some kinds of pens can move faster than others and still draw a good, clean line. For printers that don't have pens, this is ghosted out.

4.   Click Cancel to close the Pen Assignments dialog box.

Most drawings use four or five standard line weights. Using many more than that will usually begin to sabotage the clarity you were trying to achieve with line weight variation. Since most drawings use more than four or five colors, several colors are inevitably assigned the same pen weight.

The Optimization button in the Print/Plot Configuration dialog box opens a dialog box which allows you to switch on or off any of several settings that control how pen plotters operate when printing. We won't be covering these settings in this book.

Paper Size and Orientation

The Paper Size and Orientation area of the Print/Plot Configuration dialog box controls the units in which you want the sizes of sheets to be displayed—inches or millimeters. Whichever units you choose will be applied to pen width in the Pen Assignments dialog box and to the plotted units part of the scale equation.

The size button is ghosted out because with my configuration, the system printer is presently hooked up to a laser jet printer which can only print one size: 8 ½" × 11". When we print the larger drawings later in this skill, you will use a larger format printer and learn about choosing different sheet sizes.

Scale, Rotation, and Origin

The Scale, Rotation, and Origin area of the Print/Plot Configuration dialog box is where you determine how the drawing fits on the sheet. The Rotation and Origin button brings up the Plot Rotation and Origin dialog box. Click it now.

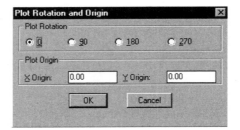

This is where you can rotate and slide the drawing relative to the sheet. Let's use Cabin11a to see how these settings work. Follow along without making any changes to your drawing.

Plot Rotation

Printers are set to print in landscape or portrait orientation. Cabin11a is in portrait orientation because it was set up to be taller than it is wide, so you will want your printer to print your drawing this way also. However, your printer may be currently set to print in landscape orientation. If you print a portrait-oriented drawing on a landscape-oriented piece of paper, the results will be like Figure 14.3a.

You need to rotate the drawing 90° by clicking the radio button marked 90. Then you will get results like Figure 14.3b.

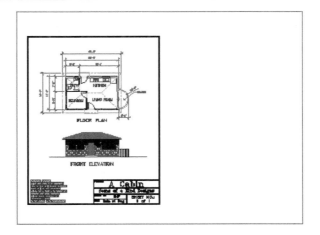

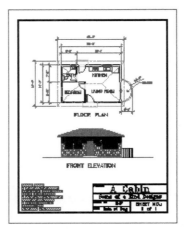

FIGURE 14.3: A print with landscape orientation (a) and with the drawing rotated 90° (b)

Plot Origin

Just as each drawing has an origin (0,0 point), each plotter creates an origin for the plot. Usually it's in the lower-left or upper-left corner, but not always. When the plot is being made, the printer first locates the origin and starts the print there, moving outward from the origin. If the origin is in the lower-left corner the print may come out looking like Figure 14.4a. If the origin is the upper-left corner, the print will look like Figure 14.4b.

By using the X Origin and Y Origin setting in the Plot Origin area of the Plot Rotation and Origin dialog box, you can center your drawing on the page (Figure 14.4c).

Setting the origin accurately will be a result of trial and error, and getting to know your printer well. We will return to this dialog box shortly, when we get ready to print. Click Cancel to close the Plot Rotation and Origin dialog box.

Setting the Scale

You can print to a scale or scale the drawing to fit on the sheet. If you click the Scaled to Fit button, AutoCAD will fill the sheet with the drawing, much like zooming to extents fills the screen with your drawing. Otherwise you enter Plotted inches and Drawing Units to define a scale. The plotted inches will be an actual distance on the drawing, while drawing units is the distance the plotted units represent, so for quarter-inch scale ($\frac{1}{4}$"=1'-0") you could enter several combinations:

Plotted Inches	Drawing Units
$\frac{1}{4}$	1'
1	4'
1	48

We'll come back to the scale after we determine what to plot.

Additional Parameters

In the Additional Parameters area, the left side has five radio buttons for specifying what to print in your drawing. We have already made some decisions about what to print by deciding which layers will be visible when the print is made, and we have frozen the layers whose objects we don't want printed. Now you must decide how you will designate the area of the drawing to be printed. As we go through the options, it will be useful to think about the choices with regard to two printing possibilities: printing the whole drawing and printing just the floor plan.

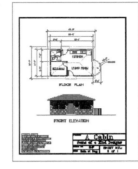

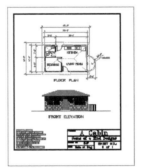

FIGURE 14.4: A print with its origin in the lower-left corner (a), in the upper-left corner (b), and with the drawing centered (c)

To illustrate how these options work, we will make a couple of assumptions: First, the Scaled to Fit option on the right side in the Scale, Rotation, and Origin area is active, so AutoCAD will try to fill the sheet with your drawing. Second, the rotation will be such that the drawing and sheet are both in portrait orientation.

Display

The display option will print what's currently on the screen, including the blank area around the drawing. With both drawing and sheet in portrait orientation, and with the origin in the lower-left corner of the sheet, the plot would look like Figure 14.5, with the dashed lines representing the edge of what was the drawing area on the screen. If the drawing were rotated, it would fit better on the sheet. Printing to Display is a good method if both drawing and sheet are in landscape orientation.

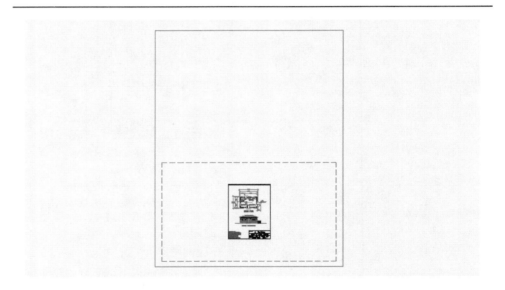

FIGURE 14.5: The Cabin11a drawing printed to Display

Extents

When you select the Extents option, AutoCAD tries to fill the sheet with the visible objects in the drawing. If you set up a print the same way as above, in terms of rotation and orientation, the results would look like Figure 14.6. This is a good method to use if the border has been drawn with the same proportions as the sheet. It was in this case because you offset a rectangle that represented the sheet, to make the border.

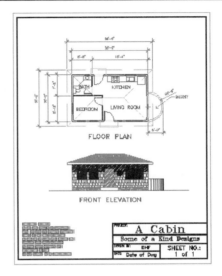

FIGURE 14.6: The Cabin11a drawing printed to Extents

Limits

Do you remember the drawing limits for the cabin drawing that you set in Skill 3, *Setting Up a Drawing*? For a reminder, perform the instructions that follow.

1. Select Cancel to cancel the plot.

2. Double-click the Grid button on the status bar to make the grid visible. It's still there, around the floor plan, just as you first set it in Skill 3 (Figure 14.7a). When you print to Limits, AutoCAD will print only what lies within the limits and it will push what's within the limits to the corner that is the origin of the print (Figure 14.7b). This doesn't work here because the limits don't cover the entire drawing. Printing to Limits can be a good tool for setting up a print, but you will usually reset the limits for the print, from their original defining coordinates.

3. Press F7 to turn off the grid.

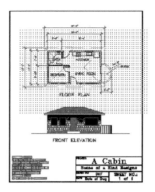

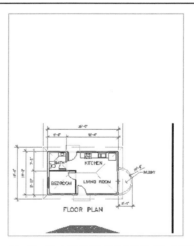

FIGURE 14.7: The grid showing the limits of Cabin11a (a) and the drawing printed to Limits (b)

View

When printing to View, you tell AutoCAD to print a previously defined view that was saved with the drawing. Right now the View radio button is ghosted because we haven't defined and saved any views yet. We'll save a view and then you'll see what the print will look like.

1. Pick View ➤ Named Views. The View control dialog box comes up.

2. Click the New button. In the Define New View dialog box, type **plot1** and click the Define Window radio button. Then click the Window button.

3. Back in the drawing make a window around the left half of the floor plan, not including the dimensions, as in Figure 14.8a.

4. Click the Save View button. The saved view called Plot1 is listed in the Views list box of the View Control dialog box.

5. Click OK to return to the drawing, then click the Print button and continue reading along.

Now, to plot the Plot1 view of this drawing, click the View button in the Print/Plot Configuration dialog box and select Plot1 from the list of saved views. At the settings for scale and orientation we have been using, the print will look like Figure 14.8b. This is a valuable tool for prints of parts of a drawing that you might want to redo at a later point in the progress of the project.

Window

Using a window to define the area of a plot is the most flexible method of the five being described. It's like using zoom window in the drawing. AutoCAD will take the area you window and put it into the print. To select this option, click the Window radio button, then click the Pick button in the Window Selection dialog box. In your drawing, make a window around the area you want to print. AutoCAD will print only what is in the window you made, regardless of how it fits on the sheet. This method is similar to the View method, discussed previously. The difference lies in the fact that the View method prints a previously defined view (one which was possibly defined by a window, but which could also be defined in other ways), and the Window method prints what is included in a window that you define as you are setting up the plot. The window used by the Window method can't be saved and recalled at a later time.

These are the five ways to specify what to print. We'll use the Extents and Window options in the following exercises.

Window ————————————————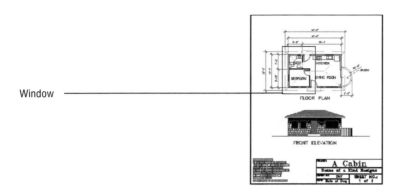

FIGURE 14.8: Using a window to define a view (a) and the print to this view (b)

Other Additional Parameters

The other checkboxes and the text box in the Additional Parameters area are for more advanced printing operations and are briefly described below:

- The Text Resolution text box and the Text Fill checkbox are for controlling the appearance of the more complex fonts.

- Hide-Lines is for 3D images.

- Adjust Area Fill is a specialized setting used when the actual area of fills and wide lines become critical in a print, as, for example, in microcircuit design.

- Plot To File allows you to make a file of the print rather than an actual print. This is used if you need to print from a different computer than your work station, or if you use a plotting service and must transfer files to them. These files use the extension `.plt`. When you select this option, the File Name button is activated and you can designate a name and folder for the `.plt` file.

- Autospool is used in an office where you are networked and several people are sending `.plt` files to several printers on the network.

We have taken a quick tour of the Print/Plot Configuration dialog box, and some of the sub-dialog boxes that go with it, and we still have a drawing—Cabin11a—to print. Let's print this drawing. As we set up the print, refer back to this section for explanation of the steps, if necessary.

Printing a Drawing

Our task is to print `Cabin11a.dwg` at a scale of ⅛"=1'-0" on an 8 ½" × 11" sheet. In this exercise, we will use the default system printer which is set up for an 8 ½" × 11" format laser jet printer. If you have an 8 ½" × 11" format printer, you should be able to follow the steps. If you don't have a printer, you can still get familiar with printing by following along with the steps in the book.

Some of the objects in the drawing are the same color but should be a different line weight. To correct this, we need to make some minor changes to the colors assigned to layers in `Cabin11a`, before we begin to set up the print.

1. Click Cancel to close the Print/Plot Configuration dialog box, then click the Layer button on the Object Properties toolbar to open the Layer & Linetype Properties dialog box.

2. Change the color of the F-elev layer to Red (1).

3. Change the color of the Tblk1 layer to Blue (5).

4. Click OK to close this dialog box.

5. Pick Format ➤ Dimension Style. In the Dimension Styles dialog box, be sure Plan1 is the current dimension style, then click the Annotation button. The Annotation dialog box comes up.

6. In the Text area (lower-right corner) click the Color button. The Select Color dialog box appears.

7. Select Red in the row of Standard colors at the top, then click OK. Click OK again to close the Annotation dialog box. Click the Save button.

8. Repeat this procedure for the Radial child style. Refer to Skill 11, *Dimensioning a Drawing*, if you need a refresher on working with the parent and child dimensioning styles.

9. In the Dimension Styles dialog box, click Save then click OK. Back in the drawing, the dimension text has turned red.

10. Use the Properties button to change the leader line text (BALCONY) to the color red.

Determining Line Weight for a Drawing

You have just made some adjustments in the colors assigned to a few of the objects in your drawing. Most of the changes you made by assigning different colors to layers. The last change was made to the dimension text. The dimension style settings allow you to assign different colors to the text, dimension lines, or extension lines. We changed the color of the dimension text so we could assign the text's color a thicker line weight. In architectural practice, the dimension lines are usually given a very thin line weight compared to those for the building lines, so the dimension and extension lines don't distract the person viewing the drawing from the building lines. But the dimension text is usually made to stand out and be easily readable, hence, the text's heavier line weight.

Looking at the Cabin11a drawing as a whole, we need to decide weights for the other lines. The floor plan is drawn as if a cut were made horizontally through the building just below the tops of the window and door openings. Everything that was cut will be given a heavy line. Objects above and below the cut will be given progressively lighter lines, depending on how far above or below the cut the objects are located. In this system, the walls, windows, and doors will be heaviest, with the roof, headers, fixtures, and steps lighter. For emphasis, we'll make the walls a little heavier than the windows and doors. In the front elevation, the hatch pattern will be very light and the outline of the various components will be heavier, for emphasis. Text and the title block information will use the default line weight.

 NOTE   These are general guidelines—weights will vary with each drawing.

We will use four line weights for this drawing:

Weight	Thickness
very light	0.005
light	0.008
medium	0.010
heavy	0.013

There are fifteen layers in Cabin11a that are visible in the drawing as it is presently set up. Their line weights will be assigned as follows:

Layer	Line Weight
Balcony	light
Dim1	very light
Doors	medium
F-elev	medium
Fixtures	light
Hatch-elev-42	very light
Hatch-elev-black	very light
Hatch-elev-gray	very light
Headers	light
Roof	very light
Steps	light
Tblk1	medium
Text	medium
Walls	heavy
Windows	medium

When we look at the colors presently assigned to these layers, and at the weights we need the lines on these layers to be, we can generate a third chart that will show us what colors need to be assigned to a particular line weight. We'll use the number of colors rather than their names because only their numbers are used in the Pen Assignments dialog box, where you will assign the line weights to the colors:

Line Weight	Colors or layers
0.005	4, 7, 8, 42, Dim1*
0.008	2, 3, 6, 9
0.010 (default)	1, Windows*, Text*
0.013	5

NOTE Assign the color of the Dim1 layer the 0.005 line weight. Whichever colors you assigned to the Windows and Text layers can be left to the default line-weight setting of 0.010.

Now it's time to assign the line weights to the colors in the drawings.

1. Click the Print button on the Standard toolbar to start the Print command. The Print/Plot Configuration dialog box appears.

NOTE If the Pen Assignments button is ghosted out, it means that your printer driver does not allow variation of line-weight. Just follow on through the text.

2. In the Pen Parameters area, click the Pen Assignments button. The Pen Assignments dialog box appears.

3. Following the table above, select color 4, then hold down Ctrl and click the following colors: 7, 8, 42 and the color you assigned to the Dim1 layer. They should all be highlighted.

4. On the right, in the Width box, change the 0.010 to 0.005, then press ↵. The selected colors are assigned the pen width of 0.005. The colors you highlighted in this step will be deselected when you pick the first color in the next group to be assigned a width.

NOTE You can always deselect all highlighted colors by clicking any color without pressing any keys.

5. Repeat steps 3 and 4 for the 0.008 line weight and the colors numbered 2, 3, 6, and 9.

6. Repeat steps 3 and 4 for the 0.013 line weight and color number 5.

7. Click OK to close the Pen Assignments dialog box.

The line weights have been assigned. When the print is complete you can judge whether these line-weight assignments are acceptable or need to be adjusted. In an office, much time is invested in developing a line weight standard that can be used in most drawings.

Setting Up the Other Parameters for the Print

Now that we have set up the pen parameters, it's time to move to the Additional Parameters and Scale, Rotation, and Origin areas of the Print/Plot Configuration dialog box. We will use the Window options for selecting what we will print.

1. Be sure Default System Printer is displayed in the Device and Default Information area. Then move to the Additional Parameters area and click the Window button. The Window Selection dialog box opens.

2. Click the Pick button.

3. In the drawing, disable any running Osnaps and pick a point just below and to the left of the border to start the window. Pick it as close to the lower-left corner of the border as you can without touching the border.

4. Click a point above and to the right of the border, also as close to the border as you can without touching the border, to complete the window.

5. When the Window Selection dialog box comes up, click OK. In the Additional Parameters area of the Print/Plot Configuration dialog box, Window is now selected.

6. In the Scale, Rotation, and Origin area, make sure the Scaled To Fit checkbox is not checked. If it is, click the checkbox to deactivate it.

7. In the text boxes above the Scaled to Fit checkbox, enter **1/8** in the left box and **1'** in the right box.

8. In the Plot Preview area, be sure the Partial radio button is selected, then click the Preview button. The Preview Effective Plotting Area dialog box appears. It has a rectangular graphic at the top, paper size and effective area displayed in the middle, and a warning box at the bottom.

Previewing a Print

The graphic at the top should look like one of the two shown below. These two diagrams represent the two possible orientations the drawing may have relative to the paper. If your printer has been previously configured to landscape orientation, you should see the diagram on the left. If portrait, the one on the right.

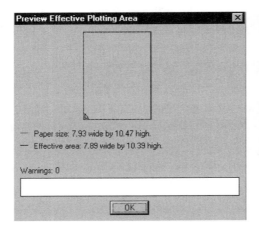 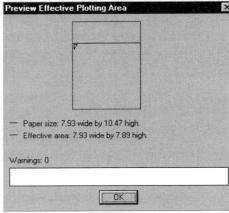

There are three elements in the graphic: a rectangle representing the sheet, another rectangle representing the area on the sheet taken up with your drawing, and a triangle indicating the lower-left corner of the drawing. In the graphic in the first dialog box (above), the two rectangles are close to being spatially coincident and the triangular icon is in the lower-left corner. Moving to the second graphic, you will see that the rectangle representing the drawing is nearly square and the lower-left corner of the drawing is in the upper-left corner of this smaller rectangle, indicating that the drawing has been turned. If your graphic looks this way you will have to rotate the print. You'll do that shortly.

The Warnings box will give you information when there are problems with the setup.

Viewing a Full Preview

To be sure how the print has been set up, make a full preview.

1. Click OK to close the Preview Effective Plotting Area dialog box.

2. In the Plot Preview area of the Print/Plot Configuration dialog box, click the Full radio button.

3. Make the same changes to colors assigned to layers that you made to Cabin11a. Refer to the beginning of the section "Printing a Drawing for the Steps."

4. Click the Preview button again. You will see how the print will look. Your full preview will look like Figure 14.9 a or b, depending upon whether your print needs rotating. If the print is sideways, note that it is also cut off at the top. With the scale set to ⅛"=1'-0", the full print cannot fit on the page in a rotated orientation. AutoCAD starts the print in the lower-left corner of the page and extends it up and to the right until there's no more room left. Then it lops off the rest.

5. Press ↵ or Esc to return to the Print/Plot Configuration dialog box. If your print was oriented correctly on the sheet, you are ready to print, so you can skip down to step 10. If your print needs rotating, complete steps 5–9 first.

6. Click the Rotation and Origin button in the Scale, Rotation, and Origin area. The Plot Rotation and Origin dialog box appears. In the Plot Rotation area the 0 or 90 radio button should be picked.

7. If the 0 button is picked, click the 90 button. If the 90 button is picked, click the 0 button.

8. Click OK.

9. Click Full in the Plot Preview area and click the Preview button. Your full preview should look like Figure 14.9a. If it does, you are ready to plot.

10. Press ↵ or Esc.

11. At the bottom of the Print/Plot Configuration dialog box, click OK. The computer will begin calculating the print and eventually send it to the printer.

NOTE   Print previews won't show you how your line weight assignments to color will appear in the final print. You have to print out the drawing to see that.

When your print comes out it should look similar to Figure 14.9a. Take a close look at the border. Is the space outside the border equal on the left and right, or up and down? If not, you can move the X and Y origin points by opening the Plot Rotation and Origin dialog box and changing the settings for the X Origin and Y Origin. Each printer has limits as to how close to the edge of the sheet it can print. These are called *hard clip limits*. When you know them, you can calculate how large a drawing can be printed on the sheets that work with the printer. It takes a little trial and error.

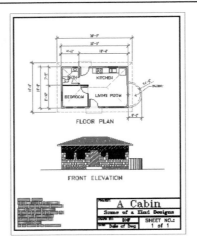

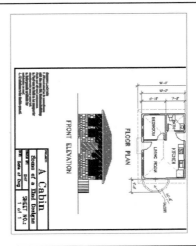

FIGURE 14.9: The full preview with the drawing correctly oriented (a) and when the drawing needs rotating (b)

TIP If you can't find the hard clip limits in your printer's manual, you can make a test plot to determine them. To make the test plot, plot this drawing using the Extents option and increase the scale to ¼"=1'-0". The print will have the lower-left corner of the border visible and the lower and left border lines will extend to the hard clip limits of your printer.

Check the line weights of the various components on the drawing. You may have to make adjustments to the pen weights for your particular printer.

Next you'll plot a similar drawing, which uses Paper Space for its border and title block.

Printing a Drawing with Paper Space

As a comparison to the previous exercise, we'll print a drawing which has Paper Space set up. When Paper Space has been set up properly and is active, you print at a scale of 1 to 1. The elements of the drawing in Paper Space are then printed actual size and the Model Space portion of the drawing is printed at the scale to which the viewport has been zoomed.

1. Save the current drawing as Cabin14a.

2. Open Cabin13a. It's appearance is identical to Cabin11a except for the outside rectangle that represents the edge of the 8 ½" × 11" sheet, but Cabin13a has its border and title block in Paper Space (Figure 14.10).

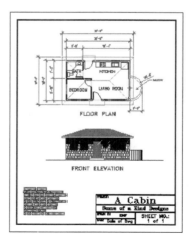

FIGURE 14.10: The Cabin13a drawing ready for printing

3. Type **print** ↵ to start the Print command. The Print/Plot Configuration dialog box appears. All the parameters you set for the last print will still be in effect, so you have to determine what settings need to be changed to accommodate Paper Space.

4. You have to specify what to print since this is a different drawing. In the Additional Parameters area, click the Window button.

5. In the Window Selection dialog box, click the Pick button, then window the border just as you did for the previous print (making a window just large enough to enclose the border). Don't window the outside rectangle.

6. Back in the Window Selection dialog box, click OK.

7. Back in the Print/Plot Configuration dialog box, the paper size can't be changed and the rotation and origin will be left the same, assuming it was set properly for the print.

8. In the Scale, Rotation, and Origin area, change the Plotted Inches to 1 and the Drawing Units to 1.

9. In the Print Preview Area, select Full and click the Preview button. Your preview should look like Figure 14.9a.

10. Press ↵ or Esc to return to the dialog box, then click OK to start the print. If you don't have a printer and/or are just following along, click Cancel to cancel the print at this point.

This exercise was intended to show you that, once Paper Space has been set up, the only difference in printing this drawing from printing a drawing without Paper Space is the scale you give the print. When Paper Space is used in a drawing, you will print to a scale of 1 to 1, or 1" = 1", while Paper Space is active. This is because you set Paper Space up in such a way that the border, title block, and any other objects in Paper Space were drawn to actual size, so you're always printing in Paper Space at a scale of 1 to 1. This greatly simplifies the printing process because the scale of the print is determined before the Print command is begun.

WARNING Make sure that Paper Space is active: If you print at 1 to 1 scale with Model Space active, the results are disastrous!

Printing a Drawing with Multiple Viewports

Multiple viewports in Paper Space don't require any special handling. The print will be made from Paper Space at a scale of 1 to 1. For the next print, you will use a different printer—one that can handle larger sheet sizes—so the procedure will be similar to the first print you made. An additional step will be required for this print, however, at the very beginning of the process. You will have to configure AutoCAD for a large format printer, assuming you don't have one already configured. If you do, you can follow along through this part of the process.

Configuring AutoCAD for a Printer

If you don't have access to a large format printer, you can still configure AutoCAD for one and preview how the print would look.

1. Save the current drawing to your training directory as Cabin14b.

2. Open Cabin13b. You will have two drawings, one of which is identical to Cabin14b and the other a 11" × 17" drawing in landscape orientation. You'll print the larger one. (If both drawings are not on the screen, zoom to extents, then zoom out a little.)

3. Pick Tools ➢ Preferences. The Preferences dialog box appears.

4. Click the Printer tab. You'll see a list of configured printers and option buttons on the right.

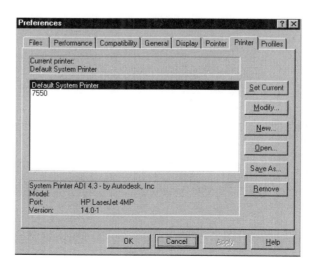

Your list may be different than the one shown here, depending on which printers you have configured to your system.

5. Click the New button. The Add a Printer dialog box appears, showing a list of available printer drivers.

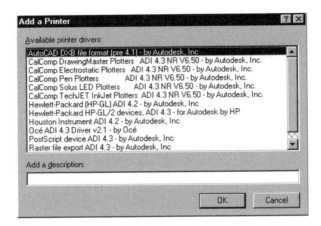

6. Highlight *Hewlett-Packard HP-GL/2 devices, ADI 4.3 - for Autodesk by HP*, and click OK. A text screen comes up displaying a list of the printers that will work with this driver. Press ↵ to see the rest of the list.

7. At the Enter selection, 1 to 21 <1>: prompt, type **3** ↵ to select the HP DesignJet 750C printer.

8. Press ↵ again. At the port specification prompts, press ↵ twice. Click OK at the warning. Then you will get a list of seven parameters for controlling the print. These are settings you can control through the Print/Plot Configuration dialog box.

9. Press ↵. You are returned to the Preferences dialog box. The HP DesignJet 750C printer is now listed as a configured printer.

10. Click OK to return to your drawing.

You now have a large format printer to work with. Now you are ready to go through approximately the same steps to set up a print that you used to print Cabin11a.

Printing with a Large Format Printer

The procedure here varies from what you have been doing only in that you will be specifying a sheet size this time. The first step is to erase the drawing on the left. Remember, both drawings have views of the same Model Space drawing, so we don't want to erase that. You will erase just the Paper Space elements of the left drawing.

1. Thaw the Vport-ps layer momentarily. The viewports appear.

2. Be sure Paper Space is active, then start the Erase command and use a window to select the title block, border, and viewport of the smaller drawing, and select the outer rectangle of the larger one. Press ↵.

3. Freeze the Vport-ps layer again. Zoom to extents, then zoom out a little (Figure 14.11). If you will be able to print this drawing, make the changes to the colors assigned to layers that you made for the previous two drawings. If you are not going to actually print, this is unnecessary.

4. Click the Print button on the Standard toolbar to start the Print command.

5. In the Print/Plot Configuration dialog box, click the Device and Default Selection button in the upper-left corner.

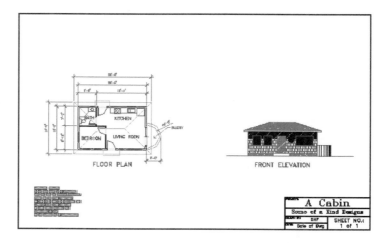

FIGURE 14.11: The 11" × 17" drawing ready to print

6. In the list of printers, highlight HP DesignJet 750C, then click OK.

NOTE If you can send this print to a large format printer, you will need to reassign the pen widths to the colors in the Pen Parameters dialog box for this new printer setup. If you cannot, it is not necessary to reassign the pen widths.

7. In the Additional Parameters area, select Extents.

8. In the Paper Size and Orientation area, click the Size button. The Paper Size dialog box appears.

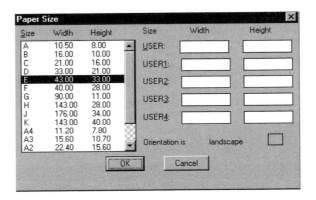

On the left is the list of preset sheet sizes, and to the right are slots for five user-defined sizes.

9. Highlight the B preset sheet size and click OK.

10. In the Scale, Rotation, and Origin area, deselect the Scaled to Fit checkbox and make the scale 1 to 1.

11. In the Plot Preview area, select Full, then click the Preview button. The preview shows that the print won't quite fit completely on the sheet (Figure 14.12).

This is a common occurrence. Often you will assume a certain standard size sheet for your drawing, only to find that the printer driver you are using doesn't offer the exact same size you need. You set the plot up for a 11" × 17" sheet and the 10.00 × 16.00 B size sheet turns out to be too small. Fortunately, you have the option of setting up user-defined sheets.

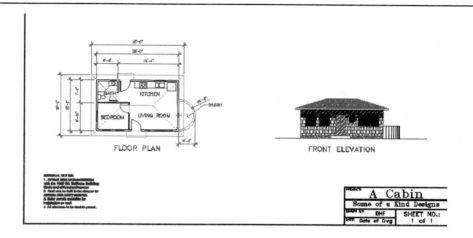

FIGURE 14.12: The print preview with the print running off the sheet

Setting Up a User-Defined Sheet Size

You'll create a 11" × 17" user-defined sheet.

1. Press ↵ or Esc to leave the preview and return to the Print/Plot Configuration dialog box, then click the Size button.

2. In the text boxes next to USER: click in the width box and type **17**, then click in the height box and type **11** ↵. The new user style is now displayed in the list on the left and it's highlighted.

3. Click OK.

4. Select Full, then click the Preview button in the Plot Preview area. The drawing's border is now completely on the sheet, but it's not centered (Figure 14.13a).

5. Press ↵ or Esc to leave the preview.

6. In the Scale, Rotation, and Origin area, click the Rotation and Origin button. The Plot Rotation and Origin dialog box appears.

7. In the Plot Origin area, change the X Origin and Y Origin to 0.50, then click OK.

8. In the Plot Preview area, Full should still be selected. If not, select it. Click the Preview button. The print is now centered on the page (Figure 14.13b).

9. Press ↵ or Esc to cancel the preview. If you have a large format printer configured and can plot this drawing on an 11" × 17" sheet, click OK to start the print. Otherwise click Cancel.

10. Save this drawing as Cabin14c.

For the last exercise in the book, you will set up a print for Site13, using the large format printer.

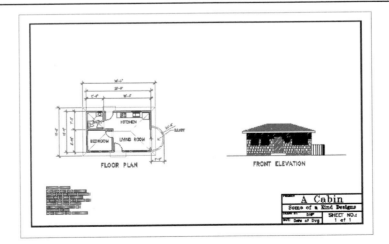

FIGURE 14.13: The print preview with a user-defined sheet (a) and with the origin adjusted (b)

Printing the Site Plan

The site plan was set up with Paper Space and based upon a 30" × 42" sheet in landscape orientation. The large format printer (HP DesignJet 750C) which we configured AutoCAD for in the last exercise will print this size sheet.

1. Open Site13. Paper Space should be active.

2. Erase the outside rectangle that represents the edge of the sheet. We won't be making any color changes for this print.

3. Start the Print command. (Type **print** ↵.) The Print/Plot Configuration dialog box comes up.

4. Be sure the HP DesignJet 750C (or your large format printer) is displayed as the current printer in the Device and Default Information area, then click the Pen Parameters button and change all pen width assignments to 0.010. Click OK.

5. In the Additional Parameters area, select Extents, then in the Paper Size and Orientation area, click the Size button.

6. In the Paper Size dialog box, look for a 42 × 30 size—or something close—in the list on the left. The E size is a bit large and F size too small. We'll make our own.

7. In the User text box, enter **30** in the left box and **42** in the right. The new user size is added to the list and highlighted. Click OK.

 NOTE   For the HP DesignJet 750C printer, there are slots for five user-defined paper sizes. The User1-4 slots can be used for permanent sizes used frequently in the office. The top User slot can then be used for the incidental size.

8. Click in the Scaled to Fit checkbox to disable that option.

9. In the Plot Preview area, select Full and click Preview. You see how the print sits on the sheet (Figure 14.14a). We want the margins to be the same top and bottom, and the right side to match those. That will leave extra on the left for the binding strip.

10. Press ↵ or Esc to return to the Print/Plot Configuration dialog box. In the Scale, Rotation, and Origin area, click the Rotation and Origin button. The Plot Rotation and Origin dialog box opens.

11. In the Plot Origin area, set the X Origin to 2 and the Y Origin to 1. Click OK. Click Preview again. The drawing is positioned fairly well (Figure 14.14b). Feel free to make minor adjustments to the origin settings.

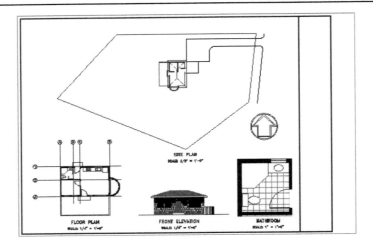

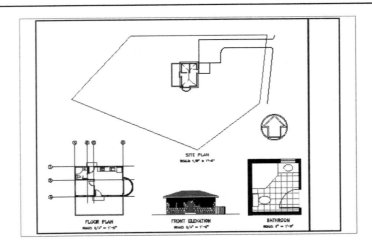

FIGURE 14.14: The first print preview (a) and the preview with the origin adjusted (b)

12. When finished making adjustments, return to the Print / Plot Configuration dialog box and click OK to start the print, or Cancel to cancel it.

13. Save this drawing as Site14a.

This concludes the exercises for this skill, and for the book. The Appendix that follows covers the concepts involved with drawing in 3D. After that, you will find a glossary of terms related to AutoCAD and building construction and design which have been mentioned in the book.

Are You Experienced?

Now you can...

- ☑ **set up a drawing to be printed**
- ☑ **choose a configured printer**
- ☑ **configure AutoCAD to a new printer**
- ☑ **assign line weights to colors in your drawing**
- ☑ **select the area of your drawing to print**
- ☑ **choose a sheet size to print your drawing on**
- ☑ **set up a user-defined sheet size**
- ☑ **control the rotation and origin of the print**
- ☑ **set the scale of the print**
- ☑ **preview a print**
- ☑ **print from Paper Space**

A Look at Drawing in 3D

Nothing in CAD is quite so fascinating as drawing in 3D. When you look at the difference between the traditional 3D rendering of a building on a drafting board, using vanishing points and projection planes, and a 3D model of a building on the computer that can be rotated and viewed from any angle, as well as from the inside, the comparison is like apples and oranges.

Constructing a 3D model of a building requires the use of many of the tools you have been using throughout this book, and some new ones that you will be introduced to in this appendix. Your competence in the use of the basic drawing, editing, and display commands is critical to your successful study of 3D for two reasons: First, drawing in 3D is more complex and difficult than drawing in 2D, and can, for this reason, be very frustrating. If you aren't familiar with the basic commands, you will become that much more frustrated. Second, accuracy is critical in 3D drawing. The effect of errors is compounded, so you must be in the habit of using tools like the Osnap modes to maximize your precision.

Don't feel discouraged, just warned. Drawing in 3D is a truly fascinating and enjoyable process, and the results you get can be astounding. I sincerely encourage you to make the effort to learn some of the basic 3D skills presented here.

There are many 3D software packages on the market today, some better for drawing buildings than others. Many times, because of the precision that Auto-CAD provides, a 3D dwg file will be exported to one of these specialized 3D packages for further work, after being laid out in AutoCAD. Other drawings will be created in 2D, converted into a 3D drawing and then refined into a shaded, colored, and textured rendering with specific lights and shadows. We will look at two basic methods of creating 3D models—surface modeling and solid modeling—but we won't be covering the rendering portion of the process. For a more in-depth discussion of the entire process, including rendering, see *Mastering AutoCAD 14* by George Omura (Sybex, 1997).

Surface Modeling

Our approach will be to begin building a 3D model of the cabin, using several techniques for creating 3D surfaces. Along the way, you will get more familiar with the User Coordinate System (UCS) and learn how it is used with 3D, and begin using a basic method of viewing a 3D model. Then you will be shown a second method of viewing 3D models and a demo of how a 3D model of the cabin can be constructed with the solid modeling commands. By then you will have had enough of a taste of this world that you can take charge of your further education in 3D techniques if you so desire.

Viewing a Drawing in 3D

We will start with Cabin6b. This version of the cabin has all the basic components of the floor plan on their respective layers, with no blocks or hatch patterns, and no front elevation or title block. If you haven't been following through the whole book and saving your work progressively, you can download this file from Sybex's Web page, at www.sybex.com. You can still follow along if you have a floor plan not too much more complex than that of the cabin, to use for the exercise.

1. Open Cabin6b. When the floor plan comes up, make the Walls layer current and freeze all other layers. Your drawing will look like Figure A.1. You need to start thinking of your drawing in three dimensions: The entire drawing is on a flat plane parallel to the monitor screen. When you add elements in the third dimension, they will project straight out of the screen towards you if they have a positive dimension, and straight back through the screen if they have a negative dimension. The line of direction is perpendicular to the plane of the screen and is called the z axis. You are familiar with the x and y axes running left-to-right, and up-to-down. Think of the z axis for a moment as running in and out of the screen.

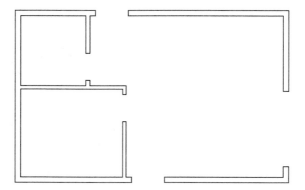

FIGURE A.1: Cabin6b with all layers frozen except Walls

2. Pick View ➤ Display ➤ UCS Icon ➤ On. The UCS Icon appears again. It's been disabled since Skill 5, when it was not used and in the way. We'll be using it in time, but, for now, just keep an eye on it as the drawing changes. Remember that the icon's arrows indicate the positive direction for the *x* and *y* axes.

3. Now you'll change the view from a plan view of the drawing—looking straight down at it—to one in which you are looking down at it from an angle. Pick View ➤ 3D Viewpoint ➤ SW Isometric. The view changes to look like Figure A.2. Notice how the UCS icon has changed with the change of view. The X and Y arrows still run parallel to the left side and bottom of the cabin, but the icon as a whole, as well as the floor plan, are at an angle to the screen.

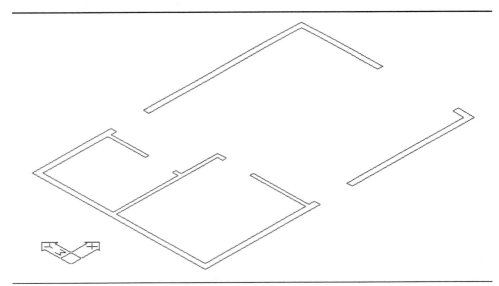

FIGURE A.2: The walls as seen from the SW Isometric view

4. Zoom out and pan down, to give yourself some room to put the walls in 3D.

Creating a Wireframe 3D Model

Your next task is to create what is called a *wireframe* of the cabin in 3D. Wireframes are drawings in 3D in which the lines represent the intersection of walls or other planes. The 2D drawing is already a kind of wireframe because the wall lines represent the intersections of the walls and jambs with the floors. We are simply going to expand on this wireframe by creating lines that extend perpendicularly up from the floor to represent the intersections of the walls with each other, and with the jambs.

1. Set Endpoint Osnap to be running, then start the Line command and pick the lowest outside corner of the building to start a line there.

2. Type **@0,0,8'** ↵↵. A line is drawn to represent the intersection of the two outside walls that meet at the corner you just picked (Figure A.3a). In this view, the positive *x* direction is diagonally up and to the right, the positive *y* direction up and to the left, and the positive *z* direction straight up. You just drew a line whose second point was 8 feet in the positive *z* direction.

3. Copy this line to the other three outside corners of the building, then draw a line connecting the upper endpoints of these four lines to each other. These lines now represent the outside walls of the building (Figure A.3b).

Now you have two tasks: Use this technique to draw the inside walls, and then draw in the doorway openings. But first, let's look at another technique for making objects in 3D, called *extrusion*.

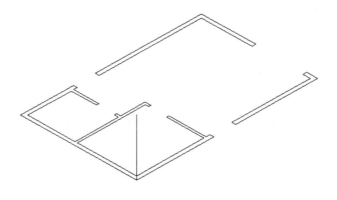

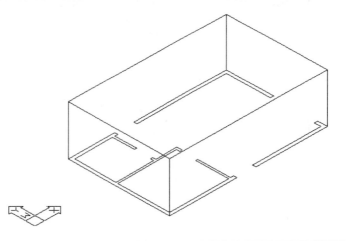

FIGURE A.3: The first line drawn in the positive *z* direction (a) and the outside walls completed (b)

Extruding Lines

Any lines drawn in the *xy* plane (in this case, any of the original wall and jamb lines) can be extended up in a direction parallel to the *z* axis, to make a 3D wall surface. This way of making walls in 3D is useful only when you don't have door or window openings in the walls. In this exercise, we'll ignore the window openings and extrude all wall lines where there are no doorway openings. In the cabin, there are seven wall surfaces without a doorway opening, all in or near the bedroom and bathroom.

Let's extrude those wall lines, then we'll discuss the process further.

1. Pick the Properties button and select the seven wall lines to be extruded (Figure A.4a). Then press ↵.

 NOTE   There is actually an eighth wall line with no doorway openings—the outside line of the exterior wall shared by the bathroom and bedroom—but we will leave it as is for now. We'll do something special with it later.

2. In the Change Properties dialog box, change the Thickness setting from 0" to 8', then click OK. The seven lines are extruded in the direction of the positive *z* axis and seven wall surfaces are created (Figure A.4b).

 NOTE   To understand how thickness is used here, think of a metal plate with holes in it. The thickness of the plate extends in the *z* direction. In a building, the same extension would be called wall height, but in AutoCAD, both are called thickness.

3. Type **hi** ↵ to start the *Hide command*. The Hide command can also be started by selecting View ➤ Hide. The extruded walls become opaque and block your view of the objects behind them (Figure A.4c).

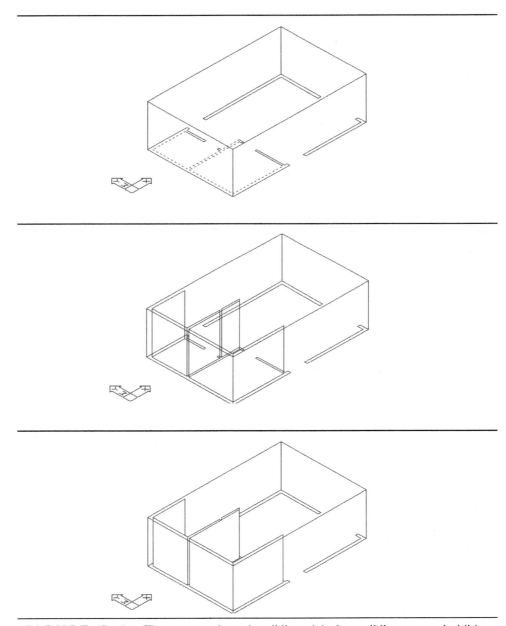

FIGURE A.4: The seven selected wall lines (a), the wall lines extruded (b), and the Hide command applied to the 3D model (c)

You have created seven interior wall surfaces in 3D, and you have created a wireframe to represent the four exterior wall surfaces. When you used the Hide command, the extruded walls became opaque, hiding objects behind them, while the wireframe didn't change. The wireframe contains no surfaces, just lines, so you can see right through the surface they're representing. The extruded wall lines look just like the wireframe lines when you first perform the extrusion, but they are actually surfaces that become opaque when the Hide command is used. Extrusions and wireframes are two of the three primary elements used to construct a 3D model with surface modeling, which is the technique of displaying 3D objects by depicting the surfaces of the objects. You'll be introduced to the third element shortly.

Lets do some more work on the wireframe model.

1. Type **regen** ↵. This regenerates the drawing from scratch and the extruded walls are no longer opaque.

2. We want to copy one of the vertical 8' lines to the other corners in the interior of the cabin, but note how the inside and outside corners coincide for some of the corners. This will make it difficult to snap to those corners. We can alleviate this problem by giving our model a slight rotation.

3. Pick View ➤ 3D Viewpoint ➤ Select. The Viewpoint Presets dialog box appears.

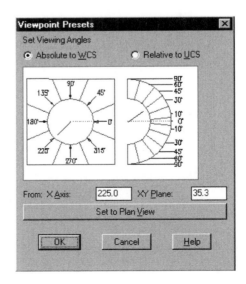

This dialog box allows you to control and change the view you have of your 3D model. You can rotate the view around the model, like a camera rotating around a person while always facing them, or you can move the camera higher or lower, again always facing the subject (in this case the cabin).

4. We just want to rotate slightly, so, in the dialog box, in the From X Axis text box, change the 225.0 to 240.0, then click OK. The model rotates slightly and the corners that were lined up no longer coincide (Figure A.5).

 TIP The Viewpoint Presets dialog box is an essential tool for working in 3D. If you learn how to use it, you will be able to view your 3D model from any viewpoint.

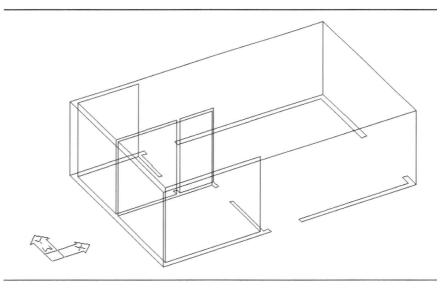

FIGURE A.5: The wireframe model slightly rotated

5. Use Copy Multiple to copy one of the 8' vertical lines in the wireframe to each of the remaining wall corners. There are four of them, all in the living room and kitchen. Don't worry about the doorway openings yet—we'll get to them shortly. Your drawing should look like Figure A.6a.

6. Draw lines to connect the upper endpoints of these lines and the corners of the extruded surfaces to complete the wireframe of the walls. You'll have to draw seven lines (Figure A.6b).

TIP Feel free to zoom and pan to facilitate picking any of the endpoints you need to pick.

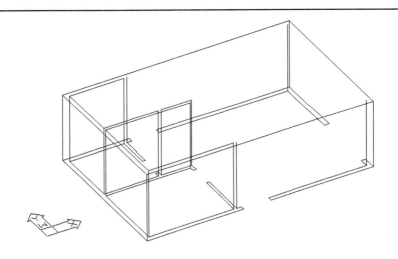

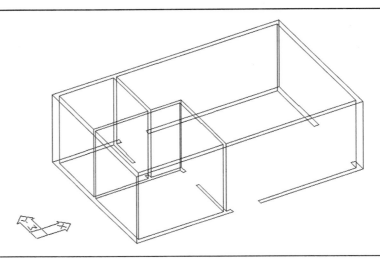

FIGURE A.6: The 8' corner copied to the remaining corners (a) and the completed wireframe of the walls (b)

Now you can begin to visualize the actual form of the cabin rooms. The next task is to draw in the doorway openings.

Making the Doorway Openings

We have to draw in the jambs and the headers in 3D. There are no openings in the jambs, so we can extrude them.

1. Use the Properties button and select all the door jamb lines. You can use regular selection windows to select most pairs of jamb lines if you're careful. Then press ↵.

2. In the Change Properties dialog box, change the thickness from 0" to 6'-6", then click OK. The jambs are all extruded (Figure A.7a).

NOTE   You can see from this task how important precision is. Be careful not to select the 6" wall lines that extend from the jamb to the corner.

3. Thaw the Headers layer, change its color to blue, just like the Walls layer, and make the Headers layer current. Then freeze the Walls layer. The drawing will look like Figure A.7b.

4. Type **change** ↵, then select the five pairs of header lines.

5. Type **p** ↵ to select the Properties option, then type **e** ↵ to select the Elevation option, then type **6'6** ↵ to set the new height for the header lines to 6'-6". Press ↵ to end the change command. The headers are raised vertically to the tops of the openings.

6. Thaw the Walls layer and make it the current layer. The doorway openings are now taking shape (Figure A.7c).

7. Type **hi** ↵ to start the Hide command. The results of the hide are shown in Figure A.8. A close inspection of this view will reveal that the extruded walls and the vertical jambs are opaque, while the rest of the model is just a wireframe. You need to put surfaces on the bare parts of the wireframe.

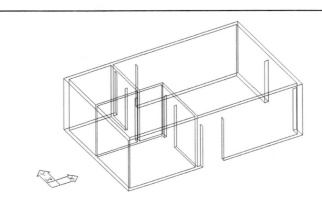

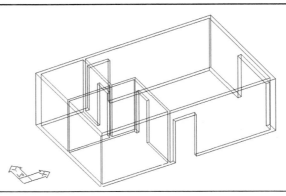

FIGURE A.7: The extruded jambs (a), the headers with the Walls layer frozen (b), and the completed wireframe of the walls (c)

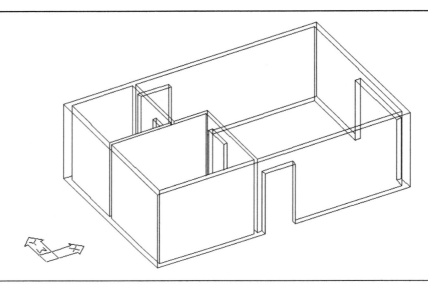

FIGURE A.8: The completed wireframe of the walls after a hide

 NOTE Extruded lines are considered part of the wireframe model before the Hide command is invoked. After the Hide command, extruded lines become part of the surface model. The wireframe becomes partially covered with surfaces.

3D Faces

We can add a new element called a 3D face to the wall surfaces that were not extruded. 3D faces are three- or four-sided areas that can be drawn over a wireframe model to make a surface model, like stretching a tent over its frame. They cannot have any openings in them, so, when applying them to a wall surface that does have an opening, the 3D faces must go around the opening. This may create joints between 3D faces that you don't want to be visible. Fortunately, you can make individual edges of a 3D face invisible. Let's put a 3D face on the front wall of the cabin to see how they work.

The front wall is no longer a rectangle after the front door opening has been cut into it. It is an upside-down U-shape that will require three 3D faces to cover it (Figure A.9a). When you draw a 3D face, you pick points in sequence around the perimeter. The command is set up to allow you to keep drawing additional faces whose first edge coincides with the last edge of the one previously drawn. If you can anticipate which edges will coincide with other faces, you can plan the sequence of points picked in such a way that you pick the fewest points necessary to define the 3D faces. For the front wall, a good sequence is shown in Figure A.9b.

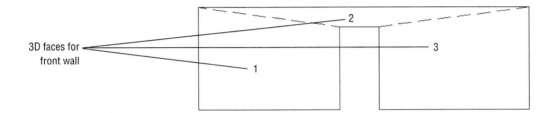

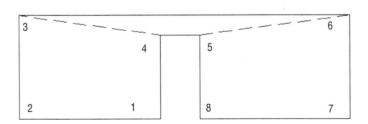

FIGURE A.9: The three 3D faces for the front wall (a) and the sequence for picking points to draw the faces (b)

1. Select Draw ➢ Surfaces ➢ 3D Face to start the 3D Face command. You can also start the command by opening the Surfaces toolbar and picking the 3D Face button, or by typing **3f** ↵.

2. Following the sequence in Figure A.9b, pick the eight pick points with Endpoint Osnap running, then press ⏎.

TIP   Having the Endpoint Osnap running is highly recommended when working in 3D.

3. Type **hi** ⏎. The front wall is opaque, but the joints between the 3D faces are visible also.

4. Pick Draw ➤ Surfaces ➤ Edge, then pick each of the two diagonal joints and press ⏎. The joints disappear (Figure A.10).

NOTE   When using the Edge command, the running Endpoint Osnap is temporarily replaced by a running Midpoint Osnap, and a colored triangle appears when you touch on the face edge. This facilitates your being able to select the edge you want.

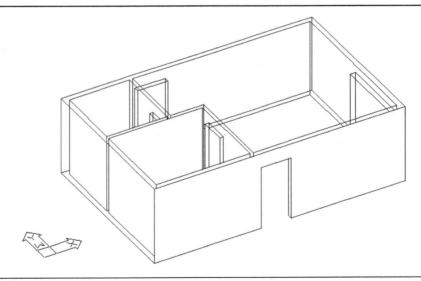

FIGURE A.10: The front wall with 3D faces and the Hide command run

This is the basic procedure for covering the wireframe with 3D faces. Each wall surface with a doorway opening needs three 3D faces and each opening has two wall surfaces—one on each side—so there are nine wall surfaces that need this procedure. We can do one of them from this view. After that we'll need to change the view to more easily pick the right points.

1. Type **regen** ↵ to regenerate the drawing. The opaqueness of the walls is gone and the whole drawing is now a wireframe model. Zoom in to a closer view of the wall containing the opening for the sliding glass door.

2. Pick Draw ➢ Surfaces ➢ 3D Face to start the 3D Face program.

3. Pick the eight points on the inside wall in the same sequence you did for the front wall, then press ↵.

4. Pick Draw ➢ Surfaces ➢ Edge, then pick each of the two diagonal joints and press ↵. You may have to use the Edge command twice and zoom in closer to be able to pick the shorter face joint. The joints disappear.

5. Hide the view (type **hi** ↵) to make the new faces opaque and check your work (Figure A.11). Now you need to rotate the view to be able to place 3D faces on other parts of the wireframe.

NOTE You should by now be realizing how important it is to know the best place to place the crosshair cursor with Endpoint Osnap running, to be able to accurately pick the correct corner.

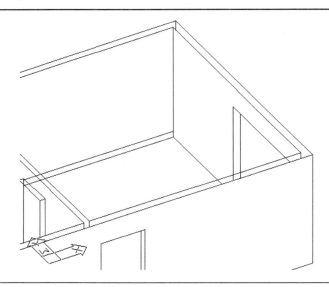

FIGURE A.11: The finished side wall after the Hide command is used

6. Pick View ➤ 3D Viewpoint ➤ Select. The Viewpoint Presets dialog box comes up. In the middle of the dialog box are two diagrams. The one on the left displays how the current view is rotated in the *xy* plane, while the one on the right shows the angle the current view is above or below the horizon. You can click in any of the pie segments in either diagram to reset the angles.

7. In the left diagram, click the 315° segment. In the right, click the 10° segment that's above the 0° segment, then click OK. Your view will look like Figure A.12. Notice the UCS icon is almost on edge. Also, note that the vertical lines representing the inside and outside corners closest to you are coinciding. We need to rotate the view slightly more.

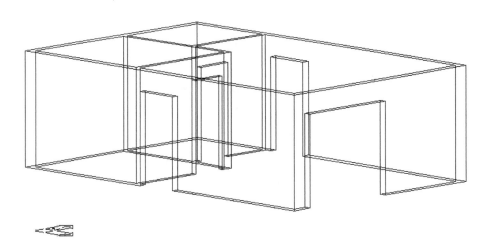

FIGURE A.12: The new view at 315° rotation and 10° angle above the horizon

8. Press ↵ to bring up the Viewpoint Presets dialog box again. Under the diagram on the left, enter **305** in the From X Axis text box, and click OK. We can take care of a couple more walls with this view.

NOTE Each time you reset the viewpoint, the model is zoomed to extents.

9. Zoom into the kitchen wall and type **3f** ↵ and pick eight points in the same locations and in the same sequence as you followed earlier, but this time for the inside back wall surface where the kitchen is. Press ↵ to end the 3D Face command.

10. Zoom previous, restart the 3D Face command, and pick eight more points the same way, this time on the outside surface of the wall with the sliding glass door. Press ↵.

11. Type **edge** ↵ and pick the four diagonal joints between the 3D faces in the two walls, then press ↵.

12. Type **hi** ↵. The drawing will look like Figure A.13.

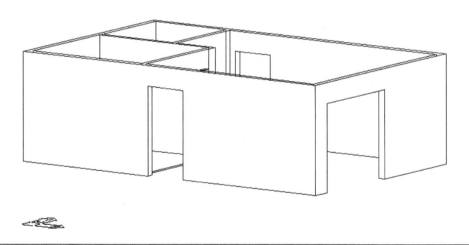

FIGURE A.13: The two new wall surfaces

N **NOTE**

You cannot use Realtime Pan or Zoom when the Hide command is in effect. Type **regen** ↵, first, then use those tools. Other zoom tools can be used, but any change of view cancels the effects of the Hide command, and your drawing reverts to the wireframe model.

Now it's your turn. Use the four commands—3D Viewpoint ➤ Select, 3D Face, Edge, and Hide to create 3D faces to cover the six remaining wall surfaces with door openings. I advise you to keep rotating the drawing approximately 90° and set the angle above the horizon at about 10° to 20°. Experiment with the Viewpoint Settings dialog box until you get familiar with how it works. You should be able to do four walls after the next rotation. Then you can finish up by rotating one more time and making the inside surfaces for the bathroom and bedroom walls that have door openings.

Here's a summary of the steps:

- Use View ➤ 3D Viewpoint ➤ Select to rotate the drawing in the *xy* plane.

- Type **3f** ↵ to start the 3D Face command and pick eight points on the wall, then press ↵.

- Type **edge** ↵ and pick the two diagonal joints between faces, then press ↵.

- Type **hi** ↵ to check your work.

- Do another wall or rotate the view, and continue.

If you make a mistake when putting on a 3D face, cancel the command, erase any incorrect faces, and try again. Faces can be a little bit of a problem to select because some of their edges coincide with lines and some coincide with edges of other faces. The regular selection window can be useful in these situations. Once selected, 3D faces will erase just like any other AutoCAD object. Take your time and be patient, as it is important to select the points of a 3D face accurately. The task of putting 3D faces on walls with openings is one of the most tedious procedures in 3D.

1. When you're finished, use the Viewpoint Presets dialog box to set the rotation to 155° and the angle above the horizon to 30°.

2. Use the Hide command. Your drawing should look like Figure A.14. The outside wall surface next to the bathroom and bedroom has not been done. We'll use this wall to take a look at how window openings can be put into walls.

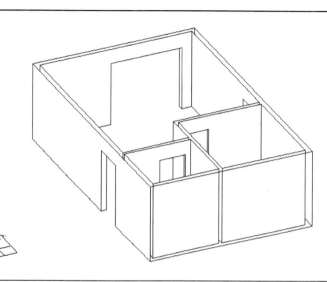

FIGURE A.14: The model at 140° rotation and 30° angle after a Hide

Creating 3D Faces around a Window Opening

We are using a drawing (Cabin6b) that was completed before Skill 7, *Using Blocks and Wblocking*, so there're no windows in the floor plan, no Windows layer, and no Win-1 block in the file. We'll create the Windows layer and insert the Win-1.dwg file that we made in Skill 7 into the exterior bedroom wall on the side of the building currently facing us.

1. Create a new layer called Windows, assign it an orange color (color number 30) and make it the current layer.

2. Select Insert ➤ Block, then click File and open your training directory and select the Win-1.dwg file. Click Open. In the Insert dialog box, click OK.

3. Zoom in to a closer view of the side wall of the cabin that includes the bedroom and bathroom.

4. In the drawing, type **.xy** ↵, then pick Midpoint Osnap to select the midpoint of the inside wall line of the exterior bedroom wall that is facing you in the current view. (This is the same location for the insertion point you used for this window in Skill 7.)

5. At the (need Z): prompt, type **3'** ↵.

6. For the X scale factor, enter **4**. For the Y scale factor, enter **1**. For the rotation angle, enter **90**. The Win-1 block is inserted inside the wall at the height of the sill (Figure A.15a).

7. Start the Copy command and select the window block, then press ↵. For the base point, pick any point on the screen. For the second point of displacement, type **@0,0,3'6** ↵. The window block is copied to a position in the wall, at a distance of 3'-6" directly above the original block insertion (Figure A.15b). You will snap to the endpoints of the jamb lines in these two blocks to create the 3D faces around this window opening in this wall. Start with the inside wall surface.

8. Click the Properties button and select the extruded inside wall surface in the bedroom where this window opening is going to go, then change the thickness of this extrusion from 8' to 0. Type **regen** ↵.

9. Now you can draw four 3D faces for the inside surface of the exterior bedroom wall. You will pick points in a sequence like this:

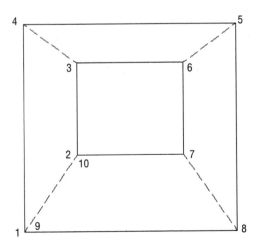

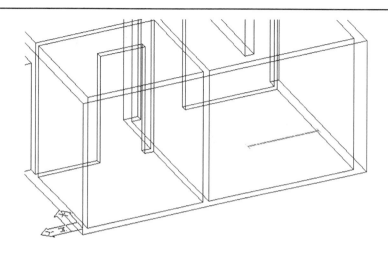

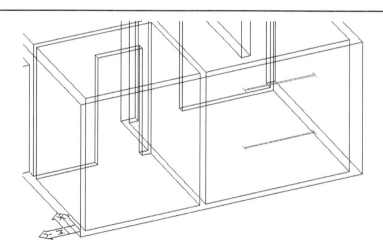

FIGURE A.15: The Win-1 block inserted in the wall (a) and the Win-1 block copied to the top of the window (b)

Start the 3D Face command (type **3f** ↵) and pick points in the sequential order shown above.

When you are finished, press ↵. The new faces will look like Figure A.16a.

10. Press ↵ to restart the 3D Face command, then repeat the same sequence of point selection for the outside wall surfaces, remembering that the left side of this wall surface extends to the left corner of the building in our current view. The results will look like Figure A.16b.

11. Type **edge** ↵, then pick the eight lines representing joints between 3D faces, then press ↵.

NOTE   You can also make any edge of a 3D face invisible as you are drawing it. Before you pick the first point of the edge you want invisible, type **i** ↵, then pick the two points to define the edge.

12. Type **hi** ↵ to use the Hide command on the view. The results will look like Figure A.16c.

NOTE   You could have drawn each face by itself rather than four in one cycle of the command. In some situations, the 3D geometry gets so complex that it's more reasonable to draw the faces individually.

To complete this window, you need to draw a 3D Face for the window sill. Because the Win-1 block is still in the wall at the top and bottom of the window opening, you can explode the bottom Win-1 block and extrude the jamb lines and one of the two glazing lines up to make the window jamb surfaces and the glass. Then you could put the glass on a special layer that you freeze or thaw, depending on whether or not you want to be able to see through the glass. Go ahead and try that if you like. We're going to move on to the next task.

You may have noticed how the second color helps to see your wireframe model more clearly. Working in 3D can be made easier by setting up additional layers for building components, or parts of building components, and assigning the layers different colors. For example, you could have a layer for interior wall faces that's assigned green and a second layer for exterior wall faces that's assigned dark green. Or you could have faces for one room be on one layer and those for another be on a second one. Using either method of organization, you can freeze layers containing the faces that you're not working on but which are in your way. This technique is also valid for working on just the wireframe, because wireframes can be full of lines that seem to coincide in a view, but which in the model are on opposite sides of the building. Making some of the lines invisible can help make snapping to points easier.

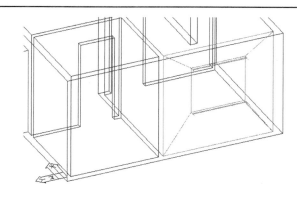

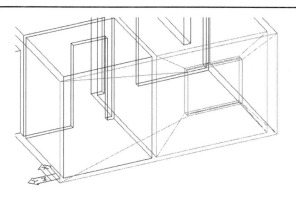

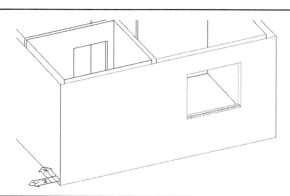

FIGURE A.16: The inside 3D faces (a), plus the outside 3D faces (b), and the view of the completed wall after using Hide (c)

If you combine the technique for drawing faces around a door opening in a wall surface with the one you just learned for windows, you can put 3D faces on walls which have both doors and windows. In a wall with two doors and three windows, the faces could have a pattern like this:

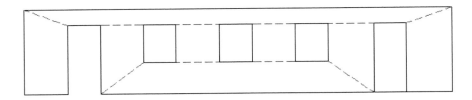

This may seem like a lot of trouble to go through to make walls with openings have the ability to be opaque after a hide, and you're right. It is a lot of trouble, and many times unnecessary. Whether it's worth the trouble will depend on whether you need the openings to really be openings. That is, would it be all right if the doors and windows were just drawings of doors and windows sitting on the surface of the wall, rather than actual holes in the wall?

Putting 2D Drawings on 3D Surfaces

Let's put the windows on the exterior front wall surface of the cabin, as 2D drawings, to see how this works. We'll get the windows from a previously saved drawing.

1. Pick View ➢ 3D Viewpoint ➢ SW Isometric to rotate the drawing around so you can see the front wall.

2. Type **vp** ↵ to bring up the Viewpoint Presets dialog box. In the From: X Axis: text box, change 225.0 to 240.0, then click OK.

3. Save this drawing as CabinB1.

4. Open Cabin8b if you have it saved. If not, open Cabin8a.

5. Zoom in to the front elevation.

6. Draw a short diagonal line from the lower-left corner of the front wall at the height of the step (Figure A.17). This will be a guideline for inserting the windows.

FIGURE A.17: The front elevation with the diagonal guideline drawn

7. Select Edit ➢ Copy, then select the four windows and the diagonal guideline. Press ⏎.

8. Open CabinB1 again, without saving changes to Cabin8b (or a).

We want to use the Windows paste tool to paste the windows on the front wall, but if we do it with the drawing set up the way it currently is, the windows will be parallel to the floor plane in the 3D model. Originally, all objects in the front elevation were drawn in the same plane as the floor plan, before any 3D objects were made. The User Coordinate System will solve this problem for us.

Setting Up a New User Coordinate System

Even though you have been drawing in 3D, the User Coordinate System (UCS) has remained the same as it was when you were drawing in 2D. This UCS is called the World Coordinate System and it's the default UCS for all new drawings. A UCS defines the orientation of the x, y, and z axes. If we set up a new UCS lined up with the front wall surface, we can paste the windows right on the 3D faces of that surface. Then we'll save that UCS so we can easily restore it anytime we want to work on the front wall.

1. Zoom out a little.

2. Type **ucs** ↵. You'll see the prompt
   `Origin/ZAxis/3point/OBject/View/X/Y/Z/Prev/Restore/Save/Del/?/`
   `<World>:`. These options give you several tools for setting up a new UCS, as well as those for saving the current UCS or restoring a previously saved one. Usually when you create a new UCS you either rotate the existing one around one of the axes, or pick points on the 3D model to define the new origin and the positive x and y directions for the new axes.

3. Type **x** ↵, then at the prompt `Rotation angle about X axis <0>:`, type **90** ↵. The UCS icon in your drawing has flipped up around the x axis and the icon is now parallel to the front wall surface (Figure A.18a). The positive x direction hasn't changed, because we rotated the UCS around the x axis, but the positive y direction is now upwards and the positive z axis comes out of the screen at an angle down and to the right.

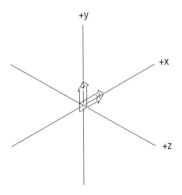

Now you can paste the window block in the correct dimension.

1. Select Edit ➤ Paste. The drawing appears in ghosted fashion with the lower-left endpoint of the guideline attached to the cursor.

2. Use Endpoint Osnap to pick the lower-left corner of the front wall, then press ↵ three times. The windows are inserted as a block and pasted onto the front wall.

3. Explode this block, then erase the diagonal guideline.

4. Type **hi** ↵. The drawing will look like Figure A.18b.

The UCS icon, by its orientation, shows you the plane defined by the x and y axes, and the two arrows in the icon show you the positive direction of these two axes. When you draw in 3D, you either snap to objects or, if you use relative coordinates, you draw in the x and y plane of the current UCS. You have seen that you can construct a good portion of the drawing without changing the default UCS, but some operations require such a change.

You will have to decide whether to construct 3D faces around openings in walls, or to place a 2D drawing of the elevation on the 3D wall. One factor that will help you make your decision is whether you need to see inside the building from the outside, or whether you need views of the interior of the building, looking through a window or door to the outside or to another interior space. There are many levels of detail in which you can work in 3D, from creating the basic shape of the building, to making openings in walls, to putting in the window details. You could take the 4-foot wide window opening you made in the wall with 3D faces, and add detail in 3D to make it look like the windows you just pasted on the front wall. Then you would have the detail and be able to see through them, but would have to spend more time to achieve that level of detail. Determining the level of detail depends on how you plan on using the 3D model.

We'll put the roof, steps, and balcony in 3D to complete this 3D surface model, then move on to other areas.

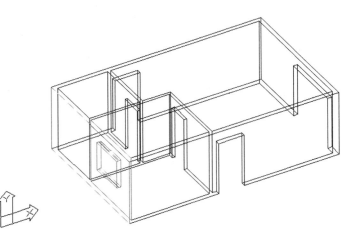

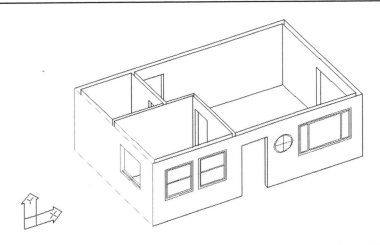

FIGURE A.18: The UCS icon rotated to its new position (a) and the windows after insertion (b)

Getting the Roof into 3D

To get the roof into 3D, you can move it up to its actual height above the walls, then extrude the edge down and stretch the ridge up.

1. Thaw the Roof layer, change its color from cyan to a darker color, change its linetype from dashed to continuous, and make it current.

2. Freeze the Walls and Headers layers, then zoom out a little (Figure A.19a).

3. Turn off any running Osnaps. Start the Move command and select the nine lines that make up the roof, then press ↵. Pick any point on the screen for the base point, then, for the point of displacement, type **@8'6<90** ↵. The roof moves up in the positive *y* direction of the current UCS (Figure A.19b).

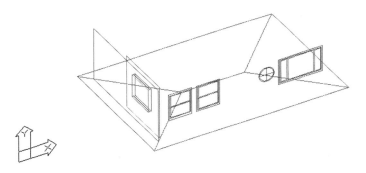

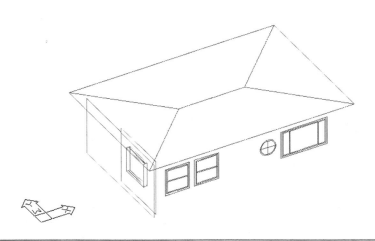

FIGURE A.19: The model with the Roof layer current and the Walls and Headers layers frozen (a) and the model after the roof is moved up (b)

4. Start the Stretch command and use a crossing window to select the ridge line of the roof, then press ↵. Pick any point on the screen for the base point, then, for the point of displacement, type **@3'<90** ↵. The ridge line is moved up and the hip lines are stretched.

5. Type **ucs** ↵, then type **s** ↵ to select the Save option. At the ?/Desired UCS name: prompt, type **front** ↵.

6. Press ↵ to restart the UCS command, then press ↵ to select the default <World> option. The UCS icon returns to its former position and the W returns to the icon.

NOTE   You don't have to save the World UCS. It's an integral part of your drawing by default. Making it the current UCS is like "going home."

7. Pick the Properties button and select the four eaves lines that form the edge of the roof, then press ↵. In the Change Properties dialog box, change the thickness from 0" to -6", then click OK. The roof's edge drops down (Figure A.20).

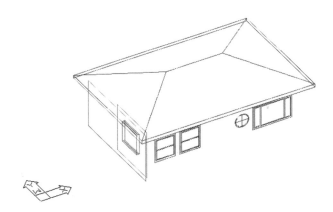

FIGURE A.20: The ridge is raised and the eaves line is dropped down.

8. Set the Endpoint Osnap to be running, then start the 3D Face command (type **3f** ↵) and put a 3D face on each of the four planes on the roof top. Do them individually, restarting the 3D Face command after each face. For the triangular areas, just click the third point twice. Press ↵ after each face is drawn to end the command, then press ↵ again to restart it.

9. Thaw the Walls and Headers layers, then type **hi** ↵. The drawing will look like Figure A.21a.

10. Type **vp** ↵, then change the XY Plane text box from 35.3 to 20 and click OK.

11. Type **hi** ↵ again. The view is flatter (Figure A.21b).

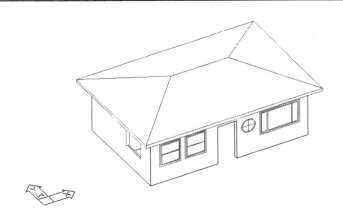

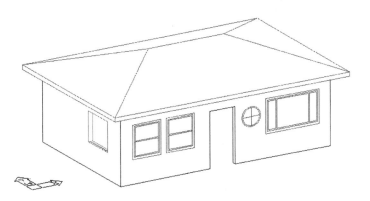

FIGURE A.21: The finished roof after a Hide (a) and the view with the angle from the *xy* plane set to 20° (b)

Some of the Modify commands are tricky to use in 3D, including the Stretch command. For the stretch to work, the direction of the stretch has to lie in the current *xy* plane. We had to have the Front UCS current, because if the World UCS were current, the direction of the stretch would have been perpendicular to the current *xy* plane, and wouldn't have worked. Other commands that behave this way are Mirror and Offset. Trim and Extend can also give unpredictable results, so it is very important that everything is set up properly.

Making a 3D Balcony

The balcony wall can be extruded just like the blank walls, but it will need a cap on the top.

1. Thaw the Balcony layer, make it current and freeze the Walls and F-elev layers.

2. Type **vp** ↵ and change the X Axis angle from 240.0 to 340.0. The view rotates.

3. Zoom in to the balcony area (Figure A.22a).

4. Pick the Properties button, select the two semi-circles, and press ↵. Change the thickness from 0" to 3', then press OK.

5. Draw a guideline between the endpoints of the outside balcony wall at the top (Figure A.22b).

6. Pick Draw ➤ Donut. Enter **9'** for the inside diameter and **10'** for the outside diameter. On the screen, pick Midpoint Osnap and select the straight guideline you just drew. The donut is placed. Press ↵.

7. Start the Trim command and select the guideline as a cutting edge, then press ↵. Pick the part of the donut that is not sitting on the balcony, then press ↵. The donut is trimmed back to a semicircle.

8. Erase the guideline and thaw the Walls layer, then type **hi** ↵. The Drawing will look like Figure A.22c.

Let's finish the drawing by putting the front and back steps into 3D.

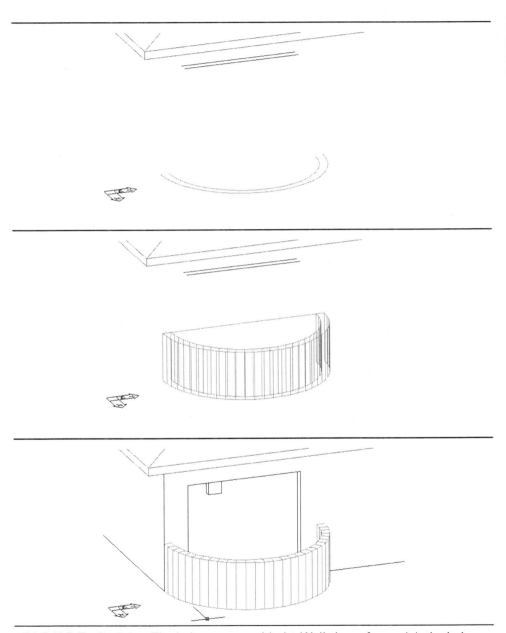

FIGURE A.22: The balcony area with the Walls layer frozen (a), the balcony walls extruded and a guideline drawn (b), and the completed balcony (c)

Bringing the Steps into the 3D Model

In the front elevation, the step starts at the floor level and extends down 12". We can extrude down by assigning a negative thickness to the lines of the step. Then we'll need to put a 3D face on the top of the step.

1. Thaw the F-elev layer. Type **vp** ⏎ and set the X Axis angle to 305.0 and the XY Axis angle to 25.0.

2. Thaw the Steps layer and make it current.

3. Zoom in to a closer view of the front and back step.

4. Click the Properties button, select the lines of the front and back steps, and press ⏎. In the Change Properties dialog box, change the thickness from 0" to -12", then click OK. The drawing will look like Figure A.23a.

5. Type **3f** ⏎ and, with Endpoint Osnap running, pick the four corners of the top of the front step. Press ⏎ to end the 3D Face command.

6. Repeat this process for the back step.

7. Zoom previous. The drawing will look like Figure A.23b.

Now we need to draw 3D faces around the perimeter of the building, extending 12" below the bottom of the walls, to represent the foundation.

1. Type **th** ⏎ to start the Thickness command, then type **-12** ⏎. Be sure Endpoint Osnap is running.

2. Start a line at the back-right corner of the front step, then pick the bottom of the right corner of the front wall. A 3D face is drawn from the back of the step to the right corner of the front wall (Figure A.24a).

3. Repeat this process for the back-right corner of the cabin, then snap to the lower-right corner of the back step. The foundation line is drawn for the right half of the building.

4. Repeat this process for the other side of the building to complete the foundation line (Figure A.24b).

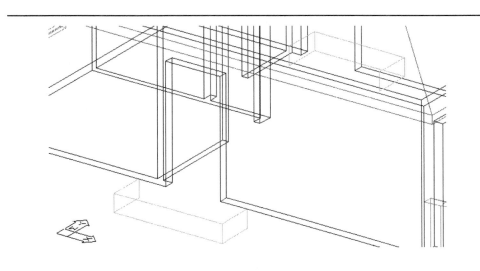

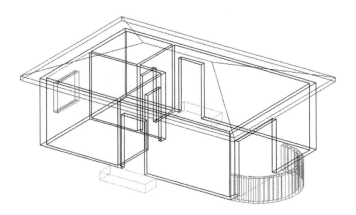

FIGURE A.23: The steps extruded 12" down (a) and the steps with 3D faces on their tops (b)

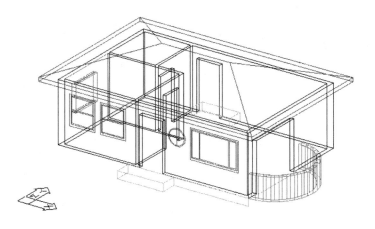

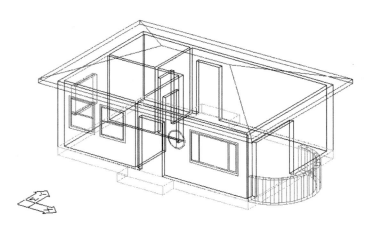

FIGURE A.24: The first segment of the foundation line (a) and the left half completed (b)

5. Type **th** ↲, then type **0** ↲ to reset the current Thickness to 0. Finally, adjust the balcony to the foundation lines.

6. Type **change** ↲, then select both of the extruded arcs that now form the vertical surfaces of the balcony wall. Press ↲. At the Properties/<Change point>:

prompt, type **p** ↵ to select the Properties option, then type **e** ↵ to select the Elevation option.

7. Type **-12** ↵ to select 12" below the floor level for the bottom of the balcony wall. (This conforms to the front elevation.)

8. Type **t** ↵ to select the thickness option, then type **4'** ↵ ↵ to adjust the height of the balcony wall back up to where it was previously.

9. Type **hi** ↵ to execute the Hide command. The resulting view is shown in Figure A.25. You may notice that you can look through the sliding glass door opening and see the foundation line of the back wall. This is because we haven't put any 3D faces in the model to serve as the floors. Go ahead and try to do that if you like.

10. Save this drawing as CabinB2.

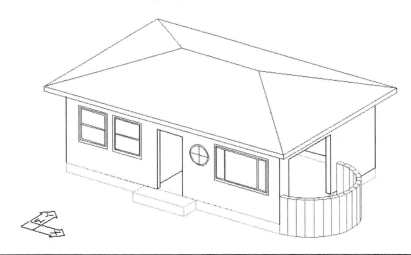

FIGURE A.25: The completed 3D model of the cabin after a Hide

With the completion of this final exercise, you have finished a whirlwind tour of the features and commands used for drawing 3D surface models. In generating a 3D model of the cabin, you have been introduced to the most basic commands for creating 3D surfaces. The following is a brief discussion about other tools for working in 3D.

3D Surface Objects

There is a set of specialized commands that let you draw 3D surface models of specific shapes.

Click Draw ➢ Surfaces ➢ 3D Surfaces. The 3D Objects dialog box appears.

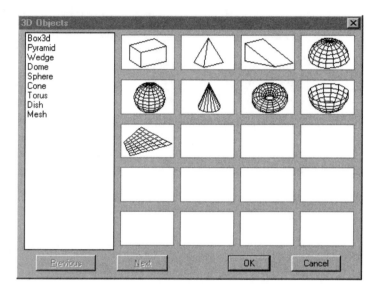

Here you will find eight geometrical shapes that will be generated when you enter specific information about a chosen shape, like height, diameter, location of center, etc.

The first three of these shapes—Box3d, Pyramid, and Wedge—are like blocks, with each side having a flat surface. The next five—Dome, Sphere, Cone, Torus, and Dish—are all 3D meshes and follow geometrical rules of regularity. 3D meshes describe a curved or undulating surface with a series of small 3D faces connected at their edges, sometimes in a regular pattern, but not always. The ninth shape—mesh—allows you to create a rectangular 3D mesh that is a composite of rectangular 3D faces. You enter a z coordinate for each vertice—the corners of the rectangular 3D faces—and thereby create a non-regular undulating surface that could describe the terrain of a parcel of land. Use of this is usually accompanied by additional software that would generate the coordinates of the faces' corners. Click Cancel to close the dialog box.

Four more 3D mesh commands allow you create a 3D mesh by defining certain geometrical aspects of the mesh, such as the lines that make up the edges, or a 2D shape that is rotated through 3D space.

Bring up the Surfaces toolbar by picking View ➤ Toolbars and clicking in the Surfaces checkbox.

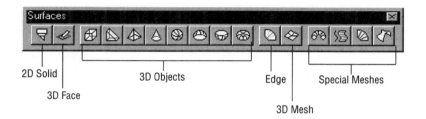

You have been introduced to some of the commands represented here (2D Solid, 3D Face, Edge) and the 3D Objects and 3D Mesh have been discussed above. The last four buttons help you create meshes by:

- Revolving a 2D shape around an axis (Revolved Surface)

- Extruding an object along a straight line (Tabulated Surface)

- Stretching a mesh between two lines (Ruled Surface)

- Stretching a mesh between four edges (Edge Surface)

Feel free to experiment with these mesh tools.

Viewing a 3D Model Dynamically

You have been using 3D Viewpoint to modify the view of the cabin while building the 3D model. There are several tools for manipulating views in this way, including the two you have used: a preset isometric view (SW Isometric) and the Viewpoint Presets dialog box. But there is another command called Dview which allows you to do much more.

1. Close the Surfaces toolbar if you haven't already done so.

2. Pick View ➤ 3D Dynamic View.

3. At the `Select objects:` prompt, select the entire cabin and press ↵. The Dview prompt
   (`CAmera/TArget/Distance/POints/PAn/Zoom/TWist/CLip/Hide/Off/Undo/<eXit>:`) appears at the command line.

4. Type **ca** ↵. As you move the mouse, the cabin rotates in all directions.

5. Try to get a view where you can look in through the sliding glass door opening and see another opening inside the cabin, then click to set the view, and type **h** ↵ (Figure A.26a).

6. Type **d** ↵ to select the Distance option, then type **60'** ↵. Type **h** ↵ (Figure A.26b). The view is a *perspective* view.

NOTE I am using perspective here to refer to a view where parallel lines appear to converge as they move away from the viewer, like railroad tracks in the distance. Up until now all your 3D views have been isometric, where parallel lines remain parallel.

---

7. Type **d** ↵, then type **8'** ↵, then type **h** ↵. Now you're inside the cabin (Figure A.26c).

8. Type **x** ↵ to end the Dview command, then type **u** ↵ to get back to the view you had when you last saved the drawing.

The Dview command will allow you to "walk through" the cabin and go out the back door. It has several other features that go beyond the scope of this book.

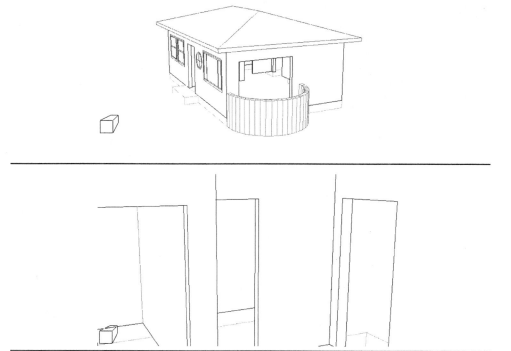

FIGURE A.26: Using Dview: the first view (a), the perspective view at 60' (b), and the view at 8' (c)

Solid Modeling

We can't leave the subject of 3D without at least mentioning *solid modeling*. For many years, this feature was an additional piece of software that you could opt to purchase with AutoCAD. It is now included as part of the AutoCAD program, and has been since release 13. While the faces and meshes are tools for surface modeling and help describe the surface of objects, solid modeling describes shapes as solid objects made up of more simple shapes that have been added together or subtracted from each other. You can read the following discussion as a demo: It's not meant to be a exercise to follow.

To construct the walls of the cabin with solid modeling, you would first make a box that was 25' long, 16' wide, and 8' high (Figure A.27a). Think of it as a solid block. Then you would make four boxes for the three rooms (two for the living room and kitchen) and put them inside the big box (Figure A.27b). Then you would subtract the four interior boxes from the big box (Figure A.27c). This creates all the 8 foot walls for the cabin. The next step would be to create boxes for the windows and door and place them in their proper location inside the walls. Then you would subtract the windows and doors from the solid object that is the walls.

Now you have openings in walls and the walls can be made opaque with the Hide command (Figure A.28). This is much easier than using the 3D faces. In addition to the boxes we just used to form the cabin walls, you have five other basic shapes you can use in combination with boxes to build up a 3D solid model: sphere, cylinder, cone, wedge, and torus. These six basic shapes are called *primitives* and the processes of adding, subtracting, and intersecting the primitives to create complex solid shapes are called *boolean* operations. Solid shapes can also be generated by extruding a 2D shape along a line or revolving it around an axis, just like the Tabulated and Revolved Surface buttons do for surface modeling with meshes. In solid modeling, however, the line of extrusion can be curved, or it can have curves and straight segments in it.

You can apply some of the standard Modify commands like Fillet to solids to produce special effects, and there is a Slice command which allows you to cut through a solid at any angle. The tools and shapes you have to work with will allow you to build any shape you want. If you experiment with these tools for a little while, you will find yourself wondering as you look at any object, "How could I build that as a solid model?"

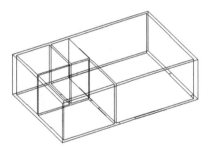

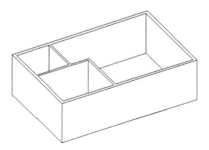

FIGURE A.27: Solid modeling the cabin walls: the outside box (a), the inside boxes added (b), and after the subtraction (c)

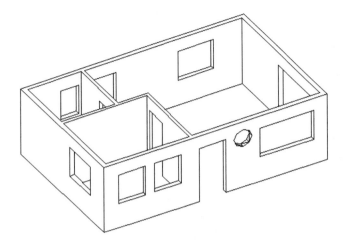

FIGURE A.28: The completed walls after subtracting window and door openings

The solid modeling commands are found on the Draw menu in a sub-menu called Solids, and the three Boolean commands (Union, Subtract, and Intersect) are found on the Modify menu, in a sub-menu called Boolean. There is also a Solids toolbar which has the primitive shapes and most of the solids modeling commands, except for the Boolean commands.

Summary

This appendix is a brief introduction to 3D drawing and its concepts. The main features covered were:

- The two methods of viewing a 3D mode—3D Viewpoint (actually called Vpoint) and Dview
- The basic surface modeling operations: wireframe construction, extrusion, and drawing 3D faces
- The User Coordinate System (UCS)
- Solid modeling concepts

GLOSSARY

Glossary

3D mesh

A set of adjacent flat surfaces which together form a geometrical depiction of a surface that occupies three dimensions.

3D model

An AutoCAD drawing file which contains AutoCAD *objects* that occupy 3D space, and represent building components or geometrical objects in the real world.

a

Absolute coordinates

Values for locating a point in space that describe its distance and direction from the *origin* (0,0,0) point of the drawing.

Alias

A shortcut for starting commands. It is a set of one or two letters which can be entered at the *command line* instead of the full command.

Aligned dimension

A linear dimension measuring the distance between two points. The dimension line for an aligned dimension is parallel to a line between the two points.

Angular Dimension

A dimension that measures the angle between two lines or the angle inscribed by an arc segment.

Angular Unit

The unit by which angle values are displayed. The choices are decimal degrees, degrees-minutes-seconds, grads, radians, or surveyor units.

Associative Dimension

A dimension that updates automatically when the object being dimensioned changes size.

Associative hatch pattern

A hatch pattern which updates automatically when the shape of the hatched area is modified.

AutoCAD object

See *Object*.

AutoSnap

A feature of AutoCAD that works with the Object Snap tools and displays a symbol on places that can be snapped to. Each *object snap mode* has a different symbol.

b

Baseline dimension

A dimensioning option that allows you to do multiple measurements from a designated baseline.

Base point

1. The initial point of reference for a number of modify commands, including Copy, Move, Rotate, Stretch, and Scale; 2. The insertion point for a drawing, as designated by the Base command.

Blip marks

Small crosses which, when enabled, mark points in the *drawing area* where points have been picked or specified, and where objects have been selected.

Block

See *Block reference*.

Block definition

The description of a grouping of AutoCAD objects that includes a name, an *insertion point*, and a listing of objects in the grouping, and is stored with the drawing file.

Block reference

An instance of a grouping of objects that is inserted into a drawing and is based upon the block definition for that grouping. Casually called a block.

BYLAYER

A property that can be assigned to colors and linetypes so that objects will receive their color and linetype properties according to the layer they are on.

c

Command line

A text window at the bottom of the screen that displays command prompts. This is where you see what you are entering through the keyboard. Also called the Command window.

Command prompt

A Command: *prompt* at the *command line*. It tells you that no commands are currently running.

Command window

See *Command line*.

Continued dimension

A dimensioning option that allows you to place sequential dimensions which are adjacent to each other in such a way that the dimension lines line up.

Crosshair cursor

A form of the *cursor* which consists of a horizontal line and vertical line intersecting at their midpoints, resembling the crosshair in a sighting device.

Crossing window

A selection tool that selects an area defined by two points acting as opposite corners of a rectangle. All objects within or crossing the rectangle are selected.

Cursor

The pointing symbol on the computer monitor that is moved by moving the mouse. It can appear as, among other things, an arrow, a *pickbox*, and a *crosshair*.

Cutting edge

The role certain objects can be temporarily assigned to play in a trimming operation. If an object is designated as a cutting edge, lines or other objects being trimmed will be trimmed back to the point where the object being trimmed intersects the cutting edge.

Default

A value or option in a command that will be used unless you designate otherwise. In AutoCAD, default values and options are enclosed in angle brackets (< >).

Dimension style

A collection of settings for *dimension variables* that is saved in a drawing under a specified name. Dimensions placed in the drawing will follow the settings of the current dimension style.

Dimension text

The text in a dimension. It expresses the measurement the dimension is displaying.

Dimension variables

A group of settings and values that control the appearance of dimensions in AutoCAD.

Donut

A 2D wide polyline drawn in a circle and resembling a ring-shaped doughnut pastry.

Drawing area

The portion of the monitor screen where you draw objects and view your drawing.

Drawing extents

A rectangular area with the same proportions as your *drawing area* that will just enclose all visible objects in your drawing. When you *zoom* to extents, the rectangular area fills the drawing area.

Drawing limits

The area in a drawing that is covered by the *grid*. It can be defined by the user and is stored as the coordinates of the lower-left corner and those of the upper-right corner of the rectangular area covered by the *grid*.

Dwg

The file extension and format for the standard AutoCAD drawing.

e

Edge

1. The side of a *3D face* or a *3D mesh*; 2. A command for controlling the visibility of edges of 3D faces.

Entity

See *Object*.

Explode

A command to undo a grouping of objects. Can be used on blocks, *multiline text*, *polylines*, and dimensions. Exploded multiline text becomes single line text. Exploded polylines become lines. Exploded blocks become the objects that made up the block.

External reference

A drawing file that has been temporarily attached to another drawing for read-only purposes. Also called an Xref.

External reference host file

The drawing file to which *external references* have been attached.

Extrusion

1. A 2D object which has been given *thickness*; 2. A 3D solid object created with the Extrude command, by sliding a closed shape along a path.

f

Face

A triangular or four-sided flat surface that is the basic unit of a 3D surface.

Fill

A display mode which can be set to on or off. When set to on, displays a solid color for shapes made with wide *polylines*, 2D solids, *donuts*, and *hatch patterns* using the Solid pattern. When set to off, the solid color area is invisible and only the boundary is displayed.

Floating viewports

Rectangular windows created in the *Paper Space* of a drawing which allow you to view a drawing in *Model Space*. See *Paper Space* and *Model Space*.

Font

A group of letters, numbers, and other symbols all sharing common features of design and appearance.

Freeze

The Off portion of a setting called Freeze/ Thaw that controls the visibility of objects on *layers* and determines whether AutoCAD calculates the geometry of these objects during a *regeneration.*

g

Graphical User Interface

See *Graphics window*.

Graphics Window

The appearance of your screen when Auto-CAD is running, consisting of the *drawing area* and surrounding *toolbars*, *menu bars*, *command window*, and *status bar*. Also called the Graphical User Interface.

Grid

1. A tool for drawing that consists of a regularly spaced set of dots in the *drawing area*;
2. A series of horizontal and vertical lines in a floor plan or section that locate the main structural elements, such as columns and walls, of a building. Also called a column grid.

Grips

An editing tool which allows you to perform six modify commands on selected objects without having to start the commands. When grips are enabled, small squares appear on selected objects. By clicking a square, you activate the first of the available commands, and can cycle through the rest of the commands by pressing the space bar.

h

Hatch patterns

Patterns of lines, dots, and other shapes that fill in a closed area.

Host file

See *External reference host file*.

i

Insertion point

A reference point that is part of a *block*, and that is used to locate the block when inserted into a drawing. It is attached to the cursor while a block is being inserted. Once a block has been inserted, the insertion point can be snapped to with the Insertion *Osnap*.

Isometric view

A view of a 3D object in which all lines that are parallel on the object appear parallel in the view. See *Perspective view*.

j

Jamb

A surface that forms the side or top of an opening in a wall for a door or window.

Justification Point

A reference point on a line of single line text, or a body of multiline text, which acts like the *insertion point* for blocks.

l

Layer

An organizing tool that operates like an electronic version of traditional transparent overlays on a drawing board. Layers can be assigned color and *linetype*, and their visibility can be controlled.

Limits

See *Drawing limits*.

Linetype

The style of appearance of a line, including continuous, dashed, dash dot, etc.

Linetype scale

A numerical value for non-continuous linetypes that controls the size of dashes and spaces between dashes and dots. In an AutoCAD drawing, there is a global and an individual linetype scale.

m

Menu bar

The set of drop-down menus at the top of the AutoCAD graphics window.

Mirror

A command that makes a copy of selected objects which are flipped around a specified line to make a mirror image of those objects.

Model Space

The portion of an AutoCAD drawing that contains the lines representing the building or object being designed, as opposed to the notes and title block information, which are kept in *Paper Space*.

Mtext

See *Multiline text*.

Multiline text

A type of text in which an entire body of text is grouped together as one object. Casually called Mtext, it can be edited with word-processing techniques, and individual characters or words can have different heights, fonts, and colors from the main body of text. *Dimension text* is Mtext. When *exploded*, Mtext becomes *single line text*.

n

Named view

A view of your drawing that is saved and given a name, to enable it to be restored later.

o

Object

A basic AutoCAD graphical element such as a line, arc, dimension, block, or text, which is created and manipulated as a part of a drawing. Also called an *entity*.

Object Snap mode

Any of a set of tools for precisely picking strategic points on an *object*, including Endpoint, Midpoint, Center, etc. Casually called *Osnap*.

Origin

The point with the coordinates 0,0,0, where the *x*, *y*, and *z* axes all meet.

Orthagonal drawing

A system of creating views in which each view shows a different side of a building or object, such as top, front, left side, right side, etc.

Ortho mode

An on/off setting which, when on, forces lines to be drawn and objects to be moved in a horizontal or vertical direction only.

Osnap

See *Object Snap mode.*

P

Pan

A command that slides the current drawing around on the drawing area without changing the magnification of the view.

Paper Space

If activated, the portion of the drawing that contains the notes and title block information, and *floating viewports* for viewing the portion of the drawing in *Model Space.* Paper Space is enabled when the *Tilemode* variable is turned off.

Path

The hierarchy of drive, folder, and sub-folders where a file is stored, along with the file's name, as in
C:\AUTOCADR14\TRAINING\CABIN8A.DWG.

Perspective view

A view of a 3D object in which parallel lines that are not parallel to the plane of the screen appear to converge as they move further away from the viewer, similar to the way objects appear in the real world, like railroad tracks in the distance. See *Isometric view.*

Pickbox

A form of the cursor as a small square that occurs when AutoCAD is in *selection mode.*

Pick button

The button on the mouse (usually the left one) which is used to pick points, buttons, or menu items, as well as select objects, on the screen.

Plan view

A view of a drawing in which the viewer is looking straight at the *xy plane,* in a direction parallel to the z axis. In Plan view, the positive *x* and *y* directions are to the right and up, respectively.

Point filters

A set of tools that allow you to specify a point in the drawing by using some of the *x, y,* and z coordinates from another point or points to generate the coordinates for the point you are specifying.

Polyline

A special type of line that (a) treats multiple segments as one object, (b) can include arcs, (c) can be smoothed into a curved line, and (d) can have width in 2D applications.

Prompt

The text at the command line that asks questions or tells you what action is necessary to continue the execution of a command. The Command: prompt tells you that no command is presently running.

r

Redraw

A command to refresh the *drawing area* or a particular *viewport*, thereby ridding it of any *blip marks* or graphic distortions caused by the monitor.

Regeneration

A process in which the geometry for the objects in the current drawing file is recalculated.

Regular window

A selection tool that selects an area defined by two points acting as opposite corners of a rectangle. All objects completely within the rectangle are selected. See also *Crossing window*.

Relative coordinates

Values for locating a point in space that describe its distance and direction from the last point picked in the drawing, rather than from the *origin*.

Rubberbanding

The effect of a line extending between the last point picked and the crosshair cursor, stretching as the cursor is moved.

Running Object Snap

An *Object Snap mode* that has been set to be continually activated until turned off.

S

Selection mode

The phase of a command that requires the user to select objects, and thereby build up a *selection set* of objects, to be modified by or otherwise used in the function of the command.

Selection set

Any object or group of objects that have been selected for modification, or to be used in a modification process.

Selection window

A tool for selecting objects whereby the user creates a rectangular window in the *drawing area* and objects are selected in two ways, depending on whether the selection window is a *crossing window* or a *regular window*.

Single line text

A type of text *object* in AutoCAD in which each line of text, whether it be a sentence, word, or letter, is treated as a single object, with its own *justification point*.

Snap mode

An on/off setting that locks the cursor onto a spatial grid, which is usually aligned with the *grid*, allowing you to draw to distances that are multiples of the grid spacing. When the grid spacing is set to 0, the grid aligns with the snap spacing.

Stud

A small upright piece of lumber or metal used in framing walls. It is usually a 2×4 or 2×6 in cross dimension and extends the height of the wall.

t

Template drawing

A drawing that has been set up to serve as a format for a new drawing. This allows the user to begin a new drawing with certain parameters already set up, because various settings have been predetermined.

Text style

A collection of settings that controls the appearance of text and is saved in a drawing under a specified name. Text placed in the drawing will follow the settings of the current text style.

Thaw

The On portion of a setting called Freeze/ Thaw which controls the visibility of objects on *layers* and determines whether AutoCAD calculates the geometry of these objects during a *regeneration*.

Thickness

The distance a 2D object is *extruded* in a direction perpendicular to the plane in which it was originally drawn, resulting in a 3D object. For a floor plan of a building, wall lines can be extruded to a thickness that is the wall's actual height.

Tiled viewports

Rectangular *viewports* that form a configuration of the *drawing area* in which the viewports all abut and are arranged side-by-side. Available as a tool only when the Tilemode variable is on, i.e., when *Paper Space* is disabled.

TILEMODE

An on/off setting controlling whether *floating viewports* (Off) or *tiled viewports* (On) are enabled.

u

UCS

See *User Coordinate System*.

UCS icon

The double-arrowed icon in the lower-left corner of the *drawing area* that indicates the positive directions of the x and y axes for the current *User Coordinate System*.

User Coordinate System (UCS)

A definition for the orientation of the x, y, and z axes in space, relative to 3D objects in the drawing or to the *world coordinate system*. UCSs can be named, saved, and restored.

v

View

A picture of the current drawing on the screen or in a *viewport*, from a particular user-defined perspective. Views may be named, saved, and restored.

Viewport

A rectangular window through which the user can view their drawing, or a portion of it. There are two kinds of viewports: *tiled viewports* and *floating viewports*.

W

Wireframe

The representation of a 3D object with lines that represent the intersections of planes or the corners of walls and other building components.

World coordinate system

The *default User Coordinate System* for all new drawing files, in which the positive directions for the *x* and *y* axes are to the right and upwards, respectively, and in which the positive direction for the *z* axis is towards the user and perpendicular to the plane of the screen.

X

XY plane

The 2D geometrical flat surface defined by the *x* and *y* axes, which is parallel to the monitor screen in a new, *default* AutoCAD drawing file.

Z

Zoom

The name of a command with several options, all of which allow the user to increase or decrease the magnification of the *view* of the current drawing, in the *drawing area* or in a *viewport*.

Glossary

Index

Note to the Reader: First level entries are in **bold**. Page numbers in **bold** indicate the principal discussion of a topic or the definition of a term. Page numbers in *italic* indicate illustrations.

m

X

Z

Aliases for AutoCAD Commands

Aliases are shortcut keys you can enter to quickly start AutoCAD commands. By typing in the alias and pressing ↵, the command is started. The following list includes commands covered in the book and commands related to material covered in the book.

Alias	Command	Informal Command Name
3F	3DFACE	3D Face
A	ARC	
AA	AREA	
AR	ARRAY	
B	BLOCK	
BH	BHATCH	Boundary Hatch
BO	BOUNDARY	
-BO	-BOUNDARY	
BR	BREAK	
C	CIRCLE	
CH	DDCHPROP	Change Properties
-CH	CHANGE	
CHA	CHAMFER	
CO	COPY	
COL	DDCOLOR	Color
D	DDIM	Dimension Styles
DAL	DIMALIGNED	Aligned Dimension
DAN	DIMANGULAR	Angular Dimension
DBA	DIMBASELINE	Baseline Dimension
DCE	DIMCENTER	Center Mark
DCO	DIMCONTINUE	Continue Dimension
DDI	DIMDIAMETER	Diameter Dimension
DED	DIMEDIT	Edit Dimension
DI	DIST	Distance
DIV	DIVIDE	
DLI	DIMLINEAR	Linear Dimension
DO	DONUT	
DOR	DIMORDINATE	Ordinate Dimension
DOV	DIMOVERRIDE	Override Dimension
DRA	DIMRADIUS	Radius Dimension
DST	DIMSTYLE	Dimension Style
DT	DTEXT	Single Line Text
DV	DVIEW	Dynamic View
E	ERASE	
ED	DDEDIT	Edit Text
EL	ELLIPSE	
EX	EXTEND	
EXIT	QUIT	
EXT	EXTRUDE	
F	FILLET	
GR	DDGRIPS	Tools ➤ Grips
H	BHATCH	Boundary Hatch
-H	HATCH	
HE	HATCHEDIT	Modify ➤ Object ➤ Hatch
HI	HIDE	
I	DDINSERT	Insert with dialog box
-I	INSERT	
IMP	IMPORT	
IN	INTERSECT	
INF	INTERFERE	
L	LINE	
LA	LAYER	
-LA	-LAYER	
LE	LEADER	
LI	LIST	
LS	LIST	
LT	LINETYPE	
-LT	-LINETYPE	
LTS	LTSCALE	Linetype Scale
M	MOVE	
ME	MEASURE	
MI	MIRROR	
ML	MLINE	Multiline